WHEN WORKERS DECIDE
Workplace Democracy Takes Root in North America

Edited by Len Krimerman and Frank Lindenfeld

NEW SOCIETY PUBLISHERS
Philadelphia, PA   Gabriola Island, BC

Inquiries regarding requests to reprint all or part of *When Workers Decide: Workplace Democracy Takes Root in North America* should be addressed to:
New Society Publishers
4527 Springfield Avenue
Philadelphia, PA 19143

ISBN USA 0-86571-200-X Hardcover
ISBN USA 0-86571-201-8 Paperback
ISBN CAN 1-55092-150-9 Hardcover
ISBN CAN 1-55092-151-7 Paperback

Printed in the United States of America on partially recycled paper by Capital City Press, Montpelier, Vermont.

Book design by Martin Kelley.

To order directly from the publisher, add $2.50 to the price for the first copy, 75¢ each additional. Send check or money order to:
New Society Publishers
4527 Springfield Avenue
Philadelphia, PA 19143
In Canada, contact:
New Society Publishers/New Catalyst
PO Box 189
Gabriola Island, BC VOR 1XO

New Society Publishers is a project of the New Society Educational Foundation, a nonprofit, tax-exempt, public foundation in the United States, and of the Catalyst Education Society, a non-profit society in Canada. Opinions expressed in this book do not necessarily represent positions of the New Society Educational Foundation, nor the Catalyst Education Society.

® GCIU

Acknowledgments

Many of the articles that appear in this book were originally prepared for or printed in *Changing Work*; others were written especially for this book. We thank the authors for allowing us to print their articles and, in many cases, preparing updates, revisions, and corrections. Special thanks are also due our co-workers and associates who helped with the editing and production of *Changing Work*.

Some articles appeared previously in other publications; we are grateful for permission from the various authors and/or publications to reprint them. The interview with Dorris Pickens and the articles on ESOPs are both reprinted with the permission of the NCB Development Corporation from the summer 1989 issue of *Cooperative Enterprises*. Karen Young's article on employee participation groups at Weirton Steel is used with permission from the National Center for Employee Ownership, Oakland, California.

The interview with Lynn Williams is reprinted from the Canadian publication *Worker Co-op*; Lars Apland's updated material on Junior Achievement originally appeared in the same publication, as did the original version of Christopher Meek's article on buyouts. Charlene Winters' article, "Earning While Learning," is reprinted from *BYU Today*, July 1990. Jackie Van Anda's article on Colt Enterprises appeared first in the February 15, 1988, issue of *Christianity and Crisis*.

Mark Satin's article on development bankers appeared first in the March 28, 1988, issue of *New Options*. Gregg Ramm's piece on Community Investment, now updated, appeared first in the spring 1987 issue of *Building Economic Alternatives*.

Frank T. Adams and Gary B. Hansen's material on education for ownership and participation is excerpted from their book, *Putting Democracy to Work* (Eugene, Oregon: Hulogosi Press, 1987). Andrew Bank's article on Dennis Walton's fight to control his union's pension fund is excerpted from a longer article that was first printed in *Labor Research Review*. Pete Leki's article, "I'd Be All for ESOPs If..." appeared first in the spring 1989 issue of *Labor Today*.

Dedications

For Marian and Kathryn

Publisher's Note

Whether in an old corrupt city like Philadelphia, or in the "New" World Order of the big money men, or even in the progressive and labor movements, "Money talks."

This tired but still potent cliché underlines a simple truth: If we are serious about changing the structural inequalities that cause so much suffering in our society, we must find ways to control the accumulation and use of capital.

Unfortunately, when many of us see or hear the word "capital," our eyes glaze over. And no wonder! "Capital" is an abstraction, a kind of code word for people's sweat and skills that have been turned into products and money and stored away in banks—to be used by those who have lots more of it to control access to food and shelter and comfort.

But if capital is stored labor, and if it means access to more labor and power, then one way to regain control of capital is to regain control of our collective labor—our sweat and skills.

Of course, it's not very exciting to think about controlling the drudgery that so many of us know as work! But one of the most captivating promises of control is that it offers the opportunity to transform work—the tasks, divisions of labor, and relationships between workers—into something more worthy of the human spirit. After all, work can and should be interesting, fulfilling and even fun!

But work will never be any of these things if we stay chained to the bottom line. Financial measures of efficiency and success are powerful and useful tools with a long history, but they are only one set of tools. To transform work into something worth doing, to find ways to turn our labor into common wealth, we must develop other tools and methods for assessing success and noting and celebrating quality.

But wait, I'm sliding into the abstract, and there's no reason to talk theory when across North America (not to mention the rest of the world) tens of thousands of people are experimenting with different ways of controlling their labor and their lives. *When Workers Decide* introduces us to the producer cooperatives, consumer cooperatives, intentional communities and democratic ESOPs that are quietly spreading through all sectors of our economy. And *When Workers Decide* goes further to explore and tie together the many experiments in community and worker control of capital and expertise, in organizing and educating for worker ownership and control, and in working with other progressive movements to create lasting and fundamental social change.

We are proud to publish *When Workers Decide* because it speaks to the heart of a constructive program for fundamental social change. It shows us how we can take control of our livelihoods and so of our dreams of the good life.

But there's another, more personal reason for our excitement about *When Workers Decide*. As worker-managers, we know first-hand some of the daily struggles and compromises involved in learning to run our own social-change business. (Publishing *When Workers Decide* certainly stretched us!) Still, while it's not always pretty or uplifting, trying to control our work lives and work is wonderfully empowering. Probably the most gratifying part of my seven years with NSP has been feeling my own—and watching my colleagues'—sense of possibility expand. By working together to articulate and realize our ideas of a good life and a just, compassionate world, we find ourselves growing in ways we didn't know were even possible.

It is in the hope that others will discover for themselves, their communities and our troubled society the transformative potential of worker control, that we are especially happy and proud to publish *When Workers Decide*.

T.L. Hill

T.L. Hill
for New Society Publishers

Table of Contents

Chapter 5
Educational Empowerment:
New Forms of Work—New Forms of Learning

Chapter 6
Worker Ownership and the Labor Movement

Chapter 7
How Far Have We Come?:
Assessing Worker Ownership

Chapter 8
Creating Democracy at Work:
Strategies for Transformation

Chapter 9
Resources for Action

1

Changing Worklife
Grassroots Activism Takes a New Turn

Salsedo Press is a busy print shop in Chicago owned and operated by its dozen or so worker-members. The press, which does a half million dollars of business annually, began in 1969 as a non-profit printer for local radical movements. It became a *for-profit worker co-op* in 1987. Many of its members earn more than $10 per hour plus benefits. It has managers for sales, production, and customer service. Policy decisions are made by the entire collective, which meets once every few months; each member has one vote.

Weirton Steel Co. is a thriving steel mill in Weirton, West Virginia, purchased from its former owners by its eight thousand workers in 1984 through an *employee stock ownership plan (ESOP)* to prevent the plant's closing. (ESOPs are legal structures designed to enable employees to buy stock in their companies through payroll deductions. A major reason for their popularity is that under existing U.S. tax laws ESOPs provide substantial tax benefits to companies that use them.) While the Weirton workers do own more than 50 percent of the stock and do elect representatives to the board of directors, they do not yet elect a majority of the board and are still struggling for more democratic control (Campbell 1989). Already, they have instituted an extensive system of shopfloor workers' representation. (Blasi 1988)

Despite their differences in size, at both Salsedo Press and Weirton Steel workers own the firm, have a say in decisions at all levels, enjoy good jobs at decent pay, and share in the profits. *When Workers Decide* is about the increasing number and viability of such worker-owned and democratically organized workplaces. Its chapters trace the growing movement for workplace democracy in the postindustrial United States and the implications of this movement for the future. This book shows how workers in many different kinds of industries have been creating and sustaining businesses that provide democratic participation, job satisfaction, decent income, and profit sharing; it also reviews some of the problems democratic workplaces have encountered.

An Outline of This Book

In this chapter, we describe some of the general features of democratic workplaces and provide an overview of the current movement for worker ownership and control in the United States. In chapter 2, we offer a sampling of democratically controlled work organizations. We move on in chapters 3 and 4 to focus on the technical assistance organizations and alternative sources of capital that have helped to ensure the success of many democratic workplaces. In chapter 5, we look at the crucial issue of education of workers and managers for democratic participation. In the more reflective second half of the book, we analyze the strengths, weaknesses, and possibilities of worker ownership and control. In chapter 6, we explore the growing compatibility of worker ownership and labor unions; in chapter 7, the successes of and obstacles to the current movement for democratic workplaces; and, in chapter 8, prospects and strategies for strengthening the movement and combining it with broader efforts at progressive social change.

Varieties of Democratic Workplaces

Democratic workplaces come in all sizes and legal forms, from two or three members to several thousand, from informal family firms and small collectives to formally organized cooperatives and companies in which voting stock is divided among all employees through an ESOP. The key questions are *Who owns the assets of the enterprise?* and *Who can make which decisions (and how)?*

One common type of democratic work organization is the *worker cooperative*, where ownership and control resides in the membership; each worker has one equal vote. Another form is the *democratically organized ESOP*, where employees purchase stock that makes them part owners of the company. A majority of the voting stock is owned by the employees, each with an equal vote and the right to exercise it.

Some hybrid democratic workplaces try to balance the interests of employees, clients or customers, and the local community by providing seats on their policy-making boards to representatives of those interests. In certain food co-ops, for example, day-to-day decisions are made by the manager and the staff, but general policies are determined by a board of directors including both staff and customer-member representatives.

In worker co-ops and democratically organized ESOPs, those who do the work determine what the company does, how the work is done, and what happens to the profits. Ideally, such organizations embody these central principles: democratic control by employees; equality of all worker-members; equitable sharing of profit and loss; voluntary, nondiscriminatory employment; meetings and records open to members; limited returns to capital; and workers' consent needed to sell the business (Adams and Hansen 1987). Most worker cooperatives have a policy-setting governing board elected directly or indirectly by members.

Democratic work organizations usually strive for certain social goals even when they may lower profits. That is, they may try to maximize the number of jobs provided, to enhance the quality of those jobs, and to take into account not only the well-being of employees but also that of customers and the wider community.

Size and the Structure of Democratic Control

Most worker-owned and operated enterprises strive to extend democracy to day-to-day operations, but how they do so often depends on the size of their workforces. While worker co-ops and democratic ESOPs vary in size from two to several thousand worker-owners, most have fewer than five hundred members, since worker participation is difficult to maintain in enterprises that are much larger.

Small collectives hold frequent group meetings to discuss policies and their implementation. Members often share tasks and rotate responsibilities. Some, like Salsedo Press, choose one or more members as managers.

Worker-owned and operated enterprises with more than fifteen or twenty members may divide into a number of work groups, each of which elects delegates to a council or governing board. Board members are "link pins" who represent the work group that elected them, transmit the suggestions of their work group to the board, and inform their group of board decisions.

In larger cooperative organizations, democratic management is usually more complex, and workers' representation on governing boards may be indirect. Work groups may be so large or numerous that the board is elected at large through a representative democratic system. In some larger co-ops, there are two or three tiers of workers' councils, each tier sending representatives to the next higher level.

Often, worker-members also belong to trade unions. Unions may set industry-wide wage rates and are especially useful in educating worker-owners and in resolving individual grievances that arise between managers and other employees. Workers sometimes also elect watchdog committees to keep an eye on the board of directors and managers and to counteract any possibility that they may become a self-serving oligarchy.

Advantages of Worker Cooperatives and Democratic ESOPs

Worker cooperatives and democratic ESOPs have a number of advantages over capitalist and state-socialist firms.

Control from Below

In worker cooperatives, members have real power and control over their workplace, often exercised through elected governing boards as well as shopfloor participation. Worker-members, their elected representatives, or managers directly responsible to them decide what goods and services to provide, by what means, and at what quality levels and prices. In contrast, employees in capitalist or state-run firms have relatively little say in their operations.

Improved Self-Respect, Happiness, and Personal Growth

More often than private corporations or state-run firms, worker co-ops strive to provide jobs that are meaningful and that allow individuals greater room to express their special talents and abilities. This, in turn, leads to greater job satisfaction and fulfillment.

In democratically controlled workplaces, members' personal and vocational growth is important; while they usually incorporate a division of labor, many deomcratic workplaces are also committed to sharing knowledge and skills as well as to demystifying professional expertise. Some even rotate jobs so that members learn new skills instead of being stuck in the same routine.

Improved Productivity

Because the members feel it is their company, they are usually motivated to work harder and smarter. Thus, the workers need fewer middle managers checking up on their work, and the co-ops generally use human and material resources more efficiently and effectively than capitalist or state-socialist firms.

As a result of better working conditions and of worker participation in decision making, co-ops have lower rates of turnover, absenteeism, and theft. When workers are owners, moreover, there is enhanced cooperation between members and their managers, and as a result, fewer strikes or informal slowdowns.

Improved productivity and good labor relations are enhanced by small or medium size, which facilitates democratic control from below.

Wage Security

In worker co-ops and democratic ESOPs, the profits belong to those who produce them with their labor. In capitalist firms, the profits go to the wealthy stockholders, whereas in government firms, the profits go to the state.

Because they are democratically controlled by their members, the lowest-level employees have greater clout than in private corporations or government-run units. Thus, cooperative organizations often raise minimum levels of pay to reduce the differential between the lowest- and highest-paid members; most also try to equalize members' opportunities to earn income.

Preserving and Creating Jobs

Democratic work organizations try to guarantee their members' jobs. When there is a recession, or a reduction in demand, members often work fewer hours so that, if possible, nobody is laid off. In fact, whereas capitalist firms try to maximize profit and managerial control, democratic work organizations typically try to maximize the number and quality of jobs.

When joined together in networks and allied with providers of technical assistance and capital, worker-owned, democratically controlled firms can be extremely effective in saving jobs and in developing new ones. This is illustrated by the dynamic cooperative network associated with Working People's Bank in the area around Mondragon, Spain, which created thousands of new jobs in industrial, service and consumer cooperatives (Whyte and Whyte 1989; Morrison 1991). This network survived the economic recession of the late 1970s and early 1980s without having to resort to any layoffs, which were massively introduced by capitalist corporations in the same situation.

Community Orientation

Worker co-ops are more likely to reflect the interests of workers, clients, and communities than are absentee-owned corporations or companies controlled by distant central governments. Because their policies are determined locally and because community interests are more likely to be represented (since the worker-owners are part of the community), democratically controlled workplaces are generally more sensitive to such issues as environmental pollution. For example, after the Vermont Asbestos Group was bought by its workers, they invested heavily in pollution control equipment.

Moreover, worker-owners have often devoted a portion of their firms' surplus to providing such benefits as health spas, day-care centers, and educational programs that are open to the wider community.

New Careers

In addition to job opportunities *in* worker co-ops, there are many careers opening up in organizations that *provide services to them*. Existing support groups and associated lending institutions already employ hundreds of persons as business developers, loan officers, lawyers, accountants, and other professionals, as well as plain old-fashioned organizers. As the movement for workplace democracy continues to expand, these opportunities should grow.

Roots of the Contemporary U.S. Movement for Worker Ownership and Control

There are today probably well over a thousand democratically organized workplaces in this country. (Counting small retail and service co-ops, their number may be closer to three thousand.) This movement for workplace democracy has a number of roots.

First, there is the long history of worker cooperatives in the United States. Curl (1980) cites a number of worker co-ops formed by striking employees in East Coast cities during the late 1700s. A century later, the Knights of Labor advocated the replacement of the capitalist wage system by industrial cooperatives. By 1886, this trade-union movement had inspired the formation of more than 130 worker cooperatives. Another wave of worker co-ops appeared in the United States during the 1930s, including a score of worker-owned plywood factories in the Pacific Northwest, most of which continued successfully for decades.

Second, the activist movements of the 1960s and 1970s led to the formation of many hundreds of worker- and consumer-run enterprises. These "new wave" co-ops included alternative schools, restaurants, print shops, food co-operatives, legal collectives, health clinics, and local newspapers, among many others.

Third, the continuing deindustrialization of the United States has led to hundreds of worker buyouts to prevent plant shutdowns.

Finally, the legislation of the 1970s facilitated the establishment of thousands of ESOPs. Some of these were plant buyouts, while others helped family owners to retire by selling their firms. Most ESOPs, however, were used by businesses to raise money, to save taxes, or to resist takeovers by other corporations. According to the **National Center for Employee Ownership**, the workforce now owns a majority of the voting stock in about one thousand ESOPs; perhaps one-third of these are democratically organized.

In general, but with ESOPs in particular, majority worker ownership does not necessarily translate into democratic management, even though it does usually lead to more worker influence. **Seymour Specialty Wire Co.** in Connecticut is a case in point. To prevent the plant's closing by its conglomerate owners, 227 workers purchased the company through an ESOP in 1985. From the beginning, workers elected the company's board of directors, but it has taken years to change old interaction patterns between managers and workers and to increase worker participation in decision making, especially at the shopfloor level (Hansen and Adams 1987).

The "new wave" of democratically owned and controlled enterprises that took off in the 1970s differs from its predecessors in five key ways. First, instead of developing largely in isolation, one at a time, *networks of worker cooperatives and supporting institutions have emerged*. Thus, in 1982 the leadership of the **United Food and Commercial Workers (UFCW)** union, with aid from consultants and from the technical assistance group **PACE**, helped workers buy two shut-down A&P markets in Philadelphia and reopen them as **O&O** (employee Owned and Operated) stores. At the same time they established an investment fund to loan start-up capital to other worker co-ops. PACE now also administers a revolving loan fund to aid worker co-ops. The **Center for Community Self-Help** in Durham, North Carolina, launched a community-development credit union in 1984 for the same purpose. Loose regional federations have formed in Ohio, Washington State, Oregon and around Chicago to provide mutual support to member co-ops. And two national groups, **Co-op America** and the **Federation for Industrial Retention and Renewal (FIRR)** began in the 1980s. Co-op America offers marketing, insurance, and other services to democratically managed workplaces. FIRR is an advocacy group that promotes worker ownership, on the local and the national level, as one solution to the problem of plant closings.

Union involvement is a second distinctive feature of the contemporary movement to democratize worklife. (For most of the twentieth century, bread-and-butter issues have headed the agenda of American unions, with little or no attention being paid to worker ownership or control.) In the late 1970s and early 1980s, locals of the **United Auto Workers** and of the **UFCW**, faced with shop closings in Connecticut, New Jersey, and Pennsylvania, helped develop worker buyouts by their members. By the end of the 1980s, these two pioneer unions had been joined by steel, bricklayer, textile, and transport-worker unions in advocating worker ownership as a means of saving jobs. Jack Sheinkman, president of the **Amalgamated Clothing and Textile Workers Union**, and Lynn Williams, President of the **United Steelworkers of America**, helped originate the **AFL-CIO**

Employee Partnership Fund, designed to help workers save jobs by buying plants through ESOPs.

A third new feature is *the spread of technical assistance or support organizations*. Previously, if workers wanted to save a closing business or start a new venture, they had to confront on their own such esoteric phenomena as business plans, feasibility studies, front end financing, cooperative bylaws, and democratic group processes. In 1978, however, two technical assistance groups were formed to fill this gap—**PACE of Philadelphia** and the Boston area **ICA Group**. By 1984 at least thirty groups specialized in financial, legal, educational, or other support services for worker-controlled firms, and today that figure has probably doubled. Additionally, there are organizations that collect and disseminate information on worker ownership such as the National Center for Employee Ownership, university centers such as the economic-development program at New Hampshire College and the doctoral program in social economy and social justice of the Boston College sociology department, and publications such as the *Grassroots Economic Organizing Newsletter (GEO)* and the Canadian journal *Worker Co-ops*. Together, these efforts provide a vital infrastructure that has aided the formation, financing, and expansion of democratically organized businesses.

Fourth, the current movement for workplace democracy *has entered the mainstream of United States business* through the proliferation of semi-cooperative quality-of-worklife (QWL) programs designed to increase worker participation in decision making, and through ESOPs, which have turned many workers into company owners. Most QWL programs, as well as most ESOPs, do not readily empower workers. Often, ESOPs are used merely as convenient gimmicks to enable corporate managements to reduce costs and save taxes. Nevertheless, ESOPs owned by a majority of their workers have provided hundreds of mainstream manufacturing and service companies an arena within which employees' struggles for a greater say in the workplace may have a better chance of success. Examples of such mainstream businesses include several steel companies, Avis car rentals, and the Publix supermarket chain.

Finally, among some worker co-ops today there is also an expanded *sense of solidarity* with other progressive causes, including environmental issues and those relating to local community control, especially among those whose members were involved in the social movements of the 1950s, 1960s, and 1970s.

U.S. Worker Co-ops Are Part of a Worldwide Movement

Worker-owned and operated enterprises are even more developed in other countries than in the United States, and many U.S. firms and technical assistance providers look overseas for inspiration and advice. We cannot do justice to the diversity of this movement abroad, but we can offer a taste—and, in chapter 9, directions to more information.

Until very recently, in Yugoslavia, the entire economy was based on worker self-management, and this idea was written into the national constitution. Even so, many enterprises were and are still dominated by managerial personnel, and the Yugoslavs are engaged in a broad debate concerning greater worker participation. Worker co-ops also exist in Russia, Hungary, Poland, Romania, and Czechoslovakia. In the past, many "cooperatives" in Socialist countries were controlled by state-appointed managers. The recent revolutionary developments in central and eastern Europe may eventually lead to an increasing spread of genuine worker control (Denitch 1990).

There is a strong worker co-op movement in several Canadian provinces, notably in Québec. Worker co-ops have spread throughout western Europe. The United Kingdom has more than fifteen hundred such cooperatives, and there are thousands more in both France and Italy. The Basques have evolved a thriving system of about a hundred industrial worker co-ops around the town of Mondragon, Spain; elsewhere in Spain other worker co-ops are thriving. In Japan, the fast-growing and ecologically committed Seikatsu consumer cooperative, with over 200,000 family members, has started about 100 worker-run cooperatives to produce such essential daily products as milk and soap.

Difficulties Facing Democratic Workplaces

Despite the advantages they offer, worker cooperatives have spread fairly slowly. We will explore in Chapter 7 many of the gaps and hurdles cooperatives must overcome. These include the disturbing facts that worker ownership of a company does not automatically lead to democratic control; that it is often difficult for democratic workplaces to find and keep competent managers; that the constraints of capitalism make it difficult for democratic alternatives to gain a foothold; and, finally, that the vast and promising terrain for worker control in the non-profit and public sectors (e.g., the postal service) remains largely unexplored.

Conclusion

It is difficult to make accurate predictions about the U.S. economy, but we think that during the 1990s democratic ESOPs and worker cooperatives will continue to proliferate, particularly during times of recession. As Mondragon has shown, democratically controlled enterprises can play an important role in helping communities combat recession. Perhaps more important, worker ownership and control offer communities and progressive movements the hope of a greater voice in their economic destinies. Now that the worker-ownership movement is wellrooted, it seems timely to explore ways it could collaborate with progressive groups within labor, environmental, and other grassroots movements. This exploration is a major theme of chaper 8 below.

Common Questions about Employee Ownership

The ICA Group, which provides technical assistance and loans to worker cooperatives, has prepared numerous publications about employee ownership and related issues. The following is an excerpt from one of them.—Eds.

What is an employee-owned company?

In an employee-owned company all of the employees (management, clerical, and shopfloor) together own a majority of the stock of the company.

If a company is employee owned, do the employees control it?

Not necessarily. Employee-owners need at least two things to ensure democratic control of their company: *voting rights*—the board of directors is elected by the employees on a one-person, one-vote basis; and *participation*—all employees receive the information with which to understand the progress of the company and have the opportunity to participate in day-to-day decisions.

If employees do not participate in the development of the corporate structure, the employee-owned company may end up being controlled by its banks or by top management. If the employees want to have a democratically controlled company, there are two types of legal structure that can be used: worker cooperatives and democratic employee stock ownership plans (ESOPs). Whether employees choose to be organized as a worker cooperative or a democratic ESOP will usually depend on the tax and financial situation of their particular company.

What is management like in a democratic, employee-owned company?

The general manager is selected by the board of directors and has responsibility for implementing policies established by the board and for coordinating day-to-day operations, much the same as in a traditional corporation. Managers in an employee-owned company should develop a participatory style, encouraging input and ideas from all people in the company.

How do employee-owned companies get started?

There are at least three ways such companies get established: start-ups, conversions, and plant closings. In a start-up a group of people decide to start a business together. A conversion occurs when the owner of a business wants to sell the business and the employees decide to buy it. An employee-owned company may result from a plant closing when the employees can operate a company more profitably or be content with less profit than could the previous owner.

Community organizations, unions, and public-sector entities often play a role in helping to start employee-owned companies. In addition, non-profit groups have formed all over the country specifically to assist employee-owned companies.

Where do employee-owned companies get their financing?

Loans—Employee-owned companies can obtain loans from commercial banks, public lending institutions, and lenders who specialize in employee-owned companies.

Equity—Financing a company is like financing a house. In order to obtain a mortgage, the home owner must make a down payment. Similarly, employees will usually have to invest equity in order to obtain loans to start the business. As new workers join the firm they also make an equity investment. Payments are sometimes made through payroll deductions. In some situations, community loan funds such as the ICA Revolving Loan Fund or a local credit union can provide financing for employees' equity investments.

Reinvestment of Profit—Each year, the company must decide what to do with its profit. Given the need for capital, particularly in the early years of a business, the majority of the profit will probably be reinvested in the company rather than distributed to owners. A portion of the reinvested profit is allocated to accounts for each employee-owner and eventually paid out to the employee-owner (after adjusting for any losses).

If the employee-owned company fails, are the employees personally liable?

No. The employees would lose their equity investment and any profit accumulated in their accounts, but they are not personally responsible for any of the debts of the company.

What is the role of the union in an employee-owned company?

In companies that have unions, union leadership often plays a critical role in setting up an employee-owned company, ensuring that the new employee-owners will also control the company. On an ongoing basis, the union represents employees in negotiating collective bargaining agreements, provides stewards for the grievance procedure, guarantees basic membership rights, ensures open channels of communication, and monitors the actions of management and the board. Ordinarily, the union-management relationship in a democratic, employee-owned company will be less adversarial than it might be in a traditional company.

2

Start from Practice
Let a Thousand Democratic Enterprises Bloom

Businesses owned or managed by their workers are by no means novel in the U.S. economy. As Adams and Hansen (1987) have pointed out, the Knights of Labor helped to organize about 135 of them more than a century ago. Moreover, waves of cooperative enterprise rose and fell in the upper Midwest, the Northwest, and several urban areas during the second, third, and fourth decades of this century. As part of the New Deal, the federal government even established a "Division of Self-Help Cooperatives," which set up such cooperative industries as a wood mill, a tractor-assembly plant, a paint factory, and hosiery mills.

There is, in short, an important—and largely overlooked—workplace democracy tradition in the United States. It is therefore not entirely surprising that, fueled in part by the anticorporate sentiments of the 1960s, we are now witnessing a new surge in cooperative economic activity. The contours of this surge are still somewhat hazy; knowledgeable observers estimate that there are between five hundred and three thousand democratic or worker-owned firms. Nonetheless, such veteran enterprises as Chicago's **Salsedo Press**, North Carolina's **Watermark Artisans**, Oregon's **Hoedads Reforestors**, and New Haven's **High School in the Community** have begun to figure out what it takes to survive and even prosper over the long haul in a generally undemocratic economy. And younger firms like Texas's **Colt Enterprises** are learning new ways to bring democracy into the workplace. We think the stories of these enterprises give a good sense of the growing day-to-day reality of contemporary worker ownership.

What these accounts do not entirely reveal is the exciting breadth of the contemporary worker-ownership movement. Democratic worker-owned firms are now found in all regions of the country and in virtually all sectors of the economy. No longer confined to retail shops, to agricultural production, to service sector firms, or to the East and West coasts, they have sprung up almost everywhere—in sectors as diverse as insurance, supermarket chains, traditional manufacturing, printing and publishing, and even public administration.

More important, contemporary democratic businesses have begun collaborating with other enterprises and organizations. These links take different forms. For example, the Watermark Association of Artisans not only provides common marketing to some 450 scattered "cottage industry" craftspersons but, through its Northeastern Education and Development Foundation, offers training and support services to its own members and to groups of artisans elsewhere who find encouragement in the Watermark model. (These include groups not only from other parts of the United States but from Central America as well.) Hoedads helps other cooperative ventures get under way by lending money or teaching what they have gleaned through direct experience. Salsedo Press is part of a Chicago group of cooperatively owned enterprises that meet regularly to support each other and a nascent country-wide association of progressive printers. And finally, Colt Enterprises is the pioneer conversion to worker ownership undertaken by the Amalgamated Clothing and Textile Workers Union (ACTWU). The union supported Colt's start-up and has since played a large role in establishing an AFL-CIO investment fund to assist worker buyouts. The Colt workers themselves have tried to make their experience useful to others who might follow by developing, in conjunction with the Texas Department of Agriculture, a handbook on worker buyouts and by using a portion of their revenues to fund educational programs for Central American textile workers, even though they compete with Colt for name-brand clothing contracts.

In short, then, links of many sorts—from common marketing, to communication and networking, to regional and industry-wide associations, to collaboration with labor unions—are central to the movement's growing strength. Later chapters will explore these links in some detail, but first let us look at some concrete examples of vibrant worker-owned and operated businesses.

Salsedo Press
Community Roots, Quality Printing

Eric Hart

Walk into Salsedo Press and you encounter a busy, professional commercial print shop—several phones ring at once, presses run eleven hours a day, and you are surrounded by purposeful workers in motion. Samples of boldly designed large posters line the walls. As you tour, the cooperative's twelve members, clearly excited about their work, tell you the story of each poster—who it was for and what particular printing challenge it presented.

One of Salsedo's recent posters, a powerful hands-in-chains graphic captioned "Freeing South Africa, Freeing Ourselves," appeared prominently in the *Chicago Sun Times*—held aloft by Bishop Desmond Tutu of South Africa. Next to Bishop Tutu stood Chicago's late mayor, Harold Washington, for whose campaigns Salsedo did substantial amounts of printing.

Salsedo member and sales manager Lauren Deutsch describes the press's mission as "operating a cooperative business that serves the Chicago community, particularly grassroots, community, and political organizations." While its roots (and over half of its printing) are in the Chicago progressive community, Salsedo serves a variety of businesses and agencies. As Deutsch describes it, customers come to Salsedo "when they get to the point where they want things to look really nice. They come here because they made a decision that quality printing is important—and because Salsedo delivers when we say it will."

Salsedo has developed into a strong business, generating $16,000 in profit on 1989 sales of $525,000. Says Deutsch, "We are all excited about having had a really good year. For a long time, we were reactive; to meet difficulties, we would simply work harder. Now we're being proactive and asserting ourselves: we're hiring new people, actively pursuing new work, and making decisions based on where we want the business to go."

Salsedo Press (the name commemorates an anarchist immigrant printer tortured and killed in Justice Department custody in the 1920s) has not always been accustomed to financial self-assertion. In 1969 the group that was to become Salsedo Press was publishing (but not yet printing) the *Walrus,* an antiwar newspaper at the University of Illinois. When the shop producing the paper was closed for zoning violations, they bought its machinery and launched themselves into the printing trade. Members believed income from printing would support their other antiwar, antiracist, and antisexist activities, but in practice the printing operation barely broke even. While sporadic wages were paid to members in need during its first four years, most members worked other jobs to pay their bills, volunteering their time to help build a press that supported antiwar and social-justice movements.

Keys to Success

Salsedo, in short, began with no printing or business experience and with little capital. What enabled it to succeed as a business and as a print shop? Several major factors stand out: the move to a large city, the pursuit of technical sophistication, and the dedication and vision of Salsedo's staff.

The decision to move to Chicago in 1973 was a critical growth step for the print shop. The movement against the Vietnam War was winding down, and with it a major source of work. Salsedo needed a larger base to survive. "We were doing all the movement work that could be printed in Champaign-Urbana, about $4,000 a month," recalls Pat Gleason, financial manager and a founding member. "We asked ourselves—how can we serve the movement and make a living? The answer was: move to a big city."

Salsedo's workers believe that, in our information-saturated society, important messages need to stand out visually in order to be noticed and read. Accordingly, Salsedo continued its growth toward high-quality printing in 1974, when it borrowed $10,000 to purchase a bigger printing press. That machine enabled Salsedo to handle the larger quantities requested by Chicago customers and to do the sophisticated multicolor work for which the shop is known.

Another important factor in Salsedo's success has been the dedication and vision of its workers. Two of Salsedo's members have been with the shop from its inception. A third member has been at Salsedo for fourteen years, a fourth for ten years, a fifth for eight, and so on. Workers have a concern for professionalism and quality and a growing understanding of business practices. They have an evolutionary, flexible approach to their structure as a co-op. Salsedo's members are willing to make sacrifices for the press and its politics and are in for the long haul.

Converting to a Co-Op

In 1987, Salsedo converted from a not-for-profit corporation to a for-profit worker cooperative. (Model bylaws were provided by the ICA Group.) This arrangement has several advantages: it makes Salsedo more attractive to lenders; it offers tax advantages over a conventional for-profit corporation; and it allows the group to match their formal structure more closely to their actual decision-making process.

The conversion brought Salsedo a direct infusion of $18,000 in capital. The Adrian Dominican Sisters, active supporters of worker ownership, loaned each worker $3,000 for the purchase of one share of common stock in the reorganized business. They used half this money to speed up payments and thereby obtained a discount on paper and supplies bills. In three years, these quick-payment discounts alone have more than paid for the original loan. At the time of the conversion, Salsedo had a negative net worth; as of 1989, it had $56,000 paid-in capital on its books (including members' shares). "I could go to a bank with this financial statement and get a loan," says Gleason, "which I couldn't do before."

Salsedo also pays less taxes as a worker cooperative. Stockholder (member) dividends are taxed only once. In a conventional for-profit corporation, dividends are taxed twice—once on the person receiving the dividend (as income) and once on the corporation itself (as corporate income, or profit). As a properly formed workers' co-op, Salsedo Press can now make a profit (useful in measuring performance or talking with banks), but it does not pay taxes on that portion of its profits (about half) that is distributed to members. (This tax advantage depends on corporate law that varies from state to state; if you are considering incorporation, consult a lawyer in your state who is familiar with worker cooperatives.)

Salsedo members feel comfortable with the co-op structure, which incorporates their tradition of democratic decision making. Before the conversion, Salsedo operated as a collective. In collectives, most decisions are made unanimously, and only in very rare cases is any decision reached without at least the assent (if not the explicit agreement) of every member. Under its new cooperative structure, Salsedo's board of directors, consisting of every shareholder (member), oversees the general management of the business. No member has a greater say than any other: it is one member, one vote (new workers must fulfill a probationary period before applying for membership). At first, the board of directors met only every few months (as the collective had done), but it now meets almost weekly on paid time. Additionally, various *ad hoc* committees look into such issues as finding a new building, buying a new press, and purchasing disability insurance. True to its roots as a collective, the press still seeks a consensus of all shareholders when making decisions. Members have never fallen back on the majority rule spelled out in their bylaws, though they accept it in principle if the need should arise.

Francisco Hernandez, the company's pressroom supervisor, contrasts the involvement of workers at Salsedo with his previous shop, where "if I thought something was wrong, the boss would say, 'Here, let me fix it.' " As Gleason puts it, "People stay because they are challenged and encouraged to learn new skills and contribute to the growth of the business."

Members know that in order to grow larger, the business needs to define job responsibilities more clearly. In 1987, Salsedo hired Victor von Schlegel, an independent consultant, to help them hammer out an organizational structure that defined each job, not the person filling it. Thus far, an organizational chart has been created that includes two new managerial positions, a sales manager and a customer-service manager. "That was hard—really difficult and very positive," says Deutsch. Clarifying job descriptions, along with other parts of the business process, has helped Salsedo expand its workforce.

A Difficult Issue: Wages

Conversion to a co-op structure forced members to face tough issues. Some have worked at Salsedo for twenty years with neither a pension plan nor seniority benefits. As a result, the board considered linking shareholder (member) dividends to years of service. Salsedo went further, however; it changed the very basis of its wage plan, paying different wages for differing jobs, skill levels, and years of experience.

Salsedo had a long-standing policy of equal pay for all workers, but has reluctantly abandoned the practice. The change began in 1985, when a highly skilled member with four children and twenty-five years printing experience approached the collective, saying that he needed more money to live on. Salsedo members realized they could not afford to pay everyone the wage that this worker needed, nor could they afford to lose his skill. After much discussion, he and several others received immediate wage increases. More workers were promised future increases, but from that point on wages were no longer held equal.

Two years later, Salsedo systematized its wages by ranking various jobs and adjusting pay accordingly. This proved to be difficult and trying. "At first we rejected such traditional ranking factors as supervisory responsibility, contact with customers, and direct financial impact on the shop," observed Deutsch. Instead, workers focused on such issues as exposure to toxic chemicals, physical effort, and the stress of dealing with customers. This resulted in a ranking of almost all production jobs (and that of the production manager) above all administrative, clerical, and customer-service positions. This went against members' own understanding of the difficulties and importance of the various jobs, however, and they called a meeting to revise the job rankings. The final result more evenly mixed production and administrative jobs, with management and supervisory positions near the top.

The new ranking specified a pay range from $4.50 to $8.25 for receptionist or general helper to $11.00 to $17.00 for production manager or large-press operator. Workers' wages within the range for a particular job depend on their level of skill and their experience in the trade. And since most members do several types of work, their wages are composite figures. Actual wages in 1989 ranged from $5.10 to $12.50 per hour, plus medical and vacation benefits.

Not all workers are entirely happy with the new scheme. Some believe they are underpaid; others would prefer a return to equality. Members are open to changing the job-ranking plan, but they realize that pay differentials allow them to hire both highly skilled workers and trainees.

Nonmember Employees

A potential pitfall—or perhaps a testament to Salsedo's flexibility and pragmatism—exists in the formal distinction between members (those workers who have purchased a $3,000 share) and nonmember employees. Before the co-op conversion, everyone working at Salsedo Press was a full member of the collective. Currently, of twelve total workers, seven are members and five are nonmember employees. (There are also two independent contractors renting space within Salsedo: a typesetter and a camera operator.) Members and employees are treated differently: members participate in board meetings, receive both dental and medical coverage, and accept lower guaranteed annual pay raises than nonmember employees.

The current bylaws require that new workers become members after nine months. This has become the subject of debate, with all sides agreeing that the rule is not perfect. Although the bylaws hold share prices constant, $3,000 is still a significant obstacle for many potential members. "It's hard enough to find good people without adding the membership requirement," Deutsch commented. As a result, some members have suggested accommodating permanent nonmembers. Other members defend the principle of universal membership, but feel that the trial period should be longer.

Flexibility is the watchword. Two nonmember employees are currently working past the nine-month limit: one employee is not sure he wants to continue living in the United States, and another plans to attend college in the fall. "It seemed crazy to tell Carla [McCarty, the firm's receptionist] that she had to leave sooner than she wanted, when we were happy with her and she was happy with us," observed Gleason. One employee has become a member since the 1987 conversion, and three current workers will be eligible for membership in the coming year. Such clear-sighted attachment to principle (workers should all be members), combined with pragmatic flexibility (better that a good person should stay longer than be forced out by a membership requirement), characterizes many of Salsedo's decisions.

Salsedo Press as a Business

Salsedo's average worker today is considerably older than she or he was in 1969, and some now have families to support. Where early workers were mostly part-time volunteers, they are now more skilled and more specialized (necessary for their ever-more-complex printing work), and most are full time. Workers increasingly depend on Salsedo for a living, even as Salsedo increasingly depends on its workers' individual skills. As a result, the cooperative must function successfully as a business in order to support and keep its workers.

Members have responded to this need by becoming impressively literate in the language and tools of conventional business and finance. According to one member, though the politics of the press agree with her own, the main reason she came to work at Salsedo was to "learn how to run a successful business." At a 1988 conference of progressive printers (described at the end of this article), Salsedo members spoke with familiarity about return on investment, costing, markup strategies, and balance sheets. Their reading list includes not only works on conflict resolution but finance textbooks and the works of such mainstream management gurus as Tom Peters.

Building a Group Culture

A diverse membership is crucial to Salsedo's political vision of serving grassroots movements. Salsedo has struggled to reflect the composition of the city and the movement of which it is a part and to move from the predominantly white, male collective of its early days to its current group, which includes five women, five Latinos, and two African-Americans. A mere head count, however, misses the challenge Salsedo has given itself: to create a truly antiracist and antisexist culture in the workplace.

Latinos and women have long filled important roles at Salsedo. Spanish is spoken freely around the office, and the jokes and banter reflect Latino and female experiences as easily as white-male experiences. On the other hand, despite Salsedo's support of Black struggles in the United States and abroad (printing for African-American community organizations and electoral campaigns, and raising money for a southern African print shop that works for majority rule), its membership and culture do not yet sufficiently reflect its commitment to the struggles of black communities.

Still, Salsedo is tackling this and other problems of diversity head on. For example, until recently, a clear sexual division of labor existed in the shop. Women did all the "front office" work (sales, customer service, financial management, job intake, and ordering), while men operated most of the machines. Salsedo intentionally took on this imbalance last year by hiring a woman to train in the previously all-male pressroom and a man to do estimating work in the front office.

Overcoming centuries of white-male domination of U.S. society is not an easy task—especially while also confronting the daily problems of keeping a small business afloat—but Salsedo is making notable progress.

Workers as Owners

When asked whether Salsedo's members' share in the press threatens their solidarity with (nonowner) workers elsewhere, Gleason replied, "That's possible in theory, but in practice, the opposite is borne out." She cited the examples of Mondragon, a network of cooperatives employing twenty thousand worker-owners, which "has always helped to develop new cooperatives and to expand the cooperative movement in the Basque region of Spain," and of Weirton Steel, a worker-owned steel mill in West Virginia, which has aided workers in failing steel plants at its own expense. Salsedo itself helped workers at another print shop in their attempt to convert to a cooperative. Gleason stressed that "co-ops need to be in the union movement" in order to maintain links with other workers. (Salsedo's production workers are members of the International Typographical Union.)

She further suggested that worker-owned companies have more concern for the communities and the environment in which their workers live than ordinary corporations do. Co-ops, she believes, are one aspect of "a larger movement for social justice, expanded democracy, and empowerment of regular people in this country."

What's the Outlook?

Salsedo's success (which they would more cautiously refer to as an "ongoing struggle") hinges on several factors: the members' willingness to make big changes when necessary; their fight to create a participatory, egalitarian culture; their adapting of conventional business tools to their purposes; their remarkable stability of location and membership; and, through it all, their flexibility.

Despite their many accomplishments, Salsedo's workers will need to draw on their growing strengths to confront a number of other substantial issues: nurturing their own political vision, continuing to diversify their membership and culture, maintaining financial stability, replacing outdated equipment, and purchasing a building. Furthermore, as Salsedo's members see it, their work and future remain intimately tied to grassroots movements in Chicago, which are still rebuilding after Mayor Washington's untimely death in 1989.

If past commitment and flexibility are a guide, Salsedo Press will overcome these new challenges. As Hernandez put it, "The biggest thing we have to do is prepare ourselves for growth and the new opportunities we've created."

Salsedo Participates in a Progressive Printers' Conference

In August 1988 the first-ever conference of North American progressive printers, hosted by Orange Blossom Press, convened at the Graphics and Communications International Union (GCIU) training facility in Cleveland. About fifty workers from fifteen shops from all over the United States and Canada attended. Most of the shops traced their beginnings to the antiwar and women's movements of the 1970s; only Salsedo Press went back to the 1960s. All share progressive political origins and values; most also share an increasing appreciation of business techniques and marketplace survival. All but a few are run as cooperatives or collectives. The shops employ between two and thirteen workers, with gross annual sales ranging from $60,000 to more than $1 million.

The participants came to extract as much experience, information, and support from each other as they could in a weekend. The workshops included Desktop Publishing, Employee Benefits, Management, Marketing, Cooperative Structure, Political Action, Capitalization, Unions, Health and Safety, and Affirmative Action and Hiring. Discussions continued late into the night. The sessions generated plenty of heat. Women expressed frustration with sexism in their workplaces and received support and advice from women and men in other shops. Presses providing equal pay for all jobs questioned Salsedo closely on its decision to institute differential wages. After discussing ruefully their gaps in objective worker evaluation, several groups listened carefully to the Press Gang's system of regular written evaluations.

The conferees freely exchanged financial data, balance sheets, and pricing information. Many of these potential competitors brought photocopies of such material to hand out to their sister and brother presses. Participants compared notes on how to deal with banks, accountants, and consultants; despite some modesty, most groups exhibited impressive levels of financial expertise.

To follow up on the meeting, the group planned a newsletter describing progress at each of the shops and began discussing "loaning" members to other shops to learn new skills and procedures. Since the conference, the participants have been calling each other for advice on pricing, computers, press operation, and work organization. A second followup conference has been scheduled for late 1991.

The print shops attending the first conference were

Common Wealth Printing, Hadley, MA
Grassroots Press, Raliegh, NC
Harbinger Publications, Columbia, SC
Inkworks, Berkeley, CA
Justice Graphics, Chicago, IL
Lakeside Press, Madison, WI
Omega Press, Philadelphia, PA
Orange Blossom Press, Cleveland, OH
Press Gang, Vancouver, BC
Prompt Press, Camden, NJ
Ragged Edge Press, New York, NY
Red Sun Press, Jamaica Plain, MA
Salsedo Press, Chicago, IL

(For addresses, etc., see resource secion—Eds.)

Watermark Artisans

A Lifetime Path of Economic and Personal Empowerment

Carolyn McKecuen

Watermark Association of Artisans, Inc., is a thirteen-year-old worker-owned craft cooperative, 97 percent composed of women. When the organization was first incorporated, it served primarily as a marketing agent for 35 women who wanted to control the business they had created in a rural, economically depressed section of northeastern North Carolina where the few jobs available for women were (and still are) at or below minimum wage.

Over the years, Watermark has grown from one small retail shop to the present busy cooperative that has more than 430 members, wholesales to more than 500 retail shops, supplies 15 retail-catalog firms with products, and operates local, state, and national training programs. However, the governance of the organization is still basically the same: our members vote at general-membership meetings on the major issues affecting the co-op; our board of directors, elected by and from the membership, convenes monthly to make decisions when the general membership does not meet; and our general manager and staff carry out the policies of the members and handle the daily activities of the organization.

Individuals may begin the process of becoming members of Watermark by completing an application form and by submitting to the Screening Committee three pieces of their work in each craft area in which they wish to be certified. If their products pass the quality, design, and craftsmanship standards, they are eligible to purchase one share of stock for $75 and to become working and voting members of the cooperative.

Once trainees are accepted as Watermark members, they are assigned to a "Watermark buddy," a Watermark member who produces crafts in the same media as the trainee and who can answer general organizational and craft-skills questions. There are several breakfast or lunch meetings each year for each craft medium so that older and newer members can meet, discuss problems, share production ideas, and be sure that everyone is adhering to agreed-upon design, material, and production criteria.

NEED: Making Self-Education Central

Recognizing the necessity to educate our members in such areas as cooperative principles, design, craftsmanship, quality control, basic business and financial practices, and self-assertion and self-esteem, Watermark created the Northeastern Education and Development (NEED) Foundation as a training center. It has three components.

First, the local program trains applicants in how to become members and in specific craft skills. The craft-skills classes NEED operates are usually taught by Watermark members, many of whom were once NEED trainees, and vary in length depending on what is taught. Usually, beginning-level classes are four to six hours long. Intermediate and advanced classes can last up to several days, but someone who learns quickly can take a basic class and receive orders from Watermark within four or five days.

The local program also offers a full array of self-employment and self-development classes to help disadvantaged individuals take more control of their lives and money-making activities. These are often taught by outside professionals.

The Statewide Technical Assistance and Marketing Training Project works with groups across North Carolina to develop their organizations, their marketing skills, and their products. It also assesses the needs of existing and developing microenterprises and creates short- and long-term strategies to assist them.

Finally, the National Internship Program responds to the various businesses and marketing organizations that contact Watermark for technical assistance. The small businesses (usually cooperatives or worker-owned organizations) selected to participate in this internship program send several staff members for hands-on training. The schooling focuses on those areas of Watermark's business structure that relate to the interns' job responsibilities in their own organizations. They receive business-theory training from NEED and work with Watermark's staff until they can perform each task competently. They then take this relevant, hands-on experience back to their own work. Because of the time required for this type of instruction, Watermark can train only one organization per month. Thus far, more than forty small businesses, from such diverse locations as Montana, Louisiana, Tennessee, Mexico, and Honduras, have participated. Government officials from Tanzania, Somalia, and the Philippines have also visited Watermark to learn from its example.

One advantage of having a training center such as NEED is flexibility. For example, if Watermark receives an order for several thousand baskets of a particular design to be shipped in thirty days, and only the person who designed the basket knows how to make it, NEED can offer a class to Watermark members using the basketmaker to do the training so that the order can be filled. Or, if several Watermark members or NEED trainees want to have a class dealing with being a working mother while coping with teenagers, NEED would offer it as soon as a qualified instructor could be found. Through having such classes, members are brought closer together; through having members instruct trainees, friendships and networks begin to develop almost automatically.

Since NEED is organized as a training center, it does not have members. The majority of the trainees join Watermark, but many people from the community take advantage of the diversity of class-workshop offerings. To help give a broad base of direction to NEED, it is governed by an elected board of directors with representatives of the communities it serves. Currently, there are three ministers, three educators, and three Watermark members, each serving a staggered three-year term.

Maintaining Cooperative Principles amid Global Competition

Because of our membership growth and the complexity of the demands from increased sales, Watermark has lost some of the personal contact and closeness of members who used to know each other intimately. For the co-op to function in the business community and to expand its share of the marketplace, we had to realize that we were competing in a global economy. The cooperative wants its members to make at least $5 per hour; however, it is selling products to shops that can buy them from China (where women who sew make $.15 per hour) or from Taiwan (where the wage is $.25 an hour). Such wages are typical for various craft media in the Far East and in most Third World countries; therefore, co-op members know they must constantly be designing and improving product lines, adopting and adapting new technologies, streamlining all aspects of the business, and learning as much about the marketplace as possible.

Complicating matters is our commitment to work on a break-even basis so that our members can take home as much of the profit as possible. This constantly challenges us to foresee and to plan for large expenditures that could put us in a cash-flow crunch. Furthermore, because NEED is a nonprofit training foundation whose primary focus is offering craft training for nominal sums (usually the cost of supplies), it must operate with a limited budget and must seek grant support.

Despite having to compete with state, regional, national, and international organizations and businesses, and having to adapt business operations to meet this competition, the co-op's members did not want to sacrifice some principles with which they had started. Chief among these is that small, rural communities must ultimately rely on themselves to create long-term economic-development projects. Another is that we deny no one who is qualified the opportunity to work through the cooperative and to make as little or as much income as she or he wants to make. We also choose to help empower all individuals to take more and better control of their lives and to develop their craft skills to the fullest.

Still, the co-op is reaching a stage in its growth where it must decide how large it wants to be and how much time it will allocate to training others. We still hold to our basic goals, but sometimes, because of having to operate in a profit-loss business environment, we are pulled in directions that make it easy to overlook the slower, less proficient individual who needs time to develop.

Feeling Ownership; Becoming Empowered

By adhering to these initial priorities, having a membership that puts the organization before personal gain, and operating an ongoing educational component for new members, new board members, and old members, Watermark has maintained its initial purposes with almost everyone feeling involved and empowered within the cooperative. The members still have high professional expectations for themselves in quality, performance, commitment, and cooperation.

A key component of Watermark's success is effort and responsibility exercised by the total membership. This concept is emphasized to NEED's trainees, and stressed again when prospective members talk to Watermark's staff at the new-member orientation session. Members learn from the beginning of their association with Watermark that this is a worker-owned, worker-managed business and that its success depends to a huge extent on them. They come to realize Watermark is *their* business. Barbara Eckert, a member of six months, expressed the idea perfectly: "Watermark is the only business I'll ever have. If it doesn't succeed, I lose. No, not just me, but we all lose. Since I can't do without the money I make through Watermark, I'm going to do everything I can to be sure Watermark is a success."

Another way most members feel ownership is through their contributions of ideas, volunteer effort, and committee work. The board members and staff frequently seek members' opinions on various operational and policy matters via phone calls, through newsletters asking for opinions, and by informal conversations when members bring in their products for shipment. Members are recruited during the year to serve as hosts for special events, to help with inventory, to give demonstrations, and the like. They are also asked to serve on the many committees that plan and conduct activities, give advice, and help set goals for the future. By having as many members as possible involved in the decision making and operation of the cooperative, each member can feel that she or he is not only supporting the organization but is also empowered within it.

Proud to Be Watermark

Most members are particularly proud of the ways we have translated our goals and ideals into reality while keeping a firm grip on the everyday marketplace. Watermark has given birth to more than four hundred jobs where there were none, while creating economic justice and democracy in the workplace that can be a model for other organizations. Also, through its training programs Watermark has helped its members and community take control over their economic lives while instructing similar organizations and creating with them a network that shares problems and solutions, sorrows and joys. Enabling others to become stronger and to solve their problems without repeating our mistakes is one of our finest contributions.

But perhaps our greatest accomplishment is how we have helped each other. Two examples from our members highlight the Watermark experience.

"I never thought I could do anything; neither did my husband or my parents. Now I am making things and people pay me for them. Now I know I can do something." This woman, the mother of three, after having been a member of Watermark for two years, went back to school, got her general-education diploma, and presently is a senior at a local college.

"I used to be afraid even to attend PTA meetings. Now I go and ask the principal questions during the meeting. Three years ago I never thought I would have been able to do such a thing." This quiet, timid woman of thirty-five went through NEED's training, became a Watermark member, left her battering husband, and soon began teaching craft skills and classes for NEED.

These women are not isolated cases. For Watermark, this is what a worker-owned cooperative is about. We do more than offer members a means of making money: we offer a path of growth and empowerment that lasts a lifetime.

The Hoedads
Building Worker Cooperatives
in the Pacific Northwest

Hal Hartzell

Many Colorful Threads

The Pacific Northwest has been home to many varied strains of worker cooperation, colorful threads woven into a gossamer history of workers striving for more control over their work lives. The longshoremen, woodworkers, plywood co-ops, Granges, and agricultural cooperatives all flourished in their own time, and all helped individuals survive certain economic pressures. Nourished by strong notions of democracy, even today consumer and electric-power co-ops, worker-owned retail outlets, factories and transportation companies, and production and labor co-ops still struggle to grow together toward a more cooperative and perhaps more productive way of doing business.

More recent cooperative efforts have their source in ideas born in the late sixties and early seventies. Many coincided with a northwestern migration of the hardier flower children. Resisting hierarchical structures, they began to experiment with worker ownership and democratic management. Eventually, in small groups they reinvented the co-op spoke of the free-enterprise wheel. In Lane County, Oregon, where I live, people have been building alternatives to business as usual as if their survival depended on it.

The Growth and Decline of Hoedads, Inc.

My personal perspective on northwestern cooperatives is formed by my eighteen years of participation in Hoedads, Inc., a worker-owned labor cooperative. In the early seventies, money for reforestation boomed through the cheap-labor market when state and federal governments, reacting to citizen alarm, began to take the dwindling forests seriously. My state created the Oregon Forest Practices Act, which required timber companies to replant clear-cut acreage before they could cut more. The federal government also began to require that public lands harvested for timber had to be reforested. It was a wide-open time, and the tree planters got close to the woods; close enough to feel the slippery mud on steep slopes and the biting cold of a winter rain in the Oregon mountains. With no pool of trained tree planters, anyone could catch some contractor's crummy at 5 A.M. at the local pickup spot and go to work.

Although tree planting may well be the hardest job on the market, back then the unskilled workers were paid less than $25 a day. The labor contractor, on the other hand, could make about $50 profit per day on each planter for doing the bookwork, raising the bond, and providing tools, crummies, and contracts. With four or five crews, a contractor could get rich. Given this structure, it did not take long for the planters to get fed up with the contractors and to form worker-owned partnerships and cooperatives to plant trees on their own.

Hoedads started as a partnership of three people in 1970. By 1974 it had transformed itself into a worker cooperative corporation with ten crews and several hundred members. From there, despite little professional assistance and no viable models to emulate, Hoedads grew quickly to a peak active membership of more than five hundred people and seventeen crews in 1977 and 1978. With Hoedads' blessing, a group broke away in the latter year to form a new cooperative called Second Growth. This separation was repeated over the next few years by six other groups within Hoedads, until by 1982 there were more than twenty such organizations. For a while, there were enough co-ops to form an association, but many of the smaller offshoot cooperatives soon failed in the face of stiff competition from large labor contractors, many of whom exploited laborers brought from other countries.

Hoedads still thrives today, though we have had to weather fierce storms, including crashing markets, problems of size and structure, intense agency scrutiny, and political struggles at the local, state, and national levels on behalf of worker ownership and cooperative business organization.

Breaking Down the Walls between Co-Ops

Despite many efforts to keep the cooperative movement vital, the U.S. free-enterprise system and people's antipathy toward the competition frequently raise walls between struggling co-ops. Perhaps small worker-owned enterprises must endure an incubation period before they can grow more aware of the larger picture and associate with other worker-controlled organizations to create new social, political, and economic agendas and strategies. Many attempts to create broad-based cooperative federations in Lane County have come to naught, bogging down in structural flaws, defective meeting process, or lack of individual cooperative skills. In contrast, the Northwest Forest Workers Association (NWFWA) was one bright spot of worker cooperation at the association level. At its height, twenty-two worker-owned forest labor cooperatives were part of what was essentially a trade association created to protect the co-ops from their business adversaries. For a while, NWFWA was also able to promote better working conditions and benefits for more than a thousand forest cooperative workers and to take over Hoedads' role as political lobbyist for various worker-owned forest-labor companies.

On the other hand, there are other examples of more ongoing regional cooperative associations. The Puget Sound Cooperative Federation (PSCF) has been extremely active and effective in and around Seattle, especially in the critical role of introducing worker ownership and democratic management to traditional labor unions and business leaders. Maybe Seattle, with a longer cooperative history than Lane County, has already gone through its incubation period.

A "School in and of the Woods": What Hoedads Achieved

Hoedads came to be because the right people came together at the right time and place. People were attracted to Hoedads by the lure of hard work in the mountains, the mystique of worker ownership, and the strong bonds that develop when people of like mind work together. More than two thousand members have passed through Hoedads, melding their experience and, in the spirit of "once a Hoedad, always a Hoedad," bringing the excitement and methods of worker ownership, democratic management, and group process to new business, political, and organizing situations. In retrospect, then, Hoedads has been like a school in and of the woods. Its open bookkeeping system, democratic meeting and management, and cooperative bylaws have been copied by other co-ops. Throughout, Hoedads has been an inspiring model—one that demonstrates for the record that worker ownership can succeed over a substantial period in the rough real world of labor contracting, that a collective perception can be articulated, that democratic decisions can be made to work in the business world. Better yet, Hoedads has been strong enough to help other cooperative ventures get under way, whether by lending money or by teaching what its members gleaned from direct experience.

Cooperatives and the Bioregional Ethic

Many former Hoedads are still very much involved in helping develop that collective perception. Here, for example, are some thoughts from a friend, himself a former Hoedad, about the Hoedads and worker ownership in the Pacific Northwest.

Jerry Rust was one of three partners to start Hoedads in the winter of 1970 and was its president through 1973, when he decided to run for county commissioner as an independent. Hoedads of course supported their favorite son with dollars and thousands of hours of voluntary campaign labor. The opposition had never seen such an organized body of volunteers! Rust was elected, and Hoedads found themselves heir to considerable attention—suddenly, politicians and government agencies began listening. Today, Jerry is in the middle of his fourth term as a Lane County commissioner. He offers the following long-term perspective on cooperation:

Ten or so years ago, there was a great deal of suspicion about cooperatives and that suspicion, while it may linger, has diminished considerably today. Democracy in the workplace, participatory management, cooperative agreements and arrangements, are all commonplace ideas now. There is a great deal of acceptance. I don't raise any eyebrows today when I talk about cooperatives as viable models for new ways of doing things. A cooperative is a private-sector entity, an entrepreneurial activity. There were various events in the seventies and eighties where intense anticooperative politics tried to smash cooperatives through adverse definitions and even defamation, but I don't see that same kind of anticooperative activity happening anymore.

I think that Hoedads has always been close to the cutting edge of change in regard to sensible work alternatives for the immediate future. I think we as a society are going through great changes toward democracy in the workplace. A lot more care is being given to the relationship between capital, labor, and management. It is good business today to make joint plans with employees and management—that is, participatory management.

The kinds of technologies we have been relating to are going to force us into smaller and more cooperative business units. The real big event which will impose profound changes on our way of doing business is the impending fuel crisis. America is based on a fuel economy. Our agriculture is based on a nonsustainable importation of oil. The distribution system for food is based on fuel. Our cities have grown and been planned to accommodate the automobile. We are not going to remain a highly mobile society moving goods to distant markets—we're not going to be able to sustain that sort of life-style. We will need smaller, more locally oriented production cooperatives, food cooperatives, farming and land cooperatives, community-economic-development corporations, and credit unions. The whole idea of self-reliant communities is going to be one of the dominant features of the very last part of this century, and I hope our efforts will pave the way for a whole new reorganization of the relationship in America between capital, management, and labor. I think it will be the only way we can survive.

What does Hoedads have to do with all of this? Well, we were on the scene before we even grasped the theories and concepts behind worker ownership and democratic management. We knew what felt right—it felt right to share, it felt right to treat women and men equally, it felt right to make democratic decisions. It felt safer: it felt more powerful in the long run to pool our meager resources into one working unit. Our early faith has paid off in many ways. Like the successful Mondragon enterprises in Spain, Hoedads were able to recycle a lot of money into the local community, as well as help start other worker-owned businesses.

It's not surprising to find that many former Hoedads, although they have branched out, still maintain similar lines of thought. Some are studying the forest ecology, some are starting a network of organic farms welded together in a cooperative marketing venture, others are publishing books on workplace democracy. We need a greater bioregional ethic in the Northwest, and I think democratic workplaces are the key if we are to deliver up any sort of future to our children.

Still Open, Democratic, and Vulnerable

Today, Hoedads has thirty members and another thirty employees, who work contract by contract. Our primary goal is still to provide work for our members. We still plant trees, but we do many other things: park, residential, bridge, and fence construction; timber-stand examination and stocking surveys; stewardship contracts; thinning; vegetation and big-game management; trail building and maintenance; cone picking; and fire fighting. We are still very definitely a worker-owned cooperative. We have two general meetings each year where most of the members get together to debate and formulate general co-op policy; our board members are elected at large and meet once a month to formulate more specific business policy; and our elected officers manage the company day by day. There are absolutely no closed aspects to the enterprise: members can participate wherever they wish, provided they respect the democratic process and cooperative structure, both of which have been fine-tuned over the years.

When I remember the struggles we have come through in the Northwest, it amazes me that any cooperatives have existed at all in this country and that any still exist. It is difficult to play the game of free enterprise from the vulnerable vantage point of democracy. Co-ops regulate themselves in ways unknown to private businesses. When the primary edge in competition depends on a company's ability to evade the rules in the battle between industry and its regulators, a many-voiced cooperative, with open meetings and elected managers, is at a distinct disadvantage. Hoedads, Inc., has survived the intense scrutiny of every agency in existence, while more traditional contractors have been running afoul of the laws for years with little notice. One can only hope that if U.S. enterprise ever does become truly free, the cooperative approach would have a chance to spread.

Many people have been involved in working out the structures and processes necessary for new models and alternatives with which to face the future. Still, there is much to be learned about the possibilities and much to be done if we are to keep our transformation growing into the 1990s. People, I think, are realizing that we need to learn once again the necessities of hard work with one another (and at all levels), and that we need to remember how to pool our labor, our time, and our resources into cooperative enterprises that will best serve our common interest in survival.

Colt Enterprises, Inc.
Union-Based Self-Determination in Texas*

Jackie Van Anda

A Grand Opening

Colt Enterprises, Inc., marked its grand opening in October 1987 with a major celebration for the 103 new worker-owners of a sewing factory and their supporters. On hand in Tyler, Texas, 100 miles east of Dallas, were then-Texas Agriculture Commissioner Jim Hightower and ACTWU (Amalgamated Clothing and Textile Workers Union) president Jack Sheinkman, as well as bank and government officials, television and newspaper reporters, and local residents. On that day, the mostly black and Hispanic unionized garment workers at Colt became the owners of the largest worker-owned sewing factory in the country and the first in Texas.

In August 1986, these women and men faced the dilemma that has become far too familiar in many small, rural towns: the Levi Strauss & Co. plant that had employed 556 people shut down. While Levi refused to discuss seriously with their employees the possibility of a conversion to worker ownership, the company did provide severance pay. Many of the workers pooled that money into a fund to finance a feasibility study for a worker-owned factory and formed a "Hands around Our Jobs" organizing committee. They then went after the expertise and the capital needed to create new jobs. Eventually, even Levi supported their efforts.

Despite careful planning and high hopes, Colt's start-up has been rocky. The worker-owners began with a pay cut to a base wage of $4.50 per hour—a rate 12 to 13 percent below that of the average Levi Strauss contract but, with incentives for production over quotas, still above the rate for even the most experienced operators in nonunion jobs in the South. The workers then faced a long series of difficulties, including layoffs of up to one-half of the workforce, a change of

* From *Christianity and Crisis*, 15 February 1988.

managers, and the loss of two name-brand contracts to low-wage plants outside the United States. Still, only three years after opening, Colt had stabilized, the workforce had increased to 130, the firm had introduced its own line of women's clothing, and the base pay had been raised to $4.80, with most workers earning 110 to 120 percent of base because of production bonuses.

Coping with Economic Crisis: New Union Strategies

Since the late 1970s, manufacturing in the United States has been in an ever-increasing crisis. Firms, and whole industries, such as steel, have faced sharper international competition. America's market share in production has declined. As companies in marginal businesses have scrambled for profits, real wages have dropped. The "supply side" economic policies of the Reagan and Bush administrations have led to the consolidation of capital into larger and larger corporate conglomerates and to the systematic dismantling of unions and affirmative-action programs.

As economic pressures forced unions to give up concessions and to lose jobs, and thus bargaining power, many, like the ACTWU, began reexamining labor's role in the economy and experimenting with new forms of worker self-determination. "I just got tired of dealing with plant closing after plant closing," says Joan Suarez, ACTWU's Southwest regional joint board manager and key organizer for the Colt project. She believes the union's role in job security must involve a broad approach that looks toward the long term.

The Colt venture represents one part of an overall effort ACTWU has undertaken in recent years to find ways of promoting job security. Union members have been active in lobbying for enforcement of import restrictions and in supporting Jim Hightower's efforts through the Texas Agriculture Commission for state revenue bonds for economic development. Other ACTWU strategies have included influencing company policies, particularly investments in South Africa, through shareholder actions and using collective bargaining to ensure notification of plant closings and retraining of workers. In some instances, unions have assisted workers in buying out plants that were about to close down or, as in the Colt venture, in opening up a new worker-owned enterprise.

All of these tactics are part of a strategy of experimentation. Many will not be successful. No one tactic is the answer, but all are part of reformulating labor's role. Labor advocates stress that the overall goal of unions is not simply collective bargaining but increasing workers' self-determination. *(Editors' note: for more on these new roles and strategies for labor unions, see chapters 4 and 6 below.)*

A Labor-Controlled and Labor-Designed ESOP

The Colt Enterprises workers took what is basically a management tool—an employee stock ownership plan (ESOP)—along with its tax advantages, and combined it with the principles of cooperatives to form their own version of worker management. They successfully joined the resources of local banks, state economic development agencies, national co-op assistance organizations, and union pension funds to finance their new experiment. And they set up a management system in which an experienced plant manager who shares the goals of the enterprise accepts his policy directives from the worker-shareholders, meets daily with a leadership team of nine plant workers, and meets monthly with a board of directors composed of three Colt workers, three local community and industry representatives, and one representative of ACTWU. The local union remains a strong voice in the plant, arbitrating disputes and grievances and doing much education. While no one can guarantee the success of any new business, Colt has taken the best of past experiments and added some new features of its own. Its record already suggests that careful groundwork is paying off.

Basic Organizing Principles

The architects of Colt Manufacturing tried to incorporate into their structure characteristics that would help Colt both compete successfully in the workplace and maintain the social goals of worker control and democratic management. Some of the original principles follow:

- Decisions are made on the basis of *one person, one vote*, regardless of how many shares a person holds;
- *All employees are members.* Often nonworking shareholders have a lower level of commitment to the business; successful firms generally keep this to a minimum;
- Workers invest a *nontrivial entrance fee*—at least $1,000—into the company;
- When members leave they must *sell back their shares* to the company—a rule that helps guarantee that worker-owners maintain control;
- All employees have *access to the financial records*, so that when decisions are to be made they can know what is possible.

Most of these principles have proven useful, but the worker-owners continue to alter them to fit their experience. For example, about one-half of the original investors no longer work at the plant, but their $1,000 fee will be held until the ESOP can repurchase their shares (but no longer than three years). Also, new recruits to the company are no longer required to invest the $1,000 but must pass a one-year probationary period before they are allowed full voting rights. A separate class of preferred stock, established to generate capital, allows nonworking investors to receive dividends and to sit in on board meetings, although they cannot vote in shareholder meetings. The board continues to guide major decisions, but monthly plantwide meetings have been replaced with weekly departmental employee participation groups (EPGs).

The Union Connection

Worker ownership is controversial to many in the ranks of labor, who view the transition to ownership as undermining unions' traditional adversarial relationship with management. At Colt, though, the buyout seems to have strengthened the local.

The ACTWU helped start Colt by offering technical support and resources. Aside from the ten months of staff time put into helping the workers organize, the union also aided in applying for several large loans from the National Cooperative Bank Development Corp. and the Cooperative Assistance Fund. The union's unemployed-workers' fund kept many people from going hungry during the planning phases.

The local also provides workers a structured grievance procedure. "With this many people you're always going to have some who don't agree," explains Essie Carter, local union president. "The union is our way of working out differences." Further, rather than operating solely from an adversarial position, "the union can now play a role of the extended family and encourage the growth and development of people" through continued education, according to ACTWU Regional Manager Suarez.

Finally, workers at Colt remain connected to larger social and labor issues through their union activities. In their unusual contract with ACTWU, Colt Enterprises agrees to promote organizing and trade unions throughout Texas, to promote cooperatives as an alternative to plant closings, and to work with ACTWU on improved workers' compensation, unemployment compensation, job training, affirmative action, child care, health care, and other issues important to workers.

Given the union's leadership and supportive role in every phase of the Colt operation and the workers' active local, identification with organized labor remains strong in the cooperative. Accepting their role as owners has proven more difficult. "Education," warns Suarez, "is a long-term process. It is difficult to require people to attend ownership meetings after work time for months and months." Instead the group has opted for fewer meetings and has developed, with the Texas Department of Agriculture, a Colt/ACTWU handbook, which is now being used as a model for other worker-owned companies in the state. New members receive one-on-one orientations, and an introductory video is under consideration. An in-plant newsletter also helps improve communication without requiring lengthy meetings.

The Management Challenge

Thorough familiarity with the clothing industry was a plus in establishing the cooperative. "You can have the best structure in the world," says Randy Barber of the Center for Economic Organizing, "but if you don't have the economics it's not going to work." An internationally recognized consulting firm conducted Colt's feasibility study and concluded that, given the increasing market for women's and girls' jeans, "a worker-owned jeans contracting company, under certain conditions, was viable and had the potential for long-term productivity."

But the biggest challenge confronting Colt was the unexpected immensity of tasks faced by their single manager. Although the workers tried to hire an experienced plant manager who was sympathetic to their cause, it proved difficult to find a single person skilled at all management responsibilities—from engineering, to financing, to marketing. Colt's first manager was an excellent engineer who became overwhelmed by the constant need for marketing and let the plant's activity slump. Faced with an off-and-on commitment from Levi Strauss and the need to bring in contract work, the owners soon found themselves sewing unfamiliar styles and missing promised deadlines. During the tenuous six-month transition between managers, an ACTWU industrial engineer, sent to assist management in technical details, had to hold the show together.

Colt finally found a new manager in September 1989, and the company has since moved back onto a smooth course, with a steady relationship with Walls Industries for hunting pants and the development of its own label. Still, the harsh realities of business competition continue to play a role—for example, in minimizing "discussion" of problems in favor of a more hard-nosed effort to discipline members who do not perform to quality standards. "We must make shipments to survive," explains manager Roy Maynard. "At this point we have the sales volume we need. Our number-one priority now is to improve quality and efficiency." Once members can see profits and the benefits of ownership, Maynard believes, they may once again feel motivated to take more leadership. However, in the short run he feels it is his job as manager to run a tight ship and guide it back into safe financial waters.

Benefits of the Colt Buyout

The Colt initiative did more than keep 130 Texas workers employed. "Colt has been a flagship within ACTWU for looking at other possible buyouts," says Joan Suarez. In order to provide crucial capital for such workers' efforts, ACTWU president Jack Sheinkman spearheaded the AFL-CIO's formation, in February 1990, of an Employee Partnership Fund. The fund plans to attract a capital pool of several hundred million dollars to enable union members to buy out troubled factories that still have a good chance of business success.

Yet, Suarez's optimism remains tempered with the caution of a seasoned organizer. Plant buyouts are not the panacea for the labor movement. "Would I do Colt again? Yeah. Would I do another Colt? That depends," she answers. Given Colt's roller-coaster past, Suarez advises others considering a buyout that "the selection of your managerial workforce is very important. Have a long line of working capital and be aware that worker-ownership education is a long-term process."

One of the Colt buyout's most impressive benefits has been the transformation of the firm's leaders. Union members have learned managerial skills as supervisory roles rotated in some departments. Suarez points to her own personal development; she sees the Colt experience as having spilled over into her other leadership roles in the union and as enabling her to better negotiate with management. For some,

Colt marked the beginning of new dreams—one former worker-owner is now a jeans designer. And managers willing to join, and risk, with the Colt workers have witnessed new levels of determination and motivation when workers become owners.

Finally, the Colt workers have shown, in several different ways, that it is possible to turn adversity into opportunity. Not only have they gradually converted a shut down plant into an increasingly successful business but they have coped with a nemesis of U.S. firms—offshore competition—in exemplary ways. When Levi's and Liz Claiborne deserted Colt in favor of competing plants operating mainly in the Dominican Republic and Guatemala, the workers developed their own line of women's (not misses') sportswear, including jeans, shorts, and skirts. "We believe we have found a special niche," says Joan Suarez. They are marketing the Colt label through Dallas clothing marts and received assistance from Jim Hightower, former Texas Commissioner of Agriculture, in setting up marketing meetings with retailers in the state.

By creating its own label, Colt Enterprises has also found a new opportunity to support Third World workers. An Austin investor who helped finance the purchase of denim fabric for the new Colt line asked—in exchange for not charging interest—that a portion of the proceeds support some form of alternative education. The Colt workers decided to put $1 of the manufacturing price of each item in their line toward worker education in the Dominican Republic; the program focuses on health, safety, and workers' rights. Rather than battling the workers who obtained their lost Levi's and Liz Claiborne contracts, Colt has resolved to work with them in solidarity. As Suarez puts it, "It's only by standing together that we can guarantee good working conditions and job stability for all in the long run."

High School in the Community
A Worker-Controlled Educational Environment

Matt Borenstein

In the late 1960s, a group of teachers at Hillhouse High School in New Haven, Connecticut, who disagreed with the administration's "clamp down" response to racial conflict, sought to effect changes in school policy. They experienced continued frustration of their efforts to exert influence and began to make plans to establish a new school based on a different set of principles.

If You Can't Change the Schools, Start Your Own

In 1970, with some support from key downtown school administrators, this group obtained a one-year grant from the Mott Foundation to establish a public "school without walls." The idea for this High School in the Community (HSC) was to use such neighborhood resources as libraries, shops, colleges, unions, and community organizations to enrich its curriculum.

The school center was located in an abandoned car-parts store, and classes were held in various community facilities. At the outset, HSC was governed, in the participatory democracy spirit of the 1960s, by teachers, parents, and students. Our initial enrollment of 150 was selected by lottery from the Hillhouse High School District. We opened in September, 1970 in the midst of a teachers' strike throughout New Haven. One HSC teacher picketed and another stayed out in sympathy. The rest of the faculty broke the strike. They felt that establishing this school was more important than their solidarity with the rest of the teachers in the public school system. This was to change!

During the 1970-71 school year, HSC obtained a federal grant to fund staff salaries, rental expenses for buildings, and costs of equipment and supplies for two of its units. The grant design included a facilitator (an administrative position) to coordinate activities for both units. The New Haven Board of Education, however, refused to designate the facilitator as an administrator, even though they did not have to fund the position. They believed that by so designating the position, the program would obtain a degree of permanence in the school system that they were unwilling to sanction.

I began teaching in the second unit of HSC in 1971. I had just received a doctorate in theoretical physics from Yale but had decided not to pursue an academic or corporate career. I was encouraged to join HSC by a few teachers I had worked with in anti-Vietnam War activities. My job began in mid-August, 1971, when I met with nine other teachers and two office assistants to plan the courses and operation of the school. We were then located in the basement of the Strauss-Adler girdle factory on Olive Street in New Haven, a facility also used by Junior Achievement on weekends and evenings.

It was clear from the beginning that this was our school. We determined the course schedule, the course content, the requirements for credit, and the disciplinary policy. We had no textbooks and no prescribed curricula. We could teach what we wanted, when we wanted, and how we wanted. We had courses in ecology, drama, human sexuality, algebra, and literature. Teachers set up programs in their areas of interest, as well as courses based on student concerns. We established our own work rules and academic policies. The first regulation I remember was a restriction on the number of courses that a teacher could present: some people were using teaching as an excuse to miss faculty meetings. We felt that the collective decision-making process was more important than teaching a few extra courses.

During the first few years of the school, staff meetings were long and difficult. Sometimes we continued our discussions into the evenings, dealing all at once with institutional racism, drugs, remediation, tracking, grades, and endlessly with individual student problems. Each teacher also acted as a counselor to about 15 students to help them decide on course selection and fulfillment of graduation requirements. Initially, students at HSC were primarily either adventurous outcasts or academic outcasts.

When we started the school, we rejected all the things we hated about traditional education: grades, calling teachers by last names, bells, attendance, the same schedule every day, and no attention to cultural and political diversity. Because we had a large chunk of federal funds, not subject to local control, our academic approach was spontaneous and exciting. The normal process for educational spending is to establish needs the previous year so that money can be budgeted and materials ordered in bulk through the city bidding process. It would thus take six months, at least, between request and receipt of materials. The federal money, on the other hand, furnished funds as ideas for projects emerged, allowing us to establish new courses in the middle of a year. We could order materials and get them the next day if they were available in New Haven. We could take field trips at almost any time and use community resources to supplement our classes.

Establishing Structures for the Long Haul

Although there was not much change in leadership over the first four years of the school, I always felt that the faculty had complete control over its operations.

During those years, our existence was always threatened, and our standing leadership was familiar with the techniques necessary for continued funding and with the politics of dealing with the downtown administration. The leadership never tried, however, to challenge the authority of the collective faculty to make the ultimate decisions concerning the operation of HSC. If there were conflicts between grant procedures and board of education policy, a collective decision determined how we would resolve the conflict.

Since our federal funding was not permanent, we had to come up with a structure that could allow us to survive the external politics of New Haven public education and the internal politics of the school. Our task was complicated when, in the spring of 1975, just as the federal funds began to run out, the New Haven Board of Education laid off two hundred first-year teachers, including four from HSC. We started 1976 devastated by the loss of staff and housed in a neglected elementary-school building. Fully dependent on local and state funds, with our two units newly combined into one (with three hundred students and twenty faculty), our collective task was to figure out how to survive.

A big part of our strategy was to create a new leadership group called the facilitating unit (FU), which was designed to permit continuity and to define more clearly the roles in the school. The FU included the facilitator, a student-membership coordinator, a community-education coordinator, and the school guidance counselor. The argument for this composition was that each member had schoolwide responsibilities. For the first time, we started calling for accountability from the leadership. For example, we asked members of the FU to make job descriptions, which we then discussed and modified.

The FU was effective in dealing with survival issues relating to the downtown school administration and the board of education. For example, when questions began to arise as to our ability to evaluate teaching, they were resolved by having the high-school supervisor for the city visit the school in June to review evaluations made by the FU.

After six years of operation, we had established an effective internal structure to operate a teacher-run school. All decisions on curriculum, discipline, and school operation were made by the faculty. The job of the leadership group remained to carry out staff decisions. As in all organizations, leadership had more information and sometimes attempted to move issues in directions based on such privileged knowledge. This technique, however, did not work at HSC. Instead, there was tremendous faculty resentment of issues and decisions sprung on them by leadership. Most often, under such conditions, we would meet extra hours (or even days) to resolve deeply felt conflicts.

From 1984 to 1986, I served as the fourth facilitator of HSC. I felt that it was my turn, but I did not enjoy an educational role so far removed from students. I spent a lot of time dealing with downtown administrators, parents, and secretaries. On my last day in that job, I received a notice that the board of education would be appointing outside administrators for HSC and for four other alternative programs in New Haven that our success had helped spawn. The administrators' union had finally prevailed with the superintendent of schools, who posted administrative positions for all of these programs.

HSC resisted this effort mightily. We organized parents to protest. We asked our union, the New Haven Federation of Teachers, to support our effort to maintain autonomy. We received national support and recognition from the American Federation of Teachers. We made the front page of the *American Teacher* and were featured at an AFT conference on educational reform. Finally, the superintendent and the administrators' union relented; more than twenty years into it, we still maintain our self-regulating structure.

Relations with the Union

When HSC first opened, most of its faculty were scabs, but this soon changed. As early as 1973, most HSC teachers honored a citywide strike, and soon HSC staff became known for their militant picketing and HSC students for their support of the teachers. Indeed, by 1975 HSC teachers made up half of the teacher strike committee. At one point, when ninety teachers from two major high schools and the negotiating committee were jailed, HSC staff maintained leadership and communication within the union in order to resolve the strike. Eventually, HSC teachers served as members of the executive board of the union, acting as grievance chairperson, stewards' chairperson, and editor of the union newspaper.

Today, the New Haven Federation of Teachers supports the establishment of teacher committees (school-planning and management teams) to take part in decisions on school operation. The union has hired a full time coordinator to support teachers in this effort, and it is has helped to start a teacher-run elementary school. Some teachers at HSC are also planning to begin yet another teacher-managed school, one with an ecologically focused curriculum that would provide students and the wider community with hands-on educational experiences and more-than-schoolroom resources.

What's So Good about It?

While efforts were under way to impose an administrator on HSC, local reporters found our story and our plight interesting. One of them asked me what difference it made for teachers to run their own school. In response, I asked the reporter to imagine a newspaper where the editors were elected by reporters from among their peers and editorial policy was decided collectively. There still would be a publication, but the product would be completely different.

At HSC, the teachers decide on all policies and aspects of the school's operation. Anyone who walks into the building immediately realizes that this is a different school, with a relaxed and friendly atmosphere. Students meet socially with teachers and other staff in the school office, where they beg to use the school phone or try to get a look at the newspaper's sports section before it disappears.

Teachers and students are called by first names and meet informally in the halls as well as in classrooms. The daily class schedule allows time for students to get snacks and to socialize. Students register for classes four times a year from catalogs prepared by the faculty, who are constantly creating new courses. Fresh teaching teams are formed and new techniques are tried.

The daily schedule is organized around three-hour classes that meet five days per week and are often team-taught and interdisciplinary. During a nine-week marking period, a full year's curriculum can be completed. Some classes are ability-grouped, while others include students of all academic levels.

Some courses have such traditional titles as Algebra I or French I, but most reflect topical interests—Technology and Culture, or Law and Statistics. One class in the spring, Ecology, meets four hours a day at the West Rock Nature Center in New Haven. Students study formal ecology, plant an organic garden, and grow and slaughter chickens for the school picnic. Besides learning academic skills, students at HSC learn how to work in groups, make decisions, resolve conflicts, and socialize with people from different neighborhoods and backgrounds.

Recently, Roger Weisberg, a Yale psychologist, introduced a curriculum for New Haven schools that systemized what HSC had been using for twenty years as our "affective" curriculum. It stresses such nonacademic skills as interpersonal relations, collective decision making, and respect for racial and ethnic diversity. Evaluations of the school have shown that HSC students do as well academically as students from other schools, but excel in these areas of social skills.

Without quotas, HSC has always maintained a racially integrated school population (40–50 percent white, 40–50 percent Black, 10–15 percent Hispanic). The faculty tries consistently to increase its own nonwhite membership; currently, there are two black faculty out of a professional staff of seventeen.

Still More Satisfying—and More Demanding

HSC receives daily requests for information from school systems all over the United States. Four or five teacher or administrator groups from other school systems visit us each year.

Working at a teacher-run school is more satisfying and more demanding than working within the traditional, hierarchical school environment. Even after twenty years, we still debate and analyze the role of leadership and the need for accountability in the school. We evaluate and revise the curriculum and course schedule every year. We are highly critical of any perceived failures, and we need to be reminded by parents and students of our successes.

My students question why I teach at HSC. Holding that doctorate in theoretical physics, I could, so they say, demand a high salary in a corporate position. I respond that working in an environment where you feel useful and creative, while having personal support and meaningful input into daily operations, is an experience offered by very few workplaces in this country!

Short Takes

Worker-owned cooperatives and employee-owned democratic businesses have made their way into virtually all sectors of our economy and all regions of our country. The short takes that follow are of necessity selective and do less than full justice to this growing terrain. We have organized them into separate categories to illustrate not only their diversity but their developing interconnections. Additional short takes, of union-led employee-owned enterprises, can be found at the end of chapter 6.

Home Care and Health Care[1]

Cooperative Home Care Associates (CHCA), in the Bronx, New York, began in 1975 with twelve part-time workers and has since expanded to over two hundred home-health aides, the greatest number of whom are full timers, older than 40, women of color, and equal shareowners in the company they own. CHCA has won recognition from such institutional clients as the Montefiore Medical Center and the Visiting Nurse Service of New York for being among their best health care providers. At the same time, they have actively advocated higher wages and better conditions throughout the home-care industry, forming coalitions with church groups, unions, and community activists to demand reforms.

In Athens, Ohio, the technical-assistance group **Worker Owned Network (WON)** met in 1984 with a group of women whose public welfare related job training as homemakers was about to run out. Surmounting personal and financial obstacles, the group opened **Home and Family Care Associates** in February 1985. Contracts with the local county's department of human services and other social service agencies have enabled the cooperative to survive. In addition, its example, together with assistance again from WON, helped spawn a similar venture in a neighboring Ohio county, **Elderly and Handicapped Resources**, which is also staffed and owned cooperatively by former welfare recipients.

Recently, efforts have begun to export these labor-intensive cooperative models to other low-income communities, particularly in Boston, Oakland, California, and the Naugatuck Valley in Connecticut. Meanwhile, in a quite different part of the health-care system, a huge (and 99 percent worker-owned) ESOP took shape in 1987, when Hospital Corporation of America (HCA) sold more than 100 acute-care hospitals to its 23,000 employees organized as **HealthTrust**. Fears that workers were being sold a lemon have subsided, inasmuch as HealthTrust bonds are currently more highly rated than those of HCA.

Retail Chains, Publishing/Communications Companies, and Taxicab Cooperatives[2]

From the **Alaska Commercial Company**, which operates general stores in 21 communities and has a seven-year-old ESOP covering all of its 470 employees, to **Publix Supermarkets**, centered in Florida, with its 40,000 workers, employee ownership has found fertile ground in the grocery and retail supply business. According to the NCEO's *Employee Ownership Report*, about 10 medium- to larger-sized chains have introduced ESOPs, apparently "as a motivational tool." They include **Dan's Supermarkets** (North Dakota), **Cost Cutter** (Washington State), **Hy-Vee** (Nebraska), and **Meatland** (Maryland). All involve substantial amounts of employee ownership, from 30 percent to 100 percent, and an "unusually high percentage provide full voting rights, considerable financial disclosure, and high levels of employee participation." Moreover, according to the article, written by former NCEO intern Eileen McCarthy, all of these ESOP companies are doing very well financially, which bodes well for the continued growth of employee ownership in this sector. Another confirming instance, reported by the National Cooperative Bank, is **Peck's Markets**, a 3-store chain along the southern tier of New York State. In 1987, their sales increased by 17 percent, with profits following suit, after employees of Peck's purchased all of the company from a retiring owner.

Outside of grocery chains, **Lowe's Home Centers** in the Southeast has been partially owned by its 15,000 employees since 1957. Then, it had only six stores; today, it is the nation's largest building- and home-supplies retailer, with annual sales of close to $3 billion from more than 300 outlets. Many credit this growth, in large measure, to the company's genuine commitment to employee ownership; this policy has also done well by Lowe's employees, allowing many on low salaries to retire with accumulated shared-profit accounts well into six figures.

A substantial number of cooperatively owned or collectively operated print shops—despite their small size and progressive politics—have weathered the rough seas of our market economy. In addition, at least three very large printers or publishers, the **Bureau of National Affairs**, **Journal Communications** (which also owns radio and television stations), and **Quad/Graphics** are employee owned. Indeed, employee ownership has been in place for more than 40 years in the first two of these highly profitable companies, a step taken by previous owners to preserve local control of their enterprises. Extensive shopfloor employee participation is the rule in all three cases. Journal Communications has developed councils to represent separate plants or departments (e.g., the *Milwaukee Journal*) within the overall corporation. Quad/Graphics is renowned for innovative and employee-empowering management. For example, it asks work groups to construct both their own areas of responsibility and appropriate entrepreneurial activities, and it encourages departments to set many policies without seeking approval from top management. (Founder and president Harry Quadracci has called his company's style "management by walking away.") The firm (its 3,000 employees own 39 percent) is also highly successful, being the printer for several major publications, including *Newsweek* and *Ms* magazine.

There appear to be some 40 or 50 employee-owned taxicab companies; many are worker-owned cooperatives, based on one person, one vote, and highly participatory principles. They range from **Capital City Co-op Cab** (serving Sacramento, California), with 80-odd members, to **Union Cab** (Madison, Wisconsin) with 140 members, to **Denver Yellow Cab**, which at its height had some 800 employee owners and an unexcelled safety record, but is presently fighting a battle to stay afloat in Denver's recession-stifled economy.

Ecologically Sound Enterprises: A Growth Field for Worker Ownership?[3]

Worker ownership has recently shown a small but noticeable presence in ecology- or environment-sustaining companies, for example, those engaged in recycling or energy conservation. One example is **Recoverable Resources/Boro Bronx (R2B2)**. Now in its second decade as a subsidiary of a nonprofit community development corporation in the South Bronx, R2B2 recycles more than 14,000 tons annually—as much as a city of 50,000 people—of glass, aluminum, newspaper, corrugated boxes, plastics, and other throwaway items. Expansion plans include doubling its present workforce of 33, opening a new plastics-recycling division with its own capacity of 16,000 tons a year (about 3 percent of New York City's entire plastic-waste stream), increasing overall capacity to 400 tons per day—and converting the business to worker ownership. Phyliss Y. Atwater, president and general manager of the company, sees this conversion as making good sense, since "from the outset, R2B2 has been a community-based enterprise."

One remarkable feature of R2B2 is its double-pronged commitment to community economic development. In its own Bronx backyard, it has created secure and well-paying employment for its mainly minority workforce, while providing more than $25,000 per month in "cash for trash" payments to local collectors—often the homeless or the chronically unemployed. In addition, this enterprise has helped export its successful operation to low-income communities in Brooklyn, Philadelphia, Miami, and Dublin, Ireland. For an account of why this sort of operation can and should be replicated, and how to do so, see the manual published in 1990 by Chicago's **Center for Neighborhood Technology**, *No Time to Waste: How Communities Can Reap Economic Benefits from the Shift to Recycling.*

Cooperatives in Democratic Intentional Communities[4]

In the United States, there are many democratic intentional communities, in which members deliberately pool resources to provide themselves with everything from child care to professional careers, homes, health care and food. (A 1990 Directory from the **Communities Publication Cooperative** and the **Fellowship for Intentional Communities** provides detailed accounts of some 350 of them.) To gain a measure of self-sufficiency, many of these communities have developed cottage industries in crafts, organic farm products, computer software, greeting cards, apparel, and the like; these are frequently organized around democratic and cooperative principles. One example is the **Federation of Egalitarian Communities**, an association of eight highly democratic communities ranging in size from households to hamlets. One of these, **Twin Oaks**, in southwestern Virginia, has supported itself over three decades in part through wood and rope furniture and an indexing business. Another, **East Wind**, of central Missouri, which began in 1973, produces rope sandals and organic nutbutters. On the West Coast, **Cerro Gordo** , an intentional community bordering on a 1,000-acre preserve in the hills of Cottage Grove, Oregon, has spawned several cooperative ecological enterprises. These include a forestry cooperative, which produces lumber in ways that preserve the forest, and **Equinox Industries**, which manufactures quality bicycle trailers, through which we can drastically reduce our dependence on cars and on fossil fuels. Equinox's "Tourlite" trailer can be used not only to carry children, groceries, or camping gear but (through kits supplied by the cooperative) converted to a running or garden cart, car-top carrier, cross-country ski sled, or carrier for rafts, kayaks, sailboards, and surfboards.

A Many-Splendored Movement

A few miscellaneous enterprises should give an even fuller sense of the contemporary movement to bring democracy into the workplace.

Fastener Industries,[5] in Berea, Ohio, is an outstanding example of active shareholder democracy. In 1980, Fastener became completely employee owned when the Whelan family decided to sell the nut and bolt factory. Shares are broadly, though not equally, distributed among the company's 125 employees. No one, including the president, owns more than 4 percent of the stock. Fastener operates through a conventional structure in which shareholders biennially elect the board of directors, who in turn appoint management. But its practice is by no means conventional, since nomination for the board is completely open: ten signatures from employee owners are enough to place a name on the ballot. Typically ten to fifteen candidates are nominated for the five seats, and employee shareholders then distribute their votes in a secret ballot among five candidates of their choice: this avoids the possibility of concentrating all one's shares on a single candidate. At least one place on the board has changed hands in each election since the first, and the majority of the board has changed twice.

Fastener has none of the committees, quality circles, or labor-management participation teams that some participation theorists espouse. Instead, an informal corporate culture of shared responsibility and mutual respect complements the formal decision-making process. The distinction between shopfloor and office workers has been blurred by putting all workers on salary and by recruiting virtually all managers from below. Both of the two current plant managers began their careers at Fastener as assistant machine operators, the usual entry-level job. Employees are asked to voice their opinions about new purchases and procedures, and some have helped to design their own machines and to develop new processes.

To an outsider schooled in conventional corporation culture, Fastener is a genuine shock. Its organizational structure is virtually flat. The company pays up to $1,500 per year to any employee taking business-related courses. It has a *no-layoff policy*, initiated during the 1980s' recession: wages are treated as a fixed cost, and during downturns production aims at increasing inventory. In good years, base pay is supplemented by bonuses and dividends.

The combination of a culture of shared ownership and management with real shareholder democracy has made Fastener one of the most financially successful ESOP firms in the United States. Its total employee compensatory package is significantly, if not embarrassingly, above the industry norm. An average machine operator, with the firm since the ESOP began in 1980, could cash out his or her shares in 1990 for close to $200,000. Thus, for the worker shareholders at Fastener, democratic governance and employee ownership within a conventional corporate structure is at least as good as winning a lottery ticket—and far more certain!

Bookpeople,[6] in Berkeley, California, converted to employee ownership in 1971. A major small-press distributor, it has grown in 19 years from 20 to 75 workers, and from a red-ink company into an efficient and profitable $15 million business. In 1988, it distributed, in equal shares, several hundred thousand dollars in profits back to its member-owners. In recent years, according to Gene Taback, the chairman, more and more employees have learned the business, so much so "that by the early 1980s we felt we could do without a general manager and decided to have our elected board manage the company." Bookpeople is organized as a genuine workers' cooperative: all new employees, after a six-months' probationary period, must purchase 50 shares of stock; this is sold back to the company when the employee departs. Governance is highly democratic, aiming at consensus wherever possible. For example, department heads are chosen and reviewed by the board, which itself is elected yearly. But all members of each department—and other members as well—are asked to identify in writing what they see as departmental weaknesses; these assessments are then shared with department heads. Planning meetings are held yearly, at which all departments present goals and ideas, the board develops a unified package, and everyone discusses all of the diverse proposals at considerable length. Despite being held during nonwork hours, these planning sessions have drawn virtually complete attendance.

Ordinarily, orchestral musicians have little or no voice in collective or artistic decisions made by their groups. This, as one Boston Symphony Orchestra musician stated in the *Wall Street Journal*, "gives [an] orchestra a kind of malaise. We're told that our opinions are irrelevant." This pattern is dramatically reversed by at least two self-managing chamber orchestras, the **Pro Arte** of Boston (150 members)[7] and **Orpheus** of New York City (26 members). In both cases, orchestra members themselves select their own program, choose soloists, and elect (rotating) directors. Orpheus members vote on a new concertmaster every week; during dress rehearsals, players take turns in the auditorium assessing how well the instruments are blending and balancing—their clarity, range, and articulation. Pro Arte's musicians have full artistic and monetary control of their enterprise, and they pay themselves union-scale salaries, while earning, as worker-owners, almost ten times as much in concert fees as they did in more conventional settings. Both groups have won widespread popular and critical acclaim. Orpheus has played at Lincoln Center and Carnegie Hall in New York City, records for Deutsche Grammophon, and has appeared on a BBC telecast. Pro Arte has commissioned and performed premieres for several young New England composers, increased its subscription base to more than 400, and now averages 750 attendees per concert.

Consumers United Insurance Company (CUIC),[8] of Washington, D.C., is a successful worker-owned and managed cooperative with about $40 million of assets and almost $50 million in annual premiums. Its growth record compares very favorably to other large insurance companies (according to Standard Analytic Service, Inc.). Beyond financial success, however, it is committed to a highly democratic and individualized work process in which departments are run by collective decision making and employees are not only owners but are given responsibility for determining their own work schedules. In addition, clients tend to be non-profit associations and groups—such as women- and minority-owned businesses—that frequently cannot obtain affordable group health insurance elsewhere. In recent years, the socially responsible standards set by CUIC for its workforce and its consumers have been extended, through its investments, to the wider community. The company has invested in low-income housing, land development, and food production in several cities, and it has set up a revolving loan fund to help finance other worker-owned enterprises.

CH2M,[9] in Corvallis, Oregon, is one of the ten largest engineering firms in this country (as judged by *Engineering News-Record*); its staff (75 percent engineers) numbers 4,000 and it has more than fifty offices worldwide. The company, a leader in environmental services, including wastewater and toxic-waste management, is fully employee-owned and has had an ESOP since 1977. Its management policies include broad ownership of stock by full-time employees, employment criteria emphasizing personal integrity; decentralization of authority, and direct communication within and between all levels of the operation. How well is all of this working? According to founding partner Jim Howland: "If you tie the goals of people together with the goals of the firm, . . . then you have a winning combination that is hard to beat." Dave Moyano, a structural engineer at CH2M, adds: "I think of it as owning my own engineering consulting firm. I take the same pride and extra time I would if I were in business for myself."

Springfield Remanufacturing Company (SRC)[10] is another employee-owned enterprise that puts its faith in the abilities of its workforce. For example, all SRC workers receive a steady flow of production and financial data; management conducts weekly financial statement meetings in small groups, throughout the plant. Employees are encouraged to take management training, and 80 percent have done so, in some cases upgrading their positions. According to John Stack, SRC's president, "Every employee knows how to run a business. We do not hire people in our factory to do elementary jobs. We hire them to learn about business." During a business downturn some years ago, SRC applied this philosophy by refusing to lay off any of its workers. Instead, it chose "to work harder than ever to keep waste down, create new products, and find new accounts."

Recently, **community development corporations (CDCs)**[11]—nonprofit groups that support and initiate local economic activity in lower-income neighborhoods—have begun to explore employee ownership. Thus, according to the *ICA Bulletin* (Fall 1990), an estimated 162 CDCs are experimenting with ESOPs or with cooperatives. Among them are the **Asian Community Development Corporation (ACDC)** in Boston, which helped establish a Vietnamese fishing cooperative, and the **Dakota Fund and Development Corporation**, which has managed a highly successful reservation school and is now developing a democratically run truck stop and motel on Sioux tribal lands in North Dakota.

Democratizing Work in the Public Sector

New Haven's High School in the Community is far from alone in developing a democratically managed public-school learning environment. There appears to be a widespread effort to move away from traditional top-down policy making in public education. Center-Hower High School in Akron, Ohio, is now largely run by a faculty senate consisting of eight elected members and the principal, who has no veto power. Similarly, Brooklyn's New School has aggressively introduced shared decision making—including a steering committee of staff and parents. And "teacher empowerment" is a priority in six schools in North Carolina, a middle school in Bedford, Massachusetts, and a high school in the Denver area, among many others.[12]

Beyond education, the public sector has recently witnessed numerous examples of employee ownership; in many cases, these have been advocated as socially responsible forms of privatization. They range from tree trimming (Kent, Ohio), to local transit (South Lake Tahoe), to waste collection (several cities in California), to fire protection and security services (Scottsdale, Arizona), to data processing (Eden Prairie, Minnesota), to electric generation and water/wastewater treatment (Pasadena, California), and to emergency medical care (Kansas City, Missouri).[13]

Notes

1. Information for this section was lifted freely from newsletters published by the Industrial Cooperative Association, the National Center for Employee Ownership, Worker Owned Network, and Cooperative Home Care Associates, as well as from an article on WON that appeared in issue 6 of *Changing Work*.

2. Much of this information came from the very useful *Employee Ownership Casebook*, available from the National Center for Employee Ownership (Oakland, California).

3. These short takes were largely drawn from materials published in the *ICA Bulletin* during 1988–90. The *Bulletin* is available from the ICA Group (Boston, Massachusetts).

4. Information here appeared previously in issue 10 of *Changing Work* and in the newsletter of Cerro Gordo, available from them (Cottage Grove, Oregon).

5. The short take on Fastener Industries is based on a report authored by Catherine Ivancic of the Northeast Ohio Employee Ownership Center.

6. Material concerning Bookpeople was drawn from an interview by Jaques Kaswan in *Democratic Business News*, summer 1989.

7. Information on Pro Arte appeared originally in the *ICA Bulletin*.

8. This short take is based on an article in *Building Economic Alternatives*, published by Co-op America (Washington, DC).

9. Quotes and material were taken from EON (*Employee Ownership Newsletter*), published by the Community Economic Stabilization Corporation (Portland, Oregon).

10. Quotes and information about SRC were drawn from the *Employee Ownership Report*, published by NCEO (Oakland, California).

11. Information about CDCs and employee ownership can be found in the *ICA Bulletin*, available from ICA Group (Boston, Massachusetts). See also the article by Kevin McQueen in chapter 7, below.

12. These and other steps toward greater teacher participation in decision making are outlined in the April 1990 issue of *Educational Leadership*.

13. For more information on these and other public-sector cases, see Philip Fixler's *Employee Ownership and the Privatization of Local Government Services* (available from the Reason Foundation in Santa Monica, California), on which we have drawn heavily.

3

Gimme Shelter
Technical Assistance Organizations

One of the most critical—and historically novel—ingredients in the current movement to bring democracy to worklife is its layer of support, or shelter, groups. Frequently referred to as "**technical assistance organizations**," they provide a wide range of services—financial, marketing, organizational, legal, educational— to clients who want to establish (or to convert existing firms to) worker-owned enterprises. Virtually unknown in this country before 1975, there are now more than fifty of them. As much as any single factor, they have contributed to the growing ranks of worker-owned start-ups and conversions over the past two decades and to the enhanced viability of these democratic enterprises. Technical assistance organizations have contributed to workplace democracy in at least three ways.

First, they offer comprehensive and continuing business consultation. At the start, they help prospective worker-owners examine the potential viability of a projected enterprise through feasibility studies; they remain around to provide assistance, where needed, at subsequent stages, such as locating competent and compatible management, developing marketing plans, applying for loans, and creating democratic and efficient work procedures.

Second, technical assistance organizations link worker-owned businesses so that they can learn from and support one another or, even better, collaborate. Some, like the **Northeast Ohio Employee Ownership Center**, the **Midwest Center for Labor Research (MCLR)**, and the **Steel Valley Authority** do this on a *regional* basis, while others, as Janet Saglio notes, have begun to link firms within a given *sector* of the economy (e.g., recycling or home health care). Using the business experience, contacts, and marketing strategies of already successful firms, they help new cooperatives enter the field. In this way, the technical assistance community aids in guiding and focusing the movement it serves, rather than simply reacting to the separate and disconnected proposals of its clients.

Third, shelter groups frequently widen the horizons of their clients by connecting them to broader issues and to other progressive organizations and coalitions. Thus, a worker-owned firm in Chicago, through being part of the MCLR network, also becomes part of the **Federation for Industrial Retention and Renewal (FIRR)**, a national coalition of labor and community groups that struggles against plant closings and for community control over economic policies. Ecological or sustainable development is a major priority for Chicago's **Center for Neighborhood Technology** and Los Angeles' **Cooperative Resources and Services Project** and, thus, for the enterprises they assist (see Short Takes). And organizations like the **ICA Group** in Massachusetts, **PACE of Philadelphia**, and many of those described in our short takes connect individual worker-owned firms with denominational, community development, and affordable housing groups around a common agenda of community empowerment.

Like their client enterprises, technical assistance groups are extremely diverse and fairly well dispersed throughout the country. They include nonprofit and for-profit organizations, as well as public agencies established by state governments. Some specialize in worker-owned cooperatives, others in ESOPs, still others in women-centered, community-based, or ecologically sustainable enterprises. But collectively they have begun to make a difference, to show that rank-and-file workers can not only learn business skills and sophistication, but can start to build the foundation for a strong and lasting democratic economy.

Rebuilding the Labor Movement and the Industrial Heartland
The Midwest Center for Labor Research

Dan Swinney

The Midwest Center for Labor Research (MCLR) began in 1982 as an act of desperation by a loose network of steelworkers seeking to cope with the storms of the industrial crisis. It is now a relatively stable and growing organization focused on a broad range of industrial-retention activities and on helping to build the labor and progressive movement for social change. In what follows, I trace MCLR's growth in size, programs, and assumptions, in the hope that this will allow others less confused than we were but who face similarly harsh conditions to replicate all or part of what we have done.

Where Is MCLR Today?

MCLR has its office in Chicago. We have a core staff of nine full-time and five part-time workers with major responsibilities, supported by additional consultants. The staff includes males and females, Blacks, Latinos, and whites and varies in age from the thirties to the sixties. Within this group there is a range of talents and skills: Project Director Frank Banks has thirty-five years of experience in the United Electrical Workers, including twenty-six years on staff and eleven on the International Executive Board; Dan Broughton has corporate experience and an M.B.A. from the Kellogg School of Management; Joanna Brown was tested in the Harold Washington campaigns; and Harvey Lyon has twenty-five years of experience in acquisitions of manufacturing companies.

Most of our staff and resources is devoted to retaining industrial jobs in Chicago. For example, we are training groups of people gathered by priests and ministers in West Town, Pilsen, Little Village, and Cicero on our "Early Warning Approach."

Most fully described in our *Early Warning Manual against Plant Closings*, this strategy seeks to develop workers and community residents as sophisticated sources of information about what is going on in the industrial companies of the city. This grassroots network gives us many types of valuable leads: about companies headed toward shutdowns or other troubles; about the potential for coalitions and mass action; and about opportunities for employee buyouts or for acquisitions by local entrepreneurs committed to keeping jobs in Chicago and to treating labor with respect.

In many situations, we assist in the formation and development of local employee-owned companies. In one of these, ownership of a small printing company facing imminent closure was transferred from an aging, sick owner with no heir to its fifteen, mostly Black (and all union) employees. We are also providing an educational program to another group of employee-owners. We have a Chicago Employee Ownership Project Board that seeks to lessen the isolation that often confronts new employee-owners as they face the special problems of this approach; it offers, as well, a place for discussion and debate. Four employee-owned companies sit on this board, along with two social investment funds.

Our research staff, led by Greg LeRoy, provides a range of research, consulting, and educational services not only in Chicago but throughout the country (and every so often in Canada). This includes social cost studies of plant closings, and evaluations of companies facing shutdowns, as well as feasibility studies of potential buyouts. We recently investigated the Diamond Tool and Horseshoe Company that was trying to flee Duluth, Minnesota. Our work, used effectively by the local union, led to an unprecedented court victory that had begun to force the company to move equipment and jobs from North Carolina back to Duluth, until it was overturned on appeal.

And then we publish the semiannual *Labor Research Review*, which is more like a book than a periodical, taking up one issue in depth from a variety of angles. Most of the authors are union organizers and activists who are themselves directly involved in practical aspects of the selected issue. Over its seven years, *LRR* has confronted such topics as worker ownership, new strategies for labor, privatization, and international labor struggles.

How We Got There

There are three distinct periods in our development. These help to explain why we are engaged in such a range of activities. Moreover, they reveal how—and the extent to which—we are still true to the original instincts and visions of our birth.

React Effectively

Those of us who formed MCLR in the early 1980s were principally local union leaders, elected to represent workers who were being sledgehammered by the demand for concession bargaining and the threat and occurrence of plant closings. I personally faced both as vice-president of United Steel Workers of America Local 8787, representing the employees of Taylor Forge, a subsidiary of Gulf &

Western that this conglomerate drained and finally closed in 1983. Most of our founding board of directors came out of basic steel, where workers were labeled greedy and falsely blamed for the crisis in the industry.

We formed MCLR in reaction to the failure of international-labor leadership to respond creatively and effectively to the very real crises surrounding us. Our frustration extended as well to government, business, and the church. We also organized MCLR to help strengthen the insurgent movement within labor. This movement, close to our hearts, was periodically capable of short-term victories against the "machine," the incumbents, or the status quo, but the insurgents repeatedly demonstrated the superficiality of their own program and their inability to build on victories or to sustain and extend their strength. Young steelworker leaders stormed the palace, then failed to translate that victory into organization and program, and were defeated and pushed back to where they started. The same happened to others in the labor and political movements.

During this early time in MCLR's history, we provided research for local unions in concession-bargaining situations, we built coalitions to fight threatened plant closings, and we developed social cost studies that documented the disastrous ripple effects of a plant closing on the rest of the community. We were *reactive* in the fullest sense in attempting to expand labor's options and tactics, in linking research and action, and in developing labor-community coalitions as a characteristic feature of our work.

We began with no financial base, no fund-raising expertise, and with limited experience in developing a not-for-profit corporation. We hired people from our immediate circle of supporters who would accept very low wages and very uncertain conditions, and who were willing to learn on the job. We expanded as resources became available.

Expand the Agenda

During the mid-1980s, we made our first, primitive assessment of an industrial company, the shut-down Wisconsin Steel. Flying in the face of both cynical politicians who cruelly promised to reopen the plant after an election and resigned steel reform movement leaders who claimed the plant could never open and that unemployed workers should demand no more than increased social services, our investigation brought to light a new option: *a state-of-the-art rolling mill to function as the core of a mini-mill anchoring perhaps seven hundred jobs.* Though this option was not realized, the study deeply influenced us.

We became interested in campaigns based on demands and objectives achievable *within the framework of the market economy.* Such campaigns deepen awareness of the social costs produced by shortsighted and greedy traditional "stewards" of the means of production—costs that are even more obvious in the framework of a changing and more competitive international economy. Moreover, these efforts point out that others in society, particularly labor and those with broad community interests, can run companies efficiently and make wise decisions that make business as well as social sense.

Later, we responded to the opportunities created by the election of Harold Washington as mayor and set up our West Side Early Warning Project, supported in part by a contract with the Chicago Department of Economic Development. This project gave some depth to the mayor's general commitment to neighborhood-based economic development and to his commitment to labor. It also helped us to sink increasingly deep and diverse roots into the industrial community—to help spawn a variety of coalitions and company-specific efforts.

During this time, we engaged in numerous debates on worker ownership. Eventually, we became comfortable with a position distinct from those who elevate this approach into a comprehensive strategy for social change (in a way we still see as utopian) and, as well, from those who attack it from the Left as opportunism that diverts workers from the struggle with the employers. Instead, we began to see workers becoming owners as a tactic that made real sense in a number of particular situations, that combined the shared desire of labor and community to retain jobs and businesses, and that affirmed the ability of a labor-based progressive movement to run at least a small part of society effectively—a seemingly obvious requirement for anyone with ambitions to run the whole society!

Organizationally and financially, we experienced rapid growth. We expanded our staff and upgraded its technical capacity by hiring people with more established professional credentials (e.g., an M.B.A.). At the same time, our inexperience in financial management led to crude and unreliable bookkeeping and to our spending money that was anticipated rather than received. This created inevitable cash-flow difficulties, which were frequently solved by mingling funds that should not have been mingled, and by borrowing, including loans from staff in the form of deferred wages. This had a predictably negative impact on staff morale and productivity. Finally, when we were almost insolvent, we got the message and confronted our problems systematically. We developed a much more sophisticated bookkeeping and financial-planning system. We evaluated our projects carefully in light of financial performance, which led to hiring a business manager for the *Review* and to finally spinning off one of our projects. We developed clearer guidelines for staff accountability and increasingly reliable cash-flow projections. After all, if we were to be effective in exposing "mismanagement" in the broader society, we had to be able to confront our own.

Toward a Competitive Alternative Strategy

By the late 1980s, MCLR (like others in the industrial-retention movement) had gone far beyond its reactive beginnings. In addition to setting up employee-owned firms and working with diverse groups to combat plant closings, we began to develop a new strategy: *arranging acquisitions of manufacturing companies by local minority owners responsive to a progressive social contract.* This strategy has led to collaboration with Chicago's Department of Economic Development and with Chicago United, a large mainstream organization that promotes racial integration and the interests of the minority business community. Through this collaborative work, we have come to understand some important realities:

- Despite our preference for the militant and the exotic (a mass campaign to keep the plant open, a worker buyout, a fight with management), we found a number of companies closing that could be effectively sustained simply by locating a more competent and socially responsible owner;
- There really is a white, old-boy network that excludes Blacks and Latinos from information about and ownership of industrial companies, even though they now live (and are predominant) in communities where these manufacturing companies are located;
- A network of Black and Latino entrepreneurs exists that often supports our desired social contract—a commitment to keeping jobs in Chicago and a willingness to treat organized and unorganized labor with respect—particularly when this contract can contribute to minorities' gaining ownership of a company. This stands in sharp relief to other segments of the business community.

We are increasingly looking for sectors of the industrial economy that can be the site of ambitious capital campaigns and that can support social entrepreneurs. But experience has also deepened our understanding of the limits of the marketplace. For example, there are large industrial sectors like steel or auto production that have problems on a scale that requires strong government intervention and investment, perhaps even some form of nationalization. The health of these sectors is a prerequisite for economic and community stability; it cannot be left entirely to management and investment practices created by the marketplace. On the other side of the scale, *hundreds of thousands* of small manufacturing companies are closing because an aging owner can't find someone to take over. The anarchy of the marketplace permits this loss of jobs and businesses, which in its aggregate is enormous. And, of course, there is outright mismanagement on a large scale in manufacturing. It does permanent and sometimes fatal damage to companies, industrial sectors, and communities. In the framework of our declining economy, we cannot passively wait for market forces to correct any of these devastating blows to the means of production and the health of our economy. Such problems have to be fought on the political front, with militancy, and with an insistence on options like government use of eminent domain to seize companies and to run them in collaboration with labor and community.

It has been this tension, this reality, that has led MCLR and other grassroots projects to form the *Federation for Industrial Retention and Renewal (FIRR)*. More than twenty local coalitions came together to found FIRR in order to increase our contact with each other, to assist each other in our separate campaigns, and to collectively construct policy options addressing these limits-of-the-marketplace problems. *(See the interview on FIRR at the end of this article —Editors' note.)*

Back to Our Initial Assumptions

In our brief history, we have maintained, while adding to, the premises that initially guided MCLR's formation.

Our movement needs organizing action guided by an increasingly profound and detailed understanding of the real facts that underlie problems and opportunities. MCLR was originally formed to provide this kind of research to grassroots organizations. Our experience and success has convinced us of the absolute need for this marriage of organizing and analysis.

Economic development activity must be guided by a new commitment to empower people to create new visions and new roles, and by a willingness to fight. This means we have had to work to make sure our staff possessed all the necessary skills and qualifications required by our various projects—whether technical, organizational, political or educational.

There are distressingly few leaders willing to address the real characteristics and causes of the crises in this country. Permanent damage is being done to our major means of production by traditional market forces. *Our movement must go beyond demands for redistribution of wealth, and go for control over production and over significant sections of the economy. To do this, however, we have to discard our fear of ownership and of responsibility for productivity, efficiency, and labor discipline.* To enter these new arenas does not imply altering our basic principles, but to apply them in creative and increasingly complex ways. Moreover, providing this kind of direction will open up the potential to gain broad support and significant power.

In order to enter this new terrain without falling into the bog of opportunism, *MCLR has had to constantly reach deeper into the community and the workforce.* We have increased our contact with organized labor locally and nationally. We have reached into unorganized plants, creating organization, and launching campaigns such as one at a closing printing company that employed 450 workers. We are now canvassing door to door to talk with workers in the Mexican community of Chicago as part of our early warning efforts.

We have had to respond seriously to criticism of our work no matter what its source. At one point, we were criticized by an investment-banking firm for shoddy work that misstated the facts in a particular situation, found that the charge was right, issued a written apology to the firm as well as our client, and took some internal disciplinary measures. We have entered debates in our publications with those who oppose our interest in worker ownership.

Organizationally, we are running MCLR more like (dare we say it?) a business. We have learned that if we don't, we will lose our ability to serve the movement and to participate in projects that require a heavy subsidy from us, e.g., our work with community organizations or local unions who cannot afford to pay us. We are also committed to increasing the wages and benefits of our own staff. In this way, we seek to break the cycles of voluntary poverty and grim conditions that often make it impossible for someone with family obligations or plans for retirement to stay within our movement's organizations for very long.

Problems and Challenges

Has everything been great, onward and upward? No. We have made progress, but there have been painful moments when we came face to face with judgments about inadequate staff skills. We have had extended periods of mismanagement, and we still struggle with our inexperience, particularly in financial planning and organizational development.

In addition, as we serve grassroots organizations and activist leaders, we are continually struck by the narrowness of sections of our movement, by its fear of going beyond the easy role of social opposition, by its comfort at being small and fragmented, and by its willingness to avoid complexity—even though our people face enormous common problems.

On the other hand, *there has been genuine growth in the breadth, depth, and skill of our movement.* There have been some remarkable chapters of success—the Naugatuck Valley Project and Seymour Specialty Wire; New Bedford, Massachusetts, and Morse Cutting Tool; the Steel Valley Authority, led by the Tri-State Conference on Steel in the Pittsburgh area; leaders like Harold Washington and Jesse Jackson, who have embraced and added depth to the struggle for industrial retention; and many valiant local campaigns against enormous odds to save companies and communities. These have more than balanced what has been slow, painful, or negative. We are excited and challenged by these developments and see increasing opportunities for resources, influence, and leadership that we would not have imagined even five years ago. We are seeing the movement of those determined to gain control over the economy in the interests of labor and local communities increasing in size and sophistication. We are glad to be part of this new movement and eager to lend organizational or programmatic assistance to those within it.

The Federation for Industrial Retention and Renewal

Developing Economic Power
through Community-Labor Alliances

Interview with Jim Benn

Changing Work: How and when did FIRR get started? What were the reasons behind its coming to life?

Jim Benn: FIRR got its start back in February 1988, at a meeting of the Interdenominational Economic Crisis Organizing Network, a national association of grassroots economic justice groups, many with religious or denominational ties. About twenty of these groups found that they had a common agenda in combating plant closings and deindustrialization; at this meeting in 1988 they decided to form a task force with two main aims. First, to explore ways of furnishing mutual support; second, to help create national policies to challenge the more-than-local conditions that had brought about the crises we all faced back home.

CW: What kind(s) of impact do you foresee FIRR having?

JB: In the short term, we are operating as a *clearinghouse*, using communication links such as PeaceNet to distribute practical research findings to our members. In addition, we will function as a *support organization*, developing cooperative funding approaches for our members and backing up local proposals to make them more fundable.

CW: How would you accomplish this?

JB: FIRR can show funding sources that what any one of our local affiliates achieves can be disseminated to, and probably replicated by, other members of the network. For example, through FIRR, the work of our Buffalo group against *maquiladoras* [US plants that shut down in order to reopen, paying much lower wages, in Mexico] can be given national impact, and thus has a better chance to obtain funding. The idea here is that, though all of our local groups fight shutdowns and are trying to build democratic alternatives to corporate irresponsibility, *each of them has carved out its own distinctive niche*. Thus, the Midwest Center for Labor

Research in Chicago has pioneered early warning systems that enable workers and communities to identify the first signs of corporate flight; Tri-State Conference's Steel Valley Authority (in Pittsburgh) has taken the legal doctrine of "eminent domain" and is applying it so that community coalitions can take over shut-down production facilities, etc. One of FIRR's important roles is to publicize these distinctive approaches, give them increased national recognition, and help make them usable throughout our network.

CW: **So much for the shorter term. What are your longer-range objectives?**

JB: Our most central long-range aim is to create greater understanding and acceptance of economic democracy, which we see as incorporating not only grassroots influences in economic decisions but the forging of regional and national coalitions.

CW: **What kinds of coalitions?**

JB: Between and among community groups, labor unions, religious organizations, unorganized (and unemployed) workers—all those concerned to build a socially responsible economy, on both the local and the national levels. Each of these diverse groups has its own assets, and its own gaps. For example, religious groups frequently have a vision of economic justice, but may have small active constituencies, while the labor movement may be longer on numbers, but shorter in regards to vision. Together they can help create the policies and conditions that bring us closer to economic democracy.

Concretely, these coalitions—both locally and nationally—can press for a *national capital fund* to promote local initiatives to retain industry or revive community economic development. Such a fund could have several different sources, federal, state, and local, public and private, union pension funds and entrepreneurial investment, the "peace dividend," etc. In addition, FIRR-supported coalitions would work for regional economic authorities, democratically elected bodies that would participate in the planning and strengthening of local economies. These regional authorities would be composed of representatives from all affected groups in a given community —unions, small businesses, churches and synagogues, neighborhoods and municipalities, the unemployed and the homeless, minorities, peace activists, etc. Together they would decide such matters as how to cope with weapons-plants layoffs, or what sectors of the economy to target for future development, how to make waste management pay off for local enterprises, etc.

CW: **Sounds like a promising agenda, and one that should keep FIRR quite busy for the foreseeable future! How many organizations do you now include, and how do new organizations become members of FIRR?**

JB: We now number twenty-two organizations, located throughout the country and connected to many major industries. Ordinarily, an organization is invited to join FIRR after we've worked or had some actual contact with it. New members, naturally, would have to share the Federation's goals of reversing deindustrialization and promoting economic justice and would need to be involved in grassroots coalitions focused on building a democratic and socially responsible economy. Any group that may be interested in joining FIRR, or in finding out more about our goals and work, can contact me at our office, 3411 W. Diversey St., #10, Chicago, IL 60647, (312) 252-7676.

CW: Jim, one final question, a bit of a curveball, perhaps. How would FIRR respond to those for whom the demise of industrialization is an opportunity rather than a problem, who see little—for either workers or their communities —in many or most of our traditional manufacturing plants, and would replace them with various sorts of ecological or planet-sustaining workplaces, e.g., ones centered on recycling, on alternative (renewable) energy sources and conservation, on labor-intensive crafts and artisanship, etc.?

JB: For FIRR, economic democracy means that people have a say in determining their own destiny. If a community wants to deindustrialize, then we would support that. But on the other hand, we have seen plant closings destroy not only jobs but whole communities, and we believe that manufacturing is often essential to community life. We also believe that industrial factories, e.g., coal-fired plants, need not bring pollution, but can be operated safely, given that they are controlled by workers and local communities. For the most part, ecologically destructive decisions come from above, not from the workers or grassroots communities, who must live with the toxic consequences.

[Since this interview was completed, we have learned that one of FIRR's affiliate coalitions—the Campaign to Keep GM Van Nuys Open—has helped spark a battle for ecological conversion of a highly toxic industry/commodity—the private auto. The Campaign has joined with other community, labor, and environmental groups in the greater Los Angeles area around a clean air fight , whose goals include "affordable public transportation, nonpolluting community economic development . . . workplace health and safety, and industrial pollution reduction." Given the auto's major contribution to L.A.'s lethal air, they also contend that "any effective clean-air plan must involve a change in automobile design and energy source." This new community-labor-environment alliance is well described in Eric Mann's article "L.A.'s Smogbusters" (the Nation, *17 September, 1990), in which the above quoted passages appear—Eds.]*

Technical Assistance for Worker-Owners Comes of Age

Interview with Janet Saglio

Changing Work: Jan, let's begin with you: how did you first get involved with worker ownership, and what led you to think of providing technical assistance to cooperatives and employee-owned businesses as a career?

Janet Saglio: I actually came into this field by three different routes. First, in college during the late 1960s, I studied our economy from a theoretical perspective. I learned about Yugoslavia and its self-managing enterprises and began to realize how much the ownership structure of companies in the United States hindered cooperation between labor and management and kept workers from contributing to or participating in their own enterprises.

Secondly, I also had some very practical experience with democratic approaches to business. For three years, I worked in the Good Bread Bakery in Mystic, Connecticut; this was a worker-owned firm. Each of us owned equal shares, and there was a real wholeness about the bakery. Thus, jobs were rotated so that everyone learned all parts of the business—from baking, to marketing, to bookkeeping. The results were not surprising: we had a stable business, but one that I feared would lose its character if it grew. The experience raised several questions for me. For example, how can an enterprise maintain both high productivity and the quality of jobs; and why do so many small businesses fail when they attempt to expand?

To get answers to questions like these I took a third route—I went to business school, to Yale's School of Organization and Management. I figured that, after three years at Good Bread Bakery, it might be time to start learning from other people's mistakes and not only from my own.

CW: Did Yale provide what you were looking for? How well did it prepare you professionally?

JS: I learned a great deal there, particularly in the Organizational Behavior Program (the very program Yale has now decimated!). Specifically, I learned several different sorts of skills that have been useful to me in assisting employee-owned businesses get launched, survive, and grow. First, in the area of job design: how to create challenging, responsible, meaningful tasks without relying on the kind of job rotation that characterized Good Bread and other similar small cooperatives. Second, communication and management skills—how to provide constructive and useful feedback, how to ensure that employees understand and maintain standards of performance, and thereby increase their productivity. And last, financial planning and analysis skills: evaluating how and when to expand a business, seeing where the risks are for different types of business plans and how best to confront them. These skills all proved immensely useful to me when I joined the ICA Group in 1980 and began working with worker-owned enterprises.

CW: **Looking back on your ten years with the ICA Group, what do you see as their high points?**

JS: What I'm most proud of? I can think of two things in particular. One is my work with Cooperative Home Care Associates (CHCA) in New York City. I consulted with them on their original business plan and loan package, and I sit on their board of directors in a nonvoting capacity. As you know, CHCA is a cooperative with over 200 workers, most of whom are also owners, and mainly women of color from a low-income community. They have had to overcome one obstacle after another, but they are now a profitable venture. Beyond that, the workers control the board, they have become well oriented to business decisions, and they provide excellent service. And while doing all of this, they have also had a remarkable impact on the field of homecare in New York City: they raised their own starting hourly wages from $4.50 an hour in 1985 to $6.50 and their model and lobbying have helped boost wages throughout the industry.

A second accomplishment I'm happy with is the manual I wrote with Richard Hackman on governance within worker-owned businesses, "The Design of Governance Systems for Small Worker Cooperatives." In it, we distinguish the separate responsibilities of managers, boards of directors, and employee-owners. In a way, this manual reflects my earlier movement away from more collective and undifferentiated approaches to business organization: it clarifies the need for and the benefits of distinct and well-defined roles for those worker-owned enterprises that want to keep growing.

CW: **Let's turn to the technical assistance field more generally : How well has it served employee-owned businesses? What do you see as its gains, its gaps, its prospects?**

JS: The employee-ownership technical assistance community has developed substantially over the past decade. We now have more experience in evaluating potential buyouts or start-ups, and we have honed our business development techniques. For example, our loan fund has learned not to give new employee-owned companies all of their loan money upfront, but to build in self-correcting mechanisms. If some aspect of the business, say, marketing, isn't working and sales are low, we'll ask that this be corrected before providing the next phase of funding. What this means is that we can now structure opportunities for employee owners to learn about business, make mistakes, and solve their problems—before they exhaust their financing and without failure.

Another indication of progress is that there are more types of places providing useful consultation to employee-owned businesses. Thus, for example, several states—New York, Michigan, Washington State, and Oregon are some—now have employee-ownership technical assistance offices. In addition, because of the broader interest in employee stock ownership plans (ESOPs), our field is expanding. Many healthy firms have begun to experiment with an ESOP as a financial mechanism, and this has increased the opportunities for educating both workers and managers about more genuine forms of employee ownership. As a result, some technical assistance groups, previously organized as not-for-profits, have set up for-profit firms. Some staff members at the ICA Group have established Employee Ownership Services (EOS); and some former staff from PACE in Philadelphia have formed PRAXIS. Both EOS and PRAXIS are for-profit consulting firms focused on converting successful businesses to employee ownership and on providing them with support services and training. A further result of this varied interest in ESOPs is that someone entering the technical assistance field today is as likely to find their way into a for-profit as a non-profit organization.

Another change in the employee-ownership field that has had a very important and positive effect on our work is the leadership role some unions have taken in buyouts. Unions like the Steelworkers and the Amalgamated Clothing and Textile Workers are establishing employee-ownership programs to identify opportunities for successful buyouts and to assist locals in developing employee-owned takeovers. In addition to increasing interest in buyouts of healthy companies—rather than just threatened businesses—union leadership strengthens employee-ownership buyouts and results in better deals for the workers represented (in terms both of control and of financial return).

Despite these gains, we still lack effective ways to extend worker ownership into low-income communities; we need more models of success, as well as greater efficiency, in creating viable cooperatives in those communities. For this, we need to find the right sector(s) of the economy, the right times to intervene—and we need some luck as well.

CW: Has anything been done along these lines, to start locating fertile areas for employee ownership in low income communities?

JS: Yes—some very exciting developments have started to take place. Working with other technical assistance organizations, ICA has selected two service industries: home health care and recycling. Not only are both of these expanding, but they can create jobs for people without extensive training or experience. Our strategy is to find or develop a successful worker-owned model in each case and then work with the original companies and local employee-ownership groups to transfer (or "franchise") it into other community settings. Thus, we're planning to utilize the experience and skills of two New York City enterprises, Cooperative Home Health Associates and R2B2 (a recycling business in the Bronx), to help build similar worker-owned businesses in other cities. We have access to their managers, their business plans, their operating systems and methods, e.g., for redesigning jobs or increasing worker involvement. All of this should help us to replicate their success—hopefully, on a wide and continuing basis. We are also exploring other service industries, such as day care, with this franchise strategy in mind.

CW: This is extremely exciting, and it illustrates a much higher level of planning and of interorganizational cooperation than did our older strategy of rescuing isolated (and often failing) companies through worker buyouts. But let's return to this question of assessing the field of democratic technical assistance.

JS: For worker ownership to thrive, there are two interrelated gaps we still need to fill: we lack good managers (and ways of locating them) and we lack ways of strengthening the boards of worker-owned enterprises. Management's role is more complex than in traditional workplaces. In addition to setting a course in the market, it must build faith in the enterprise and trust between employee owners, and it must ensure a continuous flow of information concerning all parts of the company. On the other hand, strong boards are essential so that managers can be overseen, assisted, and, where necessary, replaced. This requires experienced directors. In short, though competent and experienced managers and board members frequently make the difference between success and failure for employee-owned businesses, we do not as yet have systematic ways to locate, attract, develop, or recruit enough of them.

CW: Is anything being done to remedy this?

JS: There are some academic programs that over the years have helped to provide people with the requisite business skills: the Social Economy–Management Program at Boston College, New Hampshire College's Masters program in Community Economic Development, the MIT (formerly Tufts) Summer Institute in Community Development, what's left at Yale's School of Organization and Management. Beyond these, several technical assistance organizations, including the ICA, are now discussing ways to create a pool of qualified management candidates willing to work in employee-owned businesses within specified fields. If this pool is established, it would make our task of recruiting good managers—a vital one—less frenzied and more productive.

But perhaps the most hopeful efforts on this front may come from the franchise-development strategy we just discussed. To take the case of Cooperative Home Care Associates: their president, Rick Surpin, has had several years on the job and is an excellent manager. He developed his democratic management skills without any prior business experience or training. But now that he has those skills, he can pass them on to prospective managers or boards of newly formed worker-owned businesses in the same sector. As Mondragon illustrates, hands-on experience within a specific field of business is the best teacher: every type of business has its own unique markets, cash-flow requirements, information and labor demands, etc. As a result, the idea of franchising through replication of a successful worker-owned model should become a rich source for managers and directors. It can certainly help close the management and competency gaps we have had to contend with.

CW: All in all, then, how do you feel about the years you have spent in the new field of worker-ownership technical assistance? How far have your initial hopes or expectations been realized? And would you recommend it to others as a career?

JS: I certainly would recommend it to others. After more than ten years, working with each new employee-owned business is still fun, and each is still very different from any of the others. There's lots of struggle and hard work, of course, but there are lots of positives as well. I would have to add, though, that some of my very initial hopes have not been realized: we have just not been as wildly successful as I imagined we would be. Like others a decade or so ago, I anticipated that any obstacles out there would be fairly swiftly overcome; the reality is that the number of worker-owned businesses has indeed grown, but at a much slower pace than we hoped for.

Another difficult aspect of this line of work comes from the need to be tough minded. Not all employee-owned firms can work; some are just not going to make it. It's the business analyst who must then say "Stop," and this is bound to weigh heavily on you. But our responsibility includes leading workers away from bad start-ups or takeovers that will only drain their resources: we must trust our own judgment in these cases and give our clients the straight story.

CW: How might someone prepare to enter the field, to become a consultant to worker-owned enterprises? And what lessons might you want to pass on to those considering this as a career?

JS: As far as preparation, there are a lot of diverse routes. Some of us have liberal-arts degrees and a single year of business training, along with some business experience; others have worked in the lending or investment divisions of major banks; and the New Hampshire, Yale, and Boston College programs have all produced able graduates. What I see as crucial is to get relevant experience—to learn about business and about worker-owned enterprises firsthand, to combine real business management experience with, say, involvement with a consumer cooperative or with the board of an employee-owned firm.

Beyond this need for relevant experience, business analysts need to develop their judgment as to what can work and what won't. This comes slowly, only after lots of experience. Here, it's important to learn from seasoned people, whose judgment has had a chance to mature. Seek them out, listen to them; this can help refine your own judgment. At the same time, don't be afraid of those inevitable mistakes. We all make them, and we can all benefit and learn from them. Don't be afraid to leap forward!

Finally, I've come to see this field as a continual learning experience. We may be trained, as I was, as a business generalist, but soon find ourselves stepping temporarily into a specific business or even taking on management responsibilities for certain enterprises. Anyone entering this field should expect this, should anticipate going beyond their initial training. This is one of the field's most attractive features: it broadens us, constantly. Since our client enterprises need to know about every dimension of their new ventures, we are challenged to provide all of what they need and thus to grow and evolve.

CW: Do I hear an echo in this of the wholeness you experienced at the Good Bread Bakery?

Rustproofing the Rustbelt
Promoting Employee Ownership as Public Policy
Daniel Bell, Catherine Ivancic, and John Logue

Northeast Ohio is one of the birthplaces of the modern U.S. employee-ownership movement. The efforts in the late 1970s to rescue the Youngstown steel mills through worker and community ownership after they were shut by the Lykes conglomerate and US Steel were an education to the people of the region. Although these efforts proved unsuccessful, they inspired others. Thus, Youngstown was the location of the 1979 worker buyout of Republic Hose, one of the earliest successful efforts by employees to save a plant threatened by shutdown. Since then, the number of employee-owned companies in Ohio has grown rapidly through employee buyouts of threatened facilities, corporate divestitures of healthy plants, and retiring owners' sales of firms.

Today, approximately 275 Ohio companies use some degree of employee ownership, and there are more employee-owned firms per capita in Ohio than in any other state. Of these, perhaps 100 are significantly employee owned. Among them are **Antioch Publishing** in Yellow Springs, **Bliss** in Salem, **Dimco-Gray** in Centerville, **Davey Tree** in Kent, **Fastener Industries** in Berea, **Fluid Regulators** in Painesville, **Plymouth Locomotive** in Plymouth, **Republic Storage Systems** in Canton, **Republic Engineered Steel** in Massillon, and **Reuther Mold and Manufacturing** in Cuyahoga Falls. *(See chapter 6 for short takes on some of these companies. —Eds.)*

Creating Institutions to Support Employee Ownership

It was the failed buyouts though, not the successes, that led to the creation of the **Northeast Ohio Employee Ownership Center (NOEOC)**. For every success, in the 1970s and early 1980s, half a dozen or more buyouts failed. The reasons for failure, a 1986 Ohio study concluded, went beyond standard commercial factors to include the simple lack of timely, accurate information on how to undertake an employee buyout successfully. This study, funded by the Inter-Institutional Program of the Ohio Urban Universities Program, was followed by several others carried out by the **Employee Ownership Project (EOP)** at Kent State University. These studies cataloged existing state legislation across the country regarding employee ownership, examined the structures of workplace democracy in Ohio firms, profiled the lending environment for employee-owned companies, and assessed the general performance of Ohio employee-owned firms.

Responding to repeated requests for information, the EOP and other local groups joined the **National Center for Employee Ownership** in organizing a series of three conferences in the spring of 1986. The success of the conferences established the breadth of interest in the subject within Ohio. As the need for written materials grew, the EOP staff developed handbooks for workers and retiring owners interested in employee ownership.

By 1987, the EOP staff found itself spending more and more time providing guidance and technical assistance for those considering employee ownership. What had begun as a university research project in 1984 matured into the NOEOC in June 1987 with the financial support of the Ohio Department of Development, the Cleveland Foundation, and the George Gund Foundation.

In addition to research, the center's mission today includes information, outreach, education, and technical assistance. NOEOC staff members do everything from answering simple telephone requests for information and speaking to any community group that will sit still for a talk on employee ownership to helping business owners and employee groups who are actively considering it. The NOEOC also provides a variety of services to existing employee-owned companies, including general training in employee ownership for workers and more specific technical training for employee board representatives. Moreover, it has facilitated the development of Ohio's **Employee Owned Network**, linking a number of employee-owned firms and their resources to achieve economies of scale. The NOEOC collaborates with community-based organizations interested in employee ownership, and it runs an annual employee-ownership conference in Northeast Ohio.

The NOEOC's placement at Kent State University rather than in a government setting has its frustrations, but these are outweighed by many advantages. In addition to great autonomy, the university environment presents a wealth of resources for research, especially a pool of energetic students eager to be involved in a project that embodies a fruitful combination of theory and practice.

Learning from Buyouts

Much of the NOEOC's work has been with employee efforts to buy plants to avert shutdowns. This is the least common and most difficult use of employee ownership, but unquestionably the most prominent in the public mind. Here are some lessons we have drawn from our experience with buyouts in shutdown situations.

First, trying to avert plant shutdowns through employee ownership is not for the faint of heart or for those who like a well-ordered life. Employee and community groups seeking to buy plants to keep them open never have enough time to make the deal work properly. You will always be battling deadlines that you cannot meet. Plants close and people lose their jobs because you cannot do in four days or four weeks what it takes four months to accomplish. In many cases, our political system still permits owners to shut plants without notification and without any consideration for their employees' well-being or for grassroots efforts to buy the plant to keep it open. (Federal **WARN** legislation that went into effect in 1989 requires a minimum of sixty days advance notice of plant shutdowns. While that is helpful, particularly in forcing employees and public agencies to confront the reality of an impending closing, the sixty-day period is totally inadequate to put together a buyout.)

Another lesson is that managers who can meet the challenge of employee-owned companies are a special breed. The world is full of plants that fail because of mismanagement. Bad managers will still be bad managers after the move to employee ownership, and even good managers may not always be willing to give the necessary commitment to making the buyout happen. The employees should not hesitate to dump the current management when necessary. While difficult to do, it is easier than creating a successful company with incompetent management. Good managers for employee-owned companies need an entrepreneurial spirit and an exceptional ability to lead. Finding such people is difficult, but not impossible.

Third, we have learned that buyout attempts produce—and require—a strange mix of cultures. It is common to find steelworkers, clerical workers, and managers from a small rural town sitting in a local bar and discussing business projections with highpowered New York investment bankers, while the town's mayor, dressed in overalls, looks on. Although no one finds this mix entirely comfortable, it is the kind of team necessary to make the deal happen. There are lawyers and financial experts who are committed to the goals of saving jobs and establishing employee control. Hire them to give advice, but remember that the employees and their buyout-committee leadership will ultimately have to live with the choices. Pleasing the consultants is not the name of the game; the consultants are paid to please the employees.

A fourth lesson is that employee buyouts to avert shutdowns are basically political phenomena that require the same sort of political organization as any other major effort at mobilization. To have a chance of success, you not only need the support of the employees, you also need to organize management, local economic development experts, churches, community organizations, and, above all else, local and state elected officials. A portion of the financing of buyouts often comes from the public sector; this is so, by and large, because closed-down facilities do not inspire much confidence among commercial lenders. Public sector funding, of course, requires even more time than commercial financing, but if you have done the political mobilization properly, these delays will not kill the deal.

Fifth, a buyout can easily be perceived by many employees as being more in someone else's interest than in their own. When they are not kept informed and involved, employees grow suspicious—often rightly so—of consultants, managers, business analysts, and lawyers. Providing full and timely information to all employees is important to avert misperception, but it is even more important to structure the buyout so that its fairness and equity are immediately apparent to all. When simple and complex methods achieve the same ends, always choose the simple method.

Sixth, know when to say no. There are certain major obstacles to the success of a buyout, and when they are discovered they should be heeded as significant warnings, unless a realistic plan for overcoming them has been thought out. These red flags include: *opposition to a buyout by the seller, lack of serious interest from a significant portion of the employees, absence of a viable business (one capable of repaying the debt), a shortage of time, and the inability to find a competent manager willing to take an active role in making the deal happen.*

Last, and far from least, employee ownership is a process that continues beyond the buyout. The first day at work as employee-owners working for themselves, while of course a day of triumph, is not the final goal; it is only the beginning. If the company is to survive, the employees must become active owners. *We are convinced of the necessity for establishing systems of democratic employee participation as quickly as possible.* It is vital that the buyout committee begin discussing what kind of participation system they are going to put in place and how it will be structured *before* they actually succeed in buying the facility. Participation, moreover, is too important to leave to participation consultants. It must involve the commitment and consensus of the buyout group.

In short, buyouts of threatened facilities are about the toughest business deals imaginable. Not only do employees have to buy and run successfully a plant that experienced, conventional companies judge worthy of closing—and frequently have been unable to sell to anyone else—they have to do so within an ownership form that makes many managers and most lenders at least moderately uncomfortable. While desperately trying to make a success of the facility as a business, they also need to restructure the traditional pattern of authority in economic enterprises to make it more suitable for democratic ownership and, simultaneously, train themselves in how to become responsible owners. It is certainly no easy road.

Two crucial pieces that would make more buyouts successful are currently missing. The first is the development of an adequate, friendly employee-ownership equity pool. The pool of capital available as subordinate debt from such existing friendly lenders as the ICA Group's revolving-loan fund or the National Cooperative Bank's Development Corporation is too small to handle the demand, and friendly venture capital is virtually nonexistent. Community-based revolving-loan funds that support employee ownership certainly help in those communities where they exist, and the Employee Partnership Fund, established by the AFL-CIO in 1990 to encourage employee takeover bids, should help fill part of this gap. We hope that, in the long run, existing successful employee-owned firms will be willing individually or collectively to help provide crucial equity or subordinate debt necessary for new buyouts to succeed.

The second gap is the lack of experienced managers and of a way to train them to function well in worker-owned enterprises. While new managers can be and are hired for buyouts, they frequently have only the vaguest of ideas of how management under employee ownership works. Finding out is always painful for both manager and employees and is occasionally fatal for the new company. We think that establishing a training program will expand the pool of managers and make it easier to locate entrepreneurial leaders willing to throw themselves into making a buyout effort succeed.

Moving from Cure to Prevention: Employee Ownership as a Proactive Strategy

Buyouts to avert shutdowns more closely resemble the pound of cure than the ounce of protection or prevention. The NOEOC encourages the proactive use of employee ownership by small business and organized labor. Thus, for example, we assist owners of closely held businesses to sell to their employees when seeking to retire or otherwise withdraw from the companies. The owner benefits from tax legislation that allows the proceeds of the sale to be rolled over into other domestic securities; the employees avoid the typical alternatives of seeing their plant liquidated or sold to a competitor. The evidence is overwhelming that more jobs can be saved by using employee ownership to purchase enterprises from retiring owners than using it in plant-closing cases. Moreover, such enterprises are good commercial ventures for employees because, generally speaking, they have not been drained by their previous owners. Not surprisingly, our rate of success in helping employees buy firms from retiring owners is far greater than in cases of plants threatened by shutdown.

Employee ownership can also be a proactive strategy for the labor movement. Unions can bargain to establish employee stock ownership plans (ESOPs) and to use the financial leverage that ESOPs provide for capital improvements that will prevent a closing down the road. Where wage concessions are unavoidable, ESOPs can ensure that the employees' sacrifices will be rewarded if the company turns around. Using an ESOP purchase can also avert a sale to an undesirable or antiunion buyer. If a union local suspects that the plant will come up for sale, educating members on employee ownership and preparing for a bid *before* the plant is formally put on the block may make sense. In the construction trades, employee-owned firms may provide unions with a method to deal with nonunion competition, as illustrated by the groundbreaking bricklayers' union and other unions who have followed their example. While buyouts to avert shutdown usually lead to more democratic structures for employee participation simply because of employee mobilization and sacrifice in the buyout effort, the same is not necessarily true when employee ownership is used proactively. Here, increasing employee participation must be a conscious strategy. Our research and practical work has convinced us that it is necessary to go beyond employee representation on the legal structures of corporate governance (the board of directors and the ESOP administration committee) *to create an intermediate body—a plant steering committee—between the board and shop committees.* To be effective, the steering committee needs substantial authority and training. Indeed, education at every level—for employee board representatives, steering-committee members, and shop committees—is vital to the success of the democratic enterprise.

Fostering Collaboration among Worker-Owned Companies

When Don José Maria Arizmendiarrieta founded the first production cooperative in Mondragon in 1956, no one would have suspected that this quiet little Basque town would eventually become world famous for its development into a community of worker-owned cooperatives. Thirty years later, that first cooperative business, which in 1956 had 23 employee-owners, had grown into 120 worker-owned firms employing over 20,000 people. While the Mondragon cooperatives have to be individually successful to survive, they are aided by substantial economies of scale achieved by creating common institutions that provide them with such services as financing, training, and research and development.

Although not all the conditions that made the Mondragon cooperatives possible are present in the United States, the Mondragon example does raise the question whether common ventures among some U.S. employee-owned firms might provide similar economies of scale and thus strengthen the employee-owned sector. For the most part, Ohio's 50 or so *majority employee-owned companies* employ 50-200 people each, with sales of $8 to $15 million annually. While employee ownership has typically improved company performance—sometimes spectacularly—it has not given these firms the advantages of scale. They have competed as isolated entities against far larger conventional firms with deeper pockets. While they have often been successful, the deck has been stacked against them.

There have been a few steps toward mutually beneficial cooperation among employee-owned firms, at least in Ohio. For example, at a recent NOEOC annual conference, a round table on this issue collected more than a dozen proposals—ranging from collective purchase of liability insurance to establishing a common financing institution. Some of these proposals have been implemented:

- *Management Forums.* The NOEOC has hosted four forums on participation and communication and two forums on ESOP administration. These have brought Chief Executive Officers, key managers, and members of employee committees together from more than twenty Ohio companies to share successes and failures and to consult with a variety of experts.

- *Board of Directors Training.* Workers in democratic employee-owned firms typically elect shopfloor representatives to the board of directors and other supervisory bodies. While many are experienced in bargaining wages, hours, and terms and conditions of employment, few have enough knowledge of corporate accounting, finance, and the like to represent fully their fellow worker-owners. Frequently, even reading a balance sheet or a profit-and-loss statement seems like reading Russian. Providing such training on an in-house, single-company basis is prohibitively expensive for small businesses. The NOEOC has conducted a series of eight one-day training sessions for hourly employee-owners who have a seat on their company's board of directors or on other administrative organs. These sessions have brought 42 employees together from thirteen employee-owned companies. In addition to the technical information presented, these workers are encouraged to share experiences and to exchange responses to problems with each other as they grow more comfortable with their new roles.

- *Employee-Owner Retreats.* The NOEOC has developed a two-day leadership seminar focused on committee effectiveness training and on understanding financial information. Our first retreat brought together 35 employee owners from 11 companies.

- *Economies of Scale.* Employees from 8 companies have formed committees to explore ways for Ohio's employee-owned firms to further cooperate in the areas of training, ESOP administration, and export marketing. This work may eventually yield more concrete links among worker-owned firms.

- *Preferential Purchasing.* Finally, the NOEOC is coordinating the ongoing production of a catalog that describes the products and services of Ohio's employee-owned companies so that they can purchase from one another. Thus far, about 40 businesses have listed entries in this catalog.

In 1989, a number of firms that have been most active in these activities set up a formal network with a dues structure to support joint training programs run through the NOEOC.

How Far Can Such Cooperation Go?

All in all, the various joint activities discussed above have involved some 60 companies. At least half of them are located within a 100-mile radius in northeast Ohio. Unquestionably, additional and closer links can be forged among these firms. But how far can such cooperation between an increasing number of worker-owned enterprises lead?

Unlike Mondragon's alternative economy, Ohio's employee-owned firms were not inspired by an ideology of workplace democracy and local control. Most worker-owners here had little or nothing to say about the installation of an ESOP at their company. Those actively involved in the transition from conventional to worker ownership were more often motivated by the fear of losing their jobs than by a commitment to any ideal of democratic worklife. This does not mean that labor or management lack commitment to the equality and participation made possible by cooperative ownership. Some of Ohio's worker-owned companies are great places to work. However, left to themselves, such companies would remain just that—isolated businesses, dwarfed in the $5 trillion U.S. economy.

In the long term, the creation of local or regional networks among employee-owned firms will be necessary to give them economies of scale to compete in international markets. This, in turn, will require the development of new, cooperative institutions. Such cooperatively owned service or production facilities have long been a feature of the farmers' co-op movement; they provide cost economies in marketing, purchasing, and processing beyond what a single farmers' cooperative can attain. Our Ohio network is a mere babe in arms by comparison, but you must learn to walk before you can run.

Successful network creation will not only strengthen existing employee-owned firms but perhaps also provide a venture capital source genuinely sympathetic to the principle of democratic ownership and management. While commercial lending sources and, of course, the National Co-op Bank, are comfortable with secured lending to employee-owned firms, finding the necessary equity infusion for *100 percent employee ownership* is at best difficult. Too often, conventional venture capitalists not only want their pound of flesh but the lifeblood and the soul of potential employee-owned firms as well. Creating the mechanism to generate that equity in a friendlier fashion is one of the most important services that local or regional networks of employee-owned companies can provide for their neighbors.

From Networking to a Common Vision

While Ohio's employee-owned companies were not set up by believers in an alternative economy, this does not rule out their developing more of a common vision. After all, such firms actually *do* share an internal commitment to a more equal distribution of wealth and to greater employee participation within the firm. Though neither of these goals figured prominently on most employee-owners' *initial* list of priorities, the practice of employee ownership has been an education for many workers involved in democratically owned firms.

Can networks of worker-owned firms create a cooperative sector in the U.S. economy? Our Ohio network is no "American Mondragon." The driving force for our network is the fact that its firms have common needs, similar approaches, and some common experiences. The network's survival rides on its ability to provide needed commodities or services. These benefits alone are not sufficient cement for a cooperative economy. The sense of common values, mutual goals, and long-term vision at the very heart of Mondragon is missing. Nonetheless, the potential exists to cultivate these characteristics. Developing a long-term cooperative network from this early experimentation will require building a common vision by sharing experiences and self-analyses arising from the network's activities. If cooperation continues to produce positive results for the firms and individuals involved, there will be ample time to build that vision.

Grassroots Regional Revitalization
The Steel Valley Authority*

A Public Authority Like No Other

During the past decade, the tri-state area surrounding Pittsburgh was hit by a wave of plant shutdowns, deindustrialization, and job loss. Beginning in the 1970s with four shutdowns of mills around Youngstown, Ohio, through the closing of four major U.S. Steel facilities in the Monongahela Valley in the 1980s, plant shutdowns swept through the area like a plague, resulting in the loss of 130,000 manufacturing jobs and 40,000 steel jobs, destroying the "American Dream" for tens of thousands of families, and bankrupting entire communities.

Of course, the economic collapse that ravaged the Pittsburgh area was mirrored in nearly every part of the country, while the federal government sat by or colluded in the destruction of our country's manufacturing base. To fill the void, a number of other actors entered the arena.

Trade unions began experimenting with and initiating employee buyouts and new types of ownership of faltering companies; exploring new forms of worker participation in decision making, new displaced-worker programs, and new types of labor-management relations; and developing creative investments for union pension funds.

Local and state governments and their agencies began piloting innovative programs for revitalizing manufacturing and protecting the victims of job loss. For example, Massachusetts established the Industrial Services Program to provide substantial support and retraining opportunities to displaced workers, technical and financial assistance to troubled companies, and programs to rebuild distressed

---

* Material for this article was taken from a speech by Mike Stout of the Tri-State Conference on Steel and from brochures supplied to us by Judy Ruszkowski, Vice-President of Southbank Industry Association.

communities in various parts of the state. Michigan created a comprehensive and novel program to rebuild the local auto industry by funding and developing new technology for basic manufacturing and by using a portion of state pension funds for industrial development.

Grassroots community and church-based groups, throughout the country, also took up the fight to save jobs, revitalize manufacturing and industry, and protect the economic and social welfare of workers and communities. In Connecticut, a local coalition of labor, church, and community activists arranged the worker buyout of a major wire-producing facility, saving 250 jobs and a town's entire tax base. In Minnesota, another grassroots coalition got legislation passed that required companies using public funds to agree to plant- and job-retention initiatives and regulations. In Chicago, coalition efforts won official city support for setting up an extensive early warning network that is now being copied around the country and that has helped workers and minority entrepreneurs buy companies at risk or where owners are ready to retire. In North Carolina, women of color led a local battle that won TRA (Trade Readjustment Act) benefits and severance pay for the shutdown victims at the nonunion Schlage facility in the heart of a rural "right to work" state. And in northern California a grassroots coalition established the Redwood Employee Protection Program. This fund provides more than $100 million for 6,000 former timber workers, who receive full or partial wage replacement, medical benefits, basic education, retraining, relocation assistance, and job placement.

In the Pittsburgh area, a coalition of local labor, church, and community activists formed the **Tri-State Conference on Steel**. Early on, Tri-State spent much of its existence sounding the alarm about deindustrialization—educating workers and communities about the imminent dangers they were facing, and why, and organizing the victims of these shutdowns to survive by establishing food banks, unemployed committees, and other self-help mechanisms. From the first, however, Tri-State also began formulating strategies for saving jobs, revitalizing our manufacturing base, and empowering communities to take their destiny into their own hands. Out of this work emerged the **Steel Valley Authority (SVA)**, *a grassroots, public industrial authority*, modeled somewhat after the Tennessee Valley Authority, with state-given powers of both eminent domain and issuing revenue bonds. In the SVA, dislocated workers and distressed communities are no longer passive players, but instead sit at the economic planning table and have a voice in key economic decisions. Unlike other Authorities in the area, top-heavy with corporate officials and bureaucrats, the SVA was built from the bottom up, with community, labor, and church-group representatives on its board. As Tri-State and SVA evolved through struggles to save several plants, we discovered the potential of *coalition politics*. With each battle, we learned more about how to become players in our own economic destinies—from conducting feasibility, engineering, and marketing studies, to finding the funds to develop our programs.

Currently, the SVA, along with the Tri-State Conference, the United Steel Workers of America, and Pennsylvania state legislators, is moving toward reopening **South Side Electric Furnaces**, a plant previously owned by the LTV conglomerate. To accomplish this goal and to create a socially responsible and employee-community-investor owned facility, SVA has taken the following steps:

- Incorporated **South Side Steel of Pittsburgh** as the business entity to operate the plant, and hired experienced steel management;
- Obtained an option arrangement with LTV for exclusive development of the site;
- Commissioned an engineering firm to prepare specifications for refitting the furnaces and constructing a continuous caster to improve product quality;
- Retained an investment banking firm to pursue financing and contacted more than a dozen potential customers;
- Incorporated a nonprofit affiliate, **Southbank Industry Association**, to foster community involvement, including monitoring the new plant so as "to promote the health, safety, and welfare of the community. . . and fair and full employment opportunities for all qualified individuals." Southbank is to raise local community investment money, acquire a small ownership share in South Side Steel, and elect a representative to the new company's Board of Directors;
- Pursued $12 million in public funds to be channeled through SVA as potential holder of the land for the new facility, which it would lease to South Side Steel;
- Committed to form a partially (51 percent) worker-owned facility through an ESOP.

In brief, SVA plans to buy the mill and lease it to an operating company of worker-owners, private investors, and a community organization. This means that important decisions would be made locally, not in some remote corporate headquarters—that employees and their community would have a real voice in directing the company.

Broader Regional and National Policy Initiatives

But even the strongest local coalitions have limitations. They particularly lack sufficient resources, especially when dealing with hostile multinational corporations, which can move capital at will, with no regard for workers or communities. In this context, the need for policy initiatives on the regional and the national level is clear. Here are some of the proposals we are supporting, not as a pie-in-the-sky wish list but as concrete remedies to concrete problems that have arisen from locally based efforts:

- *Stronger plant-closing legislation*, which would require companies closing workplaces not only to give sufficient advance notice but to consult fully with labor and community groups concerning the effects of and alternatives to shutdowns;
- *Establishing a superfund* that would provide more substantial and long-term programs to assist *all* the victims of plant shutdowns, especially in regard to substantial retraining, income maintenance, job placement, and replacing social services for communities;

- *Establishing regional job authorities* and other democratic institutions modeled along the lines of SVA that enable participation of workers and of concerned community citizens in economic decision making;
- *Creating a national industrial development fund* to help finance local and regional development efforts through the use of federal monies, pension funds, and a national cooperative bank;
- *Economic conversion*, emphasizing the change from military production to civilian manufacturing and developing new technology that can improve products and production processes;
- *Managed trade policy*, which includes programs to curb unfair trade and dumping, as well as unfair labor practices on the part of antiunion and antiworker repressive regimes throughout the world.

Short Takes

The organizations profiled in this chapter are but a few of the many technical assistance groups that have been formed to help democratic businesses start and remain alive and well. The nationwide range of these support organizations is well illustrated by the directory in chapter 9. Here we describe a few more of them, starting with those that promote worker ownership explicitly and primarily, then moving to extend the circle to those that expand workplace democracy into community settings or that target specific groups now disempowered economically.

Technical Assistance for Worker-Owners

The **ICA Group,** formerly the Industrial Cooperative Association, began its work in 1977. The scope of this organization is remarkable: their clients range from Cherry Hill, a small cannery in rural Vermont, to Seymour Specialty Wire, a large, democratically owned manufacturing ESOP in Connecticut, to several home-health-care and community-recycling firms, to an interunion worker-owned shipyard in Seattle, to the Cooperativa de Muebles, a furniture-making cooperative in Puerto Rico. No sector of the economy or part of the nation seems outside its capabilities; in 1989 alone, ICA's "work with 42 companies and institutions resulted in the creation or saving of over 170 direct jobs, 550 secondary jobs, and support to another 1,800 jobs." In addition, the organization's international consultant, David Ellerman, helped two companies in the USSR convert to employee ownership using the ICA's concepts and model by-laws. ICA works in collaboration with many different types of organizations—unions, community-development groups, church-based loan funds, and state development agencies. It has assisted the startup process of newer technical assistance groups such as the Farmworkers Association in central Florida, which represents some 1,600 migrant workers, and has formed several different sorts of worker cooperatives.[1]

Utah State University Center for Productivity and Quality of Working Life. Across the country, in Logan, Utah, the **Utah State Center** provides technical assistance services including consultation, workshops, and conferences on cooperative and worker-owned enterprises, on such allied topics as "sharing the gains of productivity" and "cooperative labor-management committees," on techniques to improve organizational efficiency and the quality of worklife, and on alternative work systems, such as autonomous work groups, team building, and job sharing.

Center for Community Self-Help (CCSH). For about a decade, the CCSH in Durham, North Carolina, has worked throughout the state to help form a "network of associated worker-owned businesses in a compact geographic area." This network now totals about twenty firms, including restaurants, newspapers, a medium-sized hosiery mill in eastern North Carolina, and an outdoor-recreation center close to the Blue Ridge Parkway with more than 300 employees. In part, this network was originally designed as a multiracial coalition to extend the civil-rights movement into the workplace. In addition, the center's initial goals included motivating self-education and self-reliance within depressed communities and expanding democratic values and economic justice. Recently, CCSH has begun to provide support to a variety of women-owned businesses; in particular, it is helping women on welfare become child-care providers. To accomplish this, it has formed alliances with other community-based organizations, notably the Rural Day Care Association in Ahoskie, North Carolina, to develop a replicable model by which low-cost, high-quality day care can be created throughout poor and minority communities in the western part of the state.

One of the center's most innovative facilities is its **Self-Help Credit Union** (with assets of more than $14 million), which has provided financing for democratic businesses, cooperative housing, home ownership in minority communities, and AIDS hospices and homeless shelters. In contrast with virtually all other credit unions, SHCU is open to anyone and everyone, regardless of where they live or work; the only requirement for membership is that one share the center's commitment to promote a democratic and just economy.

Co-op America is a nationwide membership organization of democratic and environmentally sensitive businesses and people who support such enterprises that was founded in 1982. It has grown to include some 400 firms and more than 40,000 individuals. Members receive many services: access to full-coverage health plans, marketing assistance via an attractive quarterly catalog, discounts on computerized information and communication, and an excellent magazine, *Co-Op America Quarterly*, which covers a wide range of democratic economy issues. According to founder Paul Freundlich, Co-op America was initially aimed at building "an alternative marketplace." After just a decade he could claim a fair measure of success in reaching this goal: the organization had established an effective marketing and distribution system for products, services, and information. This success he attributed not merely to a high level of craft but to marketing sophistication: the increased ability to make clear to consumers that Co-op America offered *unique* products and services, ones that had special and important uses in people's lives.

Newer Technical Assistance Groups

In the past five years, many new technical assistance organizations have emerged, often to serve specific local communities. Among these are **Worker Owned Network (WON)** and **Jobs for People (JfP)**, both located in Ohio. WON, of Athens, has helped form eight enterprises, owned and controlled mainly by people who had been unable to find work. These range from a cleaning-and-maintenance operation, to a machine shop, to an innovative bicycle manufacturer. WON's organizational structure sets it apart from almost all other U.S. technical assistance groups: client businesses not only agree to recycle a percentage of their profits back to WON in order to help finance new co-ops but elect representatives to its board of directors and thus help shape its policies and direction. Recently, WON has branched out from worker co-ops to a broader and more ambitious development strategy called **flexible manufacturing networks**. This involves working with small manufacturing firms (similar to those in the Emilia-Romagna section of Italy) to form many temporary production alliances that codesign and manufacture innovative items no single firm could produce. WON has developed a comprehensive, step-by-step training program for would-be worker-owners, including such topics as Laying the Groundwork, Building the Cooperative Workgroup and Forming Business Policies, and Setting Up Shop.[2]

Jobs for People, in Cincinnati, began in 1988 as an interfaith coalition of some 40 churches and synagogues; it works primarily with the dislocated and unemployed. JfP has helped to start PFJ, Inc., a labor cooperative that provides quality services in light assembly, clerical work, house cleaning, and weatherization and is developing, along with labor and religious groups, an employee-owned construction company to help meet community needs for low-income housing.

Both WON and JfP, along with the Northeast Ohio Employee Ownership Center and other community-centered groups, have formed a statewide organization, the **Ohio Worker Owner Coalition**, that lobbies for legislation supporting the growth of worker-owned enterprises across the entire state.

In 1988, a group of business firms, housing cooperatives, and consultants formed the Democratic Business Association of Northern California in Berkeley, which now includes the book distributor Bookpeople, Modern Times Bookstore, Cheeseboard, the Northern California Land Trust, and two consulting firms for democratic enterprises in the Bay Area. The association offers technical assistance services to its members—educational, legal, financial, business—so that linkages form that can help make "democratic business a significant force in the region." Their newsletter, edited by founding members Ruth and Jaques Kaswan, keeps members informed of new cooperative developments, and provides concrete resources and accounts of practice.

Common Work, in Syracuse, New York, was formed during 1989 by community activists who believe that cooperatives and employee-owned businesses can be important tools of empowerment for low-income and working people. Its initial board of directors includes members of several different types of local co-ops (a women-run bakery, a food co-op, a cooperative credit union), as well as a staff person from the American Friends Service Committee, a lawyer, a community organizer, and a financial analyst. Common Work stresses an unusually wide range of cooperative enterprise—including housing, consumer, democratic ESOPs, and worker co-ops—and its intention is to create a membership organization in which representatives from these diverse sorts of enterprises will have ultimate control. In the past year, Common Work has worked with low-income tenants to help them consider the feasibility of establishing cooperatively owned and managed laundry facilities in their housing project, and organized a hearing, along with other community groups, before the Syracuse Common Council in an effort to get them to use the city's power of eminent domain to take over a local factory whose assets were about to be sold to outside competitors.[3]

In the Pacific Northwest, the **Community Consulting Group** and the **Puget Sound Co-operative Federation** (PSCF), both located in Seattle, provide assistance to cooperatively run enterprises. The first concentrates largely on consumer cooperatives, but many of these are now exploring a range of participatory or ownership options for their workforces. PSCF is actually an association of consumer and worker-owned enterprises whose members set up an affiliate organization, the Puget Sound Development Foundation, to help promote cooperative development within low-income and disadvantaged communities. Last year, they furnished business and educational services to 29 projects of this sort. Two of the firms recently assisted by PSCF are Fresh Herbs Cooperative, a women-owned and managed enterprise that produces several types of herbal vinegars made from its own fresh-grown herbs, and Western Cascade, a machine shop owned and operated by machinists faced with layoffs at their former plant.

Another technical assistance organization with goals similar to those of PSCF is the **Wisconsin Cooperative Development Council.**

There are also about a dozen *state-supported programs* that provide start-up financial assistance (loans or loan guarantees) to worker buyout efforts or employee-owned enterprises. States involved include *California, Connecticut, Illinois, Michigan, New Jersey, New York, Ohio, Oregon, Pennsylvania, Washington, Wisconsin, and West Virginia.* Most of these states have also passed legislation authorizing existing or newly created agencies to strengthen employee ownership by providing public outreach, feasibility studies, worker-owner education, or other forms of technical assistance.

Widening the Circle

Thus far, we have mentioned technical assistance groups that focus primarily, and sometimes exclusively, on developing worker-owned businesses. But building a democratic economy requires that all of those who are now economically disenfranchised (e.g., low-income and minority communities, and women entrepreneurs) be empowered to share in decision making about the goals and organization of production. Over the past decade, technical assistance organizations have taken form that offer services to these two groups, both now largely excluded from economic power. Such services do include support for worker ownership—but only as one of several economic development strategies.

Supporting Community-Based Development

The Naugatuck Valley in western Connecticut was a major casualty of the past two decades of plant closings, runaways, and layoffs. Once the heart of the brass industry in this country, it watched dozens of large and medium-sized plants go under. Conventional tactics, such as strikes, were of no avail. In 1984, however, an unusual coalition of religious, labor, community, and small business organizations devised a new approach, the **Naugatuck Valley Project (NVP)**, aimed at giving workers and communities greater influence in determining their economic destinies. NVP's preferred remedy for deindustrialization and job loss is broad-based local ownership. In its seven years, the project has grown to include 66 very diverse member organizations, turned the threatened closing of Bridgeport Brass into the highly successful, democratically owned and managed Seymour Specialty Wire, helped draft legislation for a state fund that now makes financing available to employees in buyout situations, established tenants' associations and cooperatively owned affordable housing, and has set up a worker-owned and managed housekeeping and home health care enterprise. It has become a major force in more than a dozen different job-saving campaigns throughout the valley, most of them in conjunction with locals of the United Auto Workers (UAW). In total, these campaigns have helped to save almost *3,000 jobs*. One of the project's most recent ventures involves the Stratford, Connecticut, Textron- Lycoming plant, which faces 1,500 layoffs because of reduced orders for M-1 tank engines. NVP has joined forces with UAW local 1010 in Stratford to develop economic conversion strategies aimed at saving jobs through shifting to nonmilitary production.

As Jeremy Brecher has pointed out, NVP is "essentially a citizens' organization in the tradition pioneered by Saul Alinsky's Industrial Areas Foundation." Thus, its constituencies are very diverse: church groups of several denominations, union locals, the Connecticut Citizens Action Group, Seymour Specialty Wire, the Chamber of Commerce of Northwestern Connecticut, and other organizations. These all work together (despite a history that includes some conflict) to save the Valley's economy through expanding local ownership and by increasing their participation in the region's economic decisions.[4]

The **Center for Neighborhood Technology (CNT)**, now more than a decade old, provides services and training, primarily in and around Chicago, in energy conservation, ecological waste management, and local food production. With its aid, neighborhood groups have established community energy centers and are using a computerized audit system to increase efficient energy use. CNT views the "working neighborhood," or "sustainable community," as the prime locus of economic activity: through coalition organizing, it has combated harmful downtown development and promoted job creation throughout the city's neighborhoods. In doing so, it has relied on a mix of strategies, including worker ownership, community incubators furnishing low-cost rentals and common services to local entrepreneurs, and community-based businesses such as those that collect and reprocess recyclables. Its monthly publication, *The Neighborhood Works*, discusses these and other neighborhood-empowering approaches in rich, concrete detail. The center publishes an excellent series of hands-on community-economic-development manuals, including *Building Sustainable Communities, Working Neighborhoods: Taking Charge of Your Local Economy, The Permanent Endowment: A Step-by-Step Energy Savings Guide,* and *The Neighborhood Toolbox: Strategies for Making Neighborhoods Work.*

In Los Angeles, the **Cooperative Resources and Services Project (CRSP)** combines deep ecological priorities (such as land stewardship and sustainable community life) with their work as a training and development center for cooperatives of many sorts—housing, child care, consumer, producer, service, and so on. Founded in 1980, CRSP publishes a bimonthly newsletter, the *Networker*, and a *Cooperative Primer and Directory*. It also runs conferences and workshops and is developing the Ecological Loan Fund to support small and earth-sustaining cooperative enterprises such as "a gray water recycling installation service, a neighborhood barter or local exchange system, and a self-help health co-op."

Nationally, there are many organizations that serve grassroots community groups seeking a greater voice in economic decision making. One of the largest and most long-lived is the **National Congress for Community Economic Development (NCCED)**, which has grown from 40 member groups in 1982 to more than 300. These members include community-action agencies, community-development corporations, community loan funds, farmworker associations, cooperatives, and other community-centered support organizations. NCCED has taken the lead in encouraging the formation of statewide federations of community economic development groups (e.g., in Ohio, Florida, Massachusetts, Wisconsin). These statewide associations get assistance of several sorts from NCCED and, in turn, help their own members to acquire the funding and expertise needed to create affordable housing, minority- and neighborhood-controlled enterprises, and, on occasion, worker or consumer cooperatives.

Two organizations that serve Native American clients are **First Nation Financial Project**, which uses small-scale economic development to diminish tribal dependence on federal funds, and **Seventh Generation Fund**, which concentrates on projects using renewable resources, for which it offers comprehensive technical and financial support and, on occasion, small seed grants.

The community-based technical assistance family also includes two groups that specialize in *economic conversion*, the transformation of military and other life-threatening forms of production to ones that enhance life and promote global security and peace. One of these is the **Center for Economic Conversion** in Mountain View, California, which has worked with several cities and states to sponsor legislation and establish projects advancing economic conversion. The Center's efforts recently bore fruit in western Massachusetts and in Burlington, Vermont, both hard hit by defense-contractor closedowns. With its assistance, these communities have now obtained state funding to explore and initiate diversified local economic planning that does not depend on military contracts.

Jobs With Peace (JWP) also seeks to promote peace and economic democracy through economic conversion. JWP has had a major impact in Minnesota, where 70,000 jobs depend on the federal military budget. They helped shape a state-funded task force, chaired by state representative Karen Clark, to "assist vulnerable and/or military dependent companies to convert to more sustainable forms of production." Equally important, JWP has provided a forum for the active discussion and serious consideration of conversion planning and has played a major role in the formation of the Minnesota Alliance for Progressive Action—a new coalition of some 20 groups representing labor, peace, human rights, farm, and environmental constituencies. Other states and cities (Pennsylvania, Connecticut, Chicago, and Baltimore among them) now have conversion committees, in part because of JWP's organizing efforts. Nationwide, JWP put together the **Housing Now!** and **Build Homes, not Bombs!** coalitions. These have included homeless people, peace activists, working families without access to home ownership, and union members threatened by shutdowns and layoffs. In short, they are broad-based coalitions, similar to the NVP, committed to working for peace through working for locally and democratically controlled conversion.[5]

Focus on Women

In their *Working Guide to Women's Self-Employment*, Sara Gould and Jing Lyman point out that both self-employment in general and in women-owned enterprises have dramatically increased over the last decade or so. Their explanation is the failure of the smokestack-chasing model of development, in which cities or states strive "to lure branch plants of large manufacturing firms by promising reduced taxes, low labor costs, and fewer environmental restrictions." In their place, new economic strategies that foster local entrepreneurs are emerging. Many of these new entrepreneurs are women, often from low-income or minority communities, whose access to ownership has been aided by what Gould and Lyman call "direct-service programs." These programs combine ordinary technical assistance promoting business skills and self-sufficiency with "a sensitivity to the life situations of the women they serve." There are now at least 60 organizations across the country focusing specifically on self-employment for low-income women.[6] Among these *woman-centered technical assistance organizations* are the following:

The **Center for Women's Economic Alternatives** in Ahoskie, North Carolina, focuses on women in the rural and very poor counties of the state. It has provided technical assistance to single proprietorships and to a sewing cooperative and is working with a statewide coalition to establish child-care centers. **Women and Employment** (Charleston, West Virginia) addresses issues of economic equity for women (e.g., by pressing for their access to jobs traditionally open only to men, and by providing business services and loan guarantees to women's cooperatives). **Women's Economic Development Corporation (WEDCO)** of St. Paul, Minnesota, provides individual consulting, workgroups for and with other businesswomen, networks of business contacts, and a loan fund that, as a last resort, offers financing to qualified applicants unable to gain assistance from banks and other financial institutions. Within its first 15 months of operation, WEDCO helped 57 low-income women begin their own business ventures.

Notes

1. Information and quote on the ICA Group is drawn from their 1989 annual report and from their newsletter, the *ICA Bulletin*.

2. This short take on WON is drawn from their newsletter, *Network News*. Their work on FMNs is written up in the May 1990 newsletter.

3. This short take was prepared by Peter Kardas, a past director and founder of Common Work.

4. Jeremy Brecher's article, on which this short take is partly based, is reprinted in *Building Bridges: The Emerging Grassroots Coalition of Labor and Community*. We are grateful, in addition, for information supplied by Kevin Bean, NVP's former staff director.

5. Information on Jobs for Peace was supplied by Mel Duncan, coordinator of their Minnesota office.

6. *The Neighborhood Works*, March–April, 1988, p. 3.

4

Common Wealth
Financing Workplace Democracy

New financial institutions have sprung up over the last decade that provide
capital for worker cooperatives, land trusts, and similar community-based efforts.
The expansion in the number of revolving loan funds and community credit unions
has led to the formation of two federations: the **National Association of
Community Development Loan Funds**, with thirty-seven members, and the
National Federation of Community Development Credit Unions, with about
100 member credit unions. These are based on what is really a remodeling of an
old idea: in many cases, individuals and organizations pool their small investments
and concentrate them for the good of the local community.

In the first section of this chapter, Mark Satin tells us about the "citizen bankers"
at Chicago's **South Shore Bank** and at New York's new **Community Capital
Bank**. Dorris Pickens describes in detail the **Neighborhood Institute**, South
Shore's non-profit, community development arm.

Community credit unions democratize banking functions even further.
Controlled by their shareholders, they can often build on close local ties to foster
effective community development. In the second section of this chapter, John
Isbister and Ron Ehrenreich explore the various possibilities and pitfalls of
community credit unions, including the strains between the demands of business,
the wider marketplace, and community development agendas.

Increasingly, both religious and secular organizations have been developing new
institutions dedicated to reversing the flow of capital from poor to rich
communities. In the third section, Christine Rico describes the efforts of churches
to redirect their substantial assets, while Gregg Ramm chronicles the exciting
growth of community revolving loan funds.

As numerous and as promising as these alternative sources of capital are, their
assets are still small compared to the need and to other sources of capital. Moreover,
few provide venture capital for new or growing worker-owned business.
Expanding democratically controlled sources of capital is one of the more crucial
tasks facing the whole movement. Recently, several labor unions have been

exploring ways of tapping (and controlling) more capital. In the fourth section of this chapter, Chris Meek talks about the various attempts by workers to use ESOPs for financing buyouts and about the AFL-CIO's buyout fund, while Andrew Banks tells the story of the Florida Operating Engineers' successful struggle to take control of their own pension fund—a huge source of capital.

In the Short Takes at the end of this chapter, we introduce readers to a number of other alternative financial institutions, including the **Center for Community Self-Help** in North Carolina and a new development bank in Arkansas. We mention several examples from abroad, particularly the **Working People's Bank** that serves the network of worker co-ops in and around the Basque town of Mondragon. We highlight the **Institute for Community Economics**, a group that has helped to popularize the idea of both land trusts and revolving loan funds, and we briefly describe two sources of financing for community development, the **Leviticus Fund** and the **Cooperative Fund of New England**. We mention the German **Ecobank's** system, which enables people to deposit money in ways that are used to promote environmental, feminist or other causes. This is but one instance of socially responsible investment, which seeks to avoid supporting companies that engage in socially harmful production, instead channeling funds to those that are socially beneficial, including worker cooperatives.

Citizen Bankers Would Rebuild the United States— Community by Community*

Mark Satin

There is an emerging alternative to the big government–big business–big labor kind of "rebuilding" of America. Its basic strategy is to get investment capital out of the hands of the big banks, the big brokerage houses, the multinationals, and the like, and into the hands of the communities. Its greatest champions are neither politicians nor oppositional political groups, but—remarkably—bankers; or more specifically, those few bankers who describe themselves as "community development bankers," or "socially responsible bankers," or some such.

We recently talked with some of these New Bankers, especially at the bank that—everyone agrees—best practices what all these bankers preach: South Shore Bank of Chicago. One of the first things we noticed is that they all started out in fields other than banking:

- Ronald Gryzwinski, chairman of the board of Shorebank Corporation (South Shore's holding company), used to sell computers;
- Joan Shapiro, senior vice president at South Shore, used to teach literature, theater, and dance. "Like many women of my generation, I am a generalist," she told *New Options*;
- Dorris Pickens, president of the Neighborhood Institute (Shorebank's nonprofit affiliate), had been a community activist. "I loved community work, and I love the neighborhood," she says;
- Mary Houghton, president of Shorebank Corporation, has a Master's degree in international relations;

---

* From *New Options*, 28 March 1988.

- Lyndon Comstock, principal organizer for the New York City–based Community Capital Bank, was a full-time antiwar activist in the sixties, "then I was involved with developing housing and small business co-ops in the early seventies both in Michigan and the Bay Area."

For decades, the political Left has been teaching that a central, overwhelming problem in this country is that most people do not have access to power. But, perhaps because of its aversion to the capitalist system, the Left never made a crucial link: in a capitalist country, access to power means not just access to the political arena but—even more importantly—access to capital.

It is access to capital that the New Bankers are seeking to win for individuals and communities. That is why their efforts may be more politically relevant today than the efforts of all the oppositional political groupuscles put together.

"In thousands of [communities like South Shore]," says Joan Shapiro,

> you have a situation of systematic disinvestment. You have a situation resulting from a deliberate decision by financial institutions and insurance companies and other providers of capital not to invest in a community—because there is a perception that the area is declining.

> You also have a situation where people put their limited savings in the local bank, and the bank lends the money outside the community. There is a net outflow of capital from less affluent to more affluent communities.

> The [beauty] of South Shore Bank is that it's essentially reversed the outflow of capital. It's saying to investors—affluent people outside of neighborhoods like South Shore—"If you put your money in this neighborhood, we will apply those resources to redevelop our disinvested community." Reversing the capital flow is, I think, one of the major innovations of South Shore Bank.

Development Deposits

South Shore Bank does not look out of the ordinary—modernistic white concrete on the outside, corporate purple-and-lavender on the inside. True: there is wallpaper, not paint, on some of the walls, and enough potted plants to serve as a statement of some kind. But it is the development deposits that separate South Shore from all other banks. It is the development deposits that support South Shore's innovative urban lending program—which has directed more than $85 million in credit to neighborhood residents to rehabilitate run-down housing, pay college tuition, and finance small businesses and non-profit organizations.

"By definition," Shapiro told *New Options*,

> a development deposit is any deposit that comes to the bank from outside its immediate neighborhood. Forty percent of South Shore's deposits are development deposits . . . . Right now it's about a $59 million portfolio.

> Now, why would some [middle-class person] in Fargo or Tucson or San Francisco put money in a medium-sized bank on the South Side of Chicago? The answer is that those people care about what's happening to their money, [what it's being used for].

According to Shapiro, development depositors need make no financial sacrifices. "The vast majority of the deposits in this portfolio are market-rate deposits. Our money-market account will equal or exceed that of other national indexes; our CDs are fully competitive with the national market."

The default rate on South Shore's loans is less than 2 percent. "So you don't lose your shirt making loans in low- to moderate-income communities," says Shapiro. "If you make a long-term commitment to it, if you put your best loan officers to it, you're going to have a very strong portfolio."

"The banks like to tell us the issue is risk," Lyndon Comstock told *New Options*. "But the idea that risk is the issue is a myth. The issue is, Where do the banks think they can make the biggest profits? That's what they're making their decisions on."

We asked Shapiro to tell us the difference between development deposits and the various social investment funds like Calvert and Working Assets. We could tell she did not want to say anything that would reflect poorly on her friends and colleagues at the funds. But she did say this: "[The social investment funds] invest in paper and securities of national intermediaries. South Shore invests directly in the community. So part of the difference is the distance of the investment from the actual direct impact."

A second basic difference, of course, is that investments in South Shore's development deposits are federally insured up to $100,000.

A third difference is that the social investment funds employ largely negative social screens. They refuse to invest in South Africa, nuclear power, and so on. Banks like South Shore and the Community Capital Bank affirmatively direct capital to community-based businesses and non-profits.

In our opinion, that is the biggest difference of all. It may be more glamorous to refuse to invest in nuclear power than to help make credit available to small-fry housing developers. But the former only says No! to what is wrong with the United States, the latter also says Yes! to what is emerging and right.

Creative Use of the Holding Company

Getting middle-class money out of national banks, brokerage houses, phony "neighborhood banks," and the like, and into development deposits at genuinely neighborhood-oriented banks like South Shore is important enough; but the development-deposits concept only represents part of South Shore's contribution to the rebuilding of the United States. What is really unique about South Shore is that its loans are part and parcel of a systemic approach to rebuilding community, fostered and supported by the bank's holding company.

"Most banks in this country are organized under a holding-company structure," Shapiro told *New Options*.

> That structure has an enormous capacity to let banks organize for community betterment, [though] very few of them have taken advantage of that capacity.

What South Shore Bank has done is, through its holding-company structure, create additional development affiliates, each of which operates its own business, if you will. The sum total [of these businesses is] a comprehensive approach to community renewal! In Shapiro's words:

> The second arm of the holding company is a real estate development company called City Lands Corporation. Its special focus is to purchase and rehabilitate more severely deteriorated buildings than the bank can do through its market-rate credit.

> [The third arm is] the Neighborhood Institute. To our knowledge, when it was organized in 1978 it was the first non- profit affiliate of a holding company in the country! It is designed to operate social and economic development programs.

> The Neighborhood Fund is the venture capital arm. It makes investments in minority- and women-owned businesses.

> Our newest affiliate is called Shorebank Advisory Services. It gives us the capacity to help others get into the business of doing development banking!

> We feel that all the arms of the holding company together create a kind of synergy . . . an impact on the market that is far greater than any of them could have alone.

The Neighborhood Institute

The holding company's non-profit affiliate, the Neighborhood Institute, is in some ways like a business, in other ways like a community organization, in still other ways like a neighborhood government.

"The Neighborhood Institute adds a new depth to the development model that was proposed by the holding company," Dorris Pickens told *New Options*.

> At first we saw our role in the community—and still do to a certain extent—as that of enabler and facilitator and connector. I think just now people would see us trying to become an economic development engine as well.

> We've been in housing development for the last four or five years. We develop housing for low-income people and we train the folks to manage the housing and take it over themselves.

> We operate an educational and vocational training facility: that's our biggest program. Training in clerical skills and word processing and carpentry . . . . The newest part of our training sequence is entrepreneurial training and development: trying to create self-employed individuals, or help self-employed individuals in the neighborhood. We take them from the concept stage to the real business plan stage. It's very intensive.

What is Pickens's ultimate goal? "I would like to see our organization help create an environment that's healthy enough for people to basically help themselves."

No Mean Politico

You would think the person who invented South Shore Bank would be an unconventional political dreamer. In fact, Ron Gryzwinski was a very conventional banker and a very successful one, president of the Hyde Park Bank while still in his thirties. The most you can say—and in truth, it is a lot—is that he is a decent person who was not afraid to learn and grow.

In 1967, he told us late one afternoon from his office, "me and another guy tried doing loans to small minority-owned businesses from out of the corner of our desks. And it turned out that the demand was greater than anything we had anticipated."

At the time, Hyde Park was changing over from a largely white to a largely Black neighborhood, and all over the United States the ghettos were seething. "I was really not familiar with racial issues. So I studied at the time a lot of Black literature. . . . There was some sensitizing going on."

In 1968, he got permission from the board of the Hyde Park Bank to start an urban development division in the bank. Its first two employees: Milton Davis, "who'd just finished being president of the Chicago chapter of CORE" (and is now vice-president of Shorebank Corporation), and Mary Houghton (now the corporation's president).

"Milton and Mary and I got involved as volunteers in a variety of community-based organizations around the city," Gryzwinski recalls.

> We saw that community-based organizations were always undercapitalized and always dependent on government or foundations giving them their next grant or contract. We thought about that, and we concluded that if this country was going to get serious about rebuilding its neighborhoods, we had better figure out some way that the activity could be adequately capitalized and become self-supporting.

Eventually, Gryzwinski lost interest in continuing as president of Hyde Park Bank. He raised $55,000 so he could spend full time figuring out how to get capital and business sense into the communities. "I hired the best consultants and lawyers we could find to help us define what this new company might be like. We did not think it would be a bank!" But it was. It opened its doors in 1973.

Two, Three, Many Banks

For fifteen years, South Shore Bank has been refining its concepts and proving its mettle. The question now—for political visionaries as much as for bankers—is, Is it replicable?

Astonishingly, it is only recently that people have started to try to replicate it—in Arkansas and in New York City, in Philadelphia and in Washington, D.C.

South Shore is setting up the effort in Arkansas. "We tried to design an organization in Arkansas that would be an adaptation of the structure we have here," Mary Houghton told *New Options*.

It'll be targeted toward generation of jobs in small rural towns. . . . We imagine that some portion of the jobs will be self-employment, some other portion will be in small- to medium-sized companies that employ five to twenty people. And we're going to try to get smart over time about which [economic] sectors have the most opportunity.

The board of Southern Development [in Arkansas] is now formed. It is three people representing the Chicago group [including herself and Gryzwinski] and the balance—seven or eight—are Arkansans. At first the staffing is going to be a mixture of Arkansans and people from outside, but in five years it'll be a permanent, professional local staff.

This is an extraordinary opportunity! It's very hard to raise capital in our society for serious long-term development initiatives. And the fact that the Winthrop Rockefeller Foundation was willing to commit a total of $5 million, and that we've been able to raise an additional $6 million, is just an extraordinary, pure opportunity for us to be able to encourage a lot of people to start working like hell to see what they can make happen.

Another way to see the opportunity is that people who live there really love Arkansas. They really want to be living there, and they speak about how great it is with enormous conviction. And the opportunity is to increase the number of options they have so they can continue living in this place that they love.

What's generally neglected in our society is all the small deals. And yet, in order to increase options there have got to be small opportunities so that people can get going with things, whether it is self-employment or small businesses or small- to medium-sized companies.

The Old-Fashioned Way

For all their innovations, there is a sense in which the New Bankers are a throwback to the old.

"Sometimes I think we're just old-fashioned good community bankers!" Gryzwinski told *New Options*.

[Our] banks were all chartered to take care of the credit needs of their local service areas. And the communities of people who've needed credit have remained essentially the same. They're the same size: neighborhoods, places like that. But the banks have become international banks. And the banks can no longer relate to the neighborhoods, because the neighborhoods' needs aren't for billions of dollars. They're for tens or hundreds of thousands of dollars per deal.

Also, I think particularly if you look at banks inside cities you'd see that bankers have very little to do with the communities in which their banks are located. The bankers typically live in the suburbs, and are sort of absentee bankers. And that wasn't true before.

"There's a proportion of what we're doing that's much more traditional, actually, than what any of the major banks in New York are doing," Comstock told us.

They're all involved in a headlong flight into investment banking—mergers and acquisitions and all that kind of stuff—and are trying to get as far away from traditional banking as possible.

They might still have a department that does small-business lending. But look at the amount that they do! Their focus on small-business lending has greatly declined compared to what it was fifteen years ago, let alone thirty years ago.

"There's parts of the old-fashioned thing that I don't like. I mean, you know, there was racism in the old banking world, there was sexism, there was classism.

The capital flow now is as classist as could be. Basically, the entire collective savings of our society are being funneled into the banking system, [which then funnels it out] into the wealthiest sectors of the economy. . . . The savings of the people of this borough are being siphoned out and taken to Japan, and to Donald Trump! I mean, how do you think Trump builds all this stuff? He didn't start out having $100 million. It's our collective savings that allows these people to do what they do!

It is outrageous. And it is entirely related to why there are so many miseries within this country.

Communities Have to Be Developed from Within*

Conversation with Dorris Pickens

The ongoing regeneration of Chicago's 80,000 population South Shore neighborhood is little short of remarkable. Since the innovative South Shore Bank initiated operations in 1973, the low- to middle-income South Shore neighborhood has gained some $170 million in new investments, and seen some 350 large apartment buildings rehabilitated.

As noted in a recent issue of the *New Republic*, the South Shore experience "demonstrates the power of combining the investment methods of the private sector with the social goals of the public sector." In addition, reports the magazine, "hundreds of businesses have started, and thousands of people have received remedial education, job training, and job placement."

Much of the credit for these human development accomplishments belongs to an organization called the Neighborhood Institute (TNI), a nonprofit affiliate of South Shore Bank that in the words of its president, Dorris Pickens, practices a "holistic" approach.

"We focus concurrently on both the human needs and the physical needs of our people," she says. "As far as we're concerned, doing one without the other is ineffective. That's why we prefer a coupling of these elements to keep both sides of the equation balanced."

All of which means that Pickens leads a comprehensive economic development organization that offers a complementary set of programs ranging from adult basic education, to small business assistance, to the rehabilitation of apartments and commercial properties.

TNI has broken ground on a new mixed-use complex, for which part of the financing was provided by the National Cooperative Bank Development

---

*   From *Cooperative Enterprise*, Summer 1989.

Corporation. With that in mind, Cooperative Enterprise spoke with Pickens about TNI's philosophy of community development.

Cooperative Enterprise: What is the approach that TNI takes toward economic development?

Dorris Pickens: Our primary role is to stimulate a climate whereby people have options and opportunities to help themselves. We have to do that on a number of different fronts. Since buildings alone don't make a community, TNI emphasizes the development of human capital by helping to obtain the tools, the resources, and perhaps most importantly the confidence to master their own destinies. This requires training, education, counseling, and support.

CE: How exactly did this approach evolve?

DP: Over time. Initially, TNI focused on advocacy and technical assistance. We started with literacy, high school equivalency diplomas, and vocational training in carpentry and office skills. From there we launched a major job placement effort so that our clients could have an opportunity to put their new skills to work. We soon recognized the need for activities aimed at job creation and started an entrepreneurial program to help people translate their ideas, hobbies, and interests into businesses and make a living from their own microenterprises.

This led to the establishment of a small business development center, which focuses on business plan development and business financing, a natural outgrowth of which was our small business incubator—the South Shore Enterprise Center. The Enterprise Center provides people just starting out in business with office and manufacturing space in a supportive environment to help them increase their chances of succeeding.

To complement our human development initiatives, we simultaneously provided a variety of housing services. Our primary objective was to help low- to moderate-income families find and maintain quality housing that was also affordable. Subsequently, our housing development efforts evolved out of the frustration of trying to place these families in homes through traditional real estate management companies. Despite our efforts, one family after another was denied residence either because they had too many children or because they were recipients of public aid. We knew that we could turn this situation around if we became housing developers in addition to being housing advocates.

CE: How do you quantify these ventures in terms of results?

DP: Just like any business, we have to be mindful of "the bottom line." Although in our business the bottom line is measured in many different terms, such as the number of housing units we develop, the number of jobs we create, the number of businesses we assist, and so on.

The majority of TNI's programs operate according to a set of performance contracts held with various government agencies. These agencies view our success according to the degree to which we comply with the objectives set forth in our contracts. If we want to stay in business, we have to perform. Over the years, we've placed several thousand people in jobs, many of whom would not otherwise have been employed. Our excellent track record enables us to get and maintain the contracts we need in order to continue to do what we do.

CE: That's sort of the answer I was looking for, but I suspect there's more to it than that.

DP: Absolutely, and that has to do with the nature of the people TNI serves. You've got to understand that a lot of people who've been unemployed for a long time, or have not been employed at all, need to have their confidence developed before they go out and look for a job. We have to serve as a connector, to provide the job readiness that people need and then connect them with jobs they can fill.

That role leads us into all kinds of areas. For example, we're now trying to develop a program called Reverse Commute. It's based on the reality that most new jobs are in the suburbs. So if the jobs are moving out that way, we have to do what we can to help our clients get those jobs. So now we're studying transportation issues so we can open up these kinds of opportunities.

CE: It's clear that TNI can turn people into employees. What about turning them into owners? Getting back to that quantification question, how do you measure the results of your entrepreneurial and small business development programs?

DP: By its very nature, that sort of thing is somewhat harder to measure, but we have evidence to show that the seeds are taking root. Please understand we're talking microenterprises here, sometimes just enough to support one person, but as far as we're concerned, that's progress.

Perhaps one of the most successful start-ups is a seamstress who once worked in a clothing factory but was laid off when the factory downsized. We helped her set up her own business, and now she's doing quite well at it. A similar situation happened with a man who was laid off from a cabinet factory. He's also in business for himself now, producing things like picture frames and plaques. There are lots of people doing little businesses like that.

In our small business incubator itself, we currently have eleven tenants. Some of these companies have real potential. For instance, there's a man in there with a wonderful cheesecake recipe. He makes them on contract for some of the major area supermarkets. We also have a company producing solar panels, a janitorial firm, a company that performs energy audits and retrofitting for apartment buildings and single family homes, a jazz production company, and a wholesale distributor.

CE: In a way, it seems you're trying to spread the entrepreneurial religion.

DP: We are, we are. The drive to succeed has to come from within. It's our role to stimulate that kind of energy and make it contagious, if you will. We have to prove to people that they can do this for themselves. At the same time, however, it is important to note that none of this could have happened without cooperation.

People who want to get something done on the neighborhood level have to learn how to work together and not be so protective of their own turf. Working alone you won't make a dent. Working together, well, that'll make a difference. Everything I've told you—I don't think could have happened if there wasn't an institutional force to bring the community together.

CE: Do you have any other thoughts you'd care to impart?

DP: Number one, you have to be patient. There are too many of us that think things are going to happen overnight. That's just not the way it is. Our whole philosophy is that our communities didn't get the way they are overnight and they're certainly not going to change overnight.

Next, communities have to be developed from within. You can bring all the money and the resources into some neighborhood and just do all the things you want. But unless the people themselves are involved in the process—cooperatively speaking, if you will—it's not going to last. The people in a community have to buy into it and feel that they are a part of it in order for it to have any meaning.

Finally, you have to learn how to adjust to the market. Whether you like it or not, market forces aren't going to go away. So use these forces to your advantage. They'll help you accomplish your goals.

The Tension between Business and Politics

The Santa Cruz Community Credit Union

John Isbister

On 17 October 1989 a major earthquake hit the central California coast, devastating the downtown business district of Santa Cruz. After they dealt with their personal emergencies, the staff and board members of the Santa Cruz Community Credit Union (SCCCU) began to fear for their financially fragile institution. They expected many of the members to pull out their deposits in order to begin rebuilding and many of the borrowers to default on their loans. The credit union building was intact, but could the institution survive?

The answer came within a few weeks. The deposit base began to grow at a rate never before experienced, loan repayments stayed steady, and new borrowers flocked to the credit union. Within four months, SCCCU's assets had increased from about $10 million to almost $15 million.

Why? Credit union staff are still scratching their heads, but perhaps the best answer came from a new member who brought in a deposit of $10,000 just a few days after the quake. "This community needs help," he said, "and I know you're the best people to give that help. I'd like to put my money where it will do some good."

What sort of an institution can evoke such a response?

The Santa Cruz Community Credit Union is a savings and lending cooperative, open to all of the residents of Santa Cruz County. Of the 18,000 credit unions in the country, the SCCCU (like a handful of others) exists for an explicitly political purpose: to promote social change in Santa Cruz County, the development of cooperative and locally controlled small businesses, and the welfare of low- and moderate-income people. Like all credit unions, it is a cooperative, owned and controlled on a one-person, one-vote basis by its members, the people who save at the credit union and who borrow from it. Unlike other credit unions, it is less interested in consumer loans (for cars, appliances, vacations, etc.) than in community development.

By community development, the SCCCU means projects that will make a permanent and progressive difference to Santa Cruz. Residents face a constant struggle to keep the community accessible to ordinary people with modest incomes from a variety of ethnic backgrounds. Since Santa Cruz is located on the California coast, its housing costs are high and rising, and there is consequently a danger that all but the affluent will be squeezed out. The credit union tries to help other people establish a stake in the community by starting or expanding their own business and by creating jobs.

As a cooperative, the credit union is particularly interested in helping other co-ops. Aside from other local credit unions, there are no longer any consumer cooperatives in the area, but dozens of businesses have been formed by local people pooling their resources, coming to SCCCU for a loan, and starting a worker cooperative. The credit union is also the lender of choice for many small businesses whose financial needs are moderate or whose track records are not yet established, and who consequently have difficulty in interesting a bank in their problems. The SCCCU offers special low-interest loans to worker cooperatives and to women- or minority-owned businesses.

The credit union was begun in 1977 by a group of activists who knew little about finance but who had strong views about their community. I joined the board in 1978, in time to experience some of the birth pains. The staff, the board, and some of the members engaged in long philosophical discussions, some of them quite acrimonious. How could we best promote the interests of poor people? Was it moral to pay interest on deposits? Should we allow our money to be used for new car purchases? How could we persuade people that they really had to pay back their loans? Was the staff a collective of equals or should there be a manager? The debates were endless.

Over the years, those early debates were resolved. The board and staff decided that the credit union should be both an effective institution for social change in the community and a thriving, successful business. It should be a full-service financial institution, but it should never lose sight of its purpose, which was community development. Those two goals are sometimes complementary but sometimes not—and so the principal theme of the credit union has been the tension between business and politics.

The dream of people at the SCCCU is to emulate the Working People's Bank in Mondragon, Spain, a bank that provides not only loans but also technical advice to a huge array of workers' cooperatives in the Basque country. The Mondragon bank actually assigns a staff member to each new cooperative, helping the fledgling institution to make the thousands of critical decisions that will spell the difference between success and failure. The credit union is a long way from having the staff resources that would allow that sort of assistance for its member businesses. Still, it has made a big difference to a lot of firms by providing loans for start-up or expansion.

A printing cooperative that began with a credit-union loan has developed into one of the leading job shops in the city. A natural juice company that was started in the same way has grown into a major supplier in northern California. Hispanic strawberry cooperatives and individual farmers in the southern part of the county come to the SCCCU for crop loans. Professionals—lawyers, accountants, therapists, consultants—often turn to the credit union to get started. We provide financing for many of the small local retailers who compete with national chains.

The board of directors is particularly proud of its work in the area of affordable housing. The credit union has jointly sponsored a major project (with fifty apartments) for low-income elderly people, and it has provided supplementary financing to allow tenants in a mobile-home park to buy their units as a cooperative.

The credit union also makes consumer loans, directly and through its VISA card. But the board's priority, since the first days, has been business and community development loans. We think that we can make a stronger contribution by promoting economic democracy—through cooperatives and locally controlled small businesses—than we can by providing consumer finance.

The credit union has five thousand members. This represents political support, since almost all of the members could if they wished find a bank that was closer to their neighborhood or that offered a more convenient array of financial services. Of course, not all members are active in the direction of the SCCCU. Beyond the staff of twenty-five, the board of eleven, and another dozen committee members, there are about a hundred people who attend annual meetings or in other ways take part in the credit union's activities. But we know from our surveys and our mail that the members really believe in what the credit union is doing. And the response after the earthquake was a remarkable confirmation of this.

While the debates of the early years have faded, the credit union has never lacked for issues and conflicts that reflect its dual goals, business and politics.

One of the most difficult dilemmas the SCCCU has faced is low-balance accounts. About fifteen hundred of the five thousand members have savings accounts of less than $100. These accounts are a drain on the credit union, because it costs money to carry out the transactions in them, although the savings are so low that the accounts contribute almost nothing to the revenues of the credit union when they are lent out at interest. So the board has instituted some penalties against low-balance accounts to protect the solvency of the institution. If it could find a way to exclude genuinely low-income persons from those penalties, imposing them only against the middle-class people who just happen to have low balances in the credit union, it would—but it cannot. Consequently, the SCCCU has found itself in the distressing position of imposing extra fees on people who can least afford to pay them.

The workplace at the credit union is under constant scrutiny. For its first six years, until 1983, the credit union was really a storefront operation, usually with a staff of just three or four people, operating more or less as a collective. Salaries were equal, and low, and job descriptions were elastic, to say the least. There was little distinction between the staff and the eleven board members in decision-making authority. Everyone came to the biweekly meetings and reached conclusions by consensus. There were lots of very hard issues and long struggles, and everyone participated in them equally.

As the credit union grew, however, the storefront collective could no longer cope with the volume of business. In 1983 a group of tellers was hired on an hourly wage basis, and the tasks of management were divided out. Since then, the organizational chart has become more complex and the salary structure more differentiated. There are twenty-five staff members now, divided into departments, including tellers, bookkeeping, computer services, lending, and marketing. There is a written personnel policy and specified channels of communication. Aside from the managers, most staff members no longer attend board meetings but send a representative instead.

As the staff structure has become more complex, the credit union has had to face the conflict between two different principles of economic democracy. It has always honored the idea of worker control; it has looked to the staff for guidance and policy. But legally, and in its heart as well, it is a member cooperative. The owners are the members whose savings make up the assets of the institution and who are invited to vote at annual meetings for the board of directors. The board takes the position, therefore, that it represents the membership and must maintain final authority for the principal decisions.

Fortunately, everyone involved understands the inherent ambiguity and is committed to finding solutions. Joint committees of the board and staff have tried to work out decision-making rules, specifying those issues that are solely the responsibility of the staff and those that must go to the board. The role of the credit union's president, Karen Zelin, is particularly ambiguous. She acts at times as an independent decision maker, at times as an advisor to the board, at times as the person deputized to carry out its decisions, and at times as the spokesperson of the staff. Meanwhile, she finds that she must spend an increasing amount of her time dealing with staff issues and the problems of the middle-level supervisors.

From a storefront collective, the credit union has evolved into a differentiated institution, with a variety of statuses, responsibilities, salaries, and levels of access to decision-making authority. Still, since its very purpose is the promotion of economic democracy in the community, it is committed to functioning so that all staff members who wish to can participate.

The people at the Santa Cruz Community Credit Union have never lacked for enthusiasm and commitment. No one can be sure how the place will evolve in the future, but no doubt the challenges and the conflicts will continue. There are many people in Santa Cruz who want to be proud of what their savings are accomplishing. The earthquake showed, once again, that the credit union is a community of people who can pull together.

Cooperation and Innovation in Credit Unions
Another Model

Ron Ehrenreich

Organizing a credit union is one more step in empowering ordinary working people and our communities, but it is not the same thing as making a social revolution. We are limited by regulation of the market and responsibility to our members. Except in very limited ways, a credit union or other democratic business cannot buck market forces and survive as a business. But with innovation, a network of cooperative relations, and basic organizing strategies we can do a great deal to serve the needs of our communities.

Rather than seeing political and business goals of community development credit unions in perpetual conflict, we have tried to understand some of the market forces that constrain us and to look at similar organizations and their experiences to reveal factors and approaches that foster achievement of both goals. Failure to understand market forces leads us to fail as businesses or to abandon or unnecessarily limit our social goals. And, by ourselves, we cannot solve the community-wide problems that a rapacious capitalism creates. Along with our work we will need other forms of struggle that go beyond the mere incremental displacement of capitalism.

Consumer Loans versus Development

Credit unions have traditionally focused on consumer loans for good reason. During the major growth wave of credit unions in the 1930s, 1940s, and 1950s, most ordinary working people were shut out of affordable credit. As the banks ignored their needs in favor of more profitable and secure business loans and investment, credit unions provided a source of consumer credit for radios, furniture, automobiles, major appliances, and emergencies.

Since this early period, there have been many changes. Banks have discovered the consumer market and have siphoned off the credit unions' best customers—secure and better-paid workers. This is at the heart of the problem. For credit unions to do well, they must have some people who have more money than they need at the time (savers) and some people who need more money than they have (borrowers). They must also balance low-risk and higher-risk loans.

The Santa Cruz Credit Union has chosen to expand member services to compete with the banks for savers and the most secure borrowers. They also make loans to higher-paid professionals (lawyers, accountants, therapists, and consultants) as part of their community development lending, which balances the riskier loans to new cooperative businesses. Savings accounts, loans, and services for better-off members should provide the funds, income, and risk balance to support loans and services to low-income members.

If a credit union cannot find the right balance in its own field of membership, there are other ways. Community development credit unions use nonmember savings to fund loans to members. Churches, socially responsible investment funds, and government supply such savings.

Credit unions can also consider alternative ways to do both development and new financial services. Instead of going the capital-intensive route of automatic-teller machines to meet members' needs for cash, credit unions can create cooperative, low-tech alternatives for member services. The Alternatives Federal Credit Union of Ithaca, New York, has a "cash-on-demand" program in which many local cooperatives and sympathetic small businesses provide cash to members. The Syracuse Cooperative Federal Credit Union used the lure of our rather substantial bank account to negotiate check-cashing services for members at the area's most socially responsible savings bank, thus adding their nineteen offices to our one. We also agreed to lend our local food co-op $1,000 at favorable rates to sustain check cashing for our members. For deposit convenience, we use a low-tech steel deposit box.

To deal with the problem of small and inactive accounts, credit unions can appeal to members who have low-balance accounts to use them or to close them. They can explain their needs regarding account-maintenance costs and the advantages of saving at the credit union. They can say that they do not want to squeeze out those who cannot afford to save; we tried this with some success. Beyond this appeal, credit unions can save money by not paying dividends on small accounts or even on the first $100 (or more) on all accounts, so that everyone contributes to costs. Small savers do not count on dividends for income, but fees are painful. To minimize the impact on low-income members, credit unions can also charge transaction fees for withdrawals but exempt withdrawals for paying rent, utilities, and other basics, or allow three or four free withdrawals per month. Credit unions can also cut costs on "lifeline" accounts by issuing statements quarterly instead of monthly.

Finally, instead of setting a fixed percentage for consumer loans versus community-development loans, credit unions can use the market to provide for both—setting high interest rates for consumer loans and lower rates for co-op development loans. Moreover, credit unions do not have to fund development with paid staffpeople on the Mondragon model. Instead, they can use volunteers, or contracted consultants from technical assistance groups like Commonworks, the ICA Group, or PACE of Philadelphia.

Some Challenges of Alternative Investment

Interview with Christine Rico

Changing Work: Tell us about your work coordinating the Clearinghouse on Alternative Investment of the Interfaith Center on Corporate Responsibility. How does the Clearinghouse function?

Christine Rico: In the simplest terms, the Clearinghouse is a coalition of religious institutional investors that helps its members find and make investments that promote development in low-income and minority communities. (Our principles are set forth in the accompanying "Vision Statement.") The Clearinghouse arose from a number of historical conditions. Back in the early 1970s, in response to James Forman's famous Manifesto demanding economic reparations for centuries of slavery and repression, churches began to set aside funds for minority groups to help start businesses and to support community organizations of many sorts. Frequently, however, loans were made directly to low-income applicants, without much if any supporting data, loan servicing, or technical support. As a result, a lot of church money was lost, investors became self-critical, wary, and eventually pulled back.

Then came the Reagan years, and with them increased pressure to fill the huge gaps in resources and funding created by the federal government's spending policies. To help meet this pressure, the Clearinghouse was set up during the early 1980s. Its aims are to promote church investment in community economic development and to demonstrate that such investments can be financially as well as socially responsible.

CW: Laudable goals, but how do you attempt to achieve them?

CR: In several ways. First, to encourage religious investment in low-income communities, we play a networking role. We bring the religious investment community together on a regular basis, send out education mailings, and run workshops and conferences. Second, we facilitate interaction, often on a face-to-face basis, between community groups seeking capital and members of the Clearinghouse who have funds to invest. Third, over the years we have assisted in the formation of several alternative investment funds such as Leviticus 25:23 and the Berakah Alternative Investment Fund. Another of our important roles is to help assemble working coalitions made up of different kinds of funding organizations. For example, our religious funders work with the National Association of Community Development Loan Funds, as well as with labor unions and the foundations that support community economic development. One of our members, the Texas Coalition for Responsible Investment, helped to start the Berakah Fund recently.

In all of these ways—networking and educating, facilitating interaction between religious investors and community borrowers, helping to form alternative investment loan funds, and working with coalitions of funders—the Clearinghouse has enabled investors to make more informed community investment decisions.

CW: But have you helped them avoid unsafe investments of the sort that initially made the investors back off from community economic development?

CR: Yes, I'm happy to be able to say that our members' investment portfolios have very low loss rates. This success can be attributed to two factors: the networking and educational functions of the Clearinghouse; and the growing sophistication of community-development groups overall. Many alternative investment funds now make loans through intermediaries, who provide loan monitoring and technical assistance services to borrowers. They are closer to borrowers and far more aware than national church investors can be of potential problems. These intermediaries are a new and valuable community investment resource.

In other words, with the aid of the Clearinghouse, religious groups need not use their alternative investment funds to make direct loans to low-income community groups. Instead, they can place them in the experienced and capable hands of organizations such as the ICA Group, the Institute for Community Economics, and the National Federation of Community Development Credit Unions. These intermediate, or "shelter," organizations manage and monitor the loans, helping when necessary to ensure that community- and worker-owned enterprises have the best chance to succeed and that the loans can be repaid. And it is working: using intermediaries and their experienced staffs to help build democratic businesses and keep them afloat has protected our investors.

CW: Can you give us some examples of this sort of success story?

CR: One that springs readily to my mind is Cooperative Home Care Associates, which was started by Community Service Society in New York City. Cooperative Home Care Associates received religious investments both directly and through the ICA Group; it now employs close to two hundred workers, of whom most are owners. In addition, several religious investment funds, including the Adrian Dominican Sisters, have recently made loans to Worker Owned Network in Athens, Ohio, to help acquire an incubator building for worker-owned enterprises. And the Center for Community Self-Help in Durham has funneled (and monitored) religious investments to North Carolina enterprises, in particular to the long-lived Workers Owned Sewing Company in Bertie, North Carolina.

CW: It certainly seems that the field of church-related alternative investment has made considerable progress. But what do you see as next steps for this field?

CR: The greatest need is still that of attracting equity for worker-owned and community based enterprises, while protecting at the same time both the investor's right to a safe investment and worker and community rights to control their own enterprises. A second challenge for the Clearinghouse is to encourage churches to use traditional investment dollars rather than segregated investment funds to make market-worthy investments in community economic development. The alternative funds are appropriate in cases involving higher risks or lower interest rates, but church groups should be willing to use traditional investment funds—for example, pension funds—where community development yields market returns and does not involve comparatively greater risks.

Third, we need to somehow link local and national church groups and coalitions much more extensively in community economic development. On the national level, we've had significant success: our members' alternative investment funds now total more than $30 million, up from $12 million only three years ago. And we know that congregations, particularly those in low-

Clearinghouse on Alternative Investments: Vision Statement

The Clearinghouse on Alternative Investments is an association of religious organizations who are interested in using their financial resources for the development of human society, especially distressed communities. Realizing that all our resources are gifts from God, our task is to use our resources for the good of many, especially the most vulnerable in society, in a just and equitable fashion.

We enter the Community Economic Development field motivated by values of justice, equality, service and human dignity.

As covenant people, we realize that the demands of that covenant require not only sharing resources with the more vulnerable in society, but even more, creating relationships between us—or systems—which are based on justice and safeguard the human dignity of each of us.

Therefore, we bond together as investors who share values and a vision. We bond together in order to strengthen that vision and promote those values. We bond together to continue to discern how we might better expand/clarify the vision of economic justice, support each other in using investments to enflesh these values, and challenge each other to continually do more. For we can never be content until the final days when all are living together in justice and peace.

income areas, are often involved in housing and unemployment issues. We need to get the body of the denominations, at national, regional, and local levels, to work together. If church efforts were coordinated and strategic, they would become increasingly effective. One model for this is the Catholic church's Campaign for Human Development, a national organization that uses the diocesan structure to support economic development. It has been successful, in part, because of having targeted coordinated support for worker-owned businesses and community organizing. It provides this support through loans, grants, and technical assistance not only from the national office but on the local level as well.

CW: All in all, you seem very enthusiastic—at times even ecstatic—about your work.

CR: Yes, I feel great about it, I'm enjoying what I do. One reason among many is that I've had the opportunity to learn on a nationwide basis, to develop and combine many sorts of strategies, and to work not only with different religious groups but with community loan funds, technical support organizations, credit unions—the entire spectrum of groups building a more just and democratic economy. In any case, for me this work in community economic development is home.

CW: How did you initially become involved in the field of socially responsible and alternative investment?

CR: When I went to college in Washington, D.C., I participated in both antiracist and Central American solidarity activities. I then worked a bit with Common Cause, but congressional lobbying didn't fit my interests: it ignored the community level where, for me at least, the most important changes take place. For a while I was at a loss to figure out just how such changes in everyday life could be promoted. I spent time in New York City learning word-processing and computer skills, and eventually became director of computer services for an investment bank that handled hospital and health care financing. This experience taught me a great deal: I discovered that the world of finance is not intimidating, and, in addition, that it could be put to service on behalf of local economic development. However, to do this, to make better use of my newfound financial capacities, I had to expand my community-development skills. The masters program at New Hampshire College in Community Economic Development had been highly recommended to me, so in June 1987 I left the investment firm and enrolled in that program. At the same time, I joined the organizing group of Community Capital Bank, which recently opened for business. That bank, modeled after South Shore Bank in Chicago, will make development loans throughout New York City.

Community Investment Comes of Age*

Gregg Ramm

The incorporation of the National Association of Community Development Loan Funds was a milestone in the evolution of community investment in the United States. It grew out of a 1985 conference organized by the Institute for Community Economics, which manages one of the largest funds in the country.

Community development loan funds (CDLFs) are nonprofit organizations that receive loans from individuals, religious organizations, and other investors. The CDLFs lend these funds to community organizations that develop housing, employment opportunities, and other resources and services for low-income, unemployed, and other economically disenfranchised people. They place a priority on projects that attack the roots of poverty and offer a unique opportunity for investors to address problems that conventional markets ignore.

The membership of the National Association of Community Development Loan Funds (NACDLF) included thirty-seven active loan funds and twenty-five associates by 1990. Some members of the NACDLF are national funds, but most are regional and local. Associate members include developing CDLFs, other community-investment institutions, and friends of the national association. The number of funds is growing rapidly.

As of 1990, the members of the NACDLF had a permanent capital of $7 million and were collectively managing a total of almost $60 million in loan capital. These funds have made more than two thousand loans representing thousands of units of housing and jobs saved or created. The development of the funds has been dramatic, with a recent growth rate among members at 40 percent per year.

The efforts of the association and its member funds are directed toward fulfilling a threefold mission:

---

* Updated version of article from *Building Economic Alternatives*, Spring 1987.

- To assist those who most need capital by providing it, together with credit and technical assistance, involving them in the process of capital allocation;
- To engage those who have capital by providing opportunities for socially responsible community investment and by stimulating a dialogue on the social and ethical responsibilities of wealth;
- By example, to encourage and challenge those who manage capital by providing information, overcoming prejudice, and broadening institutional commitments and credit standards to increase the flow of capital to projects that meet community needs.

The NACDLF and its members are committed to dispelling the myths of poverty that contribute to the credit starvation of low-income people. In many instances, the problems of the poor result not so much from a lack of resources or capabilities as from patterns of ownership—of land, housing, and employment and financial institutions—that drain resources out of lower-income communities. They are denied the credit needed to purchase homes, find security, build equity, and leave a legacy for their children.

The NACDLF and its members are committed to lending to projects and organizations operated by and for low-income communities—to projects that balance the interests of the individual resident with the interests of the whole community. Thus, CDLFs typically finance businesses owned by workers, consumers, or nonprofit organizations. They finance community land trusts, limited-equity housing cooperatives, and nonprofit corporations that provide affordable housing—often with home-ownership benefits—to those who need it most, while making sure that the housing remains affordable and does not return to the speculative market.

All CDLFs share several qualities that enable them to meet needs ignored by conventional financial institutions because of class and cultural barriers, high cost of operation, and the commitment of these institutions to profit maximization. The most important features shared by CDLFs are

- Close ties and firsthand experience with the communities, organizations, and projects in need of capital;
- A critical understanding of the various forms of community economic development;
- Low overhead, with a small staff and skilled volunteers, and a nonprofit structure;
- An ability to provide the necessary loan capital and technical assistance.

These features enable the loan funds to identify projects that address a community's problems and are financially viable. CDLFs can meet and match the needs of socially responsible investors and of those denied access to capital.

The members of the association have many stories to tell—stories of homes built and jobs saved with financing and technical assistance from CDLFs. The national directory of CDLFs lists investment offerings and the types of projects financed and describes a representative loan made by each fund. Among them are

- A $50,000 loan to Cooperative Home Care Associates, a home healthcare agency in the Bronx organized as a worker cooperative;
- A $43,000 loan to a newly formed cooperative of thirteen low-income families, who were about to be evicted from their mobile-home park in New Hampshire, to purchase the park;
- A $28,000 loan to Philadelphia Concerned About Housing (as an important part of a larger financing package) to develop shelter and transitional housing for homeless women and children;
- Three loans to the Cherry Hill Cooperative Cannery, a worker-owned cooperative in Barre, Vermont;
- A $25,000 loan to the Midwest Center for Labor Research of Chicago to help finance the Chicago Worker Ownership Project.

The association has initiated a comprehensive documentation of the lending activities of its members, analyzing both financial performance and social impact. But even a representative sampling of housing loans demonstrates the impact these funds can have. It justifies their claim of reaching those in our society who are most deprived and disenfranchised.

For example, we found that twenty-nine loans totaling $512,000 had leveraged at least five times that amount from other sources and had produced 250 units of housing. Of these households, 86 percent are very low income (with the remainder being moderate-income families in mixed-income buildings); 60 percent are Black or Hispanic; and 41 percent are single-parent, women-headed families.

The community-investment movement is still quite young—the oldest member fund began operation in 1969, and over half of the NACDLF's members began operations during the late 1980s—and its full potential is still far from realized. Nonetheless, the initial impact has been very significant. Community-development loan funds have already changed the minds of many early skeptics—those who said that while the social needs were indeed great, community investment was not financially responsible. The funds are setting an example of creative capital management and providing a vehicle through which growing numbers of investors can strike at the roots of poverty and express an affirmative vision of economic democracy.

Capital Strategies for Worker-Owners and Labor Unions*

Christopher Meek

Traditionally, employee buyouts have been confined to last-ditch efforts by workers' coalitions, aided by local government and local managers or by recruited outside entrepreneurs, to avert a plant or company closure. In the past, employees usually financed buyouts through a payroll deduction plan, an initial cash purchase of stock, or some combination of the two. These days, however, most employee buyouts are financed by ESOPs.

The central attractiveness of the ESOP is that it is a source of inexpensive capital. Under U.S. tax law, an ESOP can borrow funds from commercial lenders for a variety of purposes, ranging from purchasing of new equipment, to building new facilities, to buying all or part of a company. The entire loan repayments—both principal and interest—can be deducted from pretax profit. This is an enormous advantage over a traditional buyout, in which only the interest is deductible. ESOPs get special treatment because the repayment plan includes giving stock—a pension-like benefit—to employees.

ESOP Leveraged Buyouts

Most worker buyouts using ESOPs are leveraged—the buyers put down a small cash payment and promise to pay back the rest over time.

Some of the best-known ESOP leveraged buyout (LBO) cases have included Avis Corporation, the Dan River Textile Company, Raymond International, Phillips Petroleum, and Okonite Corporation. Some of the recent ESOP leveraged buyouts have involved billions of dollars and have been among the largest LBOs in U.S. business history. These deals sometimes have a profound impact on the national economy. For example, in October 1989 members of management and the

* Updated version of article from *Worker Co-Ops*, Spring 1989.

Airline Pilots Association made a multibillion-dollar bid for United Airlines; when major banks balked at financing the deal, United's stock dropped by half overnight, and the stock market lost 190 points. [*The employee bid to buy out United later fell through — Eds.*]

The Many Functions of Buyouts

Employees can become involved in a worker buyout in order to end control by an absentee owner. In the Avis case, management and workers bought all of the company's stock from absentee owner Wesray to get off what its chief executive officer, Joseph Vittoria, has called the "merry-go-round of owners." Avis had been controlled by ten different owners since its founding in 1946; and half of these ownership changes had taken place during the five years immediately before the employee buyout.[2]

There have probably been thousands of cases in which unionized employees have taken stock in exchange for such contract concessions as reduced wages, benefits, and protective work rules. Many of these cases have been in deregulated industries. In trucking, for example, the employees of nineteen major carriers organized by the Teamsters Union, including PIE and Transcom, accepted wage concessions in exchange for employee ownership in response to competition from new nonunion, low-price firms.

In recent years, a few unions (and in some cases joint union-management groups) have decided to control their economic destiny and arranged anticipatory buyouts of essentially healthy employers. The United Steel Workers of America and the United Auto Workers mounted one of the first such attempts. In the spring of 1986, they put together a $418 million bid, including 9 percent pay cuts, for Robertshaw Controls Company, a Richmond, Virginia, maker of thermostats. Robertshaw had shown a $25 million profit on sales of $541 million the year before. Unfortunately, a British company outbid the employees.

Problems of Power and Respect

All types of buyouts (except perhaps anticipatory buyouts, which are too new to evaluate) have suffered from common problems of power and participation, problems caused by the attempt to adopt employee ownership without making concomitant social and institutional changes. For example, when employees purchased shares through direct stock purchase instead of using an ESOP, they were almost without exception told by corporate lawyers and managers that they could not elect their own members to the board of directors. Even in cases where workers were not blocked from electing members to corporate boards, their board members were told by management, company attorneys, and outside directors not to discuss board actions and decisions with other employees because such discussions could lead to lawsuits. Although these efforts to obstruct worker participation in management were based upon false claims, they proved very effective for a while.

Similarly, early ESOP buyout deals were structured so as to ensure that management alone would appoint the trustees of the ESOP trusts that held employees' stock and that these trustees in turn would vote the stock to elect directors approved by management—a closed circle of influence completely circumventing all worker-owners. Furthermore, in buyouts involving substantial leveraged financing, employees have typically been denied voting rights until the completion of vesting periods of from five to fifteen years. In the case of some ESOP leveraged buyouts, workers have been denied voting rights altogether except on such extreme matters as a company merger or liquidation. This has been possible because only firms that trade their stock on the public market are required by law to give employee-owners full voting rights in an ESOP.

Two Purchase Prices

Voting rights are not the only way in which employees have been cheated; employees have also been flagrantly manipulated in terms of the value of their equity. Management and its self-appointed board members have given top management stock options or stock at prices well below those paid by employees, either as an incentive to work for the company or as a reward.

The most disturbing twist on this theme involved the collusion of corporate investment bankers and attorneys in some of the first major ESOP leveraged buyouts. In the case of the Dan River LBO, employees purchased 70 percent of the firm's class-A shares for $110 million ($22.50 per share) through an ESOP. The remaining 30 percent of the company's stock, called class-B shares, was sold to twenty-two managers for $2.06 a share. Furthermore, a formula was set up such that a 16 percent rise in the employees' stock prices would result in a 100 percent increase in the value of management's shares. Similar dynamics also operated when ESOP leveraged buyouts were mounted at Raymond International, Blue Bell, and Okonite Corporation—the infamous "B" shares sold to managers in these cases became known to angry workers as "Killer Bs."

The Unions: Ambivalence and Counterproductive Intervention

Surprisingly, local and especially international union officials have seldom played a positive proactive role in defending the interests of workers in employee buyouts. In fact, the response of union officials above the local level has ranged from hands off to antagonism. At South Bend Lathe, one of the first and most controversial buyouts, the United Steel Workers of America chose to have no involvement whatsoever in the effort. In the trucking buyout cases, the Teamsters, who did not support employee ownership as a quid pro quo for wage cuts, actually took a position that cost their members more money to save their jobs. Because they would not agree to wage reductions on paper, reductions that would have been diverted before taxes to purchase stock became impossible and Teamster members had to buy stock with after-tax wages.

In one of the first worker buyouts through direct stock purchase, the Herkimer Library Bureau, union officers openly opposed worker representation on the board of directors or even shopfloor participation to increase competitiveness. The union president explained, in a March 1979 interview, "We don't want any of that socialist crap. The last thing we need is to start having the monkeys telling the zoo keeper what to do."

Strikes, Slowdowns, and Stonewalling

The disempowerment and financial manipulation of workers in employee buyouts has led to anger, disillusionment, and even rebellion. Worker-owners have gone on strike and staged slowdowns at a number of companies, including South Bend Lathe, Okonite Corporation, Rath Packing Company, Jeanette Sheet Glass, and Hyatt Clark Industries. Antagonistic relations have not helped the economic success of these worker-owned companies, and have sometimes even led to failure and bankruptcy, such as at Rath, Hyatt Clark, and Eastern Air Lines.

Even where workers have had considerably more power through board representation and shopfloor involvement, management has in many instances passively resisted worker ideas and influence. At Eastern Air Lines, management simply stopped participating in labor-management problem solving groups, eventually even setting up competing "management only" committees to solve problems before joint or special committees could do the job. At Rath, management attempted to squelch the successful implementation of self-managing work teams by instructing the company's maintenance and stores supervisors to give the first autonomous team's requests for repairs or supplies the lowest possible priority. As one maintenance supervisor explained in an interview in February 1984, "They told me not to help them unless they gave the okay or it was absolutely necessary. I was told to always put it off to last."

Such conflicts ensued at the board of directors level, too. At Hyatt Clark, for example, the chief executive officer refused to share information on the compensation paid to management with worker-members of the board. Eventually, these worker board members, two of whom were also union officers, had to take their company to court to get the information.

Too Successful?

As employee buyouts have become more frequent, leaders from organized labor, management, banking, Congress, and academia have seriously questioned whether such ventures could ultimately succeed in the marketplace. The traditional worker buyout to prevent an operation from closing was heavily criticized from the political Right and Left as "lemon socialism." And indeed there were many instances in which workers, in a desperate effort to save their jobs, invested in plants, stores, and companies that had little prospect of surviving. However, many buyouts undertaken under more favorable circumstances have proven to be highly successful. Unfortunately, with economic success have also come a number of pressures which push such worker-owned firms to go public, depleting the strength of the employee equity base, or else to completely sell out to traditional capitalist business as usual.

The most obvious pressure can come from within: as the value of employee stocks rise, employees may want a more direct and immediate benefit. On a more structural level, successful employee-owned firms are often driven to the stock market by their very profitability. When success results in growth of a firm's market share, it creates pressure to expand operations with new plants, equipment, and offices. Often, the only source of capital for such expansion is the stock market. And, of course, speculation in the public markets can also result in a phenomenal increase in the value of employee stock, which tends to heighten workers' interest in selling their stock. Finally, buyout firms often have many senior workers, and as large numbers of them reach retirement age the firms are required to buy up their stock. Going to the public market often seems to be the only choice available, especially when the number of retirees is large and internally generated funds are limited.

A typical example is provided by Oregon Steel Mills, which was bought by workers in 1984 through a 100 percent leveraged ESOP and then went public in the spring of 1988 to raise enough funds to cover growth. By all other measures (such as worker participation and labor-management cooperation) Oregon Steel Mills was a success story.

In 1984 the company was purchased by employees for $22.8 million. At the time, the mill was in great economic difficulty because of heavy competition from Pacific Rim imports. Immediately after the buyout, everyone worked to make the company productive and profitable. Management invested funds in modernizing the firm's mini-mills. Employees and management worked hard to eliminate the "us-and-them" legacy of former severe labor-management strife. Profit sharing was instituted and management perks discarded. Productivity soared: steel that had taken 9.3 person-hours to make in 1983 required only 3.4 hours in 1988.

Consequently, Oregon Steel's market share grew rapidly, and they expanded to maintain it. To fund the expansion they created 2.1 million new shares and also sold 1.2 million worker-owned shares. The employees made incredible profits on their stock, the value of which increased by more than 600 percent to as much as $400,000. Given this windfall, many employees sold some stock for personal expenses or took early retirement, with little thought of the impact on their participation in and control of the firm.[3] It is, of course, preferable for employees to share in the gains made through an employee buyout rather than being cheated. But self-interest tends to make employee ownership a short-range phenomenon. Without a deeper commitment to democratic control, employee ownership will produce a more equitable distribution of quick gains but will contribute little to creating a more productive and socially responsible corporate world.

The AFL-CIO Buyout Fund: A New Era?

On 19 February 1990 the AFL-CIO announced the creation of a new leveraged buyout fund called the Employee Partnership Fund (EPF). Its purpose is to provide a positive counterresponse to the binge of mergers and acquisitions that have so devastated U.S. workers and their unions. It has the potential to support long-term employee ownership and to help workers avoid some of its abuses.

Far too often employee buyouts have failed (especially in competition with outside takeover attempts) because they have been unable to raise quickly the equity capital necessary to create an ESOP large enough to buy all of an employer's stock. In theory, the EPF should eliminate this problem in many small- and medium-sized employee buyout attempts. The fund's goal is to secure investment capital of approximately $500 to $750 million, including $200 million from pension funds.

Just as important as helping to finance employee buyouts is the EPF's role in protecting worker interests. It should be a very friendly and supportive partner that will require a fair but not exorbitant return, and the EPF will not, like many investment funds, seek to get its money out quickly. Instead, it will take a long-term interest in the firms. Its criteria for success will be company strength and employment stability.

The EPF will also seek to help ensure that workers are not cheated by greedy or power-hungry managers. "Killer B" stocks and nonvoting shares will not be tolerated. As Richard Prostin, director of bargaining for the AFL-CIO's Industrial Unions Division, explained in a February 1990 interview:

> In some respects it will be like any LBO fund. It will have to operate that way in order to raise the necessary capital. But it will also protect certain goals which are very important to us and the workers that will be involved. We want to make sure that if workers get involved in a buyout that they get a substantial chunk of ownership. We also want to make sure that they have a very real and substantial participation in company decision-making.

To make sure that the EPF plays this kind of role, Prostin said it will be monitored by an advisory board comprised of top union officials from the major U.S. international unions, as well as a group of Wall Street professionals.

The fund will be managed by two experienced investment bankers, Eugene J. Keilin and Ron A. Bloom. Both made their reputations by playing key roles in earlier worker buyout attempts.

Conclusion

Worker buyouts are not the largest segment of the employee-ownership movement in the United States, but they are very important because they often attract a great deal of media attention and present a powerful, if not accurate, image of the viability of worker ownership as an alternative to traditional capitalist forms of business. Today, many positive developments are occurring in the worker-buyout movement, such as the emergence of anticipatory buyouts of healthy firms and the decision by the AFL-CIO to create a worker-buyout fund.

At companies like Weirton Steel, Avis, Wheeling-Pittsburgh Steel, Kaiser Aluminum and Chemical Company, and many others that have been involved in more recent buyouts, considerable effort has been expended to integrate the interests of workers, management, and lenders. Worker representation on boards of directors is gradually becoming standard operating procedure for worker buyouts, as are labor-management committees and shopfloor problem-solving teams.

The movement still has a long way to go. Successful buyouts have other companies that want to buy them. Workers are now faced with the choice of making a sizable profit on their investment or remaining worker-owners.

It is nice to see the average person share in the profit from mergers and acquisitions, which have generally created financial havoc for U.S. workers. But it is also unfortunate if, rather than democratizing capitalism and revitalizing U.S. industry, worker buyouts simply become a short-term "quick fix" in which labor is duped into participating in the cannibalization of industry. Even at much-acclaimed Weirton Steel, where labor management cooperation and worker participation have been abundant, the company and its employees sold 23 percent of the stock on the public market in order to raise much-needed cash. Let us hope that this latest trend is only a temporary phenomenon, that unions and their members will invest more time and thought in the potential of worker ownership for revitalizing the labor movement, and that they will ultimately choose to build upon a foundation of self-governance, cooperation, and long-term reward.

Notes

1. In leveraged buyouts, the buyers arrange for a loan to buy all of the stock of a company, using that same company as collateral. This usually creates a huge debt burden for the company.

2. "Joining the Game: Some Workers Set-up LBO's of Their Own and Benefit Greatly," *Wall Street Journal*, 12 December 1990, pp. 1 and 4.

3. *Ibid.*

Union Pension Fund Supports Worker Ownership*

Andrew R. Banks

"If Steven Spielberg were to make a movie on how the building trades are using their pension funds to create work for their members, the film would be called 'Capital Wars' and Dennis Walton would play the part of Han Solo," says Randy Barber, union advisor and director of the Washington-based Center on Economic Organizing.

It has been more than ten years since Barber coauthored, with Jeremy Rifkin, the eye-opening exposé *The North Will Rise Again: Pensions, Politics, and Power in the 1980s*, which became a best-seller in the labor movement. Since then, trade unionists have become increasingly aware that if they sit by and let others manage the $1.3 trillion of union-negotiated pension funds, unions will in effect be financing their own destruction. Dennis Walton has become one of the most visible proponents in the labor movement of using this pension money to further the union cause.

In 1976, he had just been elected business manager of Operating Engineers Local 675 in Fort Lauderdale, Florida. Like most building trades business managers, Walton knew very little about pension funds, even though his position automatically placed him on Local 675's pension board of trustees. Like most union pension trustees then, Local 675 trustees had completely entrusted the management of the fund to a fund manager, who in turn handed over the actual investment decisions involving its $11 million assets to a large mutual insurance company.

Then, in 1978, something happened to completely change the way Walton viewed both his duties as a pension trustee and as a labor leader. "I'll never forget that day as long as I live," he recalls:

* From *Labor Research Review*, 12.

All the trades were picketing this huge nonunion construction site when an electrician came up to me and pointed to a sign on the barbed-wire fence. In big block letters for the world to see, the sign said that this nonunion project was being financed by the same company that managed my local's pension fund. I couldn't believe my eyes. Union members were walking a picket line while scabs drew paychecks. And my union and other building-trades unions were financing the whole deal by signing over control of our pension funds to these fund managers.

Becoming "Prudent"

Local 675's pension-fund managers initially told Walton that the practice of investing in nonunion projects was "prudent" and that he must remove his union hat while he was wearing his pension-trustee hat.

Not satisfied with the answer, he started to investigate. He discovered that the law governing pensions, the Employee Retirement Income Security Act (ERISA), mandated that, indeed, investments had to be "prudent." With this in mind, Walton and the other union trustees looked into the past performance of the investment company that managed Local 675's pension fund.

"Their so-called prudent investments had earned us a shameful average of 1.8 percent per year," claims Walton. "When we looked at what other funds were doing, we found the national average wasn't much better—3.2 percent. A bunch of financial wizards in pinstripe suits were milking us dry while telling us we weren't smart enough to manage our own money."

The more the trustees dug, the angrier they became. They discovered that the building trades in south Florida had pension funds totaling more than $500 million and that union pension funds nationwide accounted for more in assets than the gross national products of Great Britain and France combined. And they learned that U.S. workers' pensions provided half of all new investment dollars in this country.

Walton and the others were outraged when they found that their own money was financing the destruction of the labor movement. Union pensions owned much of the stock of such union-busting companies as the infamous textile manufacturer J.P. Stevens and the world's largest nonunion builder, Brown & Root. And as unbelievable as it sounds, they uncovered the outrage that union members' pension money helped finance the building of the National Right-To-Work Committee headquarters in Virginia. It was built nonunion, of course.

Walton took his discoveries to the members of Local 675, who endorsed the effort of the pension trustees to take back control of their fund. Walton then approached the management trustees of the pension fund. He offered proposals on how the fund could act as both developer and banker and could invest in major construction projects that would be built entirely with union labor. The management trustees (whose companies were being hurt by pension funds financing their nonunion competition) originally balked at the idea. Eventually, the persistent and forceful Walton had his way, and the pension fund trustees took their destiny into their own hands by firing the fund managers.

After hiring an economist and a staff attorney who specialized in ERISA, the Local 675 pension-fund trustees started to manage their own money. First, the pension fund set up a mortgage program so that members who could not afford the inflated rates of 15 or 16 percent could get a more realistic 10.5 percent mortgage. Next, the union started to look at investing the fund's assets in major construction projects that would be built entirely with union labor.

After carefully studying growth patterns and government plans for road extensions, the pension fund purchased 100 acres of rock quarry and swampland in northern Broward County for $2.4 million. Roads and sewage and water lines were put in, using union labor and regular Local 675 contractors.

Once the initial paving and utilities were completed, the tract was sold for $14 million to the nation's largest private commercial developer, Trammel Crow Development Company. In three years the fund had invested less than $3 million dollars, put hundreds of union members to work for tens of thousands of hours, and then sold the property for a profit of $11 million. (Before Walton would sell the property, Trammel Crow had to sign an agreement guaranteeing that all construction work on it would be union.)

Today, Park Central—an upscale office park with thirty buildings and 1.3 million square feet of office space—stands on the tract. Trammel Crow spent more than $150 million on its construction. Also located at Park Central is the union's office, where the pension fund is administered. At the other end of the property, the pension fund held onto some land to develop into an auto repair service for the occupants of the Park Central offices and a landscape service that is considered one of the best in the industry. Both companies were financed by the pension fund, are wholly union operated, and will eventually be owned by the employees.

Other Capital Strategies

Park Central is not the only property the pension fund has developed. It has leveraged more than $400 million of construction work for local building trades union members. (In 1979, the Operating Engineers Local 675 pension fund had $16 million in assets. Today, it is worth more than $60 million.)

Walton's union has demonstrated how to take back and use the power of members' pension capital to enhance their bargaining strength. He has used other capital strategies as well.

Local 675, like most building trades locals in the United States, established a labor-management committee (LMC) with contractors who signed the Local 675 bargaining agreement. The leaders of the local were determined to make LMC stand for more than "Let's Make Concessions." Walton and the others in Local 675 have used the LMC to enhance the union's bargaining position and to further the philosophy of taking wages out of competition.

The nonunion invasion of south Florida has been devastating to the trades. At one time the area boasted a 90 percent union construction rate; now, it has fallen to about 10 percent. Unemployment among union members has likewise been terrible.

To help alleviate this situation, Walton convinced the LMC to explore setting up worker-owned companies. He had three objectives.

First, Walton wanted to find work for his members. Second, he wanted to prove that a unionized company could be made more efficient and competitive if the labor-management committee were allowed to assist in the firm's management and if union members were given a voice in important decisions. Finally, worker ownership (with the assistance of the LMC) could buy out existing unionized owners who wanted to retire and sell their companies. In Florida's heavy-equipment industry, many unionized companies become nonunion when they are sold by retiring owners.

The Local 675 LMC created the Worker Ownership Project to assist unemployed members in setting up their own crane companies and to help members at unionized companies buy out owners who were ready to retire. Union members, who now own and operate United Crane, brag about being the most efficient and profitable crane company in south Florida, while paying union wages and benefits to themselves.

An important part of the LMC's worker-ownership activities is to directly involve workers. Democratically operated committees of workers are formed and trained to deal with such issues as financing, communications, and developing the by-laws and structure of the worker-owned enterprise. The LMC provides professional expertise through a full-time staff person selected by the union.

Capital Wars in the United States

At first, other unions hesitated to follow Walton's lead. Their attorneys and fund managers said it would spell real trouble and that they were better off assigning their fiduciary responsibilities to the professionals.

To make matters worse, the U.S. Labor Department, which interprets and administers the nation's pension laws, sued the Local 675 pension fund over the Park Central deal and the low-cost mortgage program. Although this temporarily scared other unions away from taking control of their pension funds, the Labor Department's plan backfired when the federal courts ruled in Walton's favor and ordered the government to pay all legal fees. The appellate courts have upheld the lower court's ruling, thus making *Ray Donovan vs. Dennis Walton* a great precedent for other unions.

Since the favorable court decisions, the pension-fund investment strategy has blossomed and spread throughout the United States. In Florida, the state Building Trades Council, under the leadership of Joe Martin from the Ironworkers and George Hudspeth of the Electrical Workers, has formed the Florida Affirmative Investment Roundtable (FAIR). Representatives of member unions literally sit at a table and are offered investment opportunities in major all-union construction projects.

Nationally, the AFL-CIO has supported developing pension-fund strategies for some time. Since 1964, its housing investment trust has invested more than $650 million in union-built single-family and multi-family housing, retirement centers, and nursing homes. In 1987, the AFL-CIO initiated a building investment trust to become a player in major commercial and industrial real-estate development.

As the Reagan-created low income housing crisis has been driving poor families into the streets, some local building trades unions have begun to join with community groups and local governments to finance affordable housing.

The New York State AFL-CIO, for example, has joined with a coalition of churches and synagogues to rehabilitate abandoned buildings in Brooklyn. Six union pension funds have invested $10 million thus far in this "New Communities" project. In Boston, the Bricklayers and Laborers have formed the B&L Non-Profit Housing Co., through which pension money is invested in government-insured certificates of deposit in a local bank. The bank, in turn, invests this money in wholly union-built housing for low- and moderate-income families. The homes can be sold at 40 percent below market value because of the unique financing and because Mayor Ray Flynn helped secure favorable prices for the land.

Building trades unions are also beginning to use their financial leverage to affect the banks and even to create new ones. In Massachusetts, the carpenters recently opened the First Trade Union Savings Bank, which attracted nearly $100 million in deposits in its first six months. Mortgage rates are slightly below those of most area lenders, and union members (who make up 60 percent of the depositors) pay half the going rate for attorney's fees at real-estate closings. The bank plans to open a trust department to manage pension funds for area unions, and it has already made many construction loans.

The list of unions becoming involved with such strategies is becoming larger every day, but people like Dennis Walton know the labor movement has barely seen the tip of the iceberg. A recent study, for example, disclosed that U.S. workers' pension funds (two-thirds of which are union-negotiated) now own half of all outstanding corporate stock in the United States.

Following the lead of Dennis Walton, the building trades have begun to demonstrate to the rest of the labor movement that by taking control of these funds (and using other capital strategies as well) maybe—just maybe—we can become the victors instead of the victims of "Capital Wars."

Short Takes

Mondragon's Working People's Bank:
A Model Development Bank

The world leader in community development banking is probably the Working People's Bank, or **Caja Laboral Popular (CLP)**, a bank launched in 1960 by the dynamic group of worker cooperatives that has grown in the Basque country of Spain in and around the town of Mondragon. Steadily enlarged by savings of the thrifty Basques and profits from loans to successful member co-ops, the CLP is a major bank with 120 branches, more than a thousand employees, and more than half a million individual member-depositors. It lends a portion of its funds to member cooperatives and also handles the Mondragon network's pension plan.

As part of its services, the bank developed an entrepreneurial division (now spun off as a separate enterprise) as a research, development, and nurturing organization. The entrepreneurial division handles every aspect of the development of new cooperative ventures, from market research to plant setup and auditing services. The CLP provides a bank "godfather" who works closely with the manager of a prospective worker co-op to help launch it. Up to two years is devoted to feasibility studies, product testing, and the like. The bank's technical experts work closely with the new cooperative for the first few years, assuring the new company of a successful start.

New Development Banks

No exact parallel to the Working People's Bank exists in the United States, though Chicago's **South Shore Bank** has some similarities. The South Shore Bank model is being copied in a number of places. In Arkansas, the **Southern Development Bancorporation** was launched in 1988 through the combined efforts of Governor Bill Clinton, the Winthrop Rockefeller Foundation, and the South Shore Bank. The bank tries to further homegrown businesses and develop local entrepreneurial skills in Arkansas. It operates a real-estate development company and a network of financial affiliates, including the **Good Faith Fund**. The latter is modeled on the successful group borrowing system developed by the **Grameen Bank** in Bangladesh. Under this system, loan applicants organize into groups of five persons who attend a two-week orientation and discuss their business plans with each other in regular meetings. The group chooses who gets the first loans and monitors loan repayments. As the first loans are repaid over several months, other members qualify for loans. Today, the limit for these loans is $5,000.

Meanwhile, in Brooklyn the **Community Capital Bank** opened for business at the end of 1990 after selling its $6 million stock offering to the public. Founding shareholders include the Brooklyn Union Gas Co., the Metropolitan Life Insurance Foundation, Morgan Guarantee Trust, and the Sisters of St. Joseph of Peace. Community Capital is a full-service commercial bank, committed to lending for affordable housing and small-business development. It works closely with local community organizations to fulfill local neighborhood needs.

Another new bank is the **Development Bank of Washington**, a community-oriented firm that emphasizes serving the needs of small businesses and minority individuals in Washington, D.C., neighborhoods. The bank will open after raising $4 million by selling shares of stock.

Borrowing-Circle Model Spreads to Women's Groups

The Grameen borrowing-circle model for financing small businesses has spread to women's groups in Chicago and Los Angeles. The **Chicago Women's Self Employment Project** had helped eighty-five women start or expand their businesses by the end of 1989. The **Los Angeles Coalition for Women's Economic Development** has begun to implement a similar program.

The Los Angeles Coalition encourages low-income women to achieve self-sufficiency by providing business training and by helping them start microenterprises. These require little capital, are frequently located in the home, and draw upon members' already existing skills and talents. For example, one group of three women has begun their own catering service. Another woman walks children of working parents from school to various after-school programs. The coalition receives money for its revolving-loan fund from foundations, individuals, and banks.

There are a number of other national and local agencies that provide financial help to worker co-ops and worker-owned firms and promote community economic development. Here we have space to mention only a few, ranging from the National Co-Op Bank and the National Federation of Community Credit Unions to lan funds, relgious groups, and those giving special help to unions and to women.

National Cooperative Bank Development Corporation (NCBDC)

The NCBDC provides financial services to employee-owned companies, housing co-ops, and community development corporations. It collaborates with developers, intermediary organizations, and others to finance existing cooperative businesses and to develop new co-ops. The NCBDC has worked with some fifty intermediary organizations—typically regional or industry-specific loan funds—that in turn re-lend monies to worker co-ops, housing co-ops, and other worthwhile cooperative ventures.

During the first five years of its existence, the NCBDC extended some $30 million in loans to more than two hundred customers, including thirteen ESOP companies and worker cooperatives.

The National Federation of Community Development Credit Unions

Established in 1974 to serve and represent financial cooperatives in low-income communities, the federation has a membership of nearly a hundred community development credit unions (CDCUs) in thirty-five states; assets range in size from $20,000 to $20 million. The federation is the national advocate for the CDCU movement on regulatory and policy issues. Apart from public-sector advocacy, the federation has raised more than $4 million in low-cost deposits for CDCUs from the private sector, particularly foundations, churches, and banks.

Unlike other credit unions, CDCUs have an explicit mission of community reinvestment, recycling their members' insured savings for loans that promote neighborhood revitalization. They help finance housing rehabilitation and acquisition, small and minority businesses, and cooperatives, along with their traditional lending for family needs. Community development credit unions help stem the cycle of disinvestment that accelerates neighborhood decline. Their market has also been expanded by the shift of banks out of low-income areas. Because of their low-overhead, nonprofit nature, CDCUs have emerged as candidates to succeed banks in many neighborhoods where the latter have closed unprofitable branches.

Institute for Community Economics (ICE)

The ICE provides technical and financial assistance to community-based groups working to produce and preserve affordable housing, jobs, and social services. Since its inception in 1966 the institute has popularized the idea of the community land trust as an answer to the growing lack of affordable housing. It works with local coalitions—religious groups, nonprofit developers, local public officials and concerned citizens—to organize land trusts.

These trusts offer an alternative to conventional public and private land ownership, blending private incentive with long-term stewardship of community resources. With ICE's help, some twenty land trusts were incorporated between 1967 and 1985. Since then, growth has been dramatic. From 1986 to 1988, thirty-two land trusts sprang up; in 1989, twenty-two new groups incorporated; at least fourteen more are in development. The institute now coordinates a national network of more than ninety community land trusts in twenty-three states. While most land trusts focus on affordable housing, some also preserve farmland and commercial space to create affordable agricultural and business opportunities.

To strengthen the community-based groups it serves, ICE established a revolving loan fund in 1979, financed by private contributors and religious organizations. It was intended to provide financing for land trusts, community-service organizations, and worker-owned businesses. By 1990, the fund had more than $10 million in capital and had made loans for more than $16 million in twenty-six states. ICE also helped establish the **National Association of Community Development Loan Funds (NACDLF)**.

Community Development Loan Funds

Two of the dozens of members and associates of the NACDLF are the **Leviticus 25:23 Alternatives Fund** and the **Cooperative Fund of New England**.

The Leviticus 25:23 Alternatives Fund is a consortium of church-related organizations that provides low-interest loans to projects that benefit the economically disadvantaged, primarily in New York, New Jersey, and Connecticut. Its first two loans were to a tenant-owned housing cooperative and a job and residence program for adult retarded persons.

The Cooperative Fund of New England supports the development of consumer, housing, marketing, and worker cooperatives in its region. Many of its loans have been extended to worker- and consumer-owned food cooperatives. It gives priority to projects that help low-income persons and provides financial services and related technical assistance.

Campaign for Human Development (CHD)

The CHD is the U.S. Catholic Bishops' education and action program to combat domestic poverty. It is the largest national funding program for self-help projects among low-income groups aimed at social change. The Campaign for Human Development is also one of the nation's largest funding programs for low-income, worker-owned, worker-managed businesses. Its annual budget of almost $10 million is raised primarily through donations from Catholic parishioners.

Working Equity, Inc.

This firm gives financial advice to unions and their members in corporate transactions, especially those involving worker buyouts.

Between 1980 and 1990 there were twenty-four union-led buyouts where the employees ended up owning more than 51 percent of the stock of their employers. The principal officers of Working Equity, Inc. (Paul D. Rusen, Craig H. Livingston, and Michael Locker) played a role in thirteen of those transactions. They cooperated with the local and international leadership of major unions, as well as the salaried work force, to turn many of these troubled companies around.

Women's World Banking

An international organization created in 1979, with local chapters in thirty-three countries, Women's World Banking is a technical assistance and support group that helps women own and operate small businesses by enabling them to qualify for loans. One of its major functions is to act as a loan guarantor; it has capital of more than $6 million for this purpose. In conjunction with local member groups, it provides business advice to women, screens loans, and guarantees 75 percent of each loan. Women's World Banking places loans with local cooperating banks, provides continuing technical assistance to recipients, and monitors their business progress and loan repayments.

Social Investment

To conclude our discussion of financing for worker co-ops and democratic employee-owned firms, we will briefly mention the principle of social investment. Ordinarily, investment is based on maximizing profits. Social investment uses ethical, ecological, and social justice criteria to screen investments in capitalist firms. Social investors seek some profit, but they also want to use their money to support businesses that meet their social criteria. Some social investors primarily want to avoid investing in companies that pollute, use unfair labor practices, discriminate against minorities, make weapons, or do business with oppressive regimes. Others try to actively promote socially responsible purposes by investing in firms whose products, services, and practices contribute to a just, healthy, and peaceful society.

Using such criteria has led an increasing number of individuals, corporations, and pension funds to support moderate- and low-income housing, worker cooperatives, and other businesses that create fulfilling jobs and help revitalize run-down communities. They have done this through direct investment, through investment funds, or through such institutions as community development credit unions, development banks, and revolving loan funds.

The **Social Investment Forum** is devoted to promoting and developing social investment. A national association of financial professionals, research and community organizations, publishers, and individual investors, it distributes a directory listing of professional members and the services they offer to the public.

Targeted Investment

Investors with a social conscience can now purchase **Community Jobs CDs**, federally insured certificates offered by the Boston-area ICA group in conjunction with the South Shore Bank. These funds will be targeted to provide equity financing for innovative, high-risk ventures that promise to create jobs for economically vulnerable groups.

Such targeted investments are also available in Europe. The **Ecobank** of Frankfurt was founded in 1988 to provide a vehicle through which investors could buy into one of several funds that lend money to specific causes. Depositors agree to lend the money at no interest in order to cover administrative costs. The Ecobank offers savings bonds for self-management, which help finance self-managed firms with at least three employees. Education bonds finance the purchase of sites for alternative schools. Women's bonds are devoted to projects that employ only women. The bonds for the mentally ill finance alternatives to institutional treatments. Some of the money is used to buy or renovate apartments for mentally ill persons and some to set up businesses that employ them and allow them to participate in managing the enterprises. Ecology bonds facilitate the development, production, and marketing of ecologically beneficial products, techniques, and services.

5

Educational Empowerment
New Forms of Work—New Forms of Learning

Education is a key to the success of worker-owned enterprises. Most schools and colleges in the United States still promote corporate and hierarchical models of work organization; if the new grassroots movement for worker ownership and control is to thrive, it will need to be supported by a growing infrastructure of educational programs. Worker-owners need to learn business skills and principles of democratic management, as well as cooperative values and attitudes. The educational process can take place at the workplace (see Karen Young's discussion of training for employee-participation groups at **Weirton Steel**) or at conference centers or college campuses removed from the day-to-day pressures of the job.

Also in this chapter, Frank Adams and Gary Hansen discuss education for ownership and participation at **Seymour Specialty Wire Company** in Connecticut and the educational program of the **Worker Owned Network**. The latter is but one example of the educational efforts of technical assistance organizations. The ICA Group, PACE, and many other groups have provided education and training for thousands of worker-owners during the last decade.

We also describe several successful college- and university-based efforts. Chuck Turner and Chris Clamp describe a **New Hampshire College** program that offers training for community development projects as part of its curriculum. Charlene Winters discusses an exciting project for students at **Brigham Young University** that involves them in running a student-owned cooperative business.

In the Short Takes, we include brief descriptions of a **Utah State** program that operates as part of that university's extension service and the doctoral program in social economy based in the **Sociology department** at **Boston College**. In addition, we look at two promising efforts to encourage students to start their own businesses—**Junior Achievement** in Saskatchewan and the **Rural Entrepreneurship Through Action Learning (REAL)** program in the U.S. South. We also briefly mention the educational programs of the **Development Training Institute**, the **Massachusetts Institute of Technology,** and the **Highlander Center in Tennessee.**

So far, there are only a handful of higher-education centers that focus on worker ownership. In addition to those described below, we may mention the **Program for Employment and Workplace Systems** and the **Program for Participation and Labor Managed Studies** at **Cornell University**, the interdisciplinary concentration in democratic management for undergraduate business students at **Guilford College**, North Carolina, and the **Northeast Ohio Employee Ownership Center**, based at the Department of Political Science, **Kent State University**. Still missing today is any educational institution with a primary focus on training for workers and managers in employee-owned enterprises, like the New School for Democratic Management, which had a brief lifespan in the late 1970s in San Francisco.

Education for Ownership and Participation*

Frank T. Adams and Gary B. Hansen

Most, if not all, workers arrive at the democratically managed worksite poorly prepared to participate in enterprise governance or to involve themselves usefully in decision making about the job. Some will never want to learn the skills it takes, but, for those who do, members, managers, and boards must be prepared to address the vexingly original issues that result when the necessities of production are mixed with the politics of democracy.

A starting point for any worker-owned cooperative is the set of assumptions taken for granted when work is organized to suit capital. Workers work for managers, and managers work for the company. Managers alone know what is best for the company. Managers give orders, workers take them. Managers and workers share few corporate goals and are separate, adversarial special-interest groups.

Where labor controls capital, and cooperation is the organizing medium for work, the assumptions differ greatly. Both workers and managers own the company. Both workers and managers have information that must be shared for optimal corporate health. Because workers and managers have information that must be shared, both must accept the responsibility for a dialogue between equals. Because they are owners, each with an equal stake and voice, workers and managers share goals that are not mutually exclusive.

Therefore, the first barrier that must fall in the ideally organized worker-owned firm is an educational one. Who gets to learn what must be redefined so that the many cognitive and vocational skills required to make a business prosper are restored to labor, ending the separation between making decisions and executing

* From Frank T. Adams and Gary B. Hansen, 1987. *Putting Democracy to Work: A Practical Guide for Starting Worker-Owned Businesses* (Eugene, OR: Hulogosi Communications).

them. In an unpublished paper from 1977, Jaroslav Vanek, an early theoretician of worker-ownership, maintains:

> The Rochdale Pioneers, forerunners of all cooperative movements today, were well aware of the significance of education for the liberation of the worker. When they wrote down the fundamental principles of their movement some one and a quarter centuries ago, they knew it was the ignorance of the wage earner of how to do things, how to organize production, that enslaved her. Thus, they resolved to allot some portion of their meager resources to education. . . . Education, and more generally, the transformation of the human consciousness, is the precondition and the very lifeblood of any successful and lasting effort to bring about self-management and economic democracy.

The place to start learning workplace self-governance is with the job itself. William "Big Bill" Haywood, the legendary organizer for the Industrial Workers of the World, never failed to bring workers to their feet shouting approval when he declared, "The bosses' brains are under the cap of the workingman [sic]." Politically and rhetorically, his assertion rang true: in reality, however, employees who have been consigned to repetitive work know principally how to carry out their job, and, generally speaking, they know little about financing, markets, or production. Since the work of creating a labor-managed enterprise begins with a feasibility study and then proceeds to a comprehensive business plan, involving workers in the process at the outset is the best way to widen the base of knowledge required, both individually and collectively.

Fashioning a way for dialogue to take place between workers who are owners and managers who are owners, too, is the second critically important step. Marty Zinn, a founder of the Worker Owned Network (based in Athens, Ohio) and Roger Wilkins, former director of the Center for Cooperative Work Relations (also in Athens) have successfully tested what they call "ground rules" and "cooperative agreements," two tools that foster collaboration.

The ground rules are three simple statements that working groups can use to lessen conflict while facilitating decision making during "moment-by-moment, face-to-face interactions" in the shop, in meetings, or at the watercooler.

First, avoid intimidation, attempts to control or manipulate a situation, threats, or, as Zinn and Wilkins call it, power plays. "To do this," they say, "we need to learn to recognize power plays, to confront people when we see them pulling power plays, and to set up cooperative ways to resolve problems. You confront a power play by saying how you feel, describe the intimidation, etc., recall how the group agreed to work cooperatively, and suggest a way that it can happen."

Second, agree to communicate openly. "This does not mean talking about everything," Zinn and Wilkins believe. "It means recognizing those things that relate to the success of our business and the health of the group. This requires us to share our feelings so that anger and resentment don't build up, and to state our needs."

Third, agree that every member's opinions are equally valued and deserve equal consideration. "Everyone's needs are not the same. Whenever there seems to be less than enough of something needed, we agree to cooperate to find more, or to compromise, or to find some other solution."

By using these easily understood ground rules—together with a clearly stated cooperative agreement that includes policies for hiring and firing, governance, working hours, and other job-related topics—Zinn and Wilkins have managed, as consultants, to help potential worker-owners un-learn ways of behaving that have sundered many start-ups or conversions.

Worker-owners at Seymour Specialty Wire Company, a large industrial ESOP, extended democratic ideals to the shop floor using a program they called Workers Solving Problems (WSP). Management and worker-owners had come to loggerheads at Seymour over issues of work organization, large and small, and the company, while prospering financially, "was its own worst enemy," according to one elected officer. Using consultants, management and worker-owners embarked on a company-wide goal-setting process that yielded four objectives, one of which surprised no one: to organize democratic ways to make decisions. "Workers Solving Problems" is the plan of action issuing from that goal.

The philosophy of the WSP program is that "any problem that is under the direct control of any working unit can be discussed. Once all the options have been considered, each shop floor working unit can make a decision about those problems." Workers and managers have agreed to focus the WSP program only on production issues. The union leadership gave its full endorsement, while insisting that any problem covered in the contract with the company could be discussed in the WSP process but that "subjects that are applicable to the Labor Agreement should be channeled through the appropriate committees for review."

The WSP program was implemented with a guide; it included spelling out each person's responsibilities and providing accountability forms and a decision-making chart. Some fifteen working units in every phase of the 250-person firm's operations were vested with decision-making and problem-solving responsibilities. While each shopfloor unit was encouraged to make as many decisions as possible, all were cautioned that two tests should be kept in mind before action is taken.

The Extensiveness Test asks about the impact a decision would have on fellow workers:

- How many persons will be affected, and how?
- How much time will be involved?
- How much money will it cost?
- How much money will be saved?

The Significance Test asks what impact a decision will have on Seymour Specialty Wire:

- Will this decision change the basic nature of Seymour?
- Will the decision affect the survival of Seymour?
- Will this decision affect the company's profits?

Implementing Education Programs

The relationship between democratic management and learning is organic. Democratic management facilitates adult learning and personal growth because all members have the right to know about the business; more important, they have the *responsibility to know* how their company works and how it can work better. This is the only way that members of a democratically managed firm can make wise decisions about its operation (Fowler and Willis 1984, 294).

More than a high-sounding principle could be at stake if worker-members omit from their participation plan a suitable educational program. The lack of education has been identified repeatedly as one of the single most frequent causes for cooperative business failure (Jackall and Levin 1984, 82). Conversely, effective workplace education has contributed directly to the success of effective cooperatives like the Mondragon network.

Developing an Educational Plan

How can a suitable educational plan be devised to deal with the problems and issues faced by worker-owners? What kind of education is needed? How should it be organized and delivered, and by whom? Any work experience can be categorized, and once categorized it can be taught. The problem with much current thinking about the workplace is that owners of capital and their hired managers have controlled how work is categorized, administered, and taught. To be consistent with the open, voluntary concepts of the labor-managed cooperative, worker-members must ensure that any education or training program derives from their collective interests and needs, and that they collaborate with competent teachers in carrying the task of learning forward.

The specific characteristics of educational plans will vary from firm to firm, but, in general, they include vocational, performance, political, and cultural elements. Vocational learning focuses on the skills needed to accomplish the tasks at hand. Performance learning aims to improve the way the firm is managed. Political learning nurtures democratic decision making and participation inside the firm and in the surrounding community. Cultural learning fosters a labor-based vision of social change, again both inside and outside the firm.

The Dungannon Sewing Co-Op in Virginia has also found that co-operatives—especially "limited resource" ones in low-income areas—need to affirm the development of people, the building of self-confidence, and the achievement of personal competence as an integral part of their social goals. "This sort of growth comes not so much from a classroom setting as it does from lived experiences discussed with a group process" (Rausch 1985, 8, 19).

Through the concept of worker-ownership, individuals assume responsibility for their workplaces; through self-defined education, workers gain control over what is to be learned, when, and how. Workers, who recognize what they need to know in order to successfully mind their own business, may need to find teachers with particular skills. Often, however, as peers, they can teach each other.

Assessing Educational Needs and Interests

Before starting an educational program, it helps to get a good picture of the needs of the worker-owners. One effective method for assessing a group's needs is to conduct a survey. Here is a survey we devised and field tested with the Guilford College Democratic Management Program.

[*Sample items from the educational needs assessment survey are listed below. The complete questionnaire is in Adams and Hansen 1987, Appendix G—Eds.*]

Assuming there was no cost to you, how much of your time would you be willing to spend (during any one year) at workshops learning skills in the following areas: (For each item, respondents are asked to circle one response.)
None   4 hours   1 day   2 days   2+ days

Governance
(a) How to develop or improve co-op by-laws.
(b) How to govern your co-op.

Decision-Making
(a) How to improve the decision-making process in your co-op.
(b) How to be a more effective member of your organization.
(c) How to chair a meeting.
(d) How to resolve conflicts in a group.

Communications
(a) How to write letters and reports.
(b) How to improve your knowledge as a worker-owner of what happens daily
    or weekly in your business.

Legal Issues
(a) How to approach legal issues facing your cooperative.
(b) How to change those laws affecting worker-owned businesses.

Outside Help
(a) How to use consultants.

Financial Management
(a) How to read and understand your co-op's financial statement.
(b) How to get the credit your business needs.

Productivity
(a) How to collect information you need to make a decision.
(b) How to lower production costs.
(c) How to plan for new products and services for your cooperative.

Sales and Marketing

(a) How to sell your co-op's product.

Personnel Management

(a) How to handle grievances.
(b) How to hire new members.
(c) How to establish co-op procedures for buying back the shares of worker-owners at retirement or termination.

General

(a) How to use a computer.
(b) How to teach other members of your co-op new skills.
(c) How to organize and run a day care center in your co-op.
(d) Why some co-ops failed.
(e) How to convert an existing business to worker-ownership.

Working Better
Employee Participation Groups at Weirton Steel
Karen Young*

The mechanics employee participation group (EPG) at Weirton Steel designed an air-evacuation system to capture the lime dust expelled when lime was unloaded at the fluxhouse. Lime is used to remove impurities during the steel-making process, but the dust is an undesirable by-product of the handling procedure because it settles on equipment and creates more frequent maintenance and higher repair costs.

Ronnie Martin, a millwright at Weirton for thirty-seven years, is one of the members of this EPG. Martin became more and more concerned as he watched the layer of dust grow on the ledge of the fluxhouse roof. He took this problem on as a personal crusade and visited lime-handling plants around the country to determine what they were doing about it.

While he and his wife were in Florida visiting their daughter, they passed a coral-products manufacturing plant. Ronnie knew that lime was involved in this process, but noticed no dust in the vicinity. He went in to speak to the company president and then rolled up his sleeves and climbed into and inspected the scrubber system. When he returned to Weirton with this new knowledge, his group proceeded to design a similar system for their plant.

* *I wrote this after visiting Weirton Steel Corporation to take part in their employee participation group (EPG) training session. This article relates information about the body of the EPGs, but the soul is in the groups of people in the mill and offices putting their muscles and their minds into making a product of highest quality with a commitment to each other, their company, and their community. The highlight of my visit came at the end of the last day of training, when one of the other participants told me that he had been a little leery of having an outsider go through the training "but you were just like one of us."*

The group included in their design the baghouse that was sitting at the now-defunct coke plant on the island on which Weirton is located. Using that baghouse eliminated the need for a capital outlay and put into service an otherwise unused piece of equipment. The next problem was what to do with the eight tons of dust the system captured each day. As steelworkers know, lime is used to neutralize the acidic discharge in some plant areas. Why buy the lime needed in one area of the mill when it is a by-product from another area, the group reasoned. Now, they recycle the lime dust within the mill, again creating a savings for their company.

The employees show so much interest and initiative in part because Weirton is literally their company. Weirton became fully employee owned in 1984, nearly two years after National Steel (now Intergroup) announced it would be downsized and eventually closed and several months after the employees voted by eight to one to establish an employee stock ownership plan (ESOP).

The lime dust episode is but one of many stories of greater employee involvement that grew out of the employee participation group program. It was developed after the establishment of the ESOP in 1984 and is a joint labor-management effort (as have been all of the relevant undertakings at Weirton since it became an employee-owned company). The program is coordinated by a management representative and a representative from the Independent Steelworkers Union and overseen by a steering committee with an equal number of management and union people. The program's object is "To establish an employee participation process throughout the corporation which will result in a better work environment and steel products of the highest quality by utilizing the experience and skills of all Weirton employees in an atmosphere of mutual trust and respect." Issues dealt with in the EPGs cannot intrude on the governing labor agreement.

The program is open to any employee at Weirton; participation is voluntary. The groups are made up of people in related work areas. They meet for one hour a week (on company time) to work on ways to improve their company and their product. Most participants attend a three-day training session on problem-solving techniques and meeting and communication tools. At least two thousand employees have been to training sessions, and there are now more than 107 groups throughout the company. There is a degree of skepticism about the participative process on the part of some, management and shopfloor alike, but as the program continues its supporters are increasing.

The training seminars run Wednesday through Friday, every week. About fifteen people attend each session. The day begins at 8 A.M. and lasts until 4 P.M., with an hour for lunch and a couple of breaks. The training takes place "up on the hill" at corporate headquarters, in the president's former dining room.

Initially, an outside consultant was hired to help establish the program; now there are ten trainers, all of whom are employees at Weirton. Eight of them formerly worked in the mill itself. The trainer teams continually update, revise, and rearrange the training methods and materials. In addition to conducting the training sessions, they facilitate work-group meetings. Consequently, some days trainers may conduct a training session all day and then meet with a work group at eleven o'clock that night if they happen to be facilitator for a work group that meets on the night shift.

The first day of EPG training began with a presentation by the management program coordinator, Alan Gould, on the history of work—beginning with Moses and the pharaohs, but quickly jumping to the Industrial Revolution and its aftermath. In the afternoon, the trainers talked about the roles of different members of a group, defining consensus decision making (what the EPGs strive for) and types of problems. They then introduced such problem-solving tools and techniques as brainstorming and cause-and-effect diagrams.

Day two began with practicing the information that had been presented the day before. The group starts with a decision-making exercise and continues with role playing. In the afternoon, the trainer discusses communications, using a number of exercises that keep the group interested and entertained.

On the last day of training, the union coordinator opened the session by delivering a talk about five other programs designed to help enhance both the company's technical and human aspects. Then the floor was opened to discussion, comments, questions, and suggestions.

At the end of the seminar, trainees were asked their reactions to the session. A couple of people said they were pleasantly surprised; one responded that he thought the effort was sincere; another said he found himself communicating even though he was not ordinarily a communicative person; and one said this experience had changed his life. We all learned a lot, laughed a lot, and came away transformed.

Building Bridges
Linking Education and Community Economic Development

Chuck Turner and Christine Clamp

The traditional spired roofs of the New Hampshire College campus give no hint of the educational experiment going on within. Nestled in the piney foothills of the White Mountains, this staid institution has for the last fifty years prepared young New Hampshire residents to enter the world of business. But today the college is undertaking a unique experiment in support of community economic development. The students who come here to receive a master's in community economic development range in age from thirty to forty-five. Half are people of color; half are women. Each is a member of either a community-based agency or an organization that focuses on community development issues, in towns and cities as far away as New York. For sixteen months they spend one weekend a month sharpening their skills, linking them to economic development, and gaining a degree—all without interrupting their work. Perhaps best of all, this innovative "work while you learn" design brings the benefits of higher education to those traditionally excluded for economic reasons. Its effectiveness is clearly demonstrated by the fact that about half of the program participants earn less than $20,000 a year while supporting their families and meeting (with the help of financial aid) the costs of the four-term program.

Linking Home, Theory, and Practice

The key to the program's success is its ability to support the growth of these students and to increase their impact on their home turf. According to the program's director, Michael Swack,

> We hope to have two primary impacts on the region and its community economic development efforts. First, we want to create a network of technically competent, politically sensitive graduates, who share a common vision of and commitment to community-based development strategies. Our second goal is to attempt to

maintain through the Institute consistent technical assistance to this network, our student body and the region in general.

To meet these objectives, the school expects its graduates to be able to guide longer-range development, as well as the initial implementation of community economic programs. Courses taught by its three full-time faculty members focus on issues of corporate structure, business development, financial analysis, capital formation, and real-estate development as well as cooperative development and land use. Seeking to balance course work and field work, the program helps students develop the ability to move easily between theory and practice. Its teachers in their own careers have been able to find and establish such balance.

The curriculum takes a learner-centered approach. Courses are designed to assist participants in developing their own abilities and in transferring them to others in their communities. Classes are focused on enhancement of participants' abilities to articulate a community-based development strategy and to design and implement projects.

It is the school's intention that graduates take home a "tool bag" of skills, an understanding of how these skills can be applied in their communities, and a developed set of attitudes regarding their role in the development process. For this reason, process is central in designing the curriculum. The manner by which the skills are transferred within the program should mirror what happens outside. This means that faculty and participants work together to assess the participants' training needs, as well as the faculty's capacity to meet them. It means that participants are continually encouraged to take active responsibility for their learning experience and examine the manner in which their perspectives on development are affected by this experience. They share in the responsibility for identifying training resources, seeking them out, adapting them, and mastering their use.

Perhaps the heart of the program is its approach to field work. One-third of the students' credits are earned through participation in an economic project of their own choosing located in their home communities. The breadth and depth of the students' efforts to link their learning process to practical problems in their communities testifies to the effectiveness of this approach. Projects initiated and implemented by students have led to the creation of community loan funds, land trusts, cooperatives, microenterprises, worker-owned businesses, and other community-based organizations.

They include: a hydroponic greenhouse in a low-income neighborhood of Hartford to demonstrate the feasibility of growing healthy food inexpensively in urban areas; a community development corporation in New York City designed and organized by a Native American student focusing on the needs of its Native American residents; a community-based grade school in Boston; the Laconia and Franklin Area Community Land Trusts in New Hampshire; the Sister Clara Muhammed School, a private Muslim school in Roxbury, Massachusetts; WAHEED Cooperative Enterprises, Inc., WAHEED Properties Management Corporation, WAHEED Housing Cooperative, and WAHEED community land trust, all evolved from a community-based organization formed to promote cooperatives and self-help in Newport, Rhode Island; the Rhode Island Community Reinvestment Association, that works with local banks and other financial institutions to explore how they can more effectively serve low-income communities in the state; and the Western Massachusetts Community Loan Fund in Springfield.

To aid the students' grassroots projects, the program has a technical assistance arm called the Institute for Cooperative Community Development. The institute also provides technical assistance to government and community organizations and to others interested in innovative approaches to improving of the economic base of their communities. Faculty from the program, as well as students and other associates, provide the assistance offered by the institute. In 1986, the college also initiated a twelve-month residential master's program in international community economic development.

Building Credibility and Confidence

A network of more than two hundred alumni provides contacts with community development organizations throughout the United States and abroad. Interviews with alumni indicate that the program is useful because it has provided them with valuable skills and credentials, as well as an opportunity to network with other practitioners every month while in the program and continued access to that network after they graduate.

Listen to Sharon Hunt of New York City, a recent graduate and a mother of four, who was on welfare when she entered the program two years ago. "All my life I've been concerned," she told *Changing Work,*

> about how to get better services for people, particularly Native Americans. When I entered New Hampshire College, I had no clear ideas about community development and what it involved. For me the issues had always been services and the confrontations necessary to get the services that were needed.
>
> The program has been a real struggle for me. I didn't even have the rhetoric when I started. However, through the program my vision has increased and I've gained the skills to bring my vision into reality. My only concern about the program now is how can we get more nontraditional education down to the grassroots—so that others can be empowered as I have been. I think that this will be the key to the regeneration of this country.

Another graduate, Paula Taylor, is the executive director of the East of Broad Community Development Corporation in Philadelphia, a recently established nonprofit focused on economic development, job placement, and housing rehabilitation. She has found, now that she has a degree from the college, that people see her differently:

> I'm looked upon now as a person that can give technical assistance. . . . Now I am asked to do speaking engagements and board training.

Finally, Teresa Prim, director of economic development for the Clarence Darrow Community Center in Chicago, would agree:

> People say that I'm more confident and they say that I'm more aggressively willing to develop and use the skills that I learned in the Community Economic Development program. When issues come up and there are problems out there in the community—I have much more confidence about going ahead and saying "Hey, we can do this." One of the skills that I think that was really stressed for me is planning—being able to plan an entire process for a project.

Still Building Bridges

With such feedback, we are confident that the New Hampshire College program is effectively providing skills, assurance, and legitimacy to practitioner-students so that they can bring about constructive changes in their communities. The program is building sturdy bridges to connect the college to cities and towns throughout this region. And across these bridges people and resources are flowing to benefit those at both ends.

Earning While Learning

A Worker Co-Op for Management Students*

Charlene Renberg Winters

Some students from the Brigham Young University (BYU) Marriott School of Management are removing their ties and getting their hands dirty to learn something about production, while a group of engineering and technology students are settling behind desks to gain a working perspective on finance and business management.

The students are participating in Equitech, a worker-owned cooperative developed by BYU faculty. Equitech gets its name from the words "equality" and "technology." Everyone has equal say and equal pay in the operation. "The objective of a democratic system, though an intriguing idea, is challenging," says Dr. Warner Woodworth, who developed Equitech with Dr. Christopher Meek and Vernon R. Dillenbeck.

Equitech provides students in the technology majors with some training in business management, finances, and cost accounting, thereby increasing their chances of succeeding in middle- and upper-management positions or in running their own businesses.

"Many of these students know how to create great products but don't know how to build and maintain a business," says Woodworth. "Conversely, we have students in business who are great with figures, but they need to learn to roll up their sleeves, get their hands dirty, and get into the trenches."

Although some students believe such a work model is unnecessary for them because they plan to work for a major corporation, Woodworth explains "The truth is that 98 percent of all businesses are small, with fewer than one hundred people. A huge entrepreneurial movement has begun in this country. That is where the new jobs are and where the new wealth is being created."

* From *BYU Today*, July 1990.

Several of the technology students involved in the program are already talking about running their own businesses. "These students are inventors and what I refer to as entrepreneurs in the embryo stage," says Dillenbeck. "Yet if they are going to do this, they need to know enough about business management to finance, produce, and market products successfully."

Equitech emerged from Dillenbeck's concern that engineering-technology students need more than just shopfloor experience and from Woodworth and Meek's concern that business schools primarily create paper entrepreneurs who know little beyond how to shuffle assets.

"Paper entrepreneurship doesn't add wealth and doesn't create new products," Woodworth explains. "Its 'strength' is with manipulating numbers and figures. If we don't like a particular set of figures, we'll just use another formula and create some other figures, but, in the process, plants are shutting down, businesses are going overseas, and international companies are buying us up left and right."

One of the reasons for this, explains Dillenbeck, is that managers and engineers, those who are designing innovative new products, have not learned how to communicate. Another reason businesses are failing, he says, is because managers either have experience in engineering or business—but not both.

> The problem is that business managers too often make decisions based on market analyses and finance costs, without ever taking into account the production process. On the other hand, some engineering managers make good production decisions—ones that will keep the production process running smoothly—but they aren't good business decisions. For example, we have found that engineering managers often fail to consider the needs of their customers, which may result in a fine product that no one wants to buy.

In seeking for an industrial renaissance, Woodworth and others have been studying worker-owned firms in northern Spain, in and around Mondragon where more than 100 firms with some 20,000 workers are part of a co-op system, and participants have their own bank, engineering school, technical-training programs, and research-and-development systems.

"As we studied ways to collaborate more with our students in integrating concepts with actual work," says Woodworth, "we thought, 'Wouldn't it be interesting to get the two elements of the Basque system into a practical education program here at BYU?' With inspiration from Spain, we developed Equitech and brought together engineering, manufacturing, business, accounting, and marketing students to see if a collaboration would be possible."

The enterprise was launched a little more than two years ago when the co-op agreed to manufacture some new weight-lifting equipment. That venture, however, never really got off the ground.

A second venture worked because the BYU co-op found and filled a local need. Students discovered that many area schools and businesses, looking for ways to bestow honors on guests or benefactors, were buying items from the East and West coasts. Equitech decided it could fill that need locally, and now it produces quality medallions, plaques, and other commemorative items at competitive prices.

The students work out of a basement lab. Three faculty representatives and three students sit on the board of directors. A dozen people form the general assembly and make decisions by majority vote. Each week students accept a new role in the company in order to share equitably in the management and the work.

On the practical side, Equitech is also providing jobs and income for students, who earn $6 per hour. Many of these students are from Third World nations and plan to return to their home nations and set up cooperatively run businesses after graduation.

Although faced with such continuing challenges as massive turnover when students graduate, the difficulties of maintaining continuity, and the responsibility of emphasizing educational rather than wealth-creation aspects for the students, Equitech has benefits on many levels, says Woodworth:

"We are training students who ask if there is a more humane way to do business. The co-op is allowing them to make mistakes now rather than when they have a spouse and five children depending on them. We are offering a grassroots experience. We're committed to them, to democracy, and to cooperation."

Short Takes

Many co-op education and technical assistance programs as well as co-op management programs have developed through North American universities over the last decade. Here we mention briefly programs at Utah State University, Boston College, the Co-op College of Canada, the Universities of Georgia and North Carolina, the University of Wisconsin, and M.I.T.

Promoting Economic Development, Worker Ownership, and Workplace Democracy at Utah State University

Since 1978, Utah State University has been providing an education, research, and technical assistance program through an extension center that promotes rural economic development, worker ownership, and workplace democracy—Business and Economic Development Services, affiliated with the College of Business and the Department of Economics. Participating faculty see the program as a natural outgrowth of the public service orientation of extension programs at such land-grant universities as Utah State.

The center has conducted research on plant closings and on ways to revitalize the local rural economy. It offers a Master of Science program in human resource administration for students interested in worker participation, workplace democracy, and industrial relations. In addition to academic courses and entrepreneurial-training workshops, the center also provides technical assistance to local residents interested in starting co-ops and worker-owned businesses. It also plans to launch a student-run worker co-op to help students finance their education and to integrate theory with practical work in a cooperative organization.

Boston College Sociology Department Specializes in Cooperative Studies

Under the leadership of Professor Severyn Bruyn, the Boston College sociology department sponsored a program in social economy and social policy that became its focus for a decade beginning in the mid-1970s. The program involved courses and research on worker self-management and the social economy. The department pioneered a joint degree program with the Boston College School of Management in 1980 and also sponsored a number of conferences on economic conversion from military to peace-promoting production, community development, and workplace democracy. The research efforts of graduate students and faculty there resulted in many books on workplace democracy, the social economy, and related themes. Recently, the department has broadened its emphasis, accenting social economy and social justice, with special studies in gender, race, and class.

Canadian Students Participate in a Junior Achievement Worker Co-Op

The Co-operative College of Canada sponsored a successful cooperative business owned and managed by a group of high-school students in Yorkton, Saskatchewan, under the auspices of the local Junior Achievement program. The project, which lasted three years, involved eighteen students in the manufacture and sale of bulletin boards.

A resource group including people from the Co-operative College and from the local cooperative sector worked with the students. The group revised some of the Junior Achievement resource materials and training manuals, incorporating principles and practices of cooperative organization. This was facilitated by the fact that the Junior Achievement program restricts the number of shares or corporate votes to one per member.

The project concluded in 1989 because project advisors could no longer keep up with the increased demands on their time. So far, the Yorkton experiment has been copied by four other Junior Achievement cooperatives in Saskatchewan.

Rural Entrepreneurship Through Action Learning (REAL)

Rural educators in Georgia, North Carolina, and South Carolina have set up a network of business-incubation centers to encourage high school and college students to start student-owned businesses. The centers provide technical assistance and training for students. The network, which currently includes three Rural Entrepreneurship through Action Learning (REAL) centers, hopes to expand to other states. The REAL centers in Georgia and North Carolina began as partnerships with the Small Business Development centers of their state universities. The North Carolina group is planning to expand its revolving-loan fund to $1 million to help provide capital for school-incubated student-operated enterprises. The Georgia center publishes a newsletter, *The REAL Story*.

Boston Area Management and Community Development Institute

The Massachusetts Institute of Technology (M.I.T.) hosts an annual week-long institute in Boston featuring courses and workshops for persons active in and concerned about low-income communities. The program began at Tufts University in 1983 and recently moved to M.I.T. The June 1990 institute was a typical example, with dozens of one- and two-day programs in five major areas: affordable housing, community economic development and finance, building community involvement and leadership, running effective community-based organizations, and strengthening our voice. Among the courses were *Developing Democratic Organizations* and *Cooperative Business Enterprise Development*.

Cooperative Management Institute at the University of Wisconsin

The University of Wisconsin's Center for Cooperatives sponsors an annual two-week institute for managers of wholesale and retail cooperative businesses. According to its coordinator, Dr. Ann Hoyt, "The Cooperative Management Institute is designed to prepare cooperative managers to complete an organizational audit, design business planning frameworks, and work with boards and staff." The courses focus on strategic planning, finance, and personnel management for cooperative firms.

Numerous other education efforts aimed at promoting worker co-ops and other grassroots economic organizations have been sponsored by private, non-university, non-governmental agencies. We single out for brief mention, the Development Training Institute, and the Highlander Center.

Development Training Institute

The institute was founded in 1981 to help those engaged in community economic development gain the technical skills to plan, finance, and manage development projects in their neighborhoods. It has provided training to more than a thousand community practitioners, bankers, and government workers in strategies and techniques of community development. It publishes the *Neighborhood Funding Bulletin Board* quarterly.

The Highlander Center

For more than fifty years, the Highlander Center has carried out education for social change among communities throughout Appalachia and the U.S. South. Highlander's history is a rich one, from education for workers in the 1930s, to Citizenship Schools for black southerners during the civil-rights movement, to building community organizations in the 1970s and 1980s.

Throughout its history, Highlander has held to a central principle: for institutional change to be effective, it must begin with the people directly affected by a problem. Grassroots leaders must be developed through an educational process that allows them to analyze their problems, test their ideas, learn from the experience of others, and strengthen their organizations.

Since 1987, Highlander has focused on three poor rural communities that have lost their traditional economic bases in coal, manufacturing, and farming—Dungannon and Ivanhoe in Virginia, and Jellico in Tennessee.

In each place, local citizens' groups have sprung up, led by low-income women. Highlander works with them, offering night classes for ten to sixteen weeks and providing technical and educational support.

In Ivanhoe, the group changed from trying to attract outside industry to developing its own plans for economic development enterprises. Out of these experiences, Highlander has published a series of manuals on education for economic development.

6

Worker Ownership and the Labor Movement

Not too long ago, union leaders thought of worker ownership as a catastrophe that would lead to workers losing their identity and to unions losing their distinctive roles and membership. They assumed that successful buyouts would lead to worker-owners fighting each other for the spoils. And they suspected that the companies most likely to be sold to workers would be marginal firms with no economic future.

While there is a core of truth to such concerns, over the past fifteen years or so these negative attitudes have gradually softened and been replaced by cautious, but increasing, support for union involvement in worker ownership. For example, after much difficult debate, the United Steel Workers of America (USWA) officially endorsed worker ownership as a desirable option under the right conditions. As union president Lynn Williams once described the process:

> The truth is, we backed into employee ownership defensively because we saw that here was an option available that at least could maintain a plant, an enterprise, a community.... But the truth is [also] that it's a wonderful experience.... Suddenly you have an enterprise that functions with some real different standards. (Conference Report, Industrial Renaissance Conference, 14-15 September 1989)

Since the decision, the USWA has supported over twenty of its locals in arranging employee buyouts, thus making steel workers a dominant force in this still very central industry. Moreover, as our Short Takes reveal, there are now some ten other unions whose members participate in worker-owned firms. Finally, the AFL-CIO has put itself squarely behind worker ownership by establishing an investment fund specifically designed to help workers become owners of their own businesses.

Unions Can Be Part of the Solution

Nonetheless, questions remain, and some labor activists are still far from convinced of the merits of worker ownership or the role of unions in firms where the distinction between workers and owners is blurred. Lance Compa, for example, a staff member for the United Electrical, Radio, and Machine Workers, argues below that, in a capitalist economy, "enterprise consciousness" is bound to overwhelm worker-owners. The need to compete, he claims, will destroy their bonds with workers in other plants and with the whole labor movement. And Pete Leki, writing in *Labor Today*, expresses still widespread (and somewhat grounded) suspicions about ESOP companies. As they are presently envisioned, he says, "ESOPs . . . are designed to lure working people into the illusion of worker ownership in order to make them work harder, produce more for less, and accept concessions."

How can this crucial controversy be resolved? One place to start is with a concrete examination of what can and does take place in actual worker-owned firms. Thus, Richard Feldman describes two recent union-backed buyouts in Washington State, one of which (Omak Wood Products) comes very close to meeting the main objections raised by Compa and Leki. And Michael Locker contends that such unions as the USWA can be part of the solution. For example, they have made worker ownership an industry-wide strategy based on such common problems as corporate flight. The next step might be to insist that worker-owned firms "recycle success" by contributing to a "fund to support other takeovers, to organize efforts among the unorganized, [and] to provide better pensions throughout the industry." In brief, the original aim of unions—to meet common needs, to support common struggles—coupled with their substantial resources and newly acquired taste for worker ownership, can make all the difference in the direction of the workplace democracy movement and in the struggle for worker control of the economy.

The Dangers of Worker Control

Lance Compa

"Worker Control" and "Workplace Democracy" as Vogue Phrases

At a time when the trade-union movement is battered by the recession and high unemployment, declining membership, layoffs in heavy industry, and militant antiunionism in business and government, the vogue phrases on the Left have become "workplace democracy" and "worker control." These slogans can mean anything from direct employee ownership ("buyout") of a failing company to increased worker participation in shopfloor-level decisions.

Daniel Zwerdling, author of *Workplace Democracy*, has written that "workplace democracy is no longer merely a rhetorical flourish invoked by radical activists. It has become a practical strategy for survival." Former United Automobile Workers counsel Stephen Schlossberg recently called on union bargainers to make tradeoffs of benefits and wages in order to win a larger voice in decisions affecting the jobs of the workers they represent. Such "nontraditional bargaining," Schlossberg said, could transform the ugliness of labor-management confrontation into "the beautiful swan of a cooperative, productive, and constructive relationship." Mark Green, head of the Democracy Project, a liberal think tank, places worker control high on the progressive agenda for the years immediately ahead.

There are a number of arguments offered by proponents of workplace democracy. One is that it can save jobs, since plant closings and runaway shops are becoming commonplace. Greater union control of pension funds offers some protection for workers faced with shutdowns and some assurance that the money will not be invested in antiunion businesses. Labor-management committees give employees more say in decisions affecting safety, job conditions, and the introduction of new technology. Appointing labor representatives to a company's board of directors can influence long-range policy. Its proponents also say that workplace democracy improves the quality of work life by encouraging employee involvement, reducing alienation, and tapping the latent creative potential of nonsupervisory personnel.

Advocates of worker buyouts admit that problems have arisen with this strategy in the past, and they readily point out the obvious pitfalls. For example, there is the danger of "lemon capitalism"—buying an undercapitalized, dying business that would have been better left to go under. Moreover, even if the business is saved, failure to introduce worker control at all levels (rather than just at the supervisory level) has often caused dissension and driven the employee-owners to sell out to private investors. Union control of pension funds creates enormous opportunities for financial chicanery. The practice of appointing union officers to corporate boards of directors has in some instances led to the estrangement of leaders from the rank and file. Worker participation in decisions made at the shopfloor level can be used by management as a ploy for speeding up output, or to prevent a union from organizing a nonunion workplace, or to co-opt an existing union into collaborating with management in order to erode employee support for their union, which might lead to its decertification.

Coming Up Short: The Problem of Enterprise Consciousness

The experiments in workplace democracy and worker control that have ended badly are easy targets for criticism. But even when looked at in the best possible light, such programs still come up short. Like full employment, another catchphrase on the Left, workplace democracy and worker control are contradictions in terms in a capitalist economic system. Employers will never willingly allow significant invasions of their prerogatives. They will agree to set up company-run worker-participation programs, appoint a union official to the board of directors, allow an occasional buyout on the periphery of the economy (an old meat-packing plant, say, or a failing auto-parts plant)—but these are essentially token gestures.

From the standpoint of the labor movement, adopting the objective of greater worker control is bad policy because it emphasizes enterprise consciousness rather than class consciousness. When workers control a firm, their interests are identical with management's. They no longer struggle for the betterment of workers in general, or for the betterment of those in a particular trade or industrial sector; they think of making their own workplace more profitable. In effect, workers become capitalists, with capitalists' problems.

As such, they are confronted with a whole new range of decisions—managerial decisions. Should we cut wages so we can buy new machinery? Should we lay off unskilled workers with seniority in favor of highly skilled workers who can do a wide range of jobs, thus increasing efficiency? Should we lay off unskilled workers with the least seniority even though they are likely to be minorities and women? Should we combine job classifications—double up the duties of current employees so we do not have to hire more people and raise costs? Should we lower piecework rates so we will get more output for the same pay? Should the pension fund lend money at 11 percent to build moderate-income housing when the going mortgage rate is 17 percent? Should we close one of our two plants in response to declining demand or should we mortgage our savings and our homes to invest $8 million in a modernization program and an advertising campaign to increase our share of the market?

It can be argued that if workers are going to run businesses, they must face up to these questions. But the time, resources, and energies of working people are severely limited, and so they have to pick their fights carefully. What are they up against now in their shops and offices and communities? An economy increasingly controlled by monopolistic conglomerates and multinational corporations. Federal and state governments that openly back business and are trying to reduce social protections, civil rights, and civil liberties. Plant closings, runaway shops, and union-busting efforts like the open-shop drives of the 1920s.

Enterprise consciousness detaches workers from the larger struggles—the battles to improve their standard of living, to organize the unorganized, to develop new forms of independent political action, to resist the Right's legislative agenda, to fight racism and sexism by employers and in their own ranks, to support workers throughout the world who are victimized by U.S. corporations. Worse, it makes it easier for corporate America to achieve its dream of a union-free environment.

Rank-and-File versus Business Unionism

The call for workplace democracy and worker control is usually accompanied by criticism, either stated or implied, of "old-fashioned" trade unionism—hard bargaining for economic gains, an aggressive antimanagement stance, contract enforcement through a strong steward system and shopfloor action, reliance on strikes, and so on. According to the critics, militant 1930s-style unionism ran out of gas in the 1970s with the entry of a new breed of worker into the work force. These new workers are better educated and skeptical of bosses and union officials alike. And they are more concerned with the quality of work life than with traditional union demands for higher wages, more benefits, and job security. Union leaders' hoary calls for militancy are falling on deaf ears.

The trouble with this view is that it does not square with reality. The labor movement put aggressive unionism on the shelf in the late 1940s when the C.I.O. purged its leftist members. Subsequently, it merged with the more conservative A.F.L., with its "business union" approach. The new breed of worker has rarely been put to the test. When young workers have been challenged, as in tough strikes or nose-to-nose shopfloor battles, they have often displayed leadership abilities they did not know they had.

Once the unions had destroyed the Left in the labor movement, they came to an understanding with management. In exchange for supporting free enterprise at home and the cold war abroad, cooperating with the Central Intelligence Agency by participating in agency-funded foreign labor "institutes," and supporting huge military budgets and the U.S. imperialist policy in the Third World, the labor movement was accepted as part of the country's power establishment. Labor leaders became labor statesmen. There were still occasional tough strikes and hard bargaining, but the basic system of power relations was not challenged. In the face of labor's compliance, business has reneged on that accord and is out to destroy the labor movement. Disarmed, confused, and foundering, many unions now engage in craven concession bargaining and try to pretend that givebacks are victories and breakthroughs. This is the ultimate in business unionism, the logical end to labor's break with its own left wing.

In our corporation-dominated economy, union involvement in experiments with workplace democracy and worker control is of a piece with business unionism. Organized labor no longer advances the interests of working people generally, and individual unions no longer advance the cause of all workers in a specific industrial sector. Rather, each union has become a company union that tries to work out the best deal with management (or itself) to keep its firm competitive. Its energies directed toward problems of worker ownership, or pension fund investment, or winning a seat on the board of directors, each union becomes a transmission belt (to borrow a metaphor often used in socialist countries) for *capitalist* values and norms—investment incentives, cost cutting, capital formation, productivity, and so on.

Strong, democratic, combative trade unions, with effective shop-steward systems providing protection for workers on the job and independent political auxiliaries for political and community action, can do more to promote *genuine* workplace democracy and worker control than all the experiments currently under way. Many labor activists are trying to revive this brand of rank-and-file unionism by getting involved in the day-to-day life of the workplace and the community that business unionism ignores.

Rank-and-file unionism addresses precisely those issues that make for a democratic or undemocratic workplace: job assignment and transfer rights, job evaluations and job descriptions, safety and health protections, the introduction of new technology, the pace of work, and freedom of speech in the workplace. The common lament of managers whose companies have strong unions is that "the union runs the shop." It is a goal worth aspiring to.

Outside the workplace, important elements of the labor movement are speaking out against nuclear weapons and military spending, against cutbacks in environmental and occupational-health programs, against U.S. intervention in the Third World, against Ku Klux Klan violence, against federal and state budget cuts. And they are speaking out for voting rights, for affirmative action, for civil liberties, for tax reform, for more unemployment benefits, for a higher minimum wage, and for food stamps. Many unions are organizing unorganized sectors of their industries, often in traditionally nonunion parts of the country. Distracted by problems of production and competition, would workers in a worker-owned and worker-run enterprise be likely to organize around such issues?

Linking Worker Control and Militant Trade Unionism

"Rank-and-file unionism" falls as trippingly off the tongue as "workplace democracy" and "worker control." But labor must not get involved in a fight over slogans. It will not advance the cause of workers to scorn old-fashioned unionism and call for workplace democracy and worker control to replace it. The job of the labor movement is still the old-fashioned one of organizing the unorganized, mobilizing the organized, and building for independent action. The best thing the Left can do is help tie the drive for workplace democracy and worker control to the movement for a militant, democratic, and politically conscious trade unionism. Then the move toward workplace democracy and worker control can be part of a drive for democracy in the whole of society, rather than a last-ditch effort to save the plant or beat the competition.

I'd Be All for ESOPs If...*

Pete Leki

Time magazine (6 February1989) featured a two-page spread on the success of ESOPs in "boosting the spirits and competitiveness of American workers." Prominently absent from the piece was the fact that in none of the ESOPs do workers *actually control* their own destiny as managers or shareholders. Avis (auto rental agency) is touted as a company bought in totality by its workers. Yet, the article admits that the company's twenty-four million shares are to be "gradually" released to the "owners" over seventeen years, while profits are used to pay off a $1.75 billion loan! Today, Avis's 12,300 workers own on average only twenty shares each, total value $200. If that's ownership, then the *Time* article should really have been on the humor page!

What are the editors of *Time* and other promoters of ESOPs trying to accomplish? They are trying to appeal to workers who are sick and tired of working for companies that don't give a damn, companies that are greedy, vicious, and ruthless. ESOPs, as presently envisaged, are designed to lure working people into the illusion of worker ownership in order to make them work harder, produce more for less, and accept concessions.

Three Ways to Make ESOPs Work for Workers and Communities

The real question is: How can we take the fraudulent abuse of ESOPs and the desperate hopes of workers and use them to fight for real worker and community takeover and ownership of industry? We need to study the experience of ESOPs and to figure out what demands, what strategies are needed to gain *actual* control.

One crucial aspect is capitalization and financing. Workers, their unions, and their communities need to demand government subsidized capitalization of their

---

* From *Labor Today*, Spring 1989.

workplaces, in order to cut out or at least neutralize the role of private banks. If the taxpayers can bankroll Lee Iacocca more than $1 million a year, do not regular folks rate some help?

This capitalization could come in the form of direct subsidies for modernizing equipment, processing, or marketing; it could include refinancing of debts on a long-term, secure low-interest or interest-free basis. After all, massive government support has been routinely granted to private industry; for example, nuclear power plant technology, developed at public expense, was basically handed over to private corporations (and look what a mess they have made of it!).

Second, the mechanisms for buyouts should include a thorough housecleaning of the original board of directors and should establish new boards with a clear social and working-class agenda. The fight for real worker ownership and control has to be waged by trade unions and their rank-and-file members and leaders.

The cynical snickering in *Time* about workers being bosses misses the point. When workers become the masters of their own workplaces, an event of extraordinary importance will have taken place. We don't want to run industry just like the previous owners. We want democracy, a cooperative and strong relationship with the community that would include integrated subsidized housing, day-care centers, clean environments with trees, parks, and swimming pools, affirmative action, apprenticeships, and research facilities. A successful fight for this sort of real change in ownership presupposes a union that is conscious of the breakthrough it is making.

Finally, a vigorous political fight needs to be waged in order to bring clarity to the uplifting, liberating, yes, revolutionary significance of a worker/community buyout. Unions and their independent political organizations at work in the factory and community, and on boards of directors, are the key to this vision.

If this were ESOPs, then I'd be for them.

State and Labor Cooperation in Designing Successful Worker Buyouts

Richard Feldman

Though the state of Washington has a rich history of worker cooperatives, before 1987 there was little knowledge of or support for employee ownership in unions, the state legislature, public agencies, or economic development organizations. Today, these groups tend to see employee ownership as a sound economic development strategy rather than a utopian dream or a desperation tactic for saving failing firms. Central to this change in attitude has been the work of the Washington State Labor Council (the statewide federation of AFL-CIO unions), the formation of the state government's Employee Ownership Program (WEOP), with its unique focus on supporting worker majority-owned cooperatives and ESOPs, and two highly publicized buyouts (Unimar International and Omak Wood Products).

A Long-Odds Buyout

When Marine Power and Equipment, the operator of a large shipbuilding and tug-and-barge corporation, finally went into bankruptcy in 1987 with $200 million of debt on $40 million of assets, another shudder of despair ran through the Puget Sound maritime and metal trades unions. The early and mid-1980s had been bad years for anyone connected with the Puget Sound shipyards, with thousands of jobs disappearing. Now, a large shipyard with superior facilities, a smaller shipyard, a tug-and-barge operation, and 450 jobs were all at stake.

Union-led efforts to save Marine Power from the auction block began immediately. After months of rocky negotiations, led by representatives from several international and West Coast unions, the bankruptcy court finally approved an employee buyout, featuring massively scaled down debt, a secured loan from Washington State, a 10 percent wage set-aside, and a labor-designed ESOP.

The result was Unimar International. It is in several respects a good model. Its ESOP controls 78 percent of company stock, and employee representatives hold six of eleven positions on the board of directors. Voting is done on a one-share, one-vote basis. Moreover, stock is allocated to employees, as the debt is paid down, according to the relative amounts that people earn. The union must approve any changes to the ESOP, and the company has a right of first refusal on the sale of the ESOP to outsiders.

On the other hand, Unimar has been beset by substantial problems. It began its first day of business $55 million in the hole, unable to borrow any cash, and forced to compete in a declining, cutthroat industry. Additionally, the local unions, organized under the Seattle Metal Trades District Council, were only indirectly involved in the negotiations. This minimized their "ownership" in the process and their familiarity with the employee-ownership option. Furthermore, despite the efforts of experienced consultants, there was little effective implementation of employee participation programs during the first year, in part because management was preoccupied with the shortage of cash and the daily crises facing Unimar and in part because of lingering animosity between the workers and the remaining owners of Marine Power who retained seats on the board of Unimar.

Despite these and other problems, Unimar still has a good chance to become a viable company. It made a large balloon payment on its debt in August 1989 and has signed a labor agreement with good and sustainable wages. Its tug-and-barge operations continue to be profitable, and it has won some major ship repair contracts. Now that it is partly out of the bankruptcy woods, it may be able to secure sounder financing and stabilize its operations.

Looking back on Unimar's shaky start, it was probably a mistake to include a long-term lease of the large shipyard as part of the deal, and it was clearly a mistake not to provide the new company with a cash cushion. Unimar's cash deficit resulted in poor marketing, poor tools for the workers, an inability to put together a significant participation plan, and workers earning substantially less than in other shipyards. This lack of cash typically plagues union-led ESOP buyouts.

Unimar's troubles reinforce the need for solid analysis of an employee buyout. The lessons learned by the Washington State Labor Council and others concerning rank-and-file involvement, independent feasibility analysis, the importance of a cash cushion, and the early development of an employee-participation plan all found application in Washington's next big buyout—Omak Wood Products.

A Dream Come True

Omak, Washington, is a company town of forty-five hundred in rural Okanogan County, 225 miles northeast of Seattle. This huge county (bigger than Connecticut) has a 14 percent unemployment rate and only three industrial wage employers: two federal dams and the mills of Omak Wood. Omak's plywood, dimensional lumber, and furniture mills once employed twelve hundred workers. Over the years, successive owners cut the labor force, reduced wages, and took profits out of the community. The second to last purchaser was Sir James Goldsmith, who acquired the plant as part of his takeover of Crown Zellerbach in 1985. The plant's most recent buyers are its employees, led by their union.

The union-led buyout of Omak represents virtually all that is possible with employee ownership and ESOPs. It secured local ownership and control of a key community economic asset so that company profits now stay within the county instead of being exported. The local union leadership took a courageous stand, and the entire community mobilized in support of the effort. With the help of the Washington Employee Ownership Program and the Washington State Labor Council, the workers had significant involvement in the buyout process, and a sophisticated system of labor-management cooperation and employee participation is being created. Even big investment bankers helped rather than harmed the workers and their company. Best of all, the company was and continues to be profitable.

Rumors of a sale or closure started circulating as early as November 1987. These rumors about Omak's lifeblood triggered separate responses from the community and the union that eventually coalesced, with WEOP's help, into an employee buyout effort. Anxiety for the future of the mill—and the union's support for an employee buyout—both increased dramatically when Louisiana-Pacific appeared as a buyer. Louisiana-Pacific is on the AFL-CIO National Boycott List because of its notorious union-busting tactics. The company buys small-town mills, shuts them down for a couple of months to starve out the workforce, and then rehires people at half their former wages.

In early 1988, the rumors were confirmed: Goldsmith had put the mill up for sale. The executive committee of the local union gave the go-ahead to bring in WEOP and to present a buyout proposal to the membership. WEOP's job was to help the workers get organized, to select the consultants they would need, and in general to prepare them to make a bid for the mill. The first step was to form a buyout committee.

The committee included not only union leaders but also a local accountant and two community businesspeople. Preliminary studies looked positive and a meeting was called that some five hundred workers attended. After outlining the buyout idea, Ron Rodriguez, of the Okanogan County Economic Development Council, asked if the membership wanted to proceed. The answer was a roaring yes. After this meeting, $10,000 was acquired from the state to cover consultants' fees. In addition, the union membership contributed $5,000, and the buyout committee raised another $5,000 from the community. Later, the union membership voted to set aside up to 10 percent of their wages for up to six years, if needed, to help pay off the buyout loans. Many local merchants supported the workers by lowering their prices by 10 percent.

After substantial lobbying from state and national legislators, Goldsmith accepted a bid from the employees, who purchased the plant for $35 million and committed to raising an additional $10 to $15 million for working capital. Through the ESOP, the employees own 57 percent of the company, with Goldsmith retaining a 10 percent interest and investors holding the rest. Major decisions, such as new products, acquisitions, and structural changes, are made on a one-person, one-vote basis. For other issues, voting is on a per-share basis. The nine-member board of directors includes three union positions, three investor positions, and seats for the chief executive officer, chief financial officer, and a representative of the plant's nonunion employees. As the outside investors are paid off, their positions will be filled by employee representatives.

Union members chose rank-and-file workers to fill several committees concerned with different aspects of the transition to employee ownership. One of these, a labor-management committee called the "six pack," oversees the entire transition process and the implementation of employee participation. Thus far, employee-owner suggestions have led to more than $1.5 million in savings, and actual performance is running far ahead of profit projections. Quality, production, and other measures of plant success are way up as well.

A potential problem for Omak is its supply of wood from federal lands. Environmental suits related to a proposed ski resort and to logging practices have blocked timber sales. It is possible, though this has not yet occurred, that the employee-owners and the environmentalists will be able to join forces around a common interest in sustainable, stewardship-oriented timber policies. After all, the employee-owners live in the community and are involved for the long haul and should not be interested in cutting and running.

The Omak buyout set several precedents. The employees bought a healthy, profitable company—not a basket case. They received tremendous union, community, and state support. While the Labor Council still looks at worker ownership as only one tool to avert job loss, it now has solid experience in establishing a labor-led employee-owned firm. As for WEOP, it is trying to expand employee ownership beyond job retention cases by marketing it as a credible option for business owners seeking to retire.

Most important, the Unimar and Omak cases indicate the leading roles the Washington Labor Council and the state government's Employee Ownership Program can play in shaping employee ownership in the state. Together, they can push highly democratized employee control, defined by majority worker ownership, restricted transferability of stock, worker representation on the board of directors, fair sharing of equity and profits, labor-management cooperation, employee participation, work redesign, and democratic voting rights. Still, the likelihood of significantly increasing the number of progressive employee-owned firms in Washington State depends on the continued support of organized labor and on the dissemination of success stories like those of Omak and Unimar.

Unions and Worker Ownership

A New Alliance?

Interview with Michael Locker

Changing Work: Michael, today you publish a highly respected newsletter on the steel industry for the United Steel Workers of America (USWA) and serve as one of their key consultants on employee buyouts, plant closings, and ESOPs. How and when did you first get into this field; and how did you develop this sort of close working relationship with one of the country's major labor unions?

Michael Locker: In the 1960s and 1970s, much of my political work involved researching U.S. corporations and their frequently irresponsible activities—and making the results known to groups attempting to change corporate behavior and priorities. Thus, in 1974, I helped create, with Steve Abrecht, the Corporate Data Exchange, a nonprofit organization that made information about corporations—public information that was difficult or expensive to access—available to community groups, to religious organizations, and on occasion to labor unions.

CW: What kinds of information?

ML: We researched a wide range of what today might be called social responsibility dimensions of corporations: labor relations and extent of unionization, job discrimination, pension fund investments, effects on the environment, concern for occupational health and safety. In addition, we used public records to identify the major investors in given companies, so that pressure to change those companies could be accurately and effectively targeted.

CW: At that time, in the middle 1970s, what sort of rapport or connection with the labor movement did you have?

ML: Quite minimal, to begin with. The labor movement, like any large social phenomenon, was (and is) a world of social relations. You could gain access to it, develop credibility, only if you already knew someone within it. But that began to soften as unions came to realize that they were faced with new and unusually severe threats: rashes of plant closings, unaccountable multinational corporations, rapidly declining memberships. Opportunities emerged; here was a gradual openness, a willingness to listen to new people with untraditional approaches.

Let me give some examples of this turnaround within the unions. One major event was the Amalgamated Clothing and Textile Workers Union's "corporate campaign" against J.P. Stevens, a nonunion textile plant in North Carolina. Under the leadership of Jack Sheinkman (now their president), the union went beyond its usual sorts of organizing drives. They researched the principal investors in this company (including banks in the Northeast), and successfully pressured them to reconsider their investments. To do this, they hired Ray Rogers, a *community*—not a labor— activist, to organize the entire campaign. But just as important, though less in the headlines, was a very different strategy: the work of people like Randy Barber and Jeremy Rifkin (set forth in their book, *The North Will Rise Again*) on labor-strengthening pension fund investments. Barber and Rifkin showed that unions controlled billions of dollars in investments that could be shifted to accomplish two aims: to provide secure retirement benefits for individual members and to penalize companies that run away or engage in other antiunion tactics.

CW: To oversimplify, was it the economic downturns of the 1970s that opened the door, and allowed you to find a place within the labor movement?

ML: To some extent. But beyond that we had to have something that worked well for unions, that offered them more than information. Unions accepted us, ultimately, because we could provide real services, real expertise. Pension fund research could shift needed investment into union-supporting companies and help open new businesses receptive to unionization; power-structure research could reveal "weak link" investors in unorganized corporations to whom community and public interest pressure could be successfully applied; examining the books of competing companies (e.g., Delta vs. Eastern) could aid union struggles by establishing that mismanagement, rather than labor costs, was undermining productivity and profitability.

What I'm saying is that crisis, by itself, was not enough. To develop mutual trust between consultants like myself and unions, to obtain the credibility we initially lacked, we had to speak to their real, immediate, and urgent needs, to deliver the kind of goods that often meant the difference between a local's surviving and not surviving. We were able to do that, for example, in the Stevens campaign and in the International Association of Machinists (IAM) dispute with Eastern Airlines. And then, having delivered in this tangible way, we could then begin to raise other kinds of issues within the labor movement.

CW: Would these include worker and community ownership of factories?

ML: Yes, it would, and today, those notions of ownership are gaining legitimacy within parts of the labor movement. They can now be seriously discussed, for example by the United Steel Workers.

CW: That's certainly a sharp contrast to the situation fifteen or even five years ago. In 1978, for example, unemployed poultry workers in Connecticut, victims of a plant closing, set up their own cooperatively run enterprise. For more than a year, they tried to get three different unions to organize this new

worker-owned plant, but none showed the slightest interest. What has brought about this shift in labor's attitude toward worker ownership?

ML: Let me concentrate on the steel industry and the USWA, both of which I know from firsthand experience. Here too, the effects of global recession, international competition, and corporate mismanagement (e.g., failure to modernize technology) have been devastating. This, coupled with the openness of steel-union leaders such as Lynn Williams [Canadian-born president of the Steel Workers International since 1983] and Jim Smith [economic assistant to the president for more than a decade], made room for new ideas and tactics. For example, early on, Williams established firm principles for concession bargaining: *something had to be gained for anything given up by the workers, and all employees had to share equally in sacrifices.* This sort of shift in collective bargaining is clearly congenial to workers getting shares of a company, becoming owners, in exchange for cuts in their hourly wages.

CW: **What role, if any, in all of this did the Weirton Steel buyout play? As I recall, it provoked a lot of controversy—despite its scope (roughly 7,000 workers owning 100 percent of the company's stock).**

ML: All in all, Weirton has been a positive influence. It is not a perfect model, but the plant has chalked up 25+ consecutive quarters of profit, repaid its original bank loan, and gone through a successful capital expansion program—all this in an industry that many had virtually given up on. Organizationally, from 1989 onward, all members of Weirton's board of directors have been elected by the workforce itself, and there seems to be a high level of commitment, on both sides, to labor-management cooperation in running day-to-day operations. Though it is not a USWA plant (having always had an independent union), there is a good deal of mutual respect and collaboration; many in the Steel Worker leadership have seen it as a useful model.

CW: **OK—we have the economic crisis in steel, we have strong, principled, and imaginative approaches to collective bargaining and concessions, and we have the generally positive experience of the Weirton buyout. Were these enough to transform union attitudes and policy—to make employee ownership an attractive and legitimate strategy for the USWA and its membership?**

ML: No. Along with the changes you've just summarized, something else was taking place at the grassroots level. We saw it in the IAM-Eastern campaign, and we saw it as well in numerous cases in the steel industry. Workers were beginning to realize that *mismanagement is rife*; in addition, they began rejecting the right of corporate owners and managers to close down irreplaceable or vital enterprises. Studies were done—I did some myself—that revealed the extent of corporate neglect and incompetence. *These studies made it clear to workers that they could do as well organizing production and running businesses as traditional management, with its distant corporate headquarters and dozens of supervisory layers.* At the USX mill in Duquesne, Pennsylvania, at Southworks in Chicago, in numerous other plants in the Steel Valley, the same political lesson was learned: These are *not* inherently unproductive or unprofitable enterprises, but they have been made so by corporate irresponsibility and management incompetence. And the same inference was drawn: *We—the workers and the communities who depend on these factories and can make them viable—should have the decisive say on whether they go down or stay up.* In short, workers in the steel industry began to view themselves in a very different light. No longer content to be passive victims of industrial policy, they began to insist on their ability and their right to shape the direction of that policy.

Take the example of Pittsburgh Forgings, a company made up of 330 workers and three plants that were once owned by AMPCO Pittsburgh Corporation. There are several noteworthy aspects of this buyout. First, it started from a threatened shutdown situation in which concessions were demanded by the previous owner. But instead of capitulating or walking out, we negotiated. We told AMPCO: "We'll accept a smaller concession, but only if you give us the right to purchase the plant after we conclude a feasibility study." This strong stand eventually led to a win-win situation: the owner got a decent selling price, and the workers saved their jobs in a plant they can make into a success. Second, once the feasibility study yielded positive results, a worker buyout committee was established that *immediately* began to restructure the company extensively: it brought in a new management team (including a former president of Bethlehem Forge), it developed a plan for labor-management cooperation, it designed a work contract and business plan. By getting an early jump in all of these areas, the committee enabled a genuinely new and hopeful process to emerge. Had they waited until *after* the buyout to start this restructuring, trust and enthusiasm might well have been damaged. Finally, top management in this new ESOP owns a *flexible* amount of stock. This flexibility arises from an incentive scheme: if Pittsburgh Forgings hits its production goals (these are set by a democratically elected board of directors), senior managers will receive 30 percent of the company's stock. In any case, however, the share held by hourly workers cannot fall below 70 percent.

CW: But how important, ultimately, are these changes? Are they more than window dressing at the margins of a still-entrenched corporate system devoid of social responsibility? Do you see anything long-lasting here?

ML: Tough question, but I think the trend connecting unions and employee ownership is here to stay. I base my (guarded) confidence on several considerations. First of all, look at the July 1988 issue of *Steelabor*, the official publication of the USWA. The lead story enthusiastically describes seven different USWA plants in which union members are "taking charge of their futures by creating ESOPs." This article reflects the strong support—of both union leadership and rank-and-file—for majority-owned, union-supported worker ownership. These seven plants, along with Weirton, have demonstrated to most steelworkers that, with careful evaluation and nurturing, ESOPs can work and can provide a positive response to the threat of shutdowns, runaways, and corporate acquisitions. In terms of projections, at the present rate of employee buyouts, *the steelworkers will very soon constitute the largest single group of stockholders in the U.S. steel industry!*

In addition, more and more mature industries, traditional kinds of manufacturing, are yielding low rates of return on investment. Rates as low as 2 or 3 percent are common not only in steel but in other metal industries, in mining, in many blue-collar sectors. So corporations and capital take flight, increasingly and in all likelihood permanently. This in turn opens up an expanded role for worker ownership, in our most basic industries, the ones on which many others depend.

CW: In short, employee ownership will shore up U.S. capitalism, and help it to limp through its current period of decline?

ML: Perhaps, but even if that is one result of the continued expansion of employee ownership into key industries, it may not be the most significant. When workers take over in cases where traditional management and ownership have failed or acted irresponsibly, and where they are backed up by their union on all levels, they begin a deep process of transformation. Their ideas about themselves, their abilities, their rights within the workplace—all of this and more are dramatically altered. A new process, a change in worker consciousness, may well emerge, and this may be what ultimately matures and endures.

CW: Perhaps so. But how would you answer those labor critics of ESOPs [such as Lance Compa and Pete Leki] who claim that worker-owners will become small-scale capitalists? That their consciousness will be cut off from its labor roots or from any broad-based solidarity, and become fixated on the profit margins of their own enterprises?

ML: Here's where the union can make all the difference. The traditional mission of unions is to develop precisely that kind of solidarity, to identify and meet common or industry-wide needs. Today's circumstances may require that this role be exercised in somewhat different ways, but at bottom the mission has not altered. Workers throughout the steel industry, for example, are all facing the same crisis: shutdowns and layoffs due to mismanagement, corporate flight, and foreign competition. They cannot combat these new conditions on their own, or even with the resources of a single factory; they need what only a strong, unified, and large-scale organization can provide.

CW: For example?

ML: For one thing, *expert, independent research*—to help evaluate the likely prospects of potential buyouts, to steer workers away from plants that lack markets, are undercapitalized, or cannot be modernized feasibly. For another, legal resources to make sense out of technical matters such as ESOP trusts, leveraged versus nonleveraged buyouts, relief from capital-gains taxes, and so forth.

Beyond all of this, unions must play a *fundamental educational role* at virtually every step. They set up employee-buyout committees, which not only transfer key skills and information to workers but negotiate with management on all aspects of pending buyouts. And in this way they begin the long process of aiding the workforce to challenge traditional management prerogatives and traditional employee roles—habits and attitudes that many generations have taken for granted.

In short, for ESOPs to have much of a chance to succeed, they will need union involvement and union resources. *With that involvement and those resources, individual workers within individual plants will not see themselves as isolated, but as one of many fragile enterprises connected and supported by the traditional vehicle of labor solidarity.*

CW: How will this connectedness get expressed, in concrete terms?

ML: One way would be through a willingness to "recycle success": some percentage of a plant's surplus earnings might be placed in a fund to support other takeovers, to organize efforts among the unorganized, to provide better pensions throughout the industry. Allocations to this fund would be separate from union dues, which would continue to cover the unions' currently standard services to members—strike benefits, lobbying, and the like.

CW: In short, then, you see a new role for unions: to build and sustain cooperation or collaboration among worker-owners in different plants and between them and other parts of the labor movement?

ML: Not a new *role*, but a new way of achieving the original aim of unions, that of meeting common needs, helping to overcome common obstacles, supporting common struggles. As we have already seen, unions like the USWA are already moving in this direction, making important and unique contributions to a democratic employee-ownership movement. At the same time, *they* are benefiting as well from their support of ESOPs: by retaining old members, by reaching out to unorganized workers, by developing new strengths to combat corporate adversaries and their attacks on working people.

Worker Ownership
A Better Alternative for the United Steel Workers*

Interview with Lynn Williams

Jack Quarter [editor, *Worker Co-ops*]: Why have there been so many worker buyouts in the U.S. steel industry?

Lynn Williams [President, United Steel Workers of America (USWA)]: The activities of our members involving buyouts in the steel industry fall into two areas—stock as recoupment of wage and benefit sacrifices, and stock in an enterprise in which the workers have purchased minority, majority, or full ownership.

The first type of case arose during the middle 1980s when the U.S. steel industry, among others, was being battered by imports and sustaining huge financial losses; this prompted the major integrated steel producers, and some smaller companies as well, to ask for our members' help. We undertook very careful analyses of these companies' financial records and, if the extent of the problems was confirmed, the workers agreed.

We insisted, however, that this help not be viewed merely as sacrifices in the form of straight wage and benefit reductions. Instead, we negotiated contracts under which sacrifices become investments. We reduced the companies' cash-flow problems by trading some of their current cash costs—wages and benefits—for deferred compensation in the form of stock ownership. Additionally, these contracts called for the major producers to join the union in a public information campaign to attack at least some of the root causes of the industry's problems—flawed trade policies that permitted, or even encouraged, much of the world's excess steel production capacity to be sold in the U.S. market.

The second area involves buyouts by employees through a qualified employee stock ownership plan (ESOP). Steelworkers now own (in whole or in part) over fifteen companies, including E.W. Bliss in Ohio, Republic Container in West

* From *Worker Co-ops*, Spring 1989.

Virginia, Republic Storage in Ohio, and McLouth Steel in Michigan. In some of these instances there was no choice but to form an ESOP or watch the companies go out of business because of their failing finances.

We also have been involved in acquiring ownership of going concerns. For example, Northwestern Steel and Wire in Sterling, Illinois, was not a distress sale; the company has been generally profitable. We will continue exploring other opportunities of this sort.

In another kind of case, the worker-owners of White Pine Copper in the Upper Peninsula of Michigan did such a good job that they attracted financial suitors and have decided to sell their company at a substantial profit. In this sale to a German mining company, which has its local headquarters in Toronto, the workers negotiated a most interesting codetermination arrangement. Half of the members of the board of directors, less one, are workers' representatives. They are not, therefore, the majority, but a special provision grants them veto power over the appointment of the general manager. A new ESOP also has been constructed that will provide the workers with 20 percent ownership.

One of the earliest buyouts in the steel industry involved a plant that was not organized by the USWA. At Weirton, West Virginia, National Steel decided that the plant required large capital investments and that the market for tin plate, its principal product, was likely to shrink in the future. If National had closed the plant at this time, it would have faced large pension and insurance costs. Instead, it sold the plant to the workers. So far the plant has been profitable. However, it recently sold some stock to the public to raise funds for the capital spending that it must do if it is to survive.

These buyouts in steel and other metal-working industries are also being abetted by a bottom-line, quick-profit mentality among the incumbent stockholders— stoked by Wall Street and the previous [Reagan] national administration. Having this mentality, they are dissatisfied with the rate of return on their investment and are willing to sell companies and reinvest the proceeds in other ventures.

JQ: Has there been a change in USWA philosophy from negotiating worker buyouts of companies with financial difficulties to negotiating buyouts of relatively healthy companies?

LW: I would not characterize our current efforts as coming from a change in philosophy as much as from a change in the world in which we live. Rather than sit idly by and permit our members to be savaged by leveraged buyouts and shutdowns, we decided that ESOPs were, in many situations, a much better alternative. Ultimately, though, the decision to participate in an ESOP—or not—is up to the members.

It is not a simple process nor a simple decision. There is an absolute need for a feasibility study to determine whether a market exists for the particular product, whether sufficient financing is available—in addition to that provided by the members—and whether the enterprise can operate profitably. We have such a situation in Pittsburgh, where the union has been involved in helping former steelworkers and community groups in the purchase of an idled LTV Steel Co. facility for the production of semifinished steel.

JQ: Is the USWA considering a total buyout of the U.S. steel industry?

LW: We are not planning to buy the entire industry, but during the industry's darkest hours it frequently looked like we were the only ones interested in maintaining a U.S. steel industry. Under current U.S. labor laws, the union itself, as an institution, cannot own a company and represent workers at other plants in that industry. The workers are the owners.

JQ: Does the USWA want to encourage the use of equity in pension funds to finance buyouts?

LW: In some industries, the pension plans covering organized workers are jointly administered by union and management representatives. Most of the plans covering USWA members, however, are administered by the individual company. We strongly favor worker input on investments of their pension plans. We support achievement of this objective either through negotiations or legislation. We have also actively supported the formation of a labor-based fund, somewhat on the model of the Solidarity Fund in Québec, to assist in employee buyouts.

Clearly, many pension plans are negotiated benefits and workers ought to have a say in their use. At the same time, we must assure the integrity of the plans and safeguard the funds so they are available for the workers upon their retirement. We do not want the future of workers' pension plans tied to the success or failure of their particular enterprise.

JQ: ESOPs have been criticized for not promoting control by workers over corporations they own, for failing to develop workplace democracy. Are those issues primary considerations in the USWA's buyouts agenda?

LW: The whole question of corporate governance is of great concern to us. In too many cases, ESOPs have been structured in such a way that employees do not have an effective say about how the company they own is to be run. This is an important concern not only for us and other unions, but for our friends in the business and academic communities, as well as in the legislature. We believe if companies are going to be afforded the various ESOP tax benefits, they should be required to structure ESOPs so as to assure meaningful participation by their worker-owners. We're not going to be party to any schemes that reward speculators at the expense of the workers.

JQ: What policy does the USWA advocate concerning worker representatives on the board of directors?

LW: We believe that if workers own the majority of the stock, they should have majority representation, directly or indirectly. One board member should be nominated by the international president in consultation with the district director, and one nominated by the bargaining unit. In addition, the union and the chief executive officer, who sits on the board, would nominate four mutually acceptable candidates.

At McLouth Steel, we have three direct representatives of the workers on the board: our District Director, Harry Lester; Douglas Fraser, the former President of the [United] Auto Workers; and Steven Hester, a Washington, DC, lawyer who has represented the USWA in a number of ESOPs. We believe both in the right of direct worker representation and, as well, the right of workers to have outside representation by qualified persons who will promote workers' interests.

JQ: Has the USWA considered the worker cooperative as a model for organizing buyouts?

LW: While there are some cooperatives in the United States, and we have given some thought to them as an alternative, we have not pursued that strategy because under current legislation they do not offer the advantages provided by ESOPs. Tax laws and individual-liability laws encourage the use of a corporation rather than a co-op, and make it more attractive for us to go in this direction. The circumstances are different in Canada. Our Canadian leadership is studying the situation, and as it develops cooperatives may well be a possible option for Canada.

JQ: Is the USWA encouraging the U.S. labor movement to be more supportive of worker buyouts?

LW: We are encouraging other unions to explore these possibilities, but each union must establish its own policy, and we would not presume to tell another international what its policy should be. More and more, however, unions and leaders of the U.S. labor movement are coming to see that developing a properly structured ESOP is not in conflict with their general responsibility to represent their members.

Inside a Union-Led
Worker-Owned Enterprise
Republic Storage Systems

Catherine Ivancic

With growing union sophistication in using employee ownership, a consensus has begun to emerge that the internal structure of firms purchased in union-initiated buyouts should reflect the existing structure of union-management relations (Olson 1982). Firms with a long history of unionization are likely to have well-articulated differences of opinion and interest between hourly employees and management. Models for democratic governance in such firms must take into account long-standing divisions but also enable both groups to work together toward common goals. Typically, such structures provide for a kind of coalition government characterized by representation for management and labor on the board of directors and co-determination on most issues. It is co-determination, American style.

Some examples of this basic model include Seymour Specialty Wire, Franklin Forge, Weirton Steel, and the long list of United Steel Workers of America (USWA) buyouts. While all differ in detail, Republic Storage Systems illustrates how the model works.

This company, in Canton, Ohio, was one of several profitable manufacturing divisions divested by LTV Steel in 1986. The profit-making locker manufacturer, sold to raise money for its cash-hungry parent conglomerate, was bought by the firm's employees through a leveraged ESOP. The employee group was committed to the buyout because it feared outside buyers would purchase the plant, ask for major wage concessions, milk the division for profit while neglecting to reinvest, or simply move production south. The hourly workforce, represented by the USWA, and the salaried workers formed an alliance with local management to purchase the firm in order to secure employment and retain a successful company in the Canton area. The international USWA played an important role in the buyout by locating competent consultants and picking up the costs for much of the legal and financial work. Because of the USWA's major role, the structure of corporate governance that developed incorporated the union-management relationship as a focal point for employee-owner participation. In addition to the traditional duties of a labor union, the two USWA locals at Republic Storage today are partners in decision making.

Governance procedures at Republic have been designed to allow employee input into company decisions at all levels. First, as owners they have the opportunity, every four years, to elect representatives to the board of directors. The salaried employees elect two representatives (thus far these have been top managers), and the membership of the union locals elects two as well. Within each group, voting is on a one-person, one-vote basis. These four elected board members then appoint three outsiders to the board; a local attorney and two local businessmen were chosen most recently. The board makes decisions on broad company policy, major investments, and acquisitions. Proposed board decisions are often circulated among employee-owners for discussion before the final decision. For example, employees were consulted in a mass meeting during May 1987 when the board voted to buy an office-mezzanine division of Rite Hite Company in Milwaukee. Though it is not required by corporate bylaws, board members feel such consultation is a necessary part of operations in an employee-owned company.

Second, an effort has been made to develop employee-owner participation in other levels of corporate decision making through a series of joint committees. Two of these—the Public Relations Committee and the Directive Committee—date to the creation of the new firm. The former is made up of equal numbers of salaried and hourly workers who deal with communications inside and outside the plant. The latter committee, composed of union officials and top management, makes policy on day-to-day operations of the firm and sets general personnel guidelines. Temporary members are added when issues related to their departments are discussed. The system does not function without friction, and there has been extensive discussion about whether Directive Committee members should be union representatives or be directly elected by employees. The 1989 contract established shop committees in all portions of the plant to assume tasks decentralized from above and to assure employee input into shop decisions.

For the unionized employees, there is a third potential channel for participation: union elections and meetings. At regular union meetings, there is an opportunity to discuss not only such traditional issues as wages, hours, and working conditions but also questions about investments, company sales, and operations.

As in many unionized employee buyouts where labor and management had previously been adversaries, Republic's first year was a honeymoon. Grievances fell 75 percent, attitudes improved, and the company picked up the cost of the union local's office. Later, however, consistent with other buyouts of this type, unions and management have had difficulty transforming themselves from adversaries into cooperators. Union strength, after all, has in the past been defined by the ability to confront management, not cooperate with it. The old adversarial relationship dies hard, even when the employees own the business. Despite problems in working together—and despite higher wage and benefit rates than its competitors—Republic Storage Systems has continued to be a profitable firm under employee ownership. The structure of governance, which both labor and management regard as imperfect, may creak, but it does work.

Short Takes

Until recently, union leaders typically viewed worker ownership with open suspicion if not downright hostility. Today, however, this situation has dramatically changed—though by no means completely. The **AFL-CIO** has established the **Employee Partnership Fund** to assist in financing worker-owned, union-supported enterprises, and several national and international unions have begun to help their locals build worker-owned enterprises.

In Alabama, a notoriously antiunion state, the International Union of Brick Layers and Allied Crafts helped establish Jefferson Masonry, Inc. (JMI), the first contemporary union-sponsored worker-owned cooperative in this country.

The United Steel Workers of America (USWA) has lent technical and legal assistance to more than twenty worker buyouts in the U.S. steel industry, including **McLouth Steel** in Trenton, Michigan; **Republic Container** in Nitro, West Virginia; **Copper Range** in White Pine, Michigan; **Chester Roofing Products** in Chester, West Virginia; **Oremet Titanium** in Albany, Oregon; **Northwestern Steel and Wire** in Sterling, Illinois; **Bliss-Salem** in Salem, Ohio; **Pittsburgh Forgings** in Coraopolis, Pennsylvania; and **Republic Storage Systems** in Canton, Ohio. (Good accounts of many of these can be found in the February and July 1988 issues of the official USWA publication, *Steelabor*.) In virtually all of these, plant workers own a majority of the stock, elect representatives to the board of directors, and participate in labor-management teams that help decide how work is organized.

According to *Steelabor*, these steelworker buyouts "reflect a new surge toward worker power in the ESOP movement." Moreover, as Warner Woodworth points out in the spring 1989 issue of *Worker Co-op*, the USWA is now entertaining "the possibility of becoming more proactive," for example, by bargaining in contract talks "for board seats and/or stock in the largest dozen steel companies" and by "getting in on the purchase of healthy steel firms."

Also in the steel industry, the more than seven thousand members of the **Independent Steel Union** own about 75 percent of Weirton Steel, a billion-dollar business and the seventh-largest steel firm in the United States. Since the worker buyout some seven years ago, productivity has increased substantially and profits-per-ton have outdistanced those of its six top rivals (*Business Week*, 23 January 1989, pp. 22-23).

The **Amalgamated Clothing and Textile Workers Union** not only provided critical financial and technical support for the Colt buyout in Tyler, Texas, but has recently assisted other worker buyouts in Toledo, Ohio, and Biddeford, Maine. Together these two buyouts saved the jobs of almost 400 workers.

Over the past ten years, several locals of the **United Auto Workers (UAW)** have begun worker-owned enterprises, including the very successful **Seymour Specialty Wire**. Not all of these have survived: two that did not are Hyatt-Clark Industries of Hyatt, New Jersey, and Atlas Chain of West Pittson, Pennsylvania. Two UAW plants that appear to be doing well are **Plymouth Locomotive**, in Plymouth, Ohio, which in its first two years of employee ownership expanded from 93 to 115 workers and provided them with the highest total compensation they ever earned from the company, and **Franklin Forge** in West Branch, Michigan, a worker-owned enterprise that began in 1984 with 20 members and annual sales of $3 million and by 1988 had more than 100 employees and sales of more than $8.5 million.

In Cleveland, Ohio, the **United Textile Workers** helped its **North American Rayon** local acquire full ownership of that ailing company in Elizabethtown, Tennessee, and in less than two years turn it into a profitable enterprise with thirteen hundred employee-owners; **Dimco-Gray**, in Centerville, Ohio, unionized by the **International Union of Electrical Workers**, has been in the black since it converted to employee-ownership in 1986. **Leslie Paper**, a **Teamster**-organized shop in Minneapolis, converted to full employee ownership in 1976, redescribing all its employees as "partners"; since that time, it has experienced an 18 percent growth in annual sales and a 504 percent increase in employee productivity. The **United Food and Commercial Workers** played a major role in the **O&O Supermarket** takeovers in the Philadelphia area, as well as in the ESOP that provides 100% employee ownership of the **Cost Cutter Stores** in Bellingham, Washington. Though the O&O story is not entirely one of long-lasting success, Cost Cutters has reduced turnover and doubled its stock price and number of stores in the decade since they established their ESOP.

The members of two **International Association of Machinists** locals have taken over their companies through ESOP arrangements; these are **Clay Equipment**, in Cedar Falls, Iowa, and **North Coast Brass and Copper** (formerly a division of Standard Oil of Ohio).

In the section that follows, Deborah Groban Olson, of Groban Olson Associates, describes a model ESOP for unions that was used in the transformation of Chase Brass into the worker-owned North Coast Brass and Copper Company.

The Employee Buyout of Chase Brass

On 29 January 1988, the 535 employees of the Chase Brass Sheet Division of Standard Oil of Ohio (Sohio) bought their company and renamed it North Coast Brass and Copper. Without the buyout, the company probably would have been closed; with it, not only were jobs saved but a new structure was established giving employees and their union more immediate control over corporate-governance issues than in any buyout yet of this size. The Chase buyout is indicative of the changing way in which employee buyouts are being handled. Unions, management, banks, and consultants have become increasingly sensitive to the fact that when employees are buying their jobs, and taking concessions to do so, they want more effective control of their new company.

The employees at Chase Brass got a good deal out of a bad situation because their leadership was vigilant and skeptical, insisted throughout on being treated as the major investor, and took on the responsibility of directing the deal and the new company.

Wage and benefit concessions were needed to make the deal feasible. In return, the unions insisted on giving employees one vote per person on all stockholder issues and having elected representatives on the board of directors and the ESOP administrative committee. Management and labor also committed themselves to creating participation programs at the shopfloor level.

One of the more unusual aspects of the deal was the way employee ownership was written into the structure of the company. In most ESOP companies, employee rights exist solely in the ESOP documents, and not in the basic corporate structure itself (in the bylaws, for instance). Generally, the board of directors has the authority to terminate the ESOP, subject to various legal constraints. Because ESOP law changes, it is always possible that the board will decide that an ESOP is no longer practical or desirable and terminate the plan or sell to someone else. To assure that North Coast remains employee owned, employee ownership was written into the basic corporate structure itself.

In addition, the buyout agreement allocated stock based on pay (as in most ESOPs), provided thirty days' notice to the union of all nonbudgeted expenditures over $1 million, required 100 percent vesting after two years of service with North Coast or prior service with Chase, and set up a profit-sharing plan. Four union representatives will serve on the initial board, with two representatives from management and three outsiders chosen jointly by labor and management. After 1990, vacant outside board seats have been filled by a majority vote of remaining board members. The ESOP committee has elected representatives from each union and from management, an at-large representative, and a representative from the International Association of Machinists district.

7

How Far Have We Come?
Assessing Worker Ownership

Now that we have looked in some detail at the worker-ownership movement in the United States, it is time to step back and begin to assess its impact and prospects. Because the movement is still young and disparate, it is difficult to describe or analyze systematically. Instead, we offer three critical approaches that, together, provide a fair sense of lessons and achievements of this movement.

We turn first to the fast-proliferating and high-profile employee stock ownership plans (ESOPs). Although they are far from pure examples of worker ownership and control, ESOPs are by far the most prevalent form of worker ownership, affecting more than ten million employees across the country. The question we ask is: Are ESOPs more hype than hope? Corey Rosen explores their impact with some optimism. Joseph Blasi offers a more critical appraisal, arguing that ESOPs are still far from being examples of true worker democracy. And Kevin McQueen suggests how ESOPs could be used as a tool by persons involved in community economic development rather than only by the corporate-finance community.

Next, we look at a concrete example of one technical assistance organization's attempts to develop a network of worker owned and operated firms at half a dozen sites in the Philadelphia area. Andrew Lamas describes PACE of Philadelphia, while Frank Lindenfeld discusses the O & O supermarkets PACE helped to launch. Although most of the O&O supermarkets failed, there is much to be learned from the experience—chiefly the crucial importance of adequate financing and well-trained management.

Finally, our own concluding article examines the current worker-ownership movement in the light both of history and of several commonly raised political objections to workplace democracy. While there are many challenges still to overcome, the current worker-ownership movement seems to have transcended many of the limitations that undercut earlier attempts at economic democracy. In chapter 8, we suggest a number of strategies to build on the current movement's strengths, to overcome its deficiencies, and to take further steps toward widespread economic democracy in the United States.

ESOPs
Hype or Hope?

Corey Rosen

There are about ten thousand employee stock ownership plans (ESOPs) in the United States with approximately ten million employees. No one knows precisely how many other employees own all or part of their companies through cooperatives, profit-sharing plans, direct-stock-purchase plans, and other arrangements, but probably at least another few million do. Such firms as Avis, HealthTrust, Parsons Engineering, Weirton Steel, and Science Applications are among the many major firms that are principally or entirely employee owned. For readers of this book, of course, the real question is whether the spread of employee ownership has changed work in positive and democratic ways. Employee ownership has not lived up to everyone's expectations and hopes, but it has changed the economic landscape of the United States in important ways. And, as by far the most prevalent form of employee ownership, ESOPs have been central to these changes.

ESOPs

An ESOP is a kind of employee-benefit plan in which a company sets up a trust to invest in its own stock. The company contributes stock to the trust outright, contributes cash to the trust to enable it to borrow money, or has the trust borrow money with the stock and the company's guarantee as collateral. In almost every case, the employees pay nothing for the stock the trust acquires; it is contributed with tax-deductible corporate dollars. If the trust borrows money, the company repays the loan, deducting from its own tax liabilities the principal and interest it repays. Because lenders can also deduct from their tax liabilities one-half of the interest income they receive on such loans, ESOPs usually receive lower loan rates.

However an ESOP acquires stock, the shares are allocated to participating employees, generally those full-time workers with a year or more of service. Union employees usually need to bargain over being included in the plan. Sometimes the employer, the union, or both, prefer *not* to have the union employees participate. In any case, participating employees build up a gradually increasing right to their allocation, although they do not receive their stock until they leave the company, at which time they can sell it back to the ESOP at an appraised value or sell it on the market if the company is public.

While they are still working, participating employees *do* get to vote their shares, at least on some issues. In private firms, they must be allowed to vote their shares at least on major issues, such as closing or relocating, but not necessarily on elections to the board. In public companies, they are allowed to vote on all issues.

ESOPs are almost always set up by profitable, ongoing firms, although in about 2 percent of the cases they have been used to rescue troubled companies. Most commonly, ESOPs are used to buy the stock of a principal owner of a privately held company, often when the owner wants to retire. They are also set up to provide a new employee-benefit plan, to divest a profitable subsidiary, or to borrow money to buy back shares on the public market. In about 4 percent of the cases, employees have taken concessions in association with an ESOP, and in about 8 percent, the ESOP replaced a pension plan. About one-third of the time, an ESOP replaced a profit-sharing plan, although the ESOP usually has a higher funding level. Despite the publicity, ESOPs are rarely used to prevent hostile takeovers or to make companies private.

ESOPs and Economic Equity

When the ESOP legislation was passed, one of its principal goals was very clearly to broaden the distribution of the ownership of wealth. Currently, about 1 percent of the population owns 50 percent of the privately held stock, and much of the public stock is controlled by a handful of investors and investment companies. For example, at one point, the five partners in the investment banking firm of Kohlberg, Kravis, Roberts owned an estimated $4 billion in equity, or $800 million *each*. Had ESOPs been used to fund their acquisition of companies, forty thousand employees could have had $100,000 each.

In a 1985 study, we found that in a typical ESOP an employee making the median wage of $18,300 would accumulate $31,000 in stock over just ten years. In many cases, employees in well-established plans have accumulated considerably more than this, often well into six figures. Compare this to the 1983 median net financial assets (other than home equity) of a family at retirement of just $11,000.

Although ESOPs have provided many employees with substantial capital stakes, they have barely scratched the surface of the inequitable distribution of wealth overall. With $20 billion in assets, ESOPs still account for only about 5 percent of the total asset value of the wealthiest four hundred U.S. families. While this is a good start, the United States still desperately needs many more ESOPs and other programs to create a more equitable economy.

ESOPs and Corporate Performance

Another critical issue is whether ESOPs contribute to corporate performance. Previous studies suggest that, in and of themselves, ESOPs make a small positive impact on performance; that participation programs alone do not yield consistent, measurable improvements of performance; but that when ESOPs and job-level participation programs are combined, there is significant improvement in growth and productivity. The combination of ownership and participation seems crucial. Ownership provides employees with a powerful financial reward; participation provides a chance to translate that incentive into the ideas and processes that can make an organization more effective.

ESOPs and Corporate Control

For many, the litmus test for ESOPs is whether they allow employees to control their companies. The controversy surrounding this, however, may be more form than substance. In one survey of twenty-seven hundred employees in thirty-five ESOP firms nationwide, the National Center for Employee Ownership found that there was no correlation between voting rights or employee board representation and employee job satisfaction, commitment to the company, or attitudes toward ownership. In a follow-up study, the Center found that having at least some board members elected by employees also had no effect, one way or another, on corporate performance. Finally, in a study of 16 companies in which employees elect a majority of the board, the Center found no discernible impact on the nature of the boards' decisions or the process by which they made them. In short, these studies suggest that corporate control is much less of an issue, at least in impact, than its proponents believe and its opponents fear.

This does not mean democracy in the workplace is a bad idea, or that if employees became more accustomed to it they might not like it more, or that it cannot be justified on ethical rather than pragmatic grounds. It may also be that blending corporate control and extensive employee participation might have more of an effect than either does alone. We just do not have the data to judge. Until we have more experience with combined employee control and participation, we can only say that control alone accomplishes little in pragmatic terms, while participation, in itself, does.

Regardless of how an ESOP company is controlled, the ESOP structure does help to prevent one of the problems employee-owned companies that are not ESOPs faced in the past: owners selling control to outsiders. By law, ESOPs have a right of first refusal on shares of departing employees and can thus ensure that an employee-owned company remains employee owned. Of course, if the employees own only part of the company through the ESOP, the company could still be bought or sold—and the stockholding employees could even vote for a sale—but so far ESOP firms have retained their ESOPs even when sold.

In many cases, ESOPs do provide for more corporate democracy. While 85 percent of private ESOP firms do not provide full voting rights to their members, and while such employees seldom vote in concert, about 40 percent of the fifteen hundred or so majority-owned ESOPs provide full voting rights. As the percentage of majority ESOPs increases, the percentage offering at least the chance for employee control should increase as well. (There are more and more majority firms because ESOPs tend to accumulate stock over time, and most ESOPs are still relatively new.)

Despite this success, there is still a long way to go. Even where employees do have legal access to control, they rarely choose to exercise it, probably because they see no reason to get involved when the company is doing well, as most of these are. Many business owners, understandably, are reluctant to give up control. Often, people think of all companies as they think of General Motors—large, public firms with active boards. But the vast majority of firms are private. The people who have built them are very skittish, not only about giving up beneficial ownership but about giving up control. Still, ESOPs are slowly and steadily becoming more than tools of corporate finance. They are beginning to change the organization of work.

Future Trends

Three significant changes seem to be occurring in the employee-ownership field. First, ESOPs are becoming more common in very large transactions. More large companies now see ESOPs as a valid alternative—although most, in the end, still resist the notion of employees as owners. All the major banks and most major investment-banking houses now have an ESOP specialty and are actively pushing the idea. These lenders have not gotten religion; instead, they see their own interests as better protected by ESOPs, both because of the tax benefits and because ESOP companies often perform better.

Second, a growing, if still minority, percentage of ESOP companies are starting employee participation programs. While only about 25 percent of the firms have any kind of program, the message is spreading that ownership and participation need to go hand in hand. The striking success of several well-publicized businesses following this approach (such as Quad Graphics, Weirton, Avis, and W.L. Gore Associates) has had a major influence on this trend.

Finally, a substantial employee-ownership infrastructure is being created. The original handful of technical assistance organizations has been bolstered by a number of state-run organizations, and more are in the works. The result should be both more and better employee ownership.

Are ESOPs Part of the Problem?

Interview with Joseph Blasi

Changing Work: In *Taking Stock*, coauthored with Michael Quarrey and Corey Rosen, you stated that most ESOPs are not democratic, though many of them are. But then you go on to claim that ESOPs are justified by having brought about a significant dispersal of ownership and by providing models of workplace democracy. What data convinced you that this earlier view should be modified? Is that view entirely consistent with your present, much more critical position?

Joseph Blasi: No, the two views are not consistent. When I helped write the earlier book, I did not have all the data in front of me, and I was responding to the newness of employee ownership and concentrating on the happier cases. What changed my mind were several findings: first, that even when ESOPs broadened the distribution of wealth within particular firms their overall impact—on our entire economy and its distribution of resources—was minimal; and second, that within individual ESOP companies, ownership was being extended mainly to people who already had greater wealth and not to those who needed it most. Beyond this, in examining the entire employee-ownership sector, it became clear to me that the laws that set it in motion are prejudiced against workplace democracy. The law is not neutral; it is written to keep ownership separate from management. And this legal prejudice, of course, severely affects the people who form ESOPs and the relations among them. Finally, there are the lessons of such defunct ESOPs as Blue Bell Jeans, which started out as employee owned and with much acclaim, but at which the employee-ownership plans were rather quickly scrapped. It seems that adopting an ESOP is of little consequence by itself: without labor-management cooperation, enhanced worker involvement, and short-term profit sharing—in short, without genuine workplace democracy— employee ownership cannot even safeguard its own perpetuation.

CW: You cite Weirton Steel as a positive example of the potential benefits of employee ownership, but other observers, such as Staughton Lynd, are more critical. Any comments?

JB: Initially, I was sympathetic to criticisms of the Weirton takeover: at the outset, workers did not have full pass-through voting rights, nor did they elect a majority of the board. Nonetheless, they've achieved something very positive. The Weirton union and top management are committed to extending employee ownership and dedicated to creating common ways of problem solving at every level. As a result, the board's power and scope have encouraged rather than discouraged labor-management cooperation; the usual antiworker attitudes and policies have not been much in evidence. And remember, Weirton's board will soon be controlled by its workforce. Keep in mind that most closely held companies like Weirton hardly ever take shareholder votes except for such matters as who will be on their board of directors. Legally speaking, Weirton, like other similar ESOPs, must pass through voting rights to employees on certain major corporate issues, such as mergers or substantial sale of assets. Additionally, Weirton was set up so that the workers, on a one-worker, one-vote basis, decide certain additional significant issues, such as any decision to eliminate the ESOP itself. But the key issue is that Weirton's managers and employees invested lots of time and money in worker-participation programs that have helped to make up for their earlier limitations.

CW: Do you see employee ownership and ESOPs as part of a strategy for making the U.S. economy more democratic along the lines of Mondragon?

JB: Yes, there is a definite potential for transformation, but it cannot depend on ESOPs alone. For even if more and more companies become 100 percent employee owned, this will change virtually nothing if we do not also find ways to attack what can be called our cultural passivity. There are rigid attitudes in our workplaces: management's condescension toward labor and labor's own refusal to exercise initiative. To alter these, ESOPs (even democratic ones) must be combined with three other conditions: extensive labor-management cooperation, short-term profit sharing, and shopfloor reorganization so that work itself is not alienating and draws on our hearts and heads as well as our hands. In short, any successful strategy for creating a new and democratic economy must provide workers with many diverse ways of shaping their work and the companies they work in.

Beyond this, a broad political movement is needed. The notion that major changes can be brought about by consultants, academics, good models, and media attention is a delusion. Innovations, however desirable, do not spread by themselves. We need to redirect congressional economic policy, obtain new legislation favoring labor-management cooperation, and create new corporate-finance, labor, and tax law. This cannot be done by individual worker-owned enterprises, nor can it be achieved by a few political leaders coming out in support of employee ownership. It will take many years of organization and struggle and the formation of groups that press for economic democracy at the national level while continuing to nurture local initiatives.

CW: Can you shed any light on the question of why some ESOPs have failed, despite what appeared to be good internal structure and adequate finances?

JB: My sense is that failed ESOPs, such as Hyatt-Clark, or Atlas Chain, are either poorly financed (Atlas), or lack any real commitment to labor-management cooperation (Hyatt-Clark). When the four conditions I have advanced are fulfilled, and there is responsible financial planning, democratic ESOPs and cooperatives are more than competitive with their nondemocratic rivals.

ESOPs and Local Control of Business*

Kevin McQueen

Recently, the president of a successful community development corporation (CDC) located in the Midwest took me on a tour of projects completed by his organization. In addition to a number of commercial and residential real estate development efforts, I also visited several thriving small businesses in which the CDC has made equity investments. These companies have been profitable, and provide employment opportunities for neighborhood residents. What is more, the dividends they return make a healthy contribution to the CDC's annual revenues.

Now, having already met the original objectives of making these investments—preserving jobs in the community—this CDC is considering selling the companies to recover its equity. Naturally, the organization's president is wondering how to best maintain the interests of the neighborhood once the businesses are sold.

Many CDCs face a similar challenge. According to a survey conducted by the National Congress for Community Economic Development, more than 60 percent of the community-based development organizations involved in commercial business development serve as owner-operators. In all, there are some 427 separate enterprises directly owned or operated by CDCs. And, during the last five years, these CDC-directed businesses have created more than twenty-seven thousand permanent positions and retained another fifteen thousand jobs.

From a straight bottom-line perspective, selling these assets may make very good sense. But CDCs are seldom animated solely by such considerations. Thus the dilemma: How can the benefits to the community created through the ownership of businesses be preserved once the company is sold? One answer may be found in

* From *Cooperative Enterprises*, Summer 1989.

the application of employee stock ownership plans (ESOPs) or other forms of employee ownership—such as worker cooperatives.

ESOPs are employee-benefit plans that provide workers with capital ownership of their companies. Since 1974, ESOPs have received favorable legislation from the U.S. Congress. Worker cooperatives have also received favorable treatment under the federal tax code. As a result, the costs of financing the conversion of a CDC-owned asset to employee control is significantly reduced.

The ESOP/worker-cooperative approach fits in well with the overall objectives of community economic development. For starters, employee ownership makes capitalists of the very people whom CDCs hoped to serve by operating these businesses in the first place.

Then, too, employee ownership helps to preserve neighborhood jobs that might otherwise be lost if the CDC sells the company to an unrelated party. In addition, since ESOPs typically gain full control over a company in phases, a CDC can maintain an ownership stake in the asset it is selling for several years after the initial stock sale to employees.

Finally, the employee-owners who reside in a given community also spend their earnings for housing and shopping in the area, which further contributes to the overall economic health of a neighborhood.

Of course, the employee-ownership door swings both ways. Just as the use of ESOPs or worker cooperatives can be an effective means for CDCs to exit from companies that they own, this development strategy can be used to acquire existing businesses.

Since CDCs usually have a relationship with companies located in their area, these organizations are well situated to take advantage of information about retiring owners, exiting stockholders, or corporations spinning off subsidiaries, and they can spearhead efforts to structure employee buyouts through ESOPs or worker cooperatives. In fact, many CDCs have decided that acquiring existing business—rather than risking the uncertainties of start-up ventures—is the most viable approach to economic development.

Naturally, the conversion of an existing company to one owned totally or in part by an ESOP is a complex transaction. But complexity is something that all of us in community development deal with every day. We are used to harvesting long-term gains from short-term difficulties. Creating employee-ownership opportunities is just one more step along the road our constituencies want to travel.

PACE of Philadelphia
The Enduring Legacy of Franklin and the Striking Carpenters

Andrew T. Lamas

Prologue

In the two hundred years between the first reading of the Declaration of Independence and the founding of PACE of Philadelphia, Inc., in 1976, Philadelphia's rich cooperative history has been shaped by forces of *social reform* and *labor struggle*. Philadelphia's most honored citizen and social innovator, Benjamin Franklin, helped to found several cooperative societies, including a cooperative fire insurance company that still exists today (Winegrad, 1990, p. 39). During the same era, the Journeymen Carpenters of the City and Liberties of Philadelphia initiated the drive for the 10-hour day and additional pay for overtime. In May 1791, these carpenters not only organized the first recorded strike of U.S. labor in the building trades but also initiated the new nation's first working-class cooperative (Bureau of Labor Statistics, 1976, p. 78; Office of the Historian, 1977, p. 19).

Franklin modeled the process of cooperative development as *social reform*. He found in cooperatives a practical means for advancing useful knowledge, promoting socially beneficial production, and enhancing the democratic culture. The striking carpenters modeled the process of cooperative development as *labor's struggle against capital*. While partnerships among skilled artisans were not uncommon in the late eighteenth and early nineteenth centuries, the worker-owned firm was often viewed as an economic weapon—or a safety net—to be used on a short-term, temporary basis during strikes and lockouts.

In the nineteenth century, local and national labor organizations emerged in Philadelphia. Many of them advocated not only continuing struggle against the capitalists, but also the formation of worker cooperatives. For example, during the 1870s and 1880s, the Knights of Labor called for an 8-hour day, multiracial unionism, equal pay for equal work by women, health and safety regulations, the abolition of contract, convict, and child labor, the public ownership of utilities, and the establishment of cooperatives (Laurie, 1989, pp. 150-51; Bureau of Labor Statistics, 1976, pp. 10-11). Worker-owned businesses, consumer-owned enterprises, popularly controlled credit unions, and even national federations of community-based cooperatives were envisioned as permanent alternatives to conventional businesses and other capitalist institutions.

One hundred years later, the traditions of social reform and labor struggle still inform cooperative experimentation. As an advocate of workplace democracy, PACE (sometimes unofficially called the Philadelphia Association for Cooperative Enterprise) joined with an innovative local union to respond to the A&P's multistore shutdown, which threatened to idle 2,000 workers. The results included the establishment of the employee owned and operated O&O Supermarkets, another bright moment in cooperative history.

For many observers, the history of PACE *is* the story of the O&O Supermarkets. PACE's organizational history may be viewed as a drama in three acts—before, during, and after the O&Os.

Act One

PACE's initial phase of operation, prior to the establishment of the O&O Supermarkets, extended from 1976-1981. During these five years, PACE developed slowly, rolling a number of foundation stones into place.

Originally, the group was a local chapter of a short-lived national organization, the Federation for Economic Democracy. Incorporated in 1976 as a Pennsylvania non-profit organization, with an all-volunteer board of directors and a budget of less than $5,000, it undertook research and writing projects on cooperatives, published a newsletter, presented public lectures and educational workshops, talked about Mondragon to anyone who would listen, and established relations with other new cooperative support groups in Boston and elsewhere.[1]

Gradually, PACE developed its internal leadership, established a coherent identity, and focused its mission. By 1981, when the organization changed to its current name of PACE of Philadelphia, Inc., it had become recognized as a technical assistance provider to existing and emerging employee-owned businesses, with a focus on unionized, private sector industries. At this time, none of the states had yet initiated employee-ownership policies or related public programs, and most unions and community-based organizations were unfamiliar with, skeptical of, or hostile to the worker-ownership concept. Despite its small size (the budget had grown to only $30,000 by 1981),[2] PACE was successful in attracting external professional resources and limited institutional support for local cooperative development projects.[3] Each of these relationships, particularly the one formed with the United Food & Commercial Workers Local 1357 (UFCW) in Philadelphia, proved crucial for PACE's later growth and accomplishments.

Act Two

The segue into PACE's "golden age" could not have been more clearly identifiable or more dramatic. The fateful month was March of 1982. The two transition events that took place that month were a PACE-sponsored conference on workplace democracy (Lamas 1983) and A&P's closing of its entire Philadelphia division of supermarkets.[4]

As a result of pre-conference publicity, Jay Guben, an advisor to Wendell Young, president of the UFCW Local 1357, had approached PACE in the late autumn of 1981 to ask for help in determining the practicality of establishing employee-owned wine and liquor outlets throughout Pennsylvania, as a job-saving strategy for union employees in the event that the commonwealth privatized its retail monopoly in this industry. This nascent working relationship soon blossomed when the union learned that a major shutdown of A&P Supermarkets was imminent.

The union began to plan its response well before the official notice of closing in February 1982. Its widely publicized announcement that it intended to arrange a worker buyout of more than twenty affected supermarkets set the stage for eventual negotiations with A&P. Meanwhile, the union's consulting team was engaged in a rapidly paced, multifaceted, enterprise-development process, including feasibility studies, business plans, and loan packages, while PACE launched a cooperative-education program for more than 700 of the affected workers.

All of this activity was undertaken on the assumption that an unprecedented agreement would be reached with A&P. By May, just such a landmark contract was negotiated. The contract specified that A&P would reopen most of its stores as the SuperFresh division, while allowing workers to buy out two of the markets. Relieved and exhilarated, the UFCW and PACE were also overwhelmed by having to perform unfamiliar, complicated roles in the public eye. The opportunity to create a network of employee-owned supermarkets had finally and suddenly arrived—and *everyone* knew it.

While the union concentrated on protecting its workers in the SuperFresh stores, PACE focused on a quick development of the O&O markets. To help the workers make the transition to the new cooperative structure, PACE facilitated a highly participatory business creation and education process.[5] The prospective O&O worker-owners met as often as four nights a week for several months to learn the principles and techniques of workplace cooperation and enterprise management and to teach each other about various supermarket operations. With technical assistance, they hired managers and crafted the details of their production and governance systems. In October and November 1982, respectively, the Roslyn and Parkwood Manor O&O Supermarkets opened, amidst national network news coverage.

With the first two O&Os securely established, and a third on the way, PACE began to attract more substantial financial resources from foundations and grant-making religious agencies. Its fee-for-service income also increased. As its budget grew, PACE was able to expand its staff and diversify its program. At its peak, PACE (and its subsidiaries and affiliates, including a revolving loan fund and a law office) had a budget of more than $500,000, offices in Philadelphia and Pittsburgh, and twelve staff who provided professional services for employee-ownership efforts and community economic development projects in five technical areas:[6]

- enterprise feasibility studies and economic development planning services;
- organizational structure analysis and comprehensive legal counsel;
- business planning, deal structuring, and loan packaging;
- worker, union, and management education, entrepreneurial development, workplace participation and productivity training, and organizational design and development; and,
- policy formulation and legislative innovations concerning employee ownership, community development, and related areas.

With the development of the O&Os, PACE transformed itself from a regional provider of technical assistance for unassociated cooperative firms into a developer of an integrated network of employee-owned, food-related enterprises. Although it was riding high, its fate was inextricably linked to that of the O&O Supermarkets.

Act Three

By late 1986, there were five O&O Supermarkets with cumulative gross sales of $30 million (although with *very* narrow margins) and a sixth store on the horizon. While these supermarkets had their strengths and competitive advantages, each also had special problems which threatened to erode their cooperative structure and business stability. Accordingly, PACE attempted a variety of interventions to stimulate growth, control costs, and promote democratic governance. In some instances, its technical assistance and shadow management contributed to the resolution of various financial, operational, and personnel problems and prolonged the existence of the stores—but PACE's efforts were largely to no avail. One by one, from 1987 to 1989, five of the six O&O Supermarkets failed.

The reasons for these failures varied with the internal circumstances of the particular O&Os (Lindenfeld 1990). Some were inadequately capitalized or structured on the basis of overly optimistic revenue projections. Others experienced poor management and operational deficiencies in various departments. At one O&O, financial success led to factional disputes that contributed to the firm's ultimate demise. At another, the failure of various stakeholders (including a local community organization, the worker-owners, and various providers of technical assistance and finance capital) to agree on and accept the limits of their respective roles and responsibilities rapidly paralyzed the supermarket's management and governance systems.

Meanwhile, significant technological changes, major corporate reorganizations, and other developments in the supermarket industry generated increasingly unfavorable conditions for independent retailers across the nation. In Philadelphia, keen competition by new and remodeled chain stores decreased each O&O's margin for error while intensifying the struggle to gain and maintain market share. Indeed, attempting to rescue the O&Os proved even more financially unprofitable and time consuming than establishing them. The O&O agenda gradually became less and less a wellspring of inspiration and more and more a pit of emotional distress.

Topping it all off, there was a destructive lawsuit, in which PACE was a primary defendant, following the bankruptcy of the Strawberry Mansion O&O Supermarket.[7] Although the dispute was eventually settled out of court, the lawsuit and related matters cast a pall over PACE's every move for the balance of the decade and inflicted nearly fatal organizational damage.

At different points, from mid-1985 through 1987, various staff members began to lose confidence in the O&O development strategy. At the same time, as the third, fourth, and fifth supermarkets failed to reach their projected sales, PACE's income from its fee-for-service arrangements with the O&Os declined.[8] The inevitable personnel reductions which followed the budget reductions only decreased staff morale as each staff member responded intensely and personally to the loss of what had been built within and with the help of PACE. Most, if not all, experienced or are still visited by powerful emotions of denial, grief, anger, and mourning. Sadly, during this period, PACE did not acknowledge explicitly the organizational trauma. Much of what might have been processed in common by the entire staff was relegated, by default, to small group discussion and private deliberation. As a consequence, the staff did not build a broad organizational consensus about either the O&O development strategy or PACE's internal objectives.

By 1990, with only one O&O Supermarket remaining, a much-diminished PACE was struggling—but still determined to meet its financial obligations, to deliver on other institutional commitments, and to redefine its organizational mission and strategies.[9] Regardless of whether PACE proves capable of self-regeneration, much of what was special about the organization will continue through the work of former staff. Beyond this, perhaps the most positive development of the post-O&O period was the creation of Praxis Associates, Inc., a new, for-profit consulting firm.[10] Several factors contributed to Praxis's formation, including frustration with PACE's supermarket-development strategy; limitations imposed by PACE's budgetary structure, financial circumstances, governance system, and organizational liabilities; and, most important, recognition of significant opportunities for a consulting practice appropriately positioned in the expanding ESOP market.

In January 1988, with PACE's endorsement and financial support, Dr. Virginia Vanderslice (from PACE's organizational development staff) and James Steiker (a PACE attorney) founded Praxis. They were soon joined by Joel Steiker (a financial consultant to PACE) and Ruth Green (PACE's office manager). With PACE reorienting toward community-based economic development and assistance to non-profit service organizations, Praxis assumed PACE's ESOP clients and proceeded to develop a broad client base (which, ironically, includes an employee-owned supermarket chain and two other food-related enterprises), primarily in New York and Pennsylvania.

Praxis's achievements since 1988 are particularly impressive. It has participated in the structuring of more than 10 ESOP transactions (most of which involve majority employee ownership), with deal sizes ranging from $500,000 to $15 million. Because of its multidisciplinary approach to service delivery as well as its emphasis on custom-designed ESOPs and workplace-participation programs, Praxis has emerged as one of the leading consulting firms to small and medium-sized ESOP companies.[11]

Through its relationship with PACE, Praxis had the benefits of incubation space and resources as well as business referrals, contacts, and marketing assistance. Through its relationship with Praxis, PACE has enjoyed the benefits of colleagueship and access—on an as-needed, project-by-project basis—to Praxis's key personnel. This symbiotic arrangement has extended the reach and capabilities of both organizations.

Epilogue

Cooperative experimentation thrived in Philadelphia during the 1980s. Challenged by a social reform agenda, and allied with an innovative labor union in a troubled economy, PACE achieved remarkable success in facilitating the development of employee-owned enterprises. Its most notable accomplishment was the creation of the O&O Supermarkets; yet, the O&O drama was not, in some key respects, the story PACE had envisioned. Business failure and cooperative degeneration were not in the original script, but neither was the unanticipated joy of Praxis.

A week that tragically began with the Polish parliament outlawing the Solidarity movement ended with the inspiring inauguration of a union-initiated, employee-owned supermarket network in Philadelphia. What is unforgettable about the Roslyn O&O's "Grand Opening" on 13 October 13, 1982 is the wonderful excitement of being present at its creation.

As the camera crew from the *CBS Evening News with Dan Rather* panned the crowded supermarket for just the right shot, their lenses focused upon Marge Bonacci, an employee-owner in the deli department. At a momentary loss for words, but with much to express, she ran to the microphone adjacent to a nearby cash register. With hundreds of shoppers (and millions of television viewers) looking on, Marge belted out "God Bless America" in a voice that would have made Kate Smith proud.

It was a perfect moment.

To the suspicious and skeptical, Marge sang a familiar song of strength and goodness. She reaffirmed that the O&O effort was a democratic experiment of, by, and for working people, wholly within the American tradition.

To the converted, Marge offered some advice. She urged presentation of progressive innovations as meaningful extensions of the American heritage. Economic democracy is not the fruit of a foreign ideological tree, but rather a delicious red apple cultivated by hard-working Americans and featured in the local supermarket.

For her fellow workers and herself, this was a plain and simple song of joy. It was their moment, and they had earned a celebration.

Their experience with employee ownership lasted seven years. By 1989, the Roslyn O&O had ceased operations. Ironically, this was also the year that a resurgent Solidarity movement restored democracy to Poland, helping to ignite the democratic revival in Eastern Europe and creating possibilities for the development of new, cooperative forms of ownership and participation.

While imperfect in many respects, the O&Os represented hope and opportunity for working people in a decade distinguished by corporate greed and government contempt. They offered good, union jobs and the experience of meaningful employee ownership in an era of plant shutdowns and unemployment.

As with the contributions of Franklin and the striking carpenters, the ultimate significance of this Philadelphia story will be determined by those seeking to extend the rich cooperative tradition of which PACE, the UFCW, and the O&Os are now a part.

Notes

1. PACE was then known as the Delaware Valley Federation for Economic Democracy.

2. With two staff members, PACE raised the majority of its revenues from local donors and grant sources, including the Philadelphia Foundation.

3. A technical advisory group composed of attorneys, financial analysts, and others was organized by PACE. Active through 1983, its role diminished as the PACE staff expanded.

4. A detailed study of the strategies employed in response to this shutdown is provided in Hochner et al. 1988.

5. Throughout the 1980s, PACE utilized a substantial portion of its resources for the education of employee-owners. For a review of its pre-opening education program with the initial O&Os, see Rosen 1987, p. 111-124.

6. A substantial portion of PACE's revenues were derived from foundations and the funding agencies of various religious denominations. PACE also generated consulting and development fees from the O&Os and other employee-owned enterprises. PACE's largest single source of funds was the Ford Foundation.

7. *Linda Banks, et al. vs. PACE of Philadelphia, Inc. et al.*, U.S. District Court for the Eastern District of Pennsylvania, Civil Action No. 87-5703.

8. As their financial circumstances worsened and their need for technical assistance increased, most of the O&Os lacked the resources to compensate PACE for its services. Rather than pursue other revenue-generating projects, PACE continued to provide significant amounts of professional support to the troubled enterprises.

9. The Parkwood Manor O&O was established in 1982 in Northeast Philadelphia, where it continues to operate as a viable enterprise in an intensely competitive market area.

10. Structured as a staff-owned organization, Praxis provides professional services in cooperation with the law office of James G. Steiker and Associates, P.C.

11. The typical ESOP transaction undertaken by Praxis involves one or more retiring owners in an established company with 25 to 250 employees. Praxis clients include numerous ESOP companies as well as private corporations, nonprofit agencies, and public institutions such as the School District of Philadelphia.

The O&O Supermarkets
Achievements and Lessons

Frank Lindenfeld

When two former A&P stores were reopened as worker-owned supermarkets in Philadelphia in 1982, hopes for their success were high. The project was launched by the United Food and Commercial Workers Union (UFCW), with the help of the technical assistance organization PACE, in response to A&P's sudden announcement that it was closing most of its Delaware Valley markets. At first, the O&O (worker Owned and Operated) markets prospered and expanded. Within several years, the two pioneer O&O stores added four additional markets. Their excellent sales record was even noted in the *Wall Street Journal* (18 August 1983). Yet by 1989, the chain had dwindled. Now only Parkwood Manor, one of the original two O&Os, remains. The rise and fall of these cooperative supermarkets provides an excellent case study of the possibilities and pitfalls of worker-owned enterprise.

Chain Supermarket Closings

In 1982, A&P laid off two thousand employees, virtually shutting down its operations in the Philadelphia area. In subsequent negotiations, the UFCW reached an agreement with A&P to reopen most of its stores as the SuperFresh chain in exchange for wage concessions. As part of the deal, SuperFresh was to institute a quality of work life (QWL) program to foster greater employee participation and to pay employees a one percent bonus, which was to be contributed to a new O&O investment fund, to finance future employee buyouts. At the same time, the union secured an option for its workers to buy two former A&P stores, which soon became the Parkwood Manor and Roslyn O&O markets.

To help with worker training and development, the union hired PACE. Soon, PACE also became involved with the expansion of the O&Os to other neighborhoods and with an attempt to start an inter-cooperative umbrella association to provide mutual aid and economies of scale in purchasing, advertising, insurance, and so on.

While the O&O network started off well, there were flaws from the beginning. For example, the better-paid meat cutters, organized in their own union local, undermined the deal negotiated by the retail clerks' local by refusing to pay "their" one percent bonus to the O&O investment fund. This resistance sparked a vote by the retail clerks to make their donation voluntary—leaving the fund with very meager income (Whyte 1986). Let's see what other roots of success and eventual failure we can find in the history of the markets.

The Original Two O&O Markets

The project was enthusiastically supported by the UFCW. Worker-owners in the Roslyn and Parkwood Manor stores participated in the planning process, helped to select their managers, and continued to take an active part in store committees afterward. They established worker-elected boards of directors to set policy and to supervise management. The first managers in both markets were chosen from among the workforce. To trim costs, the workers agreed to a temporary pay cut, with a commitment to raise their wages later and with the incentive that as owners they would share in future profits. They also agreed to flexible job descriptions, which allowed them to help out where needed, including bagging groceries and cleaning up. Finally, they reinvested their profits in modernization.

Not surprisingly, these first O&Os quickly attained higher levels of sales than the A&P markets they replaced. Indeed, Parkwood Manor did so well that it bought a former A&P in nearby Lambertville, New Jersey, which it later sold to a joint venture put together by PACE and the Roslyn O&O. Meanwhile, Roslyn expanded rapidly on its own site. As its sales climbed to the $8 to $9 million mark, the founding twenty-four full time worker-owners, all of whom were experienced supermarket employees, hired an additional twenty-four non-owner employees, most of whom had little experience and worked part time.

Unfortunately, Roslyn's success soured. In 1987, its manager, Rick Cassel, moved to Lambertville, from where he tried to manage both stores. Soon thereafter, SuperFresh and Pathmark opened competing supermarkets that drew customers away, despite Roslyn O&O's investment of $500,000 in remodeling. To make matters worse, its wholesale supplier tightened credit. These problems proved too much for the O&O, which was forced to sell to another operator in 1989.

Parkwood Manor O&O started out and stayed somewhat smaller than the Roslyn market. It began with about twenty worker-owners, and within a few years had grown to approximately thirty-six workers, with sales of roughly $5 million per year. The added employees were hired as part-timers and were not offered the opportunity to buy into ownership. From the beginning, Parkwood Manor O&O faced more adverse business conditions than did the one at Roslyn, including competition from a huge Carrefour market that opened only a half mile away. One crucial reason Parkwood Manor O&O has survived has been the competent leadership of manager Joe Offner and a team of experienced department managers; another has been the continued extra efforts of the worker-owners.

The Other Four O&O Markets

When the initial two O&O supermarkets proved successful, the UFCW and PACE promoted four additional cooperative markets. Three (Lambertville, Darby, and Upper Darby) had been closed by their former owners. Strawberry Mansion O&O was an entirely new business; it was the anchor tenant at a new shopping center sponsored by the City of Philadelphia.

The new markets lasted only a few years; the Darby O&O made it for only seventeen months. In all four, sales were lower and expenses higher than projections. They too were squeezed by a tightening credit policy of their wholesale supplier, which made them more vulnerable to relatively small unanticipated expenses. And their problems were compounded by lack of capital for modernization and, in some cases, by ineffective management.

The Strawberry Mansion O&O suffered from additional woes. When the city administration agreed to help finance the new market, it insisted that half the employees be hired from the market's neighborhood and that they be recruited through the Strawberry Mansion Citizens Participation Council. The city gave the chairperson of that group a permanent seat on the Strawberry Mansion O&O's board of directors, enabling him to dominate that body. Worse, board interference soon exacerbated problems of poor management. For example, the board paid little heed to PACE's recommendation that the number of workers be cut and a new manager hired. Eventually, PACE reluctantly withdrew from its advisory role. Not long thereafter, the Strawberry Mansion O&O filed for bankruptcy.

Achievements and Lessons

On the positive side:

- The O&Os not only maintained but increased the jobs at several markets closed by their previous owners. Moreover, almost half of the positions were full time, compared to a rate of 20 percent at most supermarkets.
- The O&Os demonstrated that worker control can lead to lower operational costs. The O&O workers took pride in their markets and consistently put in extra effort when needed. They did not hire as many supervisors as A&P—as worker-owners they did not need to be watched by bosses to perform well. With the possible exception of the Strawberry Mansion O&O, there was also less waste and less pilferage than at corporate-owned supermarkets.
- The O&Os showed that employee ownership is compatible with unionization.
- The help of external organizers was vital to the development of the O&Os. The leadership and vision of UFCW Local president Wendell Young encouraged laid-off workers to consider employee ownership as an option. PACE helped with worker education and training, as well as with financing arrangements and legal structure.

Despite these achievements, all but one of the O&Os closed; most were sold to other independent or chain operators. Some of the reasons are:

- In the retail food industry, competition is stiff, profit margins low, and modernization expensive, especially as food markets become more capital intensive (for example, because of computerized checkouts). Though the O&O markets reinvested their earnings, they still did not have enough capital to match the modernization efforts of the giant corporate chains or even to cope adequately with unanticipated expenses or tighter wholesale credit terms.

- The "me first" attitude of a majority of the SuperFresh workers (those *not* employed by the O&Os) made them unwilling to support what union officials and PACE staff had hoped would be a major alternative source of capital for future buyouts and startups, the O&O investment fund.

- Similarly, the workers at the first two O&Os became owners without developing either a sense of solidarity or a vision of extending the benefits of ownership to all future employees. Worker-owners at Roslyn and Parkwood Manor developed a worker capitalist outlook and were unwilling to accept new employees as full owners because that would have diminished their share of actual or potential profits. (At PACE's suggestion, the Strawberry Mansion, Darby, and Upper Darby O&Os tried a different system where after a sixty-day probation period, all workers became owners through an employee stock ownership plan).

Conclusion

Finding skilled managers able to work in a democratic setting is a major challenge. One thread connecting the O&O business failures seems to be poor management, especially an inability to keep costs in balance with income. Small, undercapitalized firms, including most worker cooperatives, cannot afford to make as many business mistakes as larger corporations because they do not have a cash cushion to fall back on. At some of the O&Os, optimistic sales projections led to hiring more workers than could be supported by the markets' income. At others, managers proved unable to cut labor costs in a timely way to keep expenses in line with revenues. In worker-owned firms, there is an understandable reluctance to lay off employees or to cut full-time workers' hours.

That five of the six O&Os succumbed to a lack of capital and/or poor management illustrates the acute vulnerability of small enterprises in a capitalist economy dominated by big business. And yet the persistence of the Parkwood Manor O&O despite heavy competition and a relative paucity of capital shows that, with adequate managerial leadership, worker ownership and control can nevertheless be a viable option in the supermarket industry and in similar industries throughout the United States.

Taking Stock
Workplace Democracy's Unique Potential for Progressive Change

Len Krimerman and Frank Lindenfeld

In 1988, *Changing Work* magazine began the retrospective project from which this book grew. One of our aims was to record and to celebrate the gains achieved by advocates of workplace democracy over the past two decades. As we pulled together the pieces, our excitement about worker ownership and workplace democracy grew. The more we learned, the more we began to believe that the contemporary wave of worker ownership has overcome many of the obstacles that defeated earlier cooperative movements in the United States. While a just, democratic economy is still a dream in this country, a dream for which we must still struggle long and hard, the worker-ownership and control movement seems poised to contribute mightily to that struggle. Unlike earlier waves of cooperative activity, it is *entrepreneurially competent, financially resourceful*, and, most important, *increasingly rooted* in labor, community, religious, and other grassroots movements.

As we have seen throughout this book, the strengths of the current movement include:

- **An extensive variety of viable worker-owned and cooperative enterprises.** These have taken root in many different sectors of the economy and in virtually all regions of the country.

- **A vital and growing technical assistance community.** Offering financial, business, legal, and educational expertise, its work dramatically increases the chances of creating and maintaining sound worker-owned businesses. Specifically, it has helped the worker-ownership movement gain the business sophistication needed to distinguish better from worse start-up ventures, to make loans that can be carefully monitored, to target entire congenial sectors of the economy, and to emphasize proactive strategies (such as conversions of successful businesses to employee ownership) rather than merely reacting to plant-closing crises. Finally, technical assistance groups have played a crucial role in nurturing mutually supportive networks, federations, and associations of cooperative enterprise and in linking worker ownership to labor, community, and environmental groups.

- **An extensive range of democratic financial institutions**, including socially responsible banks, community-minded credit unions and loan funds, state and national public-lending institutions, and union pension and denominational investment funds—many of which now collaborate with technical assistance groups.

- **Increasing union support.** The U.S. labor movement has begun to shift its views on worker ownership and control. Increasingly, unions see certain forms of worker ownership and control as both good for rank-and-file worker-owners and useful for rebuilding labor's mission, credibility, and strength. This change in attitude can be found on all levels, from trade union locals through to the national AFL-CIO and its newly established Employee Partnership Investment Fund. Moreover, as business sophistication and union support increase, worker ownership is spreading across whole sectors (e.g., steel), enhancing both in-plant worker control and cross-plant solidarity.

- **Increasing community support.** Religious organizations, community economic development groups, local coalitions combating plant closings, organizations of low-income women and of people of color, and grassroots environmental activists all have begun to realize that they can use worker ownership to help empower their constituents and increase their clout.

- **Contacts with overseas worker-owned and operated enterprises.** Democratically organized U.S. firms continue to learn from the plethora of well-developed worker-owned and democratically organized enterprises in Canada, Japan, western Europe, and elsewhere. Some are even exploring mutually beneficial joint ventures.

- **The accessibility of abundant resources to aid new democratic enterprises.** These include educational resources such as case studies and how-to manuals, technical assistance groups, university extension programs, community-oriented banks and revolving loan funds, and even some state agencies.

- **Career opportunities.** Unlike many volunteer social change activities, the democracy at work movement offers participants jobs that can help change society—whether in worker-owned enterprises or in the various support organizations.

The most remarkable —and hope-inspiring—aspect of these achievements is that they were virtually unknown in previous waves of cooperative activity. Taken together, they signal an historically unprecedented potential for democratic economic and social change.

Of course, the road ahead will not be smooth, straight, or easy to chart. As far as we have come, we still have much farther to go—and many formidable challenges to meet. These challenges include:

- The relatively **low level of cooperation** that persists between and among worker-owned enterprises, technical assistance providers, and democratic financial institutions;
- The **scarcity of well-developed on-site models of education** for worker-owners and managers;
- The **slow pace at which ESOPs are achieving their potential to bring democracy** into the workplace and to give worker-owners a greater voice in shaping their worklives;
- The movement's still **insufficient outreach to many of its potential allies,** such as public-sector workers, economically disenfranchised youth, women, minority workers, socially and ecologically responsible investors, and grassroots environmental groups.

These gaps are sobering, but, we think, bridgeable. How to cross them and strengthen the current movement is the subject of chapter 8. Before turning to specific future strategies, however, there are other and perhaps more fundamental challenges to worker ownership and control that have frequently been raised:[1]

- Are worker-owned enterprises viable over the long term? (Economic Viability)
- Can they resist the corrupting influences of capitalist competition and culture? (Corruptibility)
- Can worker-owners and their allies attain enough strength and coordination to effectively challenge current power relations in U.S. society? (Coordination and Power)
- Does worker ownership genuinely further democracy at work, economic justice, and a healthy environment? (Desirability)

Economic Viability

As in earlier periods of cooperative development, workers today have less capital to draw upon, as individuals, than do corporate owners and financial institutions. In the past, this lack of capital often kept co-ops small and uncompetitive, forcing them into retail and labor-intensive service sectors and away from basic manufacturing or high-technology fields. Today, however, while most sources of capital are still controlled by the undemocratic corporate status quo, there are more alternatives than ever before. As chapter 4 reveals, religious organizations, labor unions, the national AFL-CIO, community banks, credit unions, community development groups, and others have all pulled together pools of capital. Beyond these are the network of private investors developed by technical assistance groups; local, state, and federal sources; and the tax incentives furnished by ESOP legislation. Topping it all off is the vast and as yet virtually untapped reservoir of union-controlled and public-sector pension funds—some hundreds of billions of dollars in potential investment capital—waiting for more creative use.

While they still have a hard time raising essential capital, majority employee-owned firms have already begun to tap into these sources and have spread well beyond retail and marginal sectors. The steelworkers now own more than twenty separate plants—more of this capital-intensive industry than any other single group of investors. Their success indicates not only that worker-owned businesses can prosper in the harsh, capitalist marketplace but also that enterprises in other sectors facing the same conditions—low but reliable return on investment, failure by current owners to modernize technology—may be ripe for industry-wide takeovers by union-backed employee-owned enterprises.

In addition, of course, the Mondragon cooperatives offer an encouraging working model. The Basque cooperators have developed highly productive and competitive workplaces in virtually every economic sector, from durable goods to laundromats, from robots to mass transit. Some of these workplaces have now been functioning for more than three decades, and the entire cooperative community has been able to grow even during such harsh worldwide recessions as the one in the early 1980s. Indeed, the Mondragon federation has seen only 2 of its more than 125 worker cooperatives fail over its 35-year history; it has become the largest exporter of durable goods in Spain; and it outshines in productivity and efficiency comparable capitalist firms in Spain and in Europe more generally (Thomas and Logan 1982; Whyte and Whyte 1988). As George Benello emphasizes:

> The value of Mondragon is that it speaks in specific and concrete ways. Whereas the Webbs and others have long argued against the viability of worker cooperatives on the basis that they will in the end simply degenerate into capitalist enterprises, Mondragon has shown that this is not true. Not only does Mondragon work, but it works a lot better than its capitalist counterparts; it works better and it grows faster. (Benello 1988, 30)

Not surprisingly, the Mondragon cooperators have shed instructive light on many problems facing cooperatives, including that of capital. For example, they raised necessary capital by creating their own bank, the Caja Laboral Popular (Bank of the People's Labor), to tap wide regional and community support. The Caja now has close to $2 billion in assets, and its loans are supported by an Empressarial Division with highly qualified, industry-specific consultants. (The bank's surplus might even become a capital source for other worker-owned co-ops outside the Basque region.) Moreover, Mondragon's unique internal capital-account system uses the capital produced by the cooperators' labor for the good of the individual and of the group. Each worker-owner has an account at the Bank into which his or her share of the enterprise's surplus revenue is placed annually. Since worker-owners cannot draw on their accounts until they retire, the capital accumulated in their names remains available to their firms for expansion, diversification, research and development, reinvestment, and the like—thus magnifying their individual and cumulative contributions.

Mondragon's power as a model is difficult to exaggerate. Though it has roots in the Basque culture, one arguably more receptive to claims of social justice and cooperative community than is our own, "the secret of Mondragon is not ideological, but organizational: it is 'how to' knowledge that makes it work" (Benello 1988, 28), and this practical knowledge (of work organization, financing, marketing, etc.) is at last being exported. Mondragon demonstrates once and for all that—and how—cooperative firms can be economically successful without sacrificing democratic principles. The challenge becomes how to build in our own country culturally congenial, locally rooted, labor- and community-supported, Mondragon-like networks of democratically run enterprises.

Given the examples collected in this book, it should be clear that the mystique of superior capitalist efficiency and productivity is hype—inflated, self-promoting propaganda—not established fact. Industrial researchers like Seymour Melman (*Profits without Production*) have shown again and again that the U.S. corporate economy is steadily losing competitive strength and durability because it focuses on short-term profits (witness junk bonds, paper mergers and acquisitions, the S&L travesty, etc.), rather than on modernizing production processes, improving product quality, or investing in worker development. Moreover, U.S. corporations are frequently choked by excessive levels of management and extravagant headquarters costs. To a very large and increasing extent, corporate capitalism on the U.S. model is an economic dinosaur dependent for survival on government subsidies, throwaway products that consumers can neither repair nor find alternatives to, and unnecessary and globally destabilizing military production. Worse, this dinosaur is racing toward extinction (and catalyzing environmental disaster) by periodic crises of overproduction. As machines of greater capacity and sophistication replace people, productivity increases, but so also do recession, unemployment, and underemployment. This in turn spawns products for which there are fewer and fewer buyers, and thus even greater unemployment. Only through military production or war itself has our capitalist economy been able to "solve" this sort of dilemma. As the Cold War thaws, we can expect these crises to grow deeper. Perhaps, then, a more cooperative economy, one in which decisions to introduce new technology are placed on the democratic agenda, will emerge to stave off the cycles of overproduction and recession and to avert the eco-cidal crash of U.S. industrial capitalism.

Seen in this light, small-scale, flexibly networked, worker owned and operated businesses suddenly look competitive as well as desirable. Mondragon's success and efficiency is no longer an anomaly but a natural consequence of its democratic, cooperative structure. Indeed, the examples we present in this book show that appropriately scaled, democratically controlled, worker-run enterprises often need fewer managers, exhibit higher productivity, invest more prudently, and respond more flexibly to change than do traditional corporate firms. And as Chuck Turner argues in chapter 8, worker-owned and community-based enterprises are crucial building blocks for a sustainable economy featuring local self-reliance.

Corruptibility

In short, then, contemporary worker-owned enterprises, especially when supported by technical assistance and financial support organizations, are economically viable, competitive, and maybe even necessary. But can they avoid being corrupted by the capitalist system and culture in which they must compete?

It is difficult for workers to make the transition from being passive employees to being responsible owners, involved in shaping the companies they own. They face the strong temptation to cash in on success by increasing their own wages or dividends, even at the cost of failing to modernize, or, as has sometimes occurred, by selling their companies to outside corporations in order to enjoy early retirement. More subtly, they face the problem of enterprise consciousness in which worker-owners distance themselves from workers in other enterprises and cast aside solidarity to concentrate on the economic viability of their own particular enterprise. Indeed, it is all too easy to imagine the development of a kind of "self-managed capitalism" in which the pressures of competition force worker-owners to hire and to exploit second-class (non-owner) workers, perpetuate environmental degradation, produce socially damaging products, and so on. Competing with corporate capitalism on its own turf makes it hard to escape its pervasive, exploitative, and irresponsible priorities.

Admittedly, some U.S. cooperatives and ESOPs *have* hired second-class employees whose labor they have exploited and whose access to ownership and decision making they have denied. But here the past is not a reliable guide to the future. There are plenty of contrasting examples of long-lasting and economically successful democratic and majority-owned ESOPs that have not succumbed to this temptation. Furthermore, Mondragon shows once more that success can be achieved without sacrificing economic justice or democratic integrity. Not only is every Mondragon worker an owner but each owns an equal share of his or her enterprise. In addition, the Mondragon cooperators ensure solidarity with other workers by tying their own salaries to industry and regional averages, and they ensure economic justice within each enterprise by keeping the wage differential between line workers and management quite low. Finally, since the Mondragon and democratic-ESOP models are becoming widely known and respected by such influential organizations and institutions as labor unions, public agencies, community-development groups, and religious organizations, the exploitative labor practices of some worker-owned firms in the past are less likely to recur. Indeed, while there are no guarantees, so long as today's worker-owned enterprises are formed with assistance from industry-wide unions, and/or rooted in regional or citywide countereconomies, and/or aided by state, community, or religious organizations, they will be able to expand without hiring second-class labor.

But what of the other corruptions endemic to corporate-dominated capitalism: environmental decimation and degradation, production of socially harmful goods, the maldistribution of wealth? Would these persist under a system of self-managing and worker-owned enterprises?

We believe that the maximization of individual or enterprise profit need not, and probably would not, remain the fundamental economic value of a worker-owned economy. Just as worker-owned enterprises can reject (and have firmly rejected) exploitative labor practices that might augment overall enterprise profit, so also they can reject productive procedures or forms of technology that are socially or environmentally destructive. Like any other business, worker owned and operated enterprises must be profitable—but this need not mean pursuing profits at any cost or even making profits the central goal. Mondragon for example has made creating and maintaining jobs its central goal.

In fact, especially when they are connected with other worker-owned firms, worker-owners are unlikely to ignore environmental, health, or social concerns—precisely because, as *worker*-owners, they are residents of the communities in which they work, not absentee owners or managers. They are as vulnerable as other community residents to the environmental contamination and damage associated with such corporate inventions as toxic dumps, nuclear plants, coal-fired furnaces, pesticide plants, and the like. Indeed, as workers they are doubly at risk, since they must confront such hazards directly and daily on the shop floor or in the office as well as outside the workplace. As worker-*owners*, they thus have the clear incentives of their own, their families', and their friends' well-being to curb or transform life-endangering products and production processes. If in the past worker-owners have failed to do so (the allegedly poor safety record of the West Coast plywood cooperatives is sometimes cited), this may well have been because their enterprises were neither allied with nor monitored by community or labor organizations.

Moreover, when profits are distributed very widely, say among all the hundreds of thousands of employee-owners of a democratized General Motors or General Electric Co., they usually have far less motivational impact than when they are the exclusive province of a few principal shareholders or executives. The opportunity to make millions may encourage all sorts of corporate irresponsibility—from shoddy or unsafe products to secret Love Canals, to profiting from nuclear energy and warheads that make all of our lives less secure. But the opportunity to make thousands of dollars is much less likely to obscure alternatives that are environmentally and socially, as well as financially, sound.

Similarly, worker-owners, unlike corporations, have a natural bond to future generations. They are, after all, parts of families and members of local communities that they want to see perpetuated. As things are organized now, their worklives and these extrawork priorities are kept separate: in general, employees cannot use work to promote their communities, nor can they protect their homes, families, and communities from the damage or risks arising from their workplaces. In a worker-owned economy, employee-owners could more easily shape their workplaces to contribute to family and community well-being, or at least alter their production processes so that they would not threaten their own and their communities' health. Energies now suppressed or restrained—indeed not even imagined—could take form; worklife, community life, and family life could become interdependent, rather than isolated or in opposition.

Such a transition might seem difficult, particularly for such workers as nuclear engineers, pesticide chemists, or refinery employees whose jobs now depend on producing socially or environmentally harmful products. But the evidence is overwhelming that workers are both willing and able to conceive of and to produce more socially useful product lines. For example, when Lucas Aerospace, the giant

British military contractor, decided to close a factory in central England, union leaders encouraged rank-and-file workers to identify alternative products with peacetime uses that could be manufactured there with minimal retooling. Within a few months, more than 150 potential new products emerged, many designed in elaborate and precise detail. These included an on-rail, off-rail vehicle for use in developing nations; a vehicle called the HOBCART, with which severely handicapped children could propel themselves; a kidney-dialysis unit; and a bus powered by biofuels. Many of the ideas were both practical and marketable; two years after the management of Lucas vetoed all conversion strategies (and razed the plant late one night), Mercedes-Benz adopted and put into production the bus design (Cooley 1982, ch. 4).

Similarly, when the International Brotherhood of Electrical Workers' Local 2047 at Unisys' St. Paul factory was threatened with massive layoffs, the workers began "an alternative use process" in which a "survey of members on the shop floor was distributed assessing not only workers' skills and experience but also . . . alternative product ideas." A group of workers met with Amory Lovins, a specialist in environmentally sustainable technologies, and concluded that their plant could produce a number of energy-efficient products, such as fluorescent ballasts, with little or no change in the work environment. In addition, "the local's members came up with products ranging all the way from computers in cars to transportation management control centers, computer systems for personalized rapid transit, smart irrigation systems, low-powered electronic lighting, and text vocalizers for blind people" that could be produced with minimal changeover of machinery. As at Lucas, management has refused to negotiate seriously with its own workers or to consider the local's plan for converting from military to civilian production and retaining the workforce. (For more on Local 2047, see Duncan 1990.)

The point is that had either the Lucas or the Unisys plants been worker-owned, they would almost certainly have converted from weapons-related to peace-promoting production. Their example suggests that workers in a self-managing economy would not have to submit to market pressures to maintain socially dangerous forms of work; they would redirect the skills, machines, and factories over which they have control in socially useful ways. The "market" does not dictate socially or environmentally irresponsible production. The "market" is merely an abstraction based on the tension between what consumers demand or are willing to purchase and the products companies are able or willing to produce. While consumer demand does limit production on the one hand (Harrods, the London department store, recently stopped selling fur coats because of consumer opposition) and can provide powerful incentives on the other (the consumer demand for "green" products is changing production processes—or at least marketing campaigns), the range of goods and services people might want seems much greater than what companies make. Both owners and consumers influence what is produced. In an economy of worker-owners, in an economy in which the owners and consumers are the same people and in which the bottom line includes more than profit, the incentive to produce damaging products or to use destructive processes would tend to disappear.

Arguably, the public sector could help the transition to such a worker- and consumer-controlled economy. Were governments to purchase only things produced in environmentally sustainable ways or by worker-owned enterprises, were governments to convert such services as mass transit, garbage collection, and research labs to worker and community ownership, such converted enterprises could then exert tremendous influence over the market. Not only is the market subject to consumer and corporate (including worker-owned) influences; it can also be shaped by public policy.

Finally, among the best ways we can think of to avoid the corrupting influence of capitalism are expanding the scope of worker ownership education and increasing the links between worker-owned enterprises and other grassroots movements. Empowering worker-owner education has the potential to challenge and change deeply ingrained attitudes that lead to employee passivity, willingness to trade away control for short-term wage gains, and the like. And if worker-owners could be connected to, or rooted in, other progressive movements (labor, environment, and community empowerment, among others), several crops could grow from a single seed. Not only would these other social change groups gain from the economic sophistication and viability (and occasional surplus revenues) of worker-owned enterprises, but worker-owners would be less isolated, less likely to fall into "enterprise consciousness," and more apt to see participation in their company as part of a long-term struggle for social transformation rather than as merely a business venture.

Coordination and Power

However viable worker-owned firms may be, and whatever the potential for the growth of a democratic, nonexploitive, and ecologically responsible alternative to corporate capitalism, a genuinely democratic and accountable economy is not possible until corporate power can be successfully challenged. Sadly, despite the advances it has made in the past two decades, and despite its contrasts with earlier forms of cooperative enterprise, today's democracy-at-work movement remains largely fragmented. Worker-owned firms in Texas know little or nothing about those in Oregon; union-developed ESOPs in Ohio or Connecticut are disconnected from cooperatively-run print shops, home healthcare enterprises, or recycling firms. In the absence of planning, coordination, and policy making on industry-wide, regional, national, and international levels, the movement would seem to have little chance to effectively oppose the highly centralized forces now in place or even to develop a strong consensus within its own ranks that corporate capitalism should be challenged.

While the political situation looks less than promising, some of the seeds of a nationally and internationally coordinated movement have recently been sown. Worker-owned firms are increasingly linked in various and largely unprecedented ways to their counterparts and to progressive coalitions in their regions. Worker-owners have begun to join together in more explicitly promotional and political organizations, such as the Federation for Industrial Retention and Renewal, a national coalition of some twenty-five labor-community alliances. The venerable International Cooperative Association (in Geneva) now represents almost four hundred million members from about two hundred cooperative organizations in seventy nations around the world, and a new networking organization, the International Institute for Self-Management, has recently been formed to foster exchanges among worker-owned or self-managing enterprises in different countries, to encourage cooperation among them (including trade, co-production, and common marketing), and to provide education and training (vocational, business, organizational, and political) to members or prospective members of cooperatives.

Despite these beginnings, many more seeds of cooperation and coordination must still be planted if the present fragmentation is to give way to a strong and focused movement, capable of collectively planning long-term strategies and of exercising significant political power. These seeds would be well fertilized if workplace democracy became part of every progressive political agenda, along with, say, drastic reductions in nuclear weapons, mandatory and maximum recycling, and divestment from all companies still doing business with repressive governments. We agree that an essential part of challenging the power of corporate capitalism is developing counter organizations that can foster solidarity and alliances within and across industries, states, regions, and nations, that can help gain increased control over resources through which more and more democratic enterprises can be brought to life, and that can defend the ground won by worker-owners against inevitable backlashes. What form such unifying vehicles should take at this point—a new political party; caucuses within old parties; coalitions of labor, community, religious, and economically disenfranchised groups; a predominantly union-based organization; or some combination of all of these—is not clear to us. We are, however, drawn here to Jim Hightower's notion of progressive alliances, which we discuss in chapter 8. If nothing of this sort emerges, workplace democracy may once again become a marginal phenomenon.

As important as we think such coordination is, we do not believe it is time to shift the *bulk* of our energies from developing local enterprises to formulating and implementing national policy. While it may seem clear to many that if it is sufficiently democratized and linked with progressive movements worker ownership would be superior to corporate capitalism, for many others worker ownership must still prove itself to be superior not only in abstract equity and justice, and not only in Mondragon, but in workplaces in the United States. It must show that it can indeed deliver the goods, meet payrolls, fulfill pension obligations, and compete successfully. This extensive, difficult, and yet quite possible task, well begun over the past two decades, must remain the movement's first priority—at least for much of the next decade. For now, we think that the move for coordination and unity should be confined to empowering, supporting, and ensuring the viability of local initiatives.

By developing local associations, consolidating local coalitions, and winning local election campaigns (as the Tri-State Steel Authority and the Naugatuck Valley Project are doing), the movement can begin to recognize its own strength, to accumulate power, to root and grow. Once there are dozens of such grassroots authorities and democratic economy coalitions firmly in place, there will be time enough to shift our focus to statewide organizations and national and international federations. In short, we envision an incremental shifting of power, a transitional process anchored in home-grown democratic development and supported, in part, by attaining local political power and coordination.

Happily, the conditions surrounding today's worker-ownership movement are propitious to its continued growth and to its capacity to challenge the dominance of corporate capitalism. Globally, the demise of totalitarian regimes, the decentralization of the Soviet Union, and the emerging victory over South African apartheid are opening some doors for more democratic developments. Denmark has already committed itself to breaking away from huge corporate production companies in favor of small-scale, high-tech, collaborative-artisan production like that in the Emilia-Romagna region of Italy. And the Mondragon model of cooperative enterprise is being studied intensely (and in some cases implemented in small ways) by several Common Market countries.

Beyond this, corporate capitalism continues to lose credibility. Its unending ecological irresponsibility—no, *criminality*—may at last blunt its capacity to expand. Now that this criminality—from the destruction of the rain forests, to the dislocation of native peoples, to chronic oil spills, to toxic-waste dumps and life-threatening nuclear plants—is a daily target of media exposure, it has almost become a commonplace that what is good for corporate profits is dangerous to the health of consumers, workers, communities, and the planet.[2] Moreover, as Donald L. Kanter and Philip H. Mirvis show in *The Cynical Americans* (1990), U.S. workers today are more disillusioned, frustrated, and angry with employers and with the lack of meaningful and challenging work than ever before. In many cases, their cynicism with U.S. corporate capitalism is focused on the bottom-line mentality that blinds companies not only to the social costs they impose on communities but to the developmental needs of their employees. As the legitimacy of corporate America erodes and the staggering deficiencies and abuses of the command Socialist economies become clearer, some space should open up for "third way" economic approaches featuring worker ownership and control.

The success of such progressive movements as those focused on animal rights, socially responsible investing, and environmental justice is yet more evidence that the U.S. corporate system is far from invincible. While these movements have not yet shifted *capital* resources from corporations to grassroots organizations, they do involve more people than are presently employed by all majority-employee-owned firms, and they help to explain why socially responsible investments have risen from about $40 billion to more than $500 billion over the past decade. If we could forge an alliance between the budding workplace democracy movement and these other, more reactive and consumer-oriented movements, we would greatly increase the chances for genuine and far-reaching social transformation. How we might begin to do so is a subject we return to in chapter 8.

Desirability

And so we come to perhaps the most profound challenge of all. Is worker ownership really what we want? Is it an ideal worth realizing, or will it only perpetuate what is unacceptable in our present economic life?

Critics have argued that worker ownership would fail to provide genuine workplace democracy, since mere ownership is very distant from control; that a worker-owned economy might well turn out to contain severe injustices or inequities, with workers in favored regions or industries faring far better than their counterparts elsewhere; and that worker-owners might leave intact the present form of rampant, oversized, resource-depleting industrialism, rather than moving toward an ecologically sustainable economy. In short, is there any reason to think that worker ownership and control would further such ideals as genuine democratic control, equitable distribution of resources and opportunities, and ecological responsibility?

These concerns are not without force. For all its remarkable achievements (e.g., creating long-lasting jobs, expanding local housing, and promoting education), Mondragon seems so far to lack much interest in ecological sustainability; to be anxious to expand production for the global market rather than concentrating on meeting local needs; and to have replicated the wage differentials between sectors (e.g., robotics and child care) that prevail in the wider economy.

This and other examples suggest that worker ownership will not, in and of itself, lead to a more just and ecologically sustainable society. By the same token, when bent toward the kind of cooperative economy we have been advocating, one rooted in progressive grassroots movements, worker ownership and control would be a potent tool for democratic change. Toward this end, coalitions of such groups need to weave a rainbow combination of efforts, with labor stressing economic justice and equity, environmental groups stressing sustainability and home-grown development, religious and community groups stressing empowerment for the economically disenfranchised, and so on. Such a mixture would produce an enriched form of worker ownership in service of a cooperative, egalitarian, and planet-sustaining society.

At the very least, worker ownership provides a unique forum in which to explore and experiment with the ideals of justice, sustainability, and democracy. Even if these ideals are not fully built in from the start, the democratic decision-making and priority-setting process makes it possible for them to receive a serious hearing. Like humanity at its best, worker ownership is both imperfect and, to a very large and expandable extent, perfectible. Even if distributive justice, face-to-face decision making, and environmental stewardship are undervalued initially, worker ownership and control provide multiple opportunities and processes for this to be reversed.

In the last analysis, though, "the burden of proof is on the theorist. . . . If we wish to claim that something better than [grassroots worker ownership] needs to be built, theory alone simply will not do. It is incumbent on us to do it" (Benello 1988, 30).

In Review

At the very least, the typical objections to worker cooperatives—that they are no match for capitalist firms, that the successful ones are contaminated by the marketplace, that they tend to ignore political unity and coordination, and that they neglect important progressive political ideals—are undercut by the particular strengths of the contemporary movement, among them its grassroots base, its multiple allies, and its business power and sophistication. Beyond this, these strengths convince us that the *historically novel features and achievements of the contemporary worker-ownership movement provide an unparalleled opportunity to construct a new and genuinely democratic economy that can rival, perhaps even unseat, corporate capitalism.* Doing so will take years, even generations, of persistent and diversified struggle, but now is an optimum time to put our resources and energies behind this movement.

To some, the very idea of building a democratic and human-scale economy in this era of global corporate behemoths that span continents and possess greater resources than many nations may seem wildly fanciful or hopelessly naive. But as recent events in central and eastern Europe reveal, even behemoths fall. Whatever is enthroned by human hands, hearts, and minds can be dethroned by them. While worker ownership and control are *not* somehow destined to be the next stage of historical or economic development, the present form of this movement provides an unparalleled opportunity for large-scale and progressive transformation of the economy and society of the United States. The next chapter goes on to examine some ways in which we might act to seize this opportunity to dethrone corporate capitalism and to nurture an empowering and responsible alternative.

Notes

1. Beginning with Beatrice and Sidney Webb's nineteenth-century critique of worker cooperatives, there is a skeptical trail that leads to contemporary arguments against ESOPs and employee ownership (e.g., Bufe 1988; Lynd 1990).

2. The destructive impact of capitalist economies on the environment is not vitiated by the equally appalling ecological devastation fostered by command Socialist economies bent on maximizing their industrial production.

8

Creating Democracy at Work
Strategies for Transformation

As we worked on this book, and especially on chapter 7, we became more convinced than ever of the progressive potential of workplace democracy and worker ownership. This chapter, then, is devoted to strategy. How can we realize the wider promise of workplace democracy? How can we close the movement's internal gaps and overcome the external obstacles?

Reflecting on his long history with the ICA Group, formerly known as the Industrial Cooperative Association (itself cooperatively run) and his experience with the worker-ownership movement, Steve Dawson sees the opportunity for us to dive into the business mainstream and make business our medium. But to do so, he argues, we will need to overcome self-defeating reactions to business and reject "subsistence economics" in favor of creating cooperatively controlled wealth.

Chris Weiss and Chris Clamp argue that feminist organizing must begin to include women's control of economic resources. Their interviews with several women involved with worker ownership attempt to assess its potential for helping women. While their experience has been mixed, the interviewees find distinct potential for those women who choose this model. Similarly, Chuck Turner explores ways in which worker ownership, especially labor cooperatives, can help communities of color build an economic base. And he further insists that worker ownership, or indeed any serious progressive movement, cannot grow without the participation and leadership of people of color.

Finally, in our concluding essay, we put forth two sets of nuts-and-bolts strategies for cultivating worker ownership and workplace democracy. We advocate developing the movement's internal resources by such tactics as the wholesale targeting of business sectors and the strengthening of education for worker ownership. And we encourage worker-owners and their supporters to reach out to other progressive constituencies—for example, the increasingly spirited, cohesive, and successful grassroots environmental movement and the budding political populism expressed in a growing number of statewide and community-labor coalitions.

Though diverse, these proposals strike us as far more complementary than antagonistic. While each by itself may not dislodge the current corporate and socially irresponsible economy, taken together they promise transformation.

Out of the Shallows, into the Business Mainstream
A Strategy for the Co-Op Movement

Steven L. Dawson

We were pretty arrogant ten years ago, or at least pretty naive. We saw the problems of conventional business firms in the United States and believed we could build better ones. Unfortunately, that is like knowing that cars are poorly built—and then setting off to build your own! Before you can build a better business, you first have to learn how to build a business.

We have learned that much. And after ten years of work, I believe that we have mastered much of the science of business—though still too little of the art. From nonbusiness backgrounds, as teachers, students, community organizers, lawyers, and union advocates, we have come far, to the water's edge; we have even waded in the shallows. I believe, however, that we have not yet dived deeply, making business *our* medium.

I am speaking of all of us in the worker-ownership field who share a democratic vision of the economy. This vision is not simply a narrow allegiance to one-person, one-vote structures but a wider understanding that business, even in a market economy, can be a progressive vehicle binding people together. I am speaking of those who understand that business, far from being an inherent problem, has the potential for being a powerful tool for social change in the United States.

Though we share this vision, we still stand on the outside of the business world looking in. Too many of worker ownership's leaders are consultants, teachers, financiers, and grantspeople; too few are managers or entrepreneurs of major businesses. We will know when democratic ownership has come of age—when the leaders, writers, and spokespersons for democratic ownership speak primarily from inside their own profitable, democratic firms.

One person who is an important forerunner of this shift is Rick Surpin, currently chief executive officer of Cooperative Home Care Associates in the South Bronx. Rick had been an organizer and nonprofit director in New York City for more than fifteen years. Eventually his organizing work brought him to worker ownership. Several years ago he initiated, as an organizer (still on the outside looking in), a home care cooperative business.

After several failed attempts to retain a competent professional manager from the health care field, Rick directly took up the reins of the company as president. Since he took over, the cooperative has become profitable and currently employs more than two hundred members. Rick is now considered a leader, not just within the worker ownership field but in the home health care field in New York City.

Flexible Specialization: The Future for Technical Assistance Organizations

This shift to making business our own is critical, but equally important will be the continued strength of our technical assistance and development organizations. Places like the ICA Group, PACE of Philadelphia, the Center for Community Self Help (CCSH) of North Carolina, the Midwest Center for Labor Research of Chicago, and the Naugatuck Valley Project in Connecticut will remain the repositories of our shared learning—both conventional business knowledge and that which is unique to democratic organizations. These groups will change, however, and the trends are already clear:

- Their staffs will remain fairly small. Both ICA and PACE have grown smaller, and the staffing at CCSH dedicated to worker ownership has similarly been reduced. They will probably rebound somewhat, but it is unlikely we will again see nonprofit organizations of more than fifteen. They would grow large again only if the next federal government were to support explicitly democratic efforts in the workplace, something I doubt even a Democratic administration will do.

- Growth of technical assistance will more likely be spread through a proliferation of even smaller for-profit consulting groups. PACE has already created a for-profit spinoff called Praxis. Chris Mackin of ICA has created Ownership Associates in Cambridge. David Ellerman, also of ICA, formed Dragon Mountain Associates for international work. Deborah Olson, once director of the Michigan Employee Ownership Council, has shifted her efforts more toward her law firm.

For the democratic field as a whole, the resulting mix of nonprofit and for-profit firms will provide an ideal flexibility. Experimentation will continue, yet the various groups are closely connected, so they increasingly will learn from each other and work together on larger projects. We may even witness the consulting counterpart of the Italian flexible specialization, where small specialized firms alternately come together and break apart in order to combine complementary expertise for differing large projects.

- The program activities of both nonprofits and for-profits will, as Len Krimerman suggested in an issue of *Changing Work*, diversify their activities beyond worker ownership into agricultural cooperatives, housing development, and other fields.

In either case, the realities of needing fee-for-service income will continue to force diversification. Successful outreach into progressive unions, churches, and governments will also require diversification in order to meet the non-worker ownership needs of these institutions.

- Democratic worker ownership will increasingly be promoted, not as an end in itself (that is, as a benefit to employees), but as a means to an end (as a benefit to consumers). Again, Cooperative Home Care Associates is an example, where its worker ownership structure has been the means to the end of providing higher quality patient care. In short, democratic ownership has to deliver higher than average quality goods and services, or it will not succeed in the United States.

Laboring in a Shadow: The ESOP Phenomenon

For the field as a whole, the most important reality in the United States will be the continuing eclipse of democratic forms of ownership by the much larger phenomenon of nondemocratic employee ownership, that is, nondemocratic ESOPs.

Ten years ago, most of us assumed that we would labor in our own garden for quite some time. We believed that although the results might be small, worker ownership would at least be ours to manage and direct, ours to define. Little did we know that we would end up tilling a small portion of a field dominated by investment bankers and finance lawyers.

The most interesting choice in the near future for the democratic forces will be how to best adjust to this reality. Do we continue to fight for the definition of worker ownership in the hearts and minds of the United States public? Or do we instead minimize the differences, work increasingly with nondemocratic businesses, and attempt to sway them slowly toward greater democracy?

I believe our tendency will be to blend increasingly into nondemocratic forms of ownership. Conversely, a part of the nondemocratic field will, of its own accord, move toward us. A number of ESOPs, while not formally democratic, certainly have many aspects of a humane, employee-oriented business structure. As long as we do not lose our original goals, I think this blending will be for the best. Some, including myself, will still want to work with more strictly democratic businesses, but we all have much to gain and much to give by integrating ourselves into what is now obviously the dominant strain of employee ownership in the United States.

Internationally, particularly in the Third World, I think we will see greater advances in democratic forms of ownership. From within the unbridled U.S. and European capitalist traditions, democratic ownership seems cumbersome and constraining. Conversely, in socialist countries attempting to generate some entrepreneurial spark out of their nationalized economies, democratic ownership offers relatively *greater* freedom and creativity. To them, democratic worker ownership can appear an intriguing balance of "public" accountability with freedom from stultifying central control.

The Opposite of Negative Is Not Always Positive: Lessons from a Democratic Workplace

What about lessons from our experience that are unique to democratic organizations? For me, most of these come from having worked and managed within the ICA Group itself—though given our backgrounds and the complex tasks at hand, it is hardly a typical workplace. Still, the ICA has been and continues to be a successful, albeit imperfect, experiment in democratic management.

From my perspective as a manager, the ICA's struggle with its democratic forms and process stems not so much from any intrinsic aspect of democracy itself as from the phenomenon of a democratic organization trying to form itself within an overwhelmingly nondemocratic business and social culture. Ironically, the crucial problem is not so much hostility from the nondemocratic world (democratic worker ownership has enjoyed more than its share of positive publicity, for example) but the presumptions and misconceptions that we carry into our organizations from our own nondemocratic experiences.

I call the confusion we bring with us the negative role model problem. Since we have experienced conventional workplaces as unrewarding and unjust, we often want to do exactly the opposite within our democratic firms. Instead of creating new possibilities for our democratic workplaces based on a positive design, we merely react out of repulsion for the old. The results are such counterproductive myths as "management is the problem" (not bad management), "profits are the problem" (not the improper use of profits), "authority is the problem" (not illegitimate authority). It is through such myths that the outside world turns upon our democratic efforts; not so much by frontal attack, but *from within*. Let me give two examples drawn from my early experience at ICA of how reacting negatively to old models can land us in new situations that are equally thorny.

Designing Organizations for Real (Imperfect) Human Beings

We were critical of the traditional workplace for not allowing employees to be themselves, to be human beings. Management, we claimed, allowed only a narrow, dehumanized band of appropriate behavior. In reaction, we wanted an organization that let people be themselves, without authoritarian norms defining what is and is not acceptable.

This might have worked—if all people were completely rational human beings, whose past histories and current lives outside the organization were totally logical. But given the repression in all our lives, such an unbounded work environment can become a very chaotic and hurtful arena. Anger, repressed in the encircling institutions, often erupts in a democratic workplace that does not have explicit norms of acceptable behavior. The result can be a good bit of destruction to the organization and to the people within it.

One answer is to strike a balance. We want our democratic organizations to provide for a broader band of acceptable behavior, because people can not and should not leave their personal lives and histories at the workplace door, and because work can—and should—be healing. But no matter how broad the band of acceptable behavior, it helps immensely to have it clearly defined. Some of the guidelines for behavior should be codified, but most should be defined over time by the example of the organization's leadership. If the whole membership strongly disagrees with the leaders' definition of what is acceptable, and the organization's structure is democratic, then either the leaders' norms will be adjusted or new leaders will eventually emerge.

Common Wealth: Abandoning the Myth of Subsistence Politics

Progressives have for decades decried the excesses of the U. S. economic system, and yet, as we have worked to design alternatives, we have again simply reacted. Our strategic thinking seems to have been that since wealth has been a problem, the progressive institutions we create will not have much wealth. Problem solved.

How then do progressives gain resources? We either tax the wealth producers (and, we hope, control the government that directs those taxes), or we take from profits to give to wages or philanthropy. *Always, always we are on the outside and the controllers of wealth are on the inside.* Since the concept of a politically progressive institution producing wealth has been antithetical to those of us who seek fundamental change, we are left with a slender, shifting base of power in universities, nonprofits, unions, and government agencies—not one of which produces its own wealth.

In light of earlier progressive history, this is odd. The utopian communities, even the "simple" Shakers, built their efforts upon controlling their own work, and thus creating a community of abundance. Our forerunners understood (far better than we) that social change does not occur without resources, abundant resources that we ourselves must create in order to truly control. *Wealth is not bad, it is essential.* It is the *use* of wealth that is either good or bad. And wealth used well is *common wealth*: resources reinvested into the community.

I hesitate to drag out Mondragon one last time, but I believe among all the lessons it provides the one most often overlooked is the most fundamental: Mondragon's wisdom is that it built itself, block by block, business by profitable business, into a major wealth-producing system. All the aspects we now marvel at—the Caja Laboral Popular, the housing, the consumer/worker groceries, the educational support—are either second-degree support systems or wise uses of the common wealth. All came, and could only come, after several very profitable businesses were established.

Here in the United States, progressives must do the same. We must develop strategies and build institutions that create and control wealth directly. Within a market economy that means we must build and control our own major businesses. This is a fifty-year strategy, but our grandchildren will thank us. If we only tax, regulate, and win an occasional election, we will remain forever on the outside looking in.

Among progressives the democratic worker-ownership movement has come far, perhaps farthest. But we must go much farther. We must step out of the shallows of small, subsistence enterprise and dive deeply into the business mainstream. We must make business our own.

Women's Cooperatives
Part of the Answer to Poverty?

Chris Weiss and Christine Clamp

In recent years, women's organizations in the United States working with low-income women have begun to substitute economic development projects for social-service projects. Increasingly, community-based organizations headed by women are beginning to offer training and resources to support microenterprise development and worker cooperatives, to advocate nontraditional job training and placement, and to push for higher pay for women. Here, we focus on the economic development strategy of creating worker cooperatives that allow women to learn new managerial and business skills, to assume leadership roles, and to gain control over their work lives.

To learn more about this strategy, we interviewed four women active in creating women's worker co-ops. They are Carol DiMarcello (who, through the Puget Sound Cooperative Federation in Seattle, Washington, provides a range of consulting services to area cooperatives and nonprofits); June Holley, who works with the Worker Owned Network (WON) in Athens, Ohio, to develop community-based, democratic, worker-owned businesses; Maureen Fenlon, a cofounder of LYDIA, a network that provides educational services to women's cooperatives; and Peggy Powell, director of education for Cooperative Home Care Associates (CHCA) in the Bronx, New York.

The Advantages for Women of Worker Co-Ops

While each of these women reported the usual difficulties finding capital for new worker cooperatives and funds for technical assistance, they all agreed that worker cooperatives afford women a number of important benefits, including empowerment, leadership training, learning opportunities not available in traditional work settings, and increased self-esteem.

Peggy Powell emphasized cooperative workplaces' potential to promote new relationships and perspectives. Now that CHCA's Black and Latino workforce controls the board of directors and, through the assembly of worker-owners, affects decisions about pay and benefits, "The women feel that they have real input and control in this company. That clearly is going to develop their ability to speak and to assert [themselves]."

This development is enhanced by CHCA's in-house educational program. It is designed to help CHCA's worker-owners discover that

> women can make choices: women can think. One's education is not determined by whether one completed college or high school. Education is about life experience. We demonstrate that by the way that we interact with [others] and their ideas, and we demonstrate that there is a real development that happens for the women in this company.

Changing Old Attitudes

As powerful as these experiences are for the women involved, difficult challenges remain. One of the hardest is creating the kind of culture within the local community that supports worker ownership. As Carol DiMarcello points out,

> The necessary people-skills are inherent in the community but they've been covered over for so long with garbage because of systems that put people down and don't empower them that it takes some time in enterprise development to bring them forth, to foster them, which makes the learning curve longer than I had originally anticipated.

According to Maureen Fenlon, this learning is made all the more difficult when there is a cultural gap between the technical assistance providers and the co-op members. This often occurs when worker co-ops are started by community development groups for low-income people.

> It's not their idea. So it doesn't necessarily match their values unless there is lots of reeducation or rethinking (and there's usually not the luxury to think things over). They want to be in a business or some kind of an enterprise for the family. The technical assistance providers are usually well-educated, middle-class people who are in it because of their values. Worker education is still undeveloped. This form of business is an idea not yet owned by the very people with whom we are working.

CHCA has overcome this problem by providing in-house education and training. As Peggy Powell describes it:

> When you are dealing with low-income people who have a limited education, the biggest challenge is how to design training that is interactive, that people really can learn from and can feel and experience, and then to do that training in a way that real learning takes place. What I find pretty consistently is that "experts" don't know how to talk with and train nonexperts.

It takes a lot of time and commitment to develop effective training programs. For example, in preparation for a daylong session on membership development, Peggy Powell and her colleagues spent two months planning and thinking about and testing out the material. It's a very time-consuming process because we've been trained to do it a different way. Understandable materials are simple materials that people can look at and then apply the basic knowledge that they've had. They're not overwhelmed and intimidated and can, over time, feel they have real ownership and control over the company.

Beyond training, WON attempts to address this issue in part by how it positions itself in its community. Says June Holley:

We're really accepted by people in the community. We're even a member of the Chamber of Commerce, though we're not part of the old-boys network. There are real obstacles out there. But we've always worked on the theory that you always move toward anyone who appears to be even slightly interested in what you are doing.

Pay and Benefits

The cooperatives with which these women work struggle to create jobs with adequate pay. Both the Puget Sound Cooperative Federation and the Worker Owned Network use local pay rates as benchmarks for cooperative pay scales, although Carol DiMarcello points out that in making comparisons we ought to look not only at established noncooperative firms but also at newly created small businesses from which owners often draw little income for the first few years. WON will not develop a cooperative unless it will pay at least minimum wage. In part for this reason, they are very interested in creating new opportunities in nontraditional fields of employment for women and in "flexible manufacturing networks" in which small manufacturing firms come together to work on a product that none of them could produce by themselves. They hope that this model will allow more flexibility for women (e.g., to work at home), as well as more pay.

Cooperative Home Care Associates has led efforts in the New York City area to increase the compensation for and standard of care provided by home health-care providers. Starting by offering higher salaries than the norm, CHCA has also successfully pushed for increases in standard benefits and in government reimbursement to home health-care providers. As of 1991, CHCA's starting rate was $6.50 per hour, with raises for longevity, plus twelve days of paid leave per year, five vacation days for every two thousand hours worked (increasing with longevity), and a pay differential for complex care, such as for bed-bound, Alzheimer's, or AIDS patients.

Women's Co-Ops as Problem and Opportunity

These interviews reinforce our conviction that worker cooperatives can be a vital and successful part of community economic development strategies designed to improve the conditions of low-income women. Beyond providing paid work, they can help increase their members' sense of empowerment, self-esteem, skills, leadership abilities, and autonomy. Cooperatives seem particularly suitable for rural areas where opportunities for full-time employment are scarce and where marketing cooperatives can help to deliver products to a wider market, and in sectors like home health-care, in which the policies adopted by worker cooperatives can affect the entire sector.

While marginalization, lack of funding, low wages, and problems with worker training and education will probably continue to plague many women's cooperatives, feminist organizations seeking to go beyond social service and short-term approaches to problems of women's poverty would do well to look at worker-owned and democratically organized cooperatives as part of a long-term strategy.

Worker Ownership, the New Workforce, and Community Empowerment

Interview with Chuck Turner

Changing Work: Chuck, for close to a decade you worked with the Industrial Cooperative Association (currently known as the ICA Group) developing worker-owned enterprises and providing hands-on education to employees in the process of becoming owners. Do you now see this lengthy experience with worker ownership and workplace democracy as significant and useful for people of color? Is it relevant, for example, to your present work with the Center for Community Action?

Chuck Turner: Workplace democracy and democratic ownership of one's work raise critical, but largely neglected, issues for low-income communities, and in particular for communities of color. One illustration of this is the meeting that just broke up downstairs here at the Center. This was one in a series of workshops with community organizers from various Boston neighborhoods who work in either the public or nonprofit sectors. Many of them speak of feeling alienated from boards and directors who make basic decisions but do little or no work, who lack respect for them as workers with distinctive skills and responsibilities, and who go beyond establishing policy and try to determine day-to-day workplans. These organizers, for example, are often called upon to do office work, instead of the face-to-face organizing they were hired for. In short, they are disempowered by their work situations. And given this daily diminishment of their humanity, how can they be expected to encourage an attitude of empowerment in the communities where they work?

CW: Sounds familiar.

CT: Yes, in a way it's not surprising: just another dismal confirmation of the influence exerted on all sections of worklife by the prevailing forms of power and organization. Still, it reveals that the ideas behind worker democracy have very clear implications for workers in the public sector and in nonprofit organizations.

Those ideas speak to extremely important, but as yet largely unrecognized, needs of these workers, many or even most of whom are people of color.

CW: How do you see this changing? What can be done to give those needs greater legitimacy and recognition?

CT: We are working on this here at the Center—in ways that I've come to see draw heavily on my previous experience with democratic workplaces in the industrial sector. For example, we offer a kind of advanced course for these same organizers, one that applies the democratic-ownership model in an educational setting. The educator's role shifts to being a facilitator or consultant: we stipulate that our students, the organizers, tell us how they want to utilize our time and our resources. We don't determine what issues or skill-development areas are important—they do. In this way, they not only become familiar with each other's perspectives and find common threads and problems, but they get important experience establishing agendas and priorities.

CW: Beside this extension of workplace democracy to help empower public and human-service workers, how else do you see this concept as crucial, and as connected to community empowerment?

CT: If we're thinking of Black and other communities of color, there are several important connections. In the first place, consider today's minority youth. People in their teens or twenties today were born into an era of rising consciousness, an era that saw the dawning of new democratic rights and responsibilities: our young had to be affected by these vibrations all around them. One key by-product is that they are no longer willing to accept abusive or demeaning relationships, to submit docilely to corporate hierarchies. Conformity is not on their agenda. Nonetheless, these young people, like all others, *need workplaces and are needed in the workforce.*

CW: Why is that? Couldn't our economy run as well without their participation?

CT: Not any longer. The white population has been getting steadily older and smaller, while the workforce has become increasingly female, young, and of color. And it is primarily this population, these new workers, who need a different kind of workplace—one that meets their enhanced aspirations and their intuitive sense of their role and rights in a democracy.

One model with increasing potential and relevance is the labor cooperative. Instead of being hired employees, ordered about by supervisors and assistant managers, workers would collectively own enterprises that contracted with private or public organizations to provide anything from secretarial and janitorial services to carpentry and catering. They would then receive not only salaries but a fair share of year-end profits. In short, instead of what's now offered—a kind of dehumanized wage slavery—new and enhanced work relationships would be created for people who today are systematically devalued.

CW: Isn't there a danger here, though, of developing very transitory, dead-end enterprises? How would these labor cooperatives differ from the overflow of temporary positions that have recently surfaced?

CT: There are lots of differences. For one thing, while labor cooperatives might provide some of the same services now offered by temporaries, these co-ops would of course be self-managing. Workers would have the opportunity to decide together what work to take on (and how much), how best to get it accomplished, what hours to work, and so on—everything they are now kept from deciding. Second, an education-and-training component would be included, so that human development as well as business success remained a key priority. This would be good for profits as well, for it would make these labor co-ops far more flexible—adaptable to different markets, as well as to changing workforce aspirations—than temporary firms. Finally, as a labor cooperative becomes more profitable, each member's share of surplus revenues also increases. This practical incentive for worker involvement is totally absent from typical temporary employment: no matter how hard or smart they work, temporaries rarely share in the success or growth of their company.

CW: So you see the labor cooperative as providing a distinctive kind of work situation tailored to the needs and self-image of the "new workforce"—young, female, and persons of color?

CT: Yes, mainstream corporations and public agencies cannot keep pace with the changing and rising aspirations of these workers. In particular, they cannot address the issue of how to restructure work so that it is a humanizing or empowering experience for all workers in all sections of the economy. But in addition I see a more long-range role for labor cooperatives.

CW: How so?

CT: Once these labor cooperatives, which basically supply services to industry and government, start to thrive and not merely survive, they will begin accumulating capital. Furthermore, in a decade or two, they will have among them not only the capital resources but the human skills and business experience to challenge traditional corporations, even in manufacturing or industrial areas. We may then begin to see an economic withering away of capitalism in its traditional form, at least in certain sectors.

CW: That's certainly an attractive picture, but isn't it overly rosy?

CT: I don't think so. Remember that we are talking here not about isolated worker co-ops scattered in disconnected regions of the country or among many separate industries, but those created primarily by people of color in their own communities. This gives them two important advantages: they will tend to think locally, that is, to produce for local community needs; but, at the same time, these cooperatives will see themselves as participants and partners in important global and national changes. Let me spell out both of these points in some detail.

Production for local needs makes ecological and economic sense. Transportation costs are frequently a misuse of resources, and they often contribute to lowered product quality, for example, in the food industry. Beyond this, by producing for local needs, a cooperative workforce can provide itself with a steady and uniquely valuable flow of feedback from its *customers*. This sort of producer-consumer communication can only improve worker motivation and product quality.

In regard to the wider, or global, context, here the demographics will be crucial. Even in the industrial sector, and throughout the labor movement, workers of color are becoming a more and more significant influence. A growing number of them have their primary loyalties to the countries and continents of their origins—to South America, the Caribbean, and Asia—and they will look there for ideas on worklife as well as for economic partners. Models like the Mondragon association of cooperatives will continue to gain influence, for these enable planned growth while facilitating cooperation between housing, service, agricultural, and industrial enterprises.

CW: In other words, labor cooperatives are just one expression of some very far-reaching and widely diffused changes in our economy.

CT: Yes. The system initiated by Franklin Roosevelt to patch up the damage left by the Great Depression—the ruling troika of government, corporate, and union elite—is about to explode. It may take two years, or six, or ten, but it is bound to self-destruct. For decades, it's been running on subsidies, creating phony throwaway products, financing itself through junk bonds or federal deficits—pumping air, rather than new blood, into its veins. The ruling troika never did much for people of color; we were excluded from any benefits it dispersed. So as this system totters, and union leaders (as well as rank and filers) of color begin to dominate, there will be little loyalty around to keep it shored up. New models will be sought, new questions will become central. The main debate will not be over wages and benefits alone, but over how (and by whom) work is to be controlled, and over how to link it to both local community needs and those of global liberation.

CW: These are very fundamental changes. Where do you see them beginning to emerge in the next few years?

CT: One key area would be the current crisis in our youth community. Community-based labor cooperatives, with their empowering potential, might be able to help turn around the drug and gang phenomena, for example, by building viable bridges between school and worklife. They could help harness a lot of this youth energy by directing it away from short-term highs toward longer-term goals, such as gaining social, economic, and political power.

In my neighborhood, for example, a community-based security company has provided shelter and jobs for youth who had been involved in muggings. The young people are also getting their equivalency diplomas at a local community college. There are group meetings every day from 4 to 6 P.M. that bring together about twenty to twenty-five youth to think through their past and plan their future. It's not an easy process, but it illustrates how negative group energy can begin to be positively focused.

Beyond this, the wider community is beginning to edge toward a major recession. This sort of crisis period could well become an opportunity for the incubation of new ideas to rebuild our sagging and unraveling economy—ideas like that of the labor cooperative, community-based production, and regionalization. But we will need to be ready with the crucial elements—working models, training programs, technical assistance, to name just a few.

CW: How, though, do you see all of this reaching people during this coming time of turmoil? How can we start developing a wider constituency for democratic control of work?

CT: It won't be easy. But there are two promising approaches, ones that have not yet been very fully recognized or utilized by the worker-ownership movement in this country. The first of these is the development of a *land movement*, a movement that would secure homes, protect farmers and their croplands, and enable city dwellers and neighborhoods to acquire land to help meet their basic housing and food needs.

CW: Sounds like what some of us in the worker-ownership movement have called local self-reliance.

CT: Yes. However, the worker-ownership, and indeed the labor movement generally, have largely ignored their relationship to land. But without a secure home in a secure community, how can people sustain a long-term interest in work, however much improved or democratically reorganized? Land is a crucial element in all wealth, and if we view it solely as a source of profit for private developers or real-estate corporations, we risk reviving a cycle similar to that which led to the depression of 1929: farmers and others lose their lands, workers' jobs and savings dry up, the ranks of the homeless and the foodless swell. To forestall this sort of cycle, and to make room and provide stability for new forms of worklife—labor cooperatives and similar innovations—we need strong rural (and urban) land-development policies. These policies would ensure access to land for neighborhood or cooperative groups as well as for small farmers; the land thus acquired could be used for both homes and subsistence, and could in addition support numerous types of labor-intensive enterprises.

These might include, for example, remanufacturing—taking old equipment and renewing it. Or, given our food crisis, hydroponics should be carefully examined. In addition, crafts production should not be overlooked: wood and metal products, glass blowing, sweaters woven from the wool of New England sheep. Let us use our imaginations to construct an economy of the future that can be housed in buildings, and on land, owned by the community.

CW: What's the second potential path for building a wider constituency for democracy at work?

CT: This involves what I've called *education for ownership*. Up to now, surprisingly, very little of this sort of education has been introduced within worker-owned companies in the United States. Weirton Steel (in West Virginia) is perhaps a good model, since it uses worker education to enlist the consciousness of worker-owners in redesigning their own shopfloor procedures. Not only does the Weirton workforce have access to crucial company information, but they are given—through labor-management teams—the opportunity to use that information to improve both the way they work day in and day out and the larger workplace as well.

As I see it, what's essential in education for ownership is that responsibility is decentralized—planning, work schedules, resource acquisition and allocation, feedback from the firm's clients and customers—are all distributed throughout the entire enterprise. What this full-scale decentralization achieves is an increase in worker motivation. In fact, different sorts of motivation (beyond wages and benefits) come to life. Workers feel empowered, their creativity and intelligence are tapped and they become more productive, more professional, more concerned with the quality of their own work and that of the company's products. It turns out, as Richard Hackman and Greg Oldham (1980) among others have claimed, that if you treat someone as if they have a brain, they will then learn to use their capacities, but if you continually tell them what you want them to do, they'll shut down and won't do anything until they're told to do it.

In short, if we want to reach (and hold onto) more and more workers and communities, we will need more than new notions of ownership. In addition, we will have to find ways of making work empowering, of shifting key responsibilities, awakening creative powers. This in turn will require a reeducational process, one that puts the learner (and future owner of work) in the driver's seat and provides opportunities for the exercise of initiative and judgment. One illustration of this education-for-ownership model, which I've already mentioned, is our advanced workshops with community organizers in which they tell us—the students tell the teachers—what they want to learn and how they want to utilize our time and skills. In addition, labor cooperatives can provide a setting for this reeducation process. And a further example would involve blending the cooperative ethic and practice with the Junior Achievement model of youth learning business at an early age. *(Two such models are presented in the Short Takes for chapter 5 above—Eds.)*

Drawing In and Reaching Out
Strategies to Strengthen the
Workplace Democracy Movement

Len Krimerman and Frank Lindenfeld

We˙see the current worker-ownership movement as an important potential linchpin in a broader effort to build a democratic, environmentally sound, and socially responsible alternative to corporate capitalism. Worker owned and operated firms can provide a much needed economic base, opportunities for learning democratic organizational and leadership skills, and resources for bringing together diverse constituencies. On the other hand, the worker-ownership movement needs the support and widened perspective that should come from forming strong bonds with other progressive grassroots groups. With this in mind, we propose two strategies, one to consolidate and internally strengthen the current worker-ownership movement, the other designed to help it reach out and create collaborative alliances with other groups working to build a more just, democratic, and ecologically sustainable society.

Drawing In: Consolidating the Worker-Ownership Movement

To deepen the budding movement for workplace democracy and worker ownership, we suggest that its proponents:

- Increasingly *target whole economic sectors,* rather than focusing on individual plants;
- Expand and improve *education for worker ownership*;
- Build *cooperation, association, and solidarity* within the movement;
- Develop *grassroots financial institutions* to support the integrated growth of local and worker-owned enterprises.

Targeting Sectors

It makes sense, and not solely in business terms, to target specific sectors, rather than isolated firms, for the development of worker ownership. As our recycling

(R2B2) and home health care (Cooperative Home Care Associates) examples show, one successful enterprise can often be of immense value to others in the same sector by sharing its managerial expertise, production methods, accounting systems, marketing contacts, and the like. And once several such similar firms are in operation, they can naturally form—as have the progressive printers—an association to assist in developing joint ventures and cooperative marketing, bulk purchasing from common suppliers, and locating improved technology, thus enhancing the viability of each cooperative firm. As these sectors of worker owned and operated firms expand, they will naturally increase the level of cohesion and solidarity within the movement. Moreover, together they could encourage local, democratically controlled economies by adopting a common label, perhaps the old cooperative twin pine, to let consumers know that local worker-owners had produced a given item, and by pressuring the public sector to purchase the goods of local worker-owned enterprises rather than those made by distant megacorporations. This sort of public education and organized pressure would help raise the profile of worker ownership while recycling revenues within the local economy. Burlington, Vermont, is already exploring this model of publicly supported worker ownership, and the Greater London Economic Board used it for several years with considerable success before being dismantled by the Thatcher government.

What sectors lend themselves to wholesale worker ownership and control? While local conditions will of course vary, here are some that seem ripe to us:

- *Crafts cooperatives,* perhaps organized as cottage industries with a common marketing cooperative. Watermark is already an inspirational model, as well as a technical assistance provider for other would-be craft co-ops.

- *Environment-sustaining enterprises* like those relying on local and renewable energy sources, those that collect and reprocess recyclables, those that clean up hazardous wastes or help to reduce the use of toxic materials, or those that furnish less wasteful transportation (e.g., light rail manufacture). The Japanese ecological consumer-producer organization, Seikatsu, provides a fine example here. It consists of two hundred thousand households, organized into small neighborhood groups, that buy in bulk according to strict ecological criteria and that produce commodities themselves (e.g., organic milk and nontoxic soaps) where commercial products do not meet those criteria. We discuss later on why this sector is especially propitious for both worker ownership and alliance-building.

- *High-tech, small-scale artisan production,* based on the flexible manufacturing network model developed in the Emilia-Romagna section of Italy. Here, unionized shops—many, although not all, worker-owned—form temporary and shifting alliances and cooperate in their use of computer-aided design, production, and marketing methods to provide highly skilled and creative work in such fields as textiles, printing, and engineering. The Worker Owned Network (WON) in Athens, Ohio, has recently begun to develop a homegrown version of this approach, linking several firms which produce different components for accessible and affordable housing.

- *The public sector.* As many municipalities consider selling off their transportation systems, utilities, trash-collection services, emergency medical departments, and even public hospitals, employee ownership (combined perhaps with some residual degree of public ownership or supervision) may have much to offer. Good U.S. models are rare, but the large and successful transportation cooperatives in Israel, and the eight employee-owned highway service companies formed in British Columbia as a result of provincial privatization, might well prove helpful.[1]

Expanding Education for Worker Ownership

Education within the current worker-ownership movement is underdeveloped in at least four ways. First, most ESOPs and cooperatives spend too little time on work-site education designed to provide workers, managers, and board members the skills, confidence, procedures, and resources for creating and maintaining viable worker-owned firms. Second, there are very few facilities or opportunities through which management and business expertise can be developed; lacking this, worker-owned firms will operate at a distinct disadvantage. Third, even where there is ample work-site and managerial education, it is seldom accompanied by what might be called political, or solidarity-building, education. Worker-owners in Connecticut may not know about, much less feel any bond with, their counterparts in North Carolina or in Japan. And as yet they rarely look beyond democracy in their own workplace to tasks like shaping the economy of their city or industry or building local coalitions that might open more space for democratic enterprises. Political education should help to overcome enterprise consciousness, and to create links among currently fragmented worker-owned enterprises.

Finally, worker-ownership education is deficient in yet a fourth sense. Despite its progress and its future potential, the current worker-ownership movement remains largely hidden from the general public and even from many potential allies—community empowerment organizers, peace, housing, and labor activists, grassroots environmental groups, and democratic socialists. Worker ownership needs a strong education campaign to publicize its existence, the substantial gains it has made over the past two decades, and the ways it could contribute to the priorities and organizing strategies of its natural allies.

What then is to be done? To overcome these gaps, we recommend:

- *Building on and expanding the educational models presented in this book,* in particular the sort of on-site and community- or region-based programs developed by WON in Appalachian Ohio and by the Puget Sound Cooperative Federation in Washington State.
- *New university and college programs, especially land-grant university extension programs* (similar to that at Utah State University) which bring educational, technical, and financial resources directly to workers, unions, and communities involved in start-ups or conversions and which could help build statewide networks of worker-owned enterprises. As in the case of Boston

College and Kent State University, these educational programs might do well to link up with business schools or management departments, at least those—and there are some—that have begun to recognize the futility of basing economic development on remote, enormous, multinational firms.

Furthermore, such efforts can also bring the ideas—or, better, the concrete accomplishments and benefits—of worker ownership and workplace democracy to the general public and to specific interest groups who stand to gain from them. Such groups might include retiring owners of small and medium-sized firms, community development organizations, state economic development agencies, and unions faced with plant closings, among others.

- *High school (and college) fieldwork programs.* The REAL program seems an extremely valuable and replicable model, through which the next generation of workers can learn to plan and then to actually run their own enterprises. Though originally rural, it is now being extended to urban areas; although it was conceived for high school students, college students can benefit from it (and have done so, at community colleges in Georgia). Schools with so-called co-op programs could implement a REAL program by enabling students to start their own enterprises rather than simply slotting them into predetermined corporate positions. Better yet, the REAL model could be applied to community needs or problems. For example, a group in New Haven is now developing an ecology high school that would use a working farm as a vehicle for academic learning, personal growth, social integration, and community development. A recycling enterprise, or any number of environmentally responsible, locally initiated, and economy-reviving firms, would serve as well. The results of such a project could be magnified if the students and faculty joined with community and labor groups to help identify the existing pool of production skills among the under- and unemployed, and then went on to build common business ventures with them.

- *Down the Road: A Home.* If worker-ownership education is to really thrive, it will need one or more homes of its own in which ideas and programs can be continually shaped and reshaped without outside interference. Free-standing and self-managed educational centers could bring together and enhance all of the educational programs we have discussed, while avoiding most of the bureaucratic squabbles, turf wars, and ideological battles characteristic of conventional institutions. Our model here is the Highlander Folk School during the 1950s and 1960s, when it played a unique and essential role in helping consolidate and empower the civil rights movement in the South. Without some sort of similar institution to develop grassroots leaders, to nurture consciousness of shared problems, to help generate and test new tactics, and to provide the emotional support of allies, it is uncertain just how far the current movement for workplace democracy can go or whether it can develop as a whole movement, one with a soul and spirit, not merely a bottom line.

Building a More Cohesive and Unified Movement

Targeting economic sectors and developing educational programs will help to bring together worker-ownership constituencies, pave the way for geographic or industry-wide associations, and enable worker-owners to recognize common goals and problems and the need for interdependence in the face of corporate power. Beyond this, we would encourage the *formation of a nationwide democratic ESOP association*—one that could include worker-owned cooperatives that were not formally structured as ESOPs. As we envision it, this association would publicize the existence and strengths of democratic ESOPs and worker cooperatives, lobby for favorable national legislation, and advocate and support (with experience and technical assistance) the spread of democracy throughout current ESOPs and into firms seeking to convert to employee ownership. Since 90 percent of all ESOP companies are not (yet?) majority owned, and the remaining 10 percent evidence varying degrees of democracy, employee rights, participation, and so on, this association would have plenty to do. Fortunately, its work would be bolstered by the many separate studies that indicate that productivity and efficiency tend to increase only when participation by employee owners in running and governing their own enterprises is high.[2] A democratic-ESOP association, therefore, can appeal to workers in nondemocratic employee-owned firms on at least two grounds: not only is workplace democracy more equitable because all labor is respected, but it also improves the bottom line.

Finally, a democratic-ESOP association would be concerned—and very well positioned—to help overcome many of the gaps in the worker-ownership movement already discussed, such as those in worker-ownership education, technology development, targeting specific industries, developing cross-plant cooperation and solidarity, and establishing links with other progressive groups.

Developing Grassroots Sources of Capital

A major factor in the success of Mondragon, the Basque cooperative community, has been the Caja Laboral Popular (CLP), or Working People's Bank. Drawing on deposits from hundreds of thousands of members, the CLP provides entrepreneurial and financial assistance to its network of associated cooperatives. Learning from this example, and from others such as the Eco-Bank in Frankfurt and the credit union of North Carolina's Center for Community Self-Help, we suggest that local communities adopt a similar vision—that they build integrated networks of cooperatives and other local enterprises, each such network supported by a democratically controlled bank or credit union. Such capital-providing financial institutions may well be the missing link that would spur the development of worker-owned and labor-based businesses throughout the country. They might be sponsored by community development corporations, by labor unions, or, best, by *coalitions* that brought together many diverse grassroots groups. They could thus seek a wide base of member depositors and work in conjunction with union and state-controlled pension funds, as well as religious sources of investment, to channel needed capital to cooperative and community-based firms.

Reaching Out: Building Strength through Collaboration and Alliances

Worker ownership, even if it becomes more widespread, cannot by itself displace or seriously challenge corporate capitalism. For this, it will need outside help. In the apt phrase of Jeremy Brecher and Tim Costello (1990), it will need to "build bridges" and enter working coalitions with other progressive groups. Two specific sorts of alliances seem to us especially ripe, and especially crucial: an alliance with grassroots environmental groups, in particular those now calling themselves the environmental justice movement; and political coalitions designed to harness public-sector resources in order to support democratic economic activity.

Combining Worker Ownership and Environmental Justice

Over the past decade, as worker ownership has been gathering strength and sophistication, the grassroots environmental justice movement has also taken root and grown extensively. It has won a number of landmark victories against toxic waste dumps, incinerators, and corporate polluters. It owes much to the Citizens' Clearinghouse for Hazardous Waste (CCHW), an organization put together in 1981 by Lois Gibbs after the heroic battle she and her neighbors fought against Hooker Chemical's toxic dump at Love Canal. According to Will Collette, who worked as CCHW's organizing director through 1990, "there is now a genuine Grassroots Movement for Environmental Justice. By this we mean a large and growing collection of organizations—around 6500 by our latest estimate—who are fighting for the same values, often against the same opponents."[3]

Recently, this part of the environmental movement has begun reaching out to constituencies other than those primarily concerned with toxic pollution (e.g., to minorities and to labor). According to CCHW (now also called the Center for Environmental Justice), this means that the "Grassroots Environmental Justice Movement seeks common ground with low-income and minority communities, with organized workers, with churches, and with all others who stand for freedom and equality."[4]

At the same time, the environmental justice movement is shifting its focus from short-term and reactive battles to more enduring and constructive strategies. Not surprisingly, these are closely linked to workplace democracy and labor-community control over economic decisions. As CCHW puts it,

> Environmental justice is more than just preserving the environment. When we fight [for it], we fight for our homes and families and struggle to end economic, social and political domination by the strong and greedy. . . . Environmental justice is old-fashioned grassroots democracy. . . . [It] is people in action to decide, . . . no longer being the victims of somebody else's decision. [It] is the right to choose, to have options, and to act.[5]

These changes in the constituency and goals of the environmental justice movement are profound and fertile. In our view, however, they need to be strengthened by an alliance with the people involved with worker ownership and the adoption of a joint *production-centered strategy* through which rainbow constituencies could be economically empowered. Why so?

The reasons are multiple. First, environmental groups seeking common ground with organized labor, and with working people in general, need to have ways of creating or preserving jobs so that, when they challenge industrial polluters, they can offer alternatives to corporate employment. Second, a production-centered strategy offers a way of *directly* preventing or curtailing toxic releases and hazardous waste, rather than leaving this task in the unreliable, slow-moving, and readily co-opted hands of government agencies and officials. Third, grassroots movements are invariably short on capital, and they need ways to carry on their struggles continuously. A strategy of developing environmentally safe and sustainable worker-owned enterprises would help meet these needs: it could generate surplus revenue to be recycled for environmental justice battles, and/or the creation of additional nonhazardous enterprises, while providing full-time exemplary employment—rather than simply volunteer positions—for some of those engaged in the struggle.

Also, the current worker-ownership movement could offer the environmental justice movement the benefit of its growing experience with labor-community alliances. In particular, the national Federation for Industrial Retention and Renewal (FIRR), which includes some twenty-five of these coalitions, could be the meeting ground for the two movements. In addition, FIRR could provide some useful tactics, such as the use of eminent domain to counter would-be runaway polluters. Beyond this, labor-community alliances might promote various types of ecological conversion that further environmental justice while creating community-based or worker-owned jobs. Finally, as recent experience in Denmark suggests, a labor-community alliance could well force state or municipal support (research and development funding, financing, purchasing) for safe materials, toxics transition, and clean technology.

Combining worker ownership and environmental justice seems especially promising because, according to such pioneers as the Institute for Local Self-Reliance (ILSR) and the Center for Neighborhood Technology (CNT), ecologically sustainable enterprise may be a growth industry. ILSR has been working for years with municipalities as diverse as St. Paul, Minnesota, Newark, New Jersey, Toledo, Ohio, and Los Angeles on ways to "mine" (collect, reprocess, remanufacture) "urban ore" so that the waste stream yields basic materials for local manufacturing and new jobs. And CNT has recently issued *No Time for Waste*, a step-by-step manual for community groups on all aspects of recycling, which concludes that "the vision of thriving local economies fueled by garbage is within reach." [6] Moreover, as ILSR and others have repeatedly pointed out, a local economy based on recycling, reprocessing, and remanufacturing its waste stream can begin to delink from, or strengthen itself against, the pressures of the global marketplace. That is, by using local waste stream materials to produce for local needs, communities can avoid direct competition with transnational corporations and move toward self-reliance.

Consider again R2B2's "franchising" operation, which provides a model and resources for the development of similar community-based recycling enterprises elsewhere (from California, to Florida, to Ireland). This might just be the first step in a production-centered strategy that combines environmental justice and worker ownership. Imagine the impact if only 10 percent of those sixty-five hundred environmental justice groups identified by CCHW were to develop recycling cooperatives in their own localities![7]

Of course, the benefits of an environmental justice and worker-ownership alliance would flow in the opposite direction as well. By joining or expanding labor-community coalitions, environmental justice groups would add strength and diverse voices. In addition, their cohesiveness, militancy, and experience in grassroots organizing would supply much-needed energy and cross-group solidarity to a still largely disunified worker-ownership movement.

Given that an alliance would be useful, how can these groups be brought together? R2B2, ILSR, and CNT are already working toward such an alliance; and the ICA Group is now promoting, and offering technical assistance to, community-based recycling efforts. To build on these beginning steps, we propose the following:

Locally

- *Joint development and ownership (by workplace-democracy and environmental justice groups) of recycling, reprocessing, and remanufacturing firms,* as well as others that are environmentally sound. Such firms could draw support from worker-ownership technical assistance groups and common-wealth capital providers.

- *Joint development of consumer-producer cooperatives* which, following the Seikatsu model, not only purchase environmentally benign products in bulk but produce them when they are not otherwise available.

- *Creating labor-community-environmental alliances* (e.g., expanding the community-labor coalitions within FIRR) that support job retention and reindustrialization, as well as safe materials policies and ecological conversion ventures.

- *Creating banks or credit unions similar to the Eco-Bank of Frankfurt.* (Its name was chosen to convey that the bank is both an economic and an ecological alternative.) Supporters of environmental concerns (an increasingly large group) now deposit their savings almost exclusively in banks locked into unecological, as well as disenfranchising, anti-labor, and locally impoverishing, practices. In "eco banks," such deposits—together with ones from religious organizations and, possibly, pension funds—could begin to turn things around: loans could be made to recycling enterprises, to developers of safe and degradable industrial materials, to producer-consumer co-ops like Seikatsu, and so on.

Statewide, and Nationally:

* *Lobbying for legislation* requiring or favoring hazardous-waste reduction, ecological substitutes for toxic substances used in production, and new enterprises using nonpolluting, life-protecting materials.

* *Combined demands for federal policies dealing with layoffs and plant closings,* such as the "Superfund for Workers" suggested by Tony Mazzochi of the Oil, Chemical, and Atomic Workers and FIRR's proposed National Industrial Development Fund and Agency. While the Superfund would use federal monies "to help workers cope with losing work when [polluting] plants shut down or run away," FIRR's agency would provide financial assistance for buyouts or start-ups. Clearly, both concepts would support the development of ecologically sustainable industry—owned and controlled by local communities and workers.

In short, then, there is more than ample space for environmental justice and workplace democracy activists to work together, to contribute to each other's numbers, diversity, and strengths, and to expand their capacity to create a genuinely new and democratic economy.

Building a New (Populist?) Polity

How far the new workplace democracy movement can go will ultimately be decided not only by its economic viability but by whether it is supported or constrained by other key, and not strictly economic, institutions that wield power and control resources. Chief among these would be the vast array of government agencies and offices that make public policy. At present, the public sector most often supports the corporate economy by such "welfare for the wealthy" measures as subsidies, tax abatements and deferrals, favorable loans, preferential purchasing, zoning variances, and the like. Such corporation-favoring benefits—local, state, or federal—make it difficult at best for a democratic or cooperative economy to thrive. Moreover, the economic coalitions we have just been advocating may well be blocked at many points unless they can shift public policy and redirect governmental resources. But how to do this?

One promising development is the growth (or revival) of a populist conception of government. On this view, one major role of government is to actively support and promote local economic enterprise (including worker ownership), to bring grassroots groups and workers into the economic development process, and to help educate and prepare people for a locally focused and citizen-shaped economy. Jim Hightower, the former Texas agriculture commissioner and a prominent exponent of populist government, explains this concept by telling the story of a watermelon cooperative outside of Houston run by Black farmers that lost its market when previous customers, small family groceries, were displaced by huge national supermarket chains. Instead of adopting such standard liberal tactics as regulating or taxing the supermarket chains or providing supplementary income to the farmers, Hightower's populist approach changed the market structure so that Kroger's [supermarkets] could buy locally instead of nationally. . . . Kroger's bought every melon that co-op produced that year. The farmers had about a 164 percent increase in their income. Consumers paid $1.75 for the Texas melon instead of $3.50 for the Florida melon they had been buying. Kroger's made more profit and got more publicity than it had ever thought possible and now buys other products from those farmers. Today we have many more co-ops around the state and farmers have seen the advantage of local and regional marketing.[8]

Hightower goes on to describe other populist government interventions, such as:

creating direct marketing cooperatives selling to restaurants, selling to food wholesalers, selling internationally. We've been able to establish [locally owned] food processing facilities in the state [and] to promote a program of sustainable agriculture—including organic certification that a farm is pesticide- and synthetic-fertilizer free. We've been able to be an advocate for people in rural and suburban areas opposing toxic-waste dumps and pipelines and other corporate contaminating sources being located in their areas.[9]

In short, for Hightower, populist government functions neither as a bureaucratic impediment nor as a welfare provider, but as a facilitator, linking ordinary people and their enterprises with resources and markets, and catalyzing locally controlled economic development.

We would suggest several ways of extending this populist notion of government, beyond the kinds of cases described by Hightower:

- *"Cooperatizing" (rather than privatizing) much of the public sector:* that is, developing forms of shared ownership between government employees and municipalities or counties in such areas as transportation, waste disposal and recycling, parks and recreation, public health, emergency medical care, and childcare.

- *Using the public sector's vast (and largely ignored) potential as a market,* i.e., as a purchaser from locally and worker-owned enterprises of everything from recycled paper and used spare parts, to cafeteria services, to renewable energy, light-rail vehicles . . .

- *Enacting legislation which favors ecological conversion,* which supports local enterprises in producing clean and sustainable technologies or safe substitutes for toxic or nondegradable materials. Such legislation should be developed in collaboration with economic conversion groups, such as Jobs with Peace and the Center for Economic Conversion, that have long been working to redirect production away from dependence on military contracts.

Toward a Populist *Movement*

Jim Hightowers, however, are rare. We cannot count on politicians like him reappearing (or, apparently, being reelected) just when we need them. Nor could any progressive or populist individual remain long in office without the backing of a widespread constituency. Thus, if we want a populist government that will favor a decentralist, or locally empowering, economic system, we need to form a populist movement, or at the very least populist coalitions. Fortunately, such alliances have begun to take shape in several parts of the country. The Texas Populist Alliance, the Minnesota Alliance for Progressive Action, the Montana Alliance for Progressive Politics, and the Connecticut-based Legislation Electoral Action Project are all statewide coalitions with very diverse constituencies, including labor unions, community organizations, peace activists, gay and lesbian organizations, environmental groups, and religious denominations, among others.[10] Moreover, they all focus on increasing grassroots access to and influence over political decision making and on shifting government resources toward a broadly populist, or progressive, agenda. In this light, such statewide alliances may well be ideal allies for the worker-ownership movement (or ideal vehicles to create where they do not yet exist). This would be especially true where worker ownership is already linked to labor-community coalitions, as it is, for example, within FIRR. Moreover, the member organizations of FIRR, themselves already coalitions, would certainly have much to contribute to progressive alliances—for example, strategies, new constituencies, and national and local resources.

In any case, we think that the worker-ownership movement should collaborate with or work within progressive, politically focused groups like these statewide alliances. For only through this sort of strategy can government subservience to corporate interests be displaced by a populist public sector responsive to workplace democracy.

In Conclusion

We hope that we have shared our excitement about the fledgling movement for worker ownership and control: we have depicted it as a groundswell that can become increasingly cohesive and powerful while developing firm connections to other progressive grassroots groups, and that has a real chance to bring a new form of economic life into the U.S. mainstream. The current workplace democracy movement, though but two decades old, is at last developing the skills, the experience and durability, the appeal to diverse constituencies, the sources of capital, and the vision to create a genuinely democratic alternative that can meet people's immediate needs, while empowering them to create new and more fulfilling forms of worklife and community. Because worker ownership and control offer direct economic empowerment, this new movement has unprecedented transformative potential. Only when workers and communities take direct control over workplaces—and indeed over whole sectors of the economy—can they begin to "walk on two legs": that is, both survive the eroding pressures of the present system and, at the same time, move closer to a new society in which rice and beans are on every table, local economies are strong, and our citizenry is genuinely reenfranchised and has become capable of setting its own goals and shaping its own future.

NOTES

1. On the Canadian privatization efforts, see *Worker Co-op*, Toronto, Canada (Fall 1990): 4, 28–31. Two other useful sources are Severyn Bruyn's draft essay "A New Role for Government in the 1990s" and Philip E. Fixler's "Employee Ownership and the Privatization of Local Government Services." Bruyn's paper is available from him through the sociology department at Boston College, Chestnut Hill, MA; for Fixler's, write to the Reason Foundation in Santa Monica, CA.

2. For example, a recent study conducted on Michigan ESOPs showed consistent gains in employment, sales, productivity, and profits arising from "a synergy between employee involvement and ownership." *Employee Ownership Report* (November/December 1990): 4. (Oakland, CA: National Center for Employee Ownership).

3. *Everyone's Backyard* (January/February1990): 2. (Arlington, VA: Citizens' Clearinghouse for Hazardous Waste).

4. *Ibid.*

5. *Ibid.*

6. Patrick Barry, *No Time for Waste.* (Chicago: Center for Neighborhood Technology, 1989), 25.

7. For a strong beginning here, see Rev. Penny Penrose's article on Mississippi's Gulf Coast Recycling in *Everyone's Backyard* (February 1991): 6–8.

8. "Building a New Populism." Interview with Jim Hightower. *Dollars and Sense* (January/February1990): 13. (Somerville, MA).

9. *Ibid.*, 14.

10. For accounts of some of these, and other coalitions, see Brecher and Costello (1990) and Shavelson (1990).

9

Resources for Workplace Democrats

Having come this far by reading about and reflecting on workplace democracy, what next? Additional resources will probably prove helpful, regardless of whether you intend to investigate the many issues workplace democracy raises, join a worker-owned enterprise or a technical assistance group, or otherwise aid the budding movement to redirect corporate priorities more effectively. In this, our concluding chapter, you will find three sorts of resources. First, organizational: a directory containing names, addresses, and phone numbers of organizations with experience in this growing field, each part matched with one of the five types of groups highlighted in chapters 2 through 6. Second, we describe some international resources. Workplace democracy is not only a U.S. phenomenon but a global one. Over the past two decades (and in some cases much longer), it has emerged in very different forms in Japan, Italy, Canada, and many other countries. In a brief overview of these developments we attempt to sketch what is distinctive and instructive about each of them. Finally, informational: a comprehensive listing of materials (books, magazines, newsletters, manuals, and videos) on worker ownership and democracy at work.

One final note: this resource chapter will be periodically revised. If you can let us know of any additions, deletions, or corrections for the bibliography, the directories, or the international developments, we'll be wholeheartedly appreciative. Write to the editors, Len Krimerman and Frank Lindenfeld, c/o New Society Publishers, 4527 Springfield Avenue, Philadelphia, PA 19143.

Organizational Resources

Worker-Owned and Other Democratic Enterprises

Alamance Workers' Owned Knitting
737 East Davis Street
Burlington, NC 27215
(919) 226-6465

Alaska Commercial Company
1011 E. Tudor Rd. Suite 120
Anchorage, AK 99503
(907) 561-2135
(Retail chain)

Allied Plywood Corporation
4740 Eisenhower Drive
Alexandria, VA 22304
(703) 751-5800

ASEC Janitorial
P.O. Box 11515
Oakland, CA 94611
(415) 839-9044

Avis, Inc.
900 Old Country Rd.
Garden City, NY 11530
(516) 222-3000
(Car rental)

Avondale Shipyards
P.O. Box 50280
New Orleans, LA 70150
(504) 436-2121
(works primarily for the Navy Department, but is attempting to diversify.)

Bankers Print Inc.
5832 S. Green St.
Chicago, IL 60621
(312) 487-3142

Blue Dot Energy Worker Cooperative
P.O. Box 1365
Junction City, KS 66441
(913) 762-3032

Blue Mango Restaurant
330 G. St.
Davis, CA 95617
(916) 756-2616

Bookpeople
2929 5th Street
Berkeley, CA 94710
(415) 549-3030

Boston Bank of Commerce
110 Tremont
Boston, MA 02108
(617) 423-1010

Burley Design Cooperative
4080 Stewart Road
Eugene, OR 97402
(503) 687-1644
(Bicycle-gear manufacturer)

Call on Our People
25 W. Rayen Ave.
Youngstown, OH 44503
(216) 747-1633
(House-cleaning service)

Capital City Co-Op Cab, Inc.
640 E Street, P.O. Box 487
Broderick, CA 95605
(916) 371-8151

M. W. Carr and Company, Inc.
63 Gorham Street
W. Somerville, MA 02144
(617) 628-0768
(Manufactures wood and metal picture frames.)

Casa Nueva Restaurant
4 W. State St.
Athens, OH 45701
(614) 592-2016

C. C. Knitting
Box 818
Yanceyville, NC 27379
(919) 694-5824

CH2M Hill, Inc.
2300 N.W. Walnut Blvd.
Corvallis, OR 97330
(503) 752-4271
(Environmental engineering)

The Center for Human Development
332 Birnie Ave.
Springfield, MA
(413) 733-6624

Cheese Board Collective, Inc.
1504 Shattuck Ave.
Berkeley, CA 94209
(415) 549-3183

Cherry Hill Cannery
Barre-Montpelier Road,
M.R. 1
Barre, VT 05641
(800) 468-3020

Common Wealth Printing
47 East St.
Hadley, MA, 01035
(413) 584-2536

Community Market
1215 Morgan St.
Santa Rosa, CA 95401
(707) 546-1806
(Retail natural foods)

Consumers United Group
2100 M Street N.W.
Suite 207
Washington, DC 20063
(202) 872-5709
(Group-insurance plans)

**Cooperative Home Care
Associates**
349 East 149th St.
Room 706
Bronx, NY 10451
(212) 993-7104

Cost-Cutter Stores
1752 Iowa St.
Bellingham, WA 98226
(206)-773-5811
(Retail groceries)

Country Quilters
P.O. Box 248
Clay, WV 25043
(304) 587-2503
(Handmade quilts)

**George Whyte Dakotah
Handcrafts**
N. Park Ln.
Webster, SD 57274
(605) 345-4646

Davey Tree Company
1500 North Mantua Street
Kent, OH 44240
(216) 673-9511

**Denver Yellow Cab
Cooperative Association**
3455 Ringsby Court
Denver, CO 80216
(303) 292-6464

**Dungannon Sewing
Cooperative**
P.O. Box 393
Dungannon, VA 24245
(703) 467-2306

East Wind Nutbutters
East Wind Community
P.O. Box 6B2
Tecumseh, MO 65760
(417) 679-4682

EPIC Healthcare
P.O. Box 650398
Dallas, TX 75265-0398
(214) 869-0707
(Hospitals)

Equinox Industries, Inc.
Dorena Lake, Box 569
Cottage Grove, OR 97424
(503) 942-7720
(Bicycle-trailer
manufacturer)

Fastener Industries, Inc.
One Berea Common
Suite 206
Berea, OH 44017
(216) 243-0200

**Federacion para el
Dessarollo Agricola de
Puerto Rico, Inc.**
Calle Esther #E4
Royal Gardens
Bayamon, P.R. 00620
(809) 799-3025

Freedom Quilting Bee
Federation of Southern
Cooperatives
P.O. Box 95
Epes, Alabama 35460
(205) 652-9676

**Friends of the Third World
Inc./ Cooperative Trading
Project**
611 West Wayne St.
Fort Wayne, IN 46802
(219) 422-6821
(Imports Third World
products; community
printingservice)

**Ganados del Valle/Tierra
Wools**
P.O. Box 118
Los Ojos, NM 87551
(505) 588-7231

Genoa Crafts Co-op
P.O. Box 67
Genoa, WV 25517
(304) 385-4583

W. L. Gore Associates
555 Paper Mill Rd.
Newark, DE 19711
(302) 738-4880
(High-tech manufacture;
Goretex)

Grassroots Press
401-1/2 Peace St.
Raleigh, NC 27603
919-732-0557

Graybar Electric
34 N. Meramee Ave.
Clayton, MO 63105
(314) 727-3900
Electrical equipment)

Green Mountain Spinnery
Box 768, RD 2
Putney, VT 05346
(802) 254-9469
(Yarn manufacture)

Harbinger Publications
18 Bluff Rd.
Columbia, SC 29201
(803) 254-4565

HealthTrust
P.O. Box 24350
Nashville, TN 37202-4350
(615) 383-4444
(Hospital management)

**High School in the
Community**
45 Nash St.
New Haven, CT 06511
(203)787-8735

Hoedad Co-op, Inc.
P.O. Box 10107
Eugene, OR 97440
(503) 746-1125

Hulogos'i Communications
Box 1188
Eugene, OR 97440
(503) 343-0606

Icicle Seafoods
4019 21st Ave, W.
Seattle, WA 98550
(206) 754-6030

Inkworks
2827 Seventh St.
Berkeley, CA 94710.
(415) 845-7111

The Journal Company
P.O. Box 661
Milwaukee, WI 53201
(414) 224-2725

Jubilee Crafts
6117 Germantown Ave.
Philadelphia, PA 19144
(215) 849-0808

Justice Graphics
1140 W. Montrose Ave.
Chicago, IL, 60613
(312) 275-3822

Kambara—Africamerican Services, Inc.
40 Delle Ave.
Boston, MA 02120
(617) 445-4915
(Imports from African craftspeople; consults on African development)

Lakeside Press
1301 Williamson
Madison,WI 53703.
(608) 255-1800

Landmark Enterprises
P.O. Box 5685
Bellingham, WA 98227
(206) 671-9751
(Construction)

Lifetouch
400 Paramount Plaza
7831 Glenroy Road
Minneapolis, MN 55435
(218) 893-0500
(School-portrait processing)

Made in Mendocino
P.O. Box 510
Hopeland, CA 95449
(707) 744-1300
(Crafts co-op)

Milwaukee Rollers Cooperative
3480 North Pratney Street
Milwaukee, WI 53212
(414) 332-2349
(Low-cost wheelchair prototypes)

New Society Publishers
4527 Springfield Avenue
Philadelphia, PA 19143
(215) 382-6543

Noe Valley Community Store
1599 Sanchez St.
San Francisco, CA 94131

(415) 824-8022
(Retail food)

North Glenn Tax Service
11548 Community Center Dr. #53
North Glenn, CO 80233
(303) 452-7701

North Star Express
1400 Broad St.
Providence, RI 02905
(401) 781-6086
(Printing)

O&O Supermarket
12311 Academy Road
Philadelphia, PA 19154
(215) 824-3131

Omak Wood Products
Route 2, Box 54
Omak, WA 98841
(509) 826-1460

Orange Blossom Press
1935 W. 25th St.
Cleveland, OH 44113
(216) 781-8655

Orpheus Chamber Orchestra
140 W. 79th Street
New York, NY 10024
(212) 874-3710

Parsons Corporation
100 W. Walnut
Pasadena, CA 91124
(Construction and engineering)

PEP Labor Crews, Inc.
Office of Farmworker Ministry (OFM)
Farmworker Association of Central Florida
64 B. East Main St.
Apopka, FL 32703
(407) 886-5151

Playworks, Inc.
301 North Water Street
Milwaukee, WI 53202
(414) 278-8115
(Playgrounds and childrens' furniture)

Port Townsend Shipwrights Co-op
P.O. Box 1163
Port Townsend, WA 98368
(206) 385-6138

Posey Mfg. Co.
P.O. Box 418
Hoquiam, WA 98550
(206) 533-0565

Positively 3rd St. Bakery Co-op
1202 E. 3rd St.
Duluth, MN 55805
(218) 724-8619

Press Gang
603 Powell Street
Vancouver, BC V6A 1H2
Canada
(604) 253-1224

The Printshop
333 Terry Rd
Hauppauqua, NY 11288
(516) 979-7392

Pro Arte Chamber Orchestra
105 Charles St.
Box 187K
Boston, MA 02114
(617) 661-7067

Prompt Press
956 Reeves St.
Camden, NJ 08105
(609) 963-9111

Publix Supermarkets
Box 407
Lakeland, FL 33802
(813) 688-1188

Quad/Graphics
DuPlainville Road
Pewaukee, WI 53072
(414) 691-9200

Rainbow Builders
RR1, 143A Hoosoe Rd.
Conway, MA 01341
(413) 369-4144
(Construction)

Ragged Edge Press
102 Fulton St.
New York, NY, 10038
(212) 962-4488

R2B2
1809 Carter Avenue
Bronx, NY 10457
(212) 731-8666
(Community-based recycling)

Red Sun Press
94 Green St.
Jamaica Plain, MA, 02130
(617) 534-6822

Republic Storage Systems
Company, Inc.
1038 Belden Ave. NE
Canton, OH 44705
(216) 438-5800

Roots and Fruits
1929 E. 24 St.
Minneapolis, MN 55404
(612) 722-3030
(Wholesale food)

Rural/Metro Corporation
P.O. Drawer P
Scottsdale, AZ 85252
(Private fire protection,
including ambulance
service)

Salsedo Press
320 N. Damen
Chicago, IL, 60612
(312) 666-1674

Science Applications
10260 Campus Point Drive
P.O. Box 2351
San Diego, CA 92121
(619) 546-6000

Seattle Northwest Securities
Corp.
800 5th Ave., suite 3400
Seattle, WA 98401
(206) 628-2882

Seymour Specialty Wire
15 Franklin St.
Seymour, CT 06483
(203) 888-8700

Sew & Sew
Rt. 1, Box 97X
Winton, NC 27986
(919) 358-0355

Shine on Services
50 South Court
Athens, OH 45701
(614) 592-3854

South End Press
116 St. Botolph St.
Boston, MA 02115
(617) 266-0629

South Mountain Co.
P.O. Box 359
Chilmaric, MA 02535
(508) 645-2618
(Design; construction)

Space Builders
112 E. Main St.
Carrboro, NC 27510
(919) 929-7072
(Architecture and
construction)

Springfield
Remanufacturing
4860 W. Maple
Springfield, MO 65802
(406) 862-3501
(Remanufactures engines)

Starburst Computer Group
909 W. Main St.
Charlottesville, VA 22903
(804) 296-2856
(Software)

Stone Soup
50 Broadway
Asheville, NC 28801
(Restaurant)

Storefront Press
514 E. Pine,
Seattle, WA, 98122
(206) 322-3150

Through the Grapevine Gift
Shop
212 South State
Orem, UT 84058
(801) 226-8406

Touchstone Bakery
301 A N. 36 St.
Seattle, WA 99103
(206) 547-4000

Twin Oaks Wood and Rope
Furniture
Twin Oaks Community
RT. 4, Box 169-FL2
Louisa, VA 23093
(703) 894-5126

Union Cab
P.O. Box 3513
Madison, WI 53704
(608) 256-4400

The United Woodcutters
Cooperative
P.O. Box 1164.
Greenwood, MS 38930
(601) 455-4421

W.A.R.M. Construction
4835 Michigan Ave.
Detroit, MI 48210
(313) 894-1030
(Home renovation and
construction)

Warm Windows and Sunshine
304 10th St.
Port Townsend, WA 98368
(206) 385-5797
(Heating contractor;
propane delivery)

Watermark Association of
Artisans
P.O. Box 1873
Elizabeth City, NC 27909
(919) 335-1434

Weirton Steel Corporation
400 Three Springs Dr.
Weirton, WV 26062
(304) 797-2000

Whole Builders Cooperative
3160 Snelling Ave. S.
Minneapolis, MN 55406
(612) 724-1262
(Architecture; contracting)

Wild Oats Cooperative
Route 2
Colonial Shopping Center
Williamstown, MA 01267
(413) 458-8060

Workers' Owned Sewing
Company
P.O. Box 72
Windsor, NC 27983
(919) 794-2708

Wright-Gardner Insurance
49 Summit Avenue
Hagerstown, MD 21740
(301) 733-1234

WSA Community Pharmacy
341 State Street
Madison, WI 53703
(608) 251-3308

Consultants and Technical Assistance Organizations

Acacia ESOP Services Group
51 Louisiana Ave.
Washington, DC 20001
(202) 628-4506

Action Resources, Inc.
2013 N., 500 E.
Provo, UT 84604
(801) 377-7576

Alaska Commercial Co. #202
1011 E. Tudor Rd.
Anchorage, AK 99503

The Alternatives Center
2375 Shattuck Ave.
Berkeley, CA 94704
(415) 644-8336

American Capital Strategies
3 Bethesda Metro Center
Suite 350
Bethesda, MD 20814
(301) 951-6122

**Associated Pension
Consultants**
2699 Stirling Road
Ste. B-100
Ft. Lauderdale, FL 33312
(305) 624-0053

Berkman, Ruslander et al.
One Oxford Center
40th Floor
Pittsburgh, PA 15219
(412) 392-2035

Brody & Weiser
21 Woodland Street
New Haven, CT 06511
(203) 777-5375

**Brooklyn Ecumenical
Cooperative**
562 Atlantic Avenue
Brooklyn, NY 11217
(718) 858-8803

**Calumet Project for
Industrial Jobs (FIRR
affiliate)**
4012 Elm St.
E. Chicago, IN 46312
(219) 398-6393

**Campaign for Human
Development**
1312 Massachusetts Ave.
Washington, D. C. 20005
(202) 659-6650

The Catalyst Group
139 Main St., Suite 606
Brattleboro, VT 05301
(802) 254-8144

**Center for Community
Change**
1000 Wisconsin Ave., NW
Washington, DC 20007
(202) 342-0594

**Center for Community
Economic Development
Community Services
Society**
105 E. 22 St., Rm. 908
New York, NY 10010
(212) 254-8900

**Center for Community
Self-Help**
413 E. Chapel Hill St.
P.O. Box 3259
Durham, NC 27701
(919) 683-3016

Center for Cooperatives
University of California
Davis, CA 95616
(916) 752-7269

**Center for Economic
Conversion**
222-C View St.
Mountain View, CA 94041
(415) 968-8798

**Center for Neighborhood
Technology**
2125 W. North Ave.
Chicago, IL 60647
(312) 278-4800

Center for Student Business
409 Student Union
University of
Massachusetts
Amherst, MA 01003
(413) 545-2166

**Center for Women's
Economic Alternatives**
207 West Main St.
Ahoskie, NC 27910
(919) 332-4179

CESCO
522 SW 5th Ave., Suite 1010
Portland, OR 97204
(508) 228-2865

**Clearinghouse for
Community Economic
Development**
Missouri Community
Economic Development
Projects Office
628 Clark Hall
University of Missouri
Columbia, MO 65211
(314) 882-2937

**Cleveland Coalition Against
Plant Closings (FIRR
affiliate)**
1800 Euclid Ave.
Cleveland, OH 44115
(216) 566-8100

**Coalition for Women's
Economic Development**
315 West 9th St., #408
Los Angeles, CA 90015
(213) 489-4995

**Coalition for Economic
Justice (FIRR affiliate)**
167 College St.
Buffalo, NY 14201
(716) 885-2457

**Coalition to Save GM/Van
Nuys (FIRR affiliate)**
3060 St. George St.
Los Angeles, CA 90027
(213) 665-5616

Common Wealth
P.O. Box 6212
1331 Wick
Youngstown, OH 44501
(216) 744-2667

Commonworks (FIRR
affiliate)
821 Euclid Ave.
Syracuse, NY 13210
(315) 475-4822

Community Careers
Resource Center
1516 P St., NW
Washington, DC 20005
(202) 667-0661

Community Consulting
Group
4551 33d Ave. S.
Seattle, WA 98118
(206) 723-4040

Community Economic
Stabilization Corp.
(CESCO)
522 S.W. 5th Ave., #1010
Portland, OR 97204
(503) 228-2865

Community Information
Exchange
1029 Vermont Ave., NW
#710
Washington, DC 20005
(202) 628-2981

Community Service Inc.
P.O. Box 243
Yellow Springs, OH 45387
(513) 767-1461

Community Workshop on
Economic Development
100 S. Morgan St.
Chicago, IL 60607
(312) 243-0249

Consumer Cooperatives
Alliance
5645 Wayne
Kansas City, MO 64110
(816) 444-0990

Co-Op America
2100 M St., NW, Suite 310
Washington, DC 20063
(202) 872-5307

Cooperative Resources and
Services Project
3551 White House Pl.
Los Angeles, CA 90004
(213) 738-1254

Cooperative Work Relations
Program
71 South Plains Road
The Plains, OH 45780
(614) 797-2535

Corporation for Enterprise
Development
777 N. Capital St,.NE suite
801
Washington, DC 20006
(202) 408-9788

Democratic Business
Association of Northern
California
2375 Shattuck Ave.
Berkeley, CA 94704
(415) 644-8336

Democratic Management
Services
1509 Seabright Ave., Suite
A-1
Santa Cruz, CA 95062
(408) 425-7478

Detroit WARM
4835 Michigan Ave.
Detroit, MI 48210
(313) 894-1030

Displaced Homemakers
Project
Stoddard House
University of Maine,
Augusta
Augusta, ME 04330
(207) 622-7131

Employee Ownership Project
39 Phillip St.
Albany, NY 12207
(518) 463-6419

The ESOP Consulting Group
1526 18th Street, NW
Washington, DC 20036
(202) 667-2765

ESOP Services Inc.
National Bank Building
P.O. Box 400
Scottsville, VA 24590
(804) 286-3130

Fair Trade Foundation
132 Highland Ave.
Middletown, CT 06457
(203) 347-5596

Federation for Industrial
Retention and Renewal
(FIRR)*
3411 W. Diversey, #10
Chicago, IL 60647
(312) 252-7676
(*see also affiliate listings)

Federation of Egalitarian
Communities
Federation Desk
Box 6B2-FL2
Tecumseh, MO 65760
(417) 679-4682

Federation of Southern
Cooperatives
P.O. Box 95
Epes, AL 35460
(205) 652-9676

First Nations Financial
Project
Route 14, Box 74
Falmouth, VA 22405
(703) 371-5615

Grant County Cooperative
Ownership Development
Corp.
103 1/2 S. Texas
Silver City, NM 88061
(505) 388-1604

Hometowns Against
Shutdowns (FIRR affiliate)
846 Shannon Ct.
Bricktown, NJ 08723
(201) 462-3271

IKWE Community
Education Project
Route 1, Box 286
Ponsford, MN 56575
(218) 573-3411

Illinois Neighborhood
Development Corporation
South Shore Bank
71th & Jeffrey Blvd.
Chicago, IL 60649
(312) 288-1000

ICA Group
20 Park Ave. suite 1127
Boston, MA 02144
(617) 338- 0100

Institute for Local
Self-Reliance
2425 18th St., NW
Washington, DC 20009
(202) 232- 4108

Jobs for People
1216 E. McMillan Ave.
Suite 304
Cincinnati, OH 45206
(513) 861-1155

Jobs with Peace Campaign
National Office
76 Summer St.
Boston, MA 02110
(617) 338-5783

Sherman Kreiner
213 E. Sedgwick St.
Philadelphia, PA 19119
(215) 247-6905

Norman Kurland and
Associates
4318 N. 31st Street
Arlington, VA 22207
(703) 243-5155

The Labor and Religion
Taskforce (FIRR affiliate)
3210 Michigan Ave.
Kansas City, MO 64109
(816) 923-1255

Livingston Economic
Alternatives in Progress
P.O. Box 156
Old City Hall
Livingston, KY 40445
(606) 453-9800

Ludwig and Curtis
50 California St.
36th Floor
San Francisco, CA 94111
(415) 788-7200

LYDIA (A Women's
Cooperative Interchange)
1257 Siena Drive
Adrien, MI 49221
(517) 625-5135

Management and
Community Development
Institute
Lincoln Filene Center
Tufts University
Medford, MA 02155
(617) 628-5000

Manos
1941 High St.
Oakland, CA 94601
(415) 261-0717

Merrimack Valley Project
(FIRR affiliate)
198 South Broadway
Lawrence, MA 01843
(508) 452-8958

Michigan Alliance of
Cooperatives
P.O. Box 8032
Ann Arbor, MI 48107
(313) 663-3624

Midwest Center for Labor
Research
3411 W. Diversey, No. 14
Chicago, IL 60647
(312) 278-5418

Midwest Employee
Ownership Center
2550 W. Grand Blvd.
Detroit, MI 48208-1239
(313) 894-1066

Mountain Association for
Community Economic
Development
210 Center St.
Berea, KY 40403
(606) 986-2373

Mountain Women's
Exchange
P.O. Box 204
Jellico, TN 37762
(615) 784-8780

La Mujer Obrera (FIRR
affiliate)
P.O. Box 3975
El Paso, TX 79923
(915) 533-9710

National Association of
Community Development
Loan Funds
151 Montague City Rd.
Greenfield, MA 01301
(413) 774-7956

National Association of
Students of Cooperation
Box 7715
Ann Arbor, MI 48107
(313) 663-0989

National Center for
Employee Ownership
2201 Broadway, suite 807
Oakland, CA 94612
(415) 272-9461

National Congress for
Community Economic
Development
2025 Eye St., NW
Washington, DC 20006
(202) 659-8411

National Cooperative Bank
Development Corporation
1630 Connecticut Ave., NW
Washington, DC 20009
(202) 745-4670

National Cooperative
Business Association
1401 New York Avenue,
NW
Suite 1100
Washington, DC 20001
(202) 638-6222, ext. 210

National Council of La Raza
810 1st St., NE, suite 300
Washington, DC 20002
(202) 289-8173

National Council for Urban
Economic Development
1730 K Street, NW
Washington, DC 20006
(202) 223-4735

National Economic
Development and Law
Center
1950 Addison Ave.
Berkeley, CA 94704
(415) 548-2600

National Neighborhood
Coalition
810 1st St., NE, suite 300
Washington, DC 20002
(202) 289-8173

National Rural Development
and Finance Corporation
1718 Conecticut Ave., NW
Suite 400
Washington, DC 20009
(202) 797-8820

Naugatuck Valley Project
47 Central Ave.
Waterbury, CT 06702
(203) 574-2410

North Eastern Education
and Development
Foundation (NEED)
P.O. Box 1873
Elizabeth City, NC 27909
(919) 338-0853

New Hampshire College
Community Economic
Development Program
2500 North River Rd.
Manchester, NH 03104
(603) 644-3103

New York Center for
Employee Ownership
1515 Broadway, 53d Floor
New York, NY 10036
(212) 930-0451

North Country Coop
Development Services
2129-A Riverside Ave.
Minneapolis, MN 55454
(612) 371-0536

Northeast Cooperatives
P.O. Box 1120 Quinn Rd.
Brattleboro, VT 05301
(802) 257-5856

Northeast Ohio Employee
Ownership Center
Kent State University
Kent, OH 44242
(216) 672-3028

North Greenmount
Community Development
Credit Union
416 East 31st Street
Baltimore, MD 21218
(301) 243-2304

Ohio Valley Industrial
Retention and Renewal
Project (FIRR affiliate)
Wheeling College
Wheeling, WV 26003
(304) 243-2270

Deborah Groban Olson &
Associates
1880 Penobscot Building
Detroit, MI 48226
(313) 964-2460

Ownership Associates, Inc.
17 Dunster St., suite 203
Cambridge, MA 02138
(617) 868-4600

Ozark Cooperative
Warehouse, Inc.
Box 1528
Fayetteville, AR 72702
(501) 521-2667

PACE of Philadelphia
2100 Chestnut St., 2nd Fl.
Philadelphia, PA 19103
(215) 561-7079

Participation Associates
2555 N. Clark St.
Chicago, IL 60614
(312) 332-5100

Phenneger and Morgan
West 815 7th Avenue
Spokane, WA 99204
(509) 624-1933

Plant Closures Project
(FIRR Affiliate)
518 17th St.
Suite 200-A
Oakland, CA 94612
(415) 763-6585

Program for Employment
and Workplace Systems
Industrial and Labor
Relations School
Cornell University
Ithaca, NY 14853-3901
(607) 255-3266

Praxis
2100 Chestnut St.
Philadelphia, PA 19103
(215) 561-7079

Puget Sound Cooperative
Federation
4201 Roosevelt Way, NE
Seattle, WA 98105
(206) 632-4559

Ramah Navajo Weavers
Association
P.O. Box 153
Pine Hill, NM 87357
(505) 775-3254

The Regeneration Project
33 E. Minor St.
Emmaus, PA 18049
(215) 967-5171

Rural Coalition
20001 S Street, NW
Washington, DC 20009
(202) 483-1500

Seattle Workers Center
(FIRR affiliate)
2411 Western Ave.
Seattle, WA 98121
(206) 461-8408

Southbank Industry
Association
c/o Bradshear Association
2005 Sarah St.
Pittsburgh, PA 15203
(412) 421-1980

Southerners for Economic
Justice (FIRR affiliate)
P.O. Box 79
Dayton, KY
(606) 261-3266

Storey & Green Associates
230 California St., #500
San Francisco, CA 94111
(415) 398-3950

Telecommunications
Cooperative Network
1333 H St., NW, #1155
Washington, DC 20005
(202) 682-0949

Tennessee Industrial
Renewal Network (FIRR
affiliate)
P.O. Box 5447
Knoxville, TN 37928
(615) 687-7926

Tompkins-Cortland Labor
Coalition (FIRR affiliate)
109 W. State St.
Ithaca, NY 14850
(607) 277-5670

Tri-State Conference on
Steel (FIRR affiliate)
300 Saline St.
Pittsburgh, PA 15207
(412) 421-1980

University Center for
Cooperatives
Lowell Hall
University of Wisconsin
610 Langdon St.
Madison, WI 53703
(608) 262-7390

Utah Center for Productivity
and Quality of Working
Life
Utah State University
UMC 35
Logan, UT 84322
(801) 750-2283

Washington Employee
Ownership Program
Washington Dept. of
Community Development
Ninth & Columbia Bldg.
Olympia, WA 98504-4151
(206) 586-8984

Washington State Labor
Council
201 Elliot Ave., West
Seattle, WA 98119
(206) 281-8901

Waterhouse & Associates
328 Kellogg Blvd. West
St. Paul, MN 55102-1900
(612) 341-0455

Western Earth Support
Co-op
P.O. Box 800
LaPorte, CO 80521
(303) 224-5196

Wisconsin Cooperative
Development Council
Suite 401
30 West Miflin Street
Madison, WI 53703
(608) 258-4395

Women and Employment,
Inc.
1217 Lee Street
Charleston, WV 25301
(304) 345-1298

Women's Business
Development Center
230 N. Michigan
Suite 1800
Chicago, IL 60601
(312) 853-3477

Women's Economic
Development Corporation
Iris Park Place, Suite 315
85 University Ave., West
St. Paul, MN 55104
(612) 646-3808

Women's Self-Employment
Project
166 W. Washington, #730
Chicago, IL 60602
(312) 606-8260

Worker Owned Network
94 N. Columbus Rd.
Athens, OH 47501
(614) 592-3854

Working Equity
198 Broadway, 7th floor
New York, NY 10038
(212) 571-7000

Working Group on
Economic Dislocation
(FIRR affiliate)
821 Raymond Ave., Rm. 160
St. Paul, MN 55114
(612) 644-4472

Canadian Technical Assistance Groups

Coady Consulting
88 Coady Ave.
Toronto, Ontario M4M 2Y8
(416) 778-4744

The Community
Development Cooperative
of Nova Scotia
c/o R.R. #2
St. Peter's, Nova Scotia
B0E 3B0

La Conference Des
Cooperatives Forestieres
915 St. Cyrille Blvd., #102
Sillery, Québec G1S 1T8
(418) 681-6201

Conseil des Cooperative de
l'Outaouais
100 rue Edmonton
Bureau 265
Hull, Québec J8Y 6N2
(819) 777-4003

Cooperative de
Developpement de l'Estrie
37 rue Brooks
Sherbrooke, Québec
J1H 4X7
(819) 566-0234

Cooperative de
Developpement de
Lanaudiere
643 rue Notre-Dame
Joliette, Québec J1H 4X7
(514) 759-8488

Cooperative de
Developpement Regional
de Montreal-Laval
3514 avenue Lacombe
Montreal, Québec
H3T 6N2
(514) 340-6060

The Confederation des
Syndicats Nationaux
(CSN)
1601 DeLormier Ave.
Montreal, Québec
H2K 4M5
(514) 598-2275

Cooperative de
Developpement Regional
de Québec
230 Marie de l'Incarnation
Québec, Québec G1N 3G4
(418) 687-1354

Cooperative de
Developpement Regional
du Saguenay/Lac St. Jean
545 rue Sacre-Coeur ouest
Alma, Québec G8B 1M4
(418) 662-4045

The Organic Resource Co-Op
32 Mountview Ave.
Toronto, Ontario M6P 2L3
(416) 766-3056

The Social Investment
Organization
#447-366 Adelaide St. East
Toronto, Ontario M5A 3X9
(416) 869-1915

La Societe de Developpement
des Cooperatives
430 Chemin Ste. Foy
Québec City, Québec
G1S 2J5
(418) 687-9221

The Worker Ownership
Development Foundation
348 Danforth Ave.
Toronto, Ontario M4K 1N8
(416) 466-2129

Worker Ownership
Resource Centre
102-713 Columbia St.
New Westminster, B.C.
V3M 1B2
(604) 520-3341

Funding and Financial Sources

Adrian Dominican Sisters
1320 Fenwick Lane, #600
Silver Spring, MD 20910
(301) 565-0053

Alternatives Federal Credit
Union
301 W. State St.
Ithaca, NY 14850
(607) 273-4666

American Indian National
Bank
1700 K Street, NW
Banksuite 2000
Washington, DC 20006
(202) 887-5252
(800) 368-5732

Anawim Fund of the Midwest
1517 W. 7th St.
P.O. Box 4022
Davenport, IA 52808
(219) 324-6632

Association for Regional
Agriculture Building the
Local Economy
1175 Chamelton St.
Eugene, OR 97401
(503) 485-7630

Berakah Alternative
Investment Fund
P.O. Box 15765
San Antonio, TX 78212
(512) 344-6778

Blackfeet National Bank
P.O. Box 730
Browning, MT 59417-0730
(406) 338-7000

Boston Community Loan
Fund
30 Germania St.
Jamaica Plain, MA 02130
(617) 522-6768

Calvert Social Investment
Fund
4550 Montgomery Ave.,
#1000
Bethesda, MD 20814
(800) 368-2750

Campaign for Human
Development
1312 Massachusetts Ave., NW
Washington, DC 20005
(202) 659-6650

Capital District Community
Loan Fund
33 Clinton Ave.
Albany, NY 12202
(518) 436-8586

Cascadia Revolving Fund
4649 Sunnyside North
Suite 348
Seattle, WA 98103
(206) 547-5183

Catherine McAuley Housing
Foundation
3005 East 16th Ave.
Suite 260
Denver, CO 80206
(303) 393-3806

Catskill Mountain Housing
Development Corp.
Revolving Loan Fund
P.O. Box 473
Catskill, NY 12414
(518) 943-6700

Central Appalachian Peoples
Federal Credit Union
P.O. Box 504
Berea, KY 40403
(606) 986-8423

Common Good Loan Fund
1320 Fenwick Lane, #600
Silver Spring, MD 20910
(301) 565-0053

Common Wealth Revolving
Loan Fund
P.O. Box 6212
Youngstown, OH 44501
(216) 744-2667

Community Capital Bank
111 Livinston St.
Brooklyn, NY 11201-9215
(718) 802-1212

Community Loan Fund of
New Jersey
126 N. Montgomery St.
Trenton, NJ 08608
(609) 989-7766

Cooperative Fund of New
England
108 Kenyon St.
Hartford, CT 06105
(203) 523-4305

Cornerstone Loan Fund
PO Box 8974
Cincinnati, OH 45208
(513) 871-3899

Delaware Valley Community
Reinvestment Fund
924 Cherry St.
Philadelphia, PA 19107
(215) 925-1130

Ecumenical Development
Cooperative Society
155 N. Michigan, Suite 627
Chicago, IL 60601
(312) 938-0884

Elk Horn Bank
605 Main St.
Arkadelphia, AR 71923
(501) 246-5811

Employee Partnership Fund
c/o Keilin and Bloom
230 Park Ave, suite 1455
New York, NY 10069
(212) 661-3208

Enterprise Loan Fund, Inc.
505 American City Bldg.
Columbia, MD 21044
(301) 964-1230

Federation of Appalachian
Housing Enterprises
Drawer B
Berea, KY 40403
(606) 986-2321

First Affirmative Financial
Network
410 N. 21st St., suite 203
Colorado Springs, CO 80904
(800) 422-7284

Friends of Women's World
Banking/USA, Inc.
684 Park Avenue
New York, NY 10021
(212) 744-0202

Fund for an OPEN Society
311 S. Juniper St.
Suite 400
Philadelphia, PA 19107
(215) 735-6915

The Good Faith Fund
1210 Cherry St., Suite 9
Pine Bluff, AR 71601
(501) 535-6233

Grameen Bank
2G Shyamoli, Dhaka—7
Bangladesh

Greater New Haven
Community Loan Fund
5 Elm St.
New Haven, CT 06510
(203) 789-8690

Human/Economic
Appalachian Development
(HEAD) Community
Loan Fund
P.O. Box 504
Berea, KY 40403
(606) 986-1651

ICA Revolving Loan Fund
20 Park Ave., Suite 1127
Boston, MA 02116
(617) 338-0010

Institute for Community
Economics
57 School St.
Springfield, MA 01105
(413) 746-8880

Interfaith Center for
Corporate Responsibility/
Clearinghouse for
Alternative Investments
475 Riverside Dr., Rm. 566
New York, NY 10115
(212) 870-2936

Koinonia Partners Fund for
Humanity
Route 2
Americus, GA 31709
(912) 924-0391

Lakota Fund
P.O. Box 340
Kyle, SD 55752
(605) 455-2500

Leviticus 25:23 Alternative
Fund
Box 1200
Mariandale Center
Ossining, NY 10562
(914) 941-9422

Local Initiative Support
Corporation
666 Third Ave.
New York, NY 10017
(212) 949-8560

Low Income Housing Fund
605 Market St.
Suite 709
San Francisco, CA 94105
(415) 777-9804

McAuley Institute
1320 Fenwick Ln.
Suite 600
Silver Spring, MD 20910
(301) 588-8110

Michigan Housing Trust
Fund
122 S. Grand Ave.
Suite 206
Lansing, MI 48933
(517) 485-8801

National Association of
Community Development
Loan Funds
924 Cherry St., 3rd floor
Philadelphia, PA 19107-5085
(215) 923-4754

National Business
Association Credit Union
3807 Otter St.
Bristol, PA 19007
(800) 441-0878

National Cooperative Bank
Corporate Headquarters
1630 Connecticut Ave., NW
Washington, DC 20009
(202) 745-4600

National Cooperative Bank
Northeast Region
101 E. 52d Street
16th Floor
New York, NY 10022
(212) 888-8444

National Cooperative Bank
Midwest Region
Plaza VII
45 South 7th Street
Suite 3032
Minneapolis, MN 55402
(612) 332-0032

National Cooperative Bank
Western Region
Seatac Office Center
18000 Pacific Highway
Suite 404
Seattle, WA 98188
(206) 243-4115

National Federation of
Community Development
Credit Unions
59 John Street, 8th floor
New York, NY 10038
(212) 513-7191
(800) 437-8711

National Network of
Women's Funds
1821 University Avenue
Suite 221 South
St. Paul, MN 55104
(612) 641-0742
(The Network distributes a
directory of women's
funds.)

National Rural Development
and Finance Corporation
1718 Connecticut Ave., NW
suite 400
Washington, DC 20009
(202) 797-8820

The Neighborhood Institute
1750 E. 71st St.
Chicago, IL 60649
(312) 684-4610

New Alternatives Fund
295 Northern Blvd.
Great Neck, NY 11021
(516) 466-0808 (call
collect)

New Hampshire Community
Loan Fund
P.O. Box 666
Concord, NH 03301
(603) 224-6669

Northcountry Cooperative
Development Fund
2129-A Riverside Ave.
Minneapolis, MN 55454
(612) 371-0325

Northern California
Community Loan Fund
14 Precita Ave.
San Francisco, CA 94110
(415) 285-3909

Pax World Fund
224 State Street
Portsmouth, NH 03801
(603) 431-8022

Rural Community
Assistance Corporation
2125 19th St.
Suite 203
Sacramento, CA 95818
(916) 447-2854

Santa Cruz Community
Credit Union
P.O. Box 552
Santa Cruz, CA 95061
(408) 425-7708

Self-Help Credit Union
413 East Chapel Hill Street
P.O. Box 31619C
Durham, NC 27702-3619
(919) 683-3016
(800) 476-7428

Seventh Generation Fund
Office of Native Women
Box 72, Nixon, NV 89424
(702) 574-0157

Social Investment Forum
430 1st Ave, N., #204
Minneapolis, MN 55401
(612) 333-8338

South Shore Bank of Chicago
71st and Jeffrey Blvd.
Chicago, IL 60649-2096
(312) 228-7017
(800) 669-7725

Southeastern Reinvestment
Ventures
159 Ralph McGill Blvd.
Suite 412
Atlanta, GA 30365
(404) 659-0002

Syracuse Cooperative
Federal Credit Union
618 Kensington Road
Syracuse, NY 13210

Texas Coalition for
Responsible Investment
P.O. Box 15765
San Antonio, TX
78212-8965
(512) 344-6838

United Methodist Church
475 Riverside Drive, Rm.
341
New York, NY 10115
(212) 870-3820

Vermont Community Loan
Fund
Box 827
Monpelier, VT 05602
(802) 223-1448

Vermont National Bank,
Socially Responsible
Banking Fund
P.O. Box 804
Brattleboro, VT
05302-9987
(800) 544-7108, ext. 244
(802) 257-7151

Washington Area
Community Investment
Fund
2201 P Street, NW
Washington, DC 20037
(202) 462-4727

Wisconsin Partnership for
Housing Development
1045 E. Dayton St.
Madison, WI 53703
(608) 255-1558

Women's World Banking
104 East 40th Street
Suite 607-A
New York, NY 10016
(212) 953-2390

Women's World Banking
West Virginia Affiliate
1217 Lee Street
E. Charleston, WV 25301
(304) 345-1298

Women's Way
125 S. Ninth St., #602
Philadelphia, Pa 19107
(215) 342-2081

Woodstock Institute
53 W. Jackson Blvd.
Suite 304
Chicago, IL 60604
(312) 427-8070

Worcester Community Loan
Fund
P.O. Box 271
Mid Town Mall
Worcester, MA 01614
(508) 799-6106

Working Assets Money Fund
230 California St.
San Francisco, CA 94111
(800) 543-8800

Education for Workplace Democracy Resources*

Alliance for Cultural
Democracy
P.O. Box 7442
Minneapolis, MN 55407

Chinook Learning
Community
P.O. Box 57
Clinton, WA 98236
(206) 321-1884

Cooperative College
141 105th Street West
Saskatoon, Sask. S7N 1N3
Canada
(306) 373-0474

Development Training
Institute
4806 Seton Drive
Baltimore, MD 21215
(301) 764-0780

Eastern Cooperative
Recreation School
49 W. 96th St., #4C
New York, NY 10025
(212) 866-5362

Grindstone Co-op
202-427 Bloor St. West
Toronto, Ontario, M5S 1X7
Canada
(416) 968-9187

Guilford College Program in
Democratic Management
and Employee Ownership
5800 W. Friendly Ave.
Greensboro, NC 27410
(919) 292-5511, ext. 330

Highlander Center
Route 3, Box 370
New Market, TN 37820
(615) 933-3443

LYDIA (A Women's
Cooperative Interchange)
1257 Siena Drive
Adrien, MI 49221
(517) 625-5135

Multi-Cultural Community
High School
430 E.Garfield St.
Milwaukee, WI 53212
(414) 263-3855

New College of California
766 Valencia St.
San Francisco, CA 94110
(415) 626- 0884

New Hampshire College,
School of Human Services
2500 N. River Road
Manchester, NH
03104-1394
(603) 668-2211

Program in Social Economy
and Social Justice
Sociology Department
Boston College
Chestnut Hill, MA 02167
(617) 552-4134

REAL Enterprises
Chicopee Complex
1180 East Broad St.
Athens, GA 30602
(404) 542-6806

SEADS Solar Center
P.O. Box 192
Harrington, ME 04643
(207) 483-9763

Tufts University, Urban and
Environmental Policy
Program
Medford, MA 02155
(617) 381-3394

University of Wisconsin-
Madison, Center for
Cooperatives, Cooperative
Management Institute
513 Lowell Hall
610 Langdon St.
Madison, WI 53703
(608) 262-3981

University of Saskatchewan
Centre for the Study of
Cooperatives
Saskatoon, Sask. S7N 0W0
Canada
(306) 966-8503

---

* Note: For additional educational resources, see groups listed under technical assistance providers, e.g., Workers Owned Network, Puget Sound Cooperative Federation, ICA Group, Praxis, and the Utah Center for Productivity and Quality of Working Life.

Labor-Based or Union Resources

Amalgamated Clothing and Textile Workers Union (ACTWU)
15 Union Square
New York, NY 10003
(212) 242-0700

American Capital Strategies
3 Metro Center
Bethesda, MD 20814
(301) 951-6122

Bliss-Salem
530 Ellsworth
Salem, OH 44460
(216)337-3444
[United Steel Workers of America (USWA) local]

Bureau of National Affairs, Inc.
1231 25th Street, NW
Washington, DC 20037
(202) 452-4200
(The Newspaper Guild)

Center for Economic Organizing
1522 K Street, NW
Suite 406
Washington, DC 20005
(202) 775-9072

Channellock
1306-16 S. Main
Meadville, PA 16335
(814) 724-8700
(USWA local)

Colt Enterprises
1106 N. Glenwood Blvd.
Tyler, TX 75701
(903) 593-8261
(ACTWU local)

Confederation des Syndicats Nationaux (CSN)
1601 DeLormier Ave.
Montréal, Québec H2K 4M5
Canada
(514) 598-2275

Copper Range Company
Box 100
White Pine, MI 49971
(906) 885-5111
(USWA local)

Employee Ownership Inc.
25 Greentree Road
Wheeling, WV 26003
(304) 242-8763

Employee Partnership Fund (AFL-CIO)
c/o Keilin and Bloom
230 Park Avenue, suite 1455
New York, NY 10069
(212 661-3208

First Trade Union Savings Bank
10 Drydock Ave.
P.O. Box 9063
Boston, MA 02205-9063
(617) 482-4000

Franklin Forge
4747-T S.M. 76
West Branch, MI 48661
(517) 345-3850
[United Auto Workers (UAW) local]

James O. Hall, Atty.
30 Newbury Street
Boston, MA 02116
(617) 247-4800

Industrial Union Department, AFL-CIO
815 16th St., NW
Washington, DC 20006
(202) 637-5000

Robert Kantor
Northeastern Connecticut Community Development Corp.
P.O. Box 156
Danielson, CT 06239

Kerotest Manufacturing Corp.
2525 Liberty Avenue
Pittsburgh, PA 15222
(412) 392-4200
(USWA local)

Leslie Paper Products
P. O. Box 1351
Minneapolis, MN 55440
(612) 540-0700
(Teamster local, mainly)

McLouth Steel Products Corporation
1491 W. Jefferson
Trenton, MI 48183
(313) 285-1200
(USWA local)

Machine Action Project
1176 Main Street
Springfield, MA 01103
(413) 781-6900

Midwest Center for Labor Research; Federation for Industrial Retention and Renewal
3411 W. Diversey
Chicago, IL 60647
(312) 278-5418

National Center for Employee Ownership
2201 Broadway, #807
Oakland, CA 94612
(415) 272-9461

National Writers Union
13 Astor Pl., 7th Floor
New York, NY 10003
(212) 254-0279

New York State AFL-CIO
Pension Investment Group
48 East 21st St., 12th floor
New York, NY 10010
(718) 591-2000

North American Rayon
West Elk Avenue
Elizabethtown, TN 37643
(615) 542-2141
[United Textile Workers local]

Deborah Groban Olson and Associates
1880 Penobscot Bldg.
Detroit, MI 48226
(313) 964-2460

Operating Engineers, Local 675
1200 Park Central Blvd.,
S. Pompano Beach, FL 33064
(305) 979-1700

Oregon Metallurgical Corporation (OREMET)
530 S.W. 34th St.
Albany, OR 97321
(USWA local)

Pittsburgh Forgings Company
301 Thorn St.
Corapolis, PA 15108
(412) 264-4000
(USWA local)

Republic Container
Viscose Road
Nitro, WV 25143
(304) 755-4325
(USWA local)

Republic Engineered Steel
410 Oberlin Road
Massillon, OH 44748-0579
(216) 837-6000
(USWA local)

Republic Storage
1038 Belden Ave. NE
Canton, OH 44705
(216) 438- 5800
(USWA local)

Seymour Specialty Wire
15 Franklin Street
Seymour, CT 06483
(203) 888- 8700
(UAW local)

Textileather Co.
3729 Twining St.
Toledo, OH 43608
(419) 729-3731
(ACTWU local)

United Steel Workers of America
Five Gateway Center
Pittsburgh, PA 15222
(412) 562-2442

Washington State Labor Council
201 Elliot Ave West
Seattle, WA 98119
(206) 281-8901

Weirton Steel Corporation
Department of Public Relations
400 Three Springs Dr.
Weirton, WV 26062
(304) 797-2000
(Independent Steel Workers Union)

Wheeling-Pittsburgh Steel
500 Main St.
Wheeling, WV 26003
(304) 234-2400
(USWA local)

Workplace Democracy Worldwide

We have already touched on certain recent and remarkable international illustrations of workplace democracy, such as Bangladesh's Grameen Bank (a model now imported into the United States and elsewhere), the Eco-Bank in Germany, and, of course, Euskadi's Mondragon cooperative consortium. These are not isolated or atypical phenomena: we have much to learn from many other countries about the diverse forms democracy at work can take and the steps by which our own movement can gather greater strength. This can be seen by even a brief examination of developments in three countries—Canada, Italy, and Japan.

Canadian Cooperatives

Our northern neighbor, more precisely the province of Québec, provides what some observers have termed "the most successful North American example of worker cooperatives contributing to job creation and workplace democracy." (Adams and Hansen 1987, 7) As with Mondragon, one source of worker ownership in *la belle province* was severely rising unemployment and economic hardship. Today, after barely a decade of expansion, Québec's cooperatives number close to three hundred with more than 10,000 worker-owners. These are agricultural, industrial, service, and high tech; they include as well a "second-tier," industry-specific umbrella cooperative formed by over thirty forest co-ops in the province. A crucial role in this encouraging story has been played by the Québec provincial government, which helped to establish three different sorts of shelter organizations for worker-owned enterprises:

- *Group Conseils (GC)*, or *advisory groups*, which assist workers who already have business ideas "with feasibility studies, financial projections, aid requests, and development of internal structures." (Adams and Hansen 1987, 7)

- *Cooperatives de development regional (CDR)*, or regional development co-ops, which, as developers, identify the most promising business options for worker-owners in the province and then recruit worker-entrepreneurs who can bring those options to life. CDRs also serve as "resource banks," linking worker co-ops to one another and to educational, labor, and community development organizations.

- *Societe de Development Cooperatif (SDC)*, or cooperative development society, was established in 1979 to provide financial assistance to worker-owned enterprises: it has since invested over $7 million in more than 100 co-ops and is authorized as well to guarantee loans made by commercial institutions.

Québec has been joined by other Canadian provincial governments in backing worker ownership. Manitoba, Saskatchewan, and the Maritimes, for example, have all provided public support, including gap and feasibility-study financing, educational materials and training programs, technical assistance, and low-interest development loans and loan guarantees. Besides this relatively high level of provincial government support, however, Canada's cooperative movement has at least three other distinctive features. First, it very recently formed a nationwide federation which will seek to expand cooperative enterprise and workplace democracy by, for example, "providing leadership and a voice for worker cooperatives in Canada" and by "creating a vision and a strategy for the development of Canadian worker cooperatives" (Quarter 1990, 9). Second, one of Canada's largest labor federations (representing numerous labor unions), the CSN *(Confederation des Syndicates Nationaux)*, established its own GC to actively develop worker co-ops. And it is doing so not only within its own ranks but with unorganized workers as well.

The CSN's major project has been the conversion of Québec's privately owned ambulance businesses into worker cooperatives: "It is anticipated that within several years [of 1990] all of these will be operated by worker cooperatives" (Quarter and Wilkenson, forthcoming).

And last, Canada is home to the "uncontested co-op capital of North America, at least on a per capita basis." In *Evangeline*, a small area on Prince Edward Island, 2,500 Acadians participate in a rich cooperative tradition that touches almost everyone in the community and reaches back some four generations. This lively cooperative community includes a fish-processing enterprise, the "Olde Barrel" preservative-free potato chip company, a cooperative community health clinic, numerous consumer co-ops, and several youth employment cooperatives. The financial backbone for Evangeline's cooperative community is its credit union (Caisse Populaire), with 2,900 members and $10 million of assets, which for five decades has channeled local deposits into community economic development. Evangeline sees its cooperatives in a cultural as well as economic light: not only do they provide employment for over 25 percent of their adult population, but they are a "major contributor to the survival of the French language in the area." (Arsenault 1988, 7)

Cooperative Development, Italian Style

Across the Atlantic, and over many generations, Italians have built what may well be the largest and most elaborate cooperative economy in the world. Prior chapters have described Italy's influential flexible manufacturing networks (FMNs): the hundreds of thousands of small-scale, high-tech, computerized design and production, artisan-managed enterprises that, over the past two decades, have sprung up in the northern Emilia-Romagna region. With their ready capacity to adjust to even minuscule market fluctuations and their high utilization of worker inventiveness, FMNs have inspired similar sorts of enterprise networks in other countries, including the United States and Denmark.

Beyond (and in some cases including) these, however, is a much older cooperative movement, one which predates World War I and has cultivated richly integrated cooperative communities in such cities as Bologna, Imola, Modena, and Ravenna. Consider *Imola*, for example: with a population of around 60,000, it boasts some 65 cooperatives of many different sorts, with 28,000 members and composite annual sales in 1989 of almost $1 billion. In addition, Imola is the home of *SACMI (Societa Anonima Cooperativa Maccanici di Imola)*, the largest and one of the oldest co-ops in Italy, with an annual turnover (1989) of some $300 million, and foreign subsidiaries in six countries, including Germany and Argentina. For over seventy years, SACMI has been the acknowledged "world leader against capitalist competition in the supply of equipment and the erection of plants for the ceramics industry" (Earle 1990, 24).

Most of Italy's cooperatives belong to one of three national umbrella organizations—the *Lega* (League), the *Confederazione* (Confederation), or the *Associazione* (Association). The first two of these have about the same number of individual members, 3 million, whereas the last is much smaller, with only 200,000. In 1989, annual sales for the Lega rang in at about $30 billion, while the Confederazione's turnover was about $20 billion and that of the Associazione about $4 billion. The Confederazione has links to the Catholic church and to a national network of rural savings banks. The Lega, on the other hand, is known to have a tradition of trade-union involvement and progressive political engagement. SACMI belongs to it, as do the majority of northern Italian cooperatives. In addition, within the Lega numerous local cooperative associations have formed in such sectors as retail shops, construction, housing, and tourism. Recently, the Lega established a large insurance company and a cooperative bank, and it is developing its own network of financial services.

"Woman Democracy" Comes to Life in Japan: Seikatsu

In 1965, a group of Tokyo housewives set up a buying club to purchase milk at better prices. What was to grow out of this initial venture was not then foreseeable:

the remarkable *Seikatsu Consumer Cooperative Club*, which now comprises over 200,000 families and over 500,000 individuals. Seikatsu has gradually developed "a philosophy encompassing the whole of life" through which it "is committed to a host of social concerns, including the environment, the empowerment of women, and workers' conditions."[1]

We first became aware of Seikatsu in 1989, when this Japanese movement received the highly esteemed Right Livelihood Award in honor of being

the most successful model of production and consumption in the industrialized world, aiming to change society by promoting self-managing and less wasteful lifestyles.[2]

Seikatsu members will only purchase products safe for the environment and for human health; where these are not commercially available, they establish production co-ops to fill the gap. The organization thus operates about 100 worker-owned enterprises, and markets about 60 original-brand items, including several types of nontoxic soap and organically produced dairy products. This combination of ecological responsibility and cooperative productive enterprise is rare, if not unparalleled, in the world.

Seikatsu is unique in other ways. Over twenty-five years, it has developed a radically face-to-face internal democratic structure, one based on what are called *hans*—local groups which average about eight member families. Each han manages its own activities, develops its own priorities, and sends delegates to the Seikatsu General Assembly to help make overall federation policy. Beyond this, Seikatsu has moved further by developing what it calls "woman democracy." By this they mean, in part, that 80 percent of the group's own board members are female. More important, woman democracy signifies an approach to collective life that is holistic and does not isolate work from family life, ecological concerns from political ones. For Seikatsu, *Political Reform from the Kitchen* and *From Collective Buying to All of Life* are more than catchy and original slogans. Rather, they give expression to a basic "belief that housewives can begin to create a society that is harmonious with nature by taking action in the home." To the question of where social reconstruction should start, Seikatsu would respond, "Anywhere, not only in the workplace, and especially in the home." To the question of what needs to be transformed, they would answer, "Everything, not just work, but family life as well." Woman democracy is a way of extending and enriching workplace democracy.

Seikatsu's wholeness is revealed in its campaigns to gain political power ("From Soap to City Council"). Forming independent networks, it has run candidates in dozens of localities, managing to elect some seventy councillors in cities throughout Japan. Their campaigns and manifestos resemble those of the European Greens—stressing strong environmental, antinuclear, and peace objectives, equal status for women, and an integrated, enhanced, and highly localized conception of democratic community life.

Seikatsu intends to keep growing: over the past decade, membership has expanded by an average of about 5 percent every year, and they now have branch cooperatives in Korea. With a full-time staff of 700, they have set themselves the goals of spreading to at least ten percent of all Japanese households and of winning ever-increasing political representation. Given what they have already done to challenge male-dominated politics and culture in Japan, and to integrate consumption, production, politics, and ecology, who can say that these goals are unrealistic?

An Encouraging Conclusion

Three countries, three very different approaches to the democratic reconstruction of work. Which is right or best for the United States is not really the issue. Rather, they all—along with Mondragon and other international models—can offer us fertile suggestions, instructive lessons, paths to ponder, assess, and build upon. We may be impressed by the level of provincial government support in Canada for worker ownership, or by the Italian Lega's long-lasting, highly integrated, sectionally refined, and artisan-based cooperatives, or again by the full spectrum wholeness and local self-determination of Seikatsu's woman democracy. Or we may want to combine elements of all three. In any case, these global stories point to one encouraging conclusion: living models of grassrooted economic democracy have now taken root within otherwise capitalistic and hostile environments, and these are growing in size, stability, and worldwide impact. If elsewhere, why not here as well?

Far from the Whole Story

This account has of necessity been selective, omitting several important global expressions of workplace democracy. These include, for example, the kibbutzim and Histradut (labor federation)-managed cooperatives of Israel; the regional Cooperative Development Agencies established throughout the British isles which "parent" budding enterprises; the 800+ collective cooperatives (up from 72 in 1982), containing some 50,000 members, of Zimbabwe; and Iceland's cooperative movement (over 45,000 members), which is that country's largest employer.

Beyond this, there are cross-national umbrella and support organizations for cooperatives. These include the *International Cooperative Alliance*, housed in Geneva, which began networking among cooperatives about a century ago. It now represents close to 375 million members from 170 cooperative organizations in 70 nations. A newer cross-national organization, formed in 1988, is the *International Institute for Self-Management (IIS)*. Since it began, the IIS has assisted in the founding of Frankfurt's Eco-bank, in developing an international consortium of alternative finance funds, and in creating common marketing facilities in places such as London and Paris for women's crafts cooperatives located in remote areas of Europe. In addition, it is also working within several eastern European countries with groups interested in starting worker-owned or self-managing enterprises.

For more information on these and other international developments in workplace democracy, we suggest contacting the following organizations directly:

Association for Employee Ownership in Australia, PO Box 1135, North Sydney, NSW 2059, Australia.

Confederation Generale des Societe Cooperatives Ouvrieres de Productions, Rue 37 Jean LeClere, Paris, France 75017.

Cooperative Research Unit, The Open University, Walton Hall, Milton Keynes, United Kingdom MK7 6AA.

International Co-operative Alliance, 15 Route des Morellons, CH-1218, Grand-Saconnex, Geneva, Switzerland.

International Institute for Selfmanagement, Wolfsmunster 52, D- 8781 Grafendorf, Germany.

Organization of Collective Co-operatives, PO Box 66102, Kopje, 25 Forbes Ave., 103 Emekay House, Harare, Zimbabwe.

Seikatsu Club Consumers Co-operative, 2-26-17, Miyasaka, Setagaya, Tokyo—156 Japan.

Worker Co-op Magazine, PO Box 101, Station G, Toronto, Ontario, Canada M4M 3E8.

Notes

1. The Seikatsu Club. Tokyo, Japan: Seikatsu Consumers Club Cooperative, 1988; p. 6.

2. The Right Livelihood Awards Foundation, press release, 4 October 1989; p. 1.

References and Bibliography on Workers' Participation, Worker Ownership, and Workplace Democracy, 1979-1991

A. North America, Western Europe, and General References

Adams, Frank T., 1982. *Making Production, Making Democracy: A Case Study of Teaching in the Workplace* (Chapel Hill, NC: Twin Stream Educational Center).

Adams, Frank T., and Gary B. Hansen, 1987. *Putting Democracy to Work: A Practical Guide for Starting Worker-Owned Businesses* (Eugene, OR: Hulogosi Communications). P.O. Box 1188, Eugene, OR 97440.

Albert, Michael, and Robin Hahnel, 1991. *Looking Forward: A Participatory Economy for the Twenty-First Century* (Boston: South End Press).

Albert, Michael, and Robin Hahnel, 1991. *The Political Economy of Participatory Economics* (Princeton: Princeton University Press).

Antoni, Antoine, and Alastair Campbell, 1983. *The Cooperative Way! Worker Co-ops in France, Spain, and Eastern Europe* (Oxford: Plunkett Foundation for Cooperative Studies). Available through State Mutual Books, 521 Fifth Ave. New York, NY 10175.

Arsenault, Raymond, 1988. "Evangeline, Prince Edward Island, the Uncontested Co-op Capital," *Worker Co-op*, 7,3 (Winter).

Axelrod, Robert, 1984. *The Evolution of Cooperation* (New York: Basic Books).

Barber, Benjamin R., 1984. *Strong Democracy: Participatory Politics for a New Age* (Berkeley: University of California Press).

Bell, Daniel, 1988. *Bringing Your Employees into the Business: An Employee Ownership Handbook for Small Business* (Kent, OH: Kent Popular Press). P.O. Box 905, Kent, OH 44240.

Benello, George, 1988. "The Challenge of Mondragon." *Changing Work*, 7 (Winter). Reprinted in Krimerman, Lindenfeld, Korty, and Benello, *From the Ground Up*.

Benello, George, et al., 1989. *Building Sustainable Communities: Tools and Concepts for Self-Reliant Economic Change* (New York: Bootstrap Press).

Bensman, David, and Roberta Lynch, 1988. *Rusted Dreams: Hard Times in a Steel Community* (Berkeley: University of California Press).

Bernstein, Paul, 1980. *Workplace Democratization* (New Brunswick, NJ: Transaction Books).

Berry, John, and Mark Roberts, 1984. *Co-op Management and Employment* (London: ICOM Publications).

Blasi, Joseph R., 1988. *Employee Ownership: Revolution or Ripoff?* (Cambridge, MA: Ballinger).

Blasi, Joseph, and Douglas Kruse, 1991. *New Owners* (New York: HarperCollins).

Bloom, Steven M., 1986. *Employee Ownership and Firm Performance*. Ph.D. dissertation, Department of Economics, Harvard University

Bluestone, Barry, and Bennett Harrison, 1982. *The Deindustrialization of America: Plant Closings, Community Abandonment, and the Dismantling of Basic Industry* (New York: Basic Books).

Bookchin, Murray, 1980. *Post Scarcity Anarchism* (Palo Alto, CA: Ramparts Press).

Bowles, Samuel, and Herbert Gintis, 1986. *Democracy and Capitalism* (New York: Basic Books).

Bowles, Samuel D., Michael Gordon, and Thomas E. Weisskopf, 1983. *Beyond the Wasteland: A Democratic Alternative to Economic Decline* (Garden City, NY: Anchor Press).

Bradley, Keith, and Alan Gelb, 1983. *Cooperation at Work: The Mondragon Experience* (London: Heinemann).

Bradley, Keith, and Alan Gelb, 1983. *Worker Capitalism: The New Industrial Relations* (Cambridge, MA: MIT Press).

Bradley, Keith, and Alan Gelb, 1986. *Share Ownership for Employees* (London: Public Policy Centre).

Brandow, Karen, and Jim McDonnell, 1981. *No Bosses Here: A Manual on Working Collectively,* 2d ed. (Copublished by Alyson Publications, P.O. Box 2783, Boston, MA 02208, and Vocations for Social Change, P.O. Box 211, Essex Station, Boston, MA 02112).

Brecher, Jeremy, and Tim Costello (eds.), 1990. *Building Bridges: The Emerging Grassroots Coalition of Labor and Community* (New York: Monthly Review Press).

Bruyn, Severyn T., 1987. *The Field of Social Investment* (Cambridge, MA: Cambridge University Press).

Bruyn, Severyn T., 1991. *A Future for the American Economy: The Social Market* (Stanford, CA: Stanford University Press).

Bruyn, Severyn T., and James Meehan, 1987. *Beyond the Market and the State* (Philadelphia: Temple University Press).

Bruyn, Severyn T., and Litsa Nicolaou-Smokoviti, 1989. *International Issues in Social Economy* (New York: Praeger).

Bufe, Chaz, 1988. "Limits of the Cooperative Movement." *Ideas and Action*, 9 (Spring).

Bureau of Labor Statistics, U.S. Department of Labor, 1976. *Brief History of the American Labor Movement* Bulletin 1000 (Washington, DC: U.S. Government Printing Office).

Burns, Tom, Lars Erik Karlsson, and Velijko Rus (eds.), 1979. *Work and Power: The Liberation of Work and the Control of Political Power* (Beverly Hills, CA: Sage).

Campbell, Alistair, 1987. *The Democratic Control of Work* (Oxford: Plunkett Foundation for Co-operative Studies). Available through State Mutual Books, 521 Fifth Ave., New York, NY 10175.

Campbell, Thomas Nelson, 1989. *The Community Stock Ownership Plan: Lessons of Weirton Steel*, M.A. dissertation, Cornell University.

Carnoy, Martin, and Derek Shearer, 1980. *Economic Democracy: The Challenge of the 1980s* (White Plains, NY: M.E. Sharpe).

Carnoy, Martin, Derek Shearer, and Russell Rumberger, 1983. *A New Social Contract: The Economy and Government after Reagan* (New York: Harper and Row).

Case, John, and Rosemary C. R. Taylor (eds.), 1979. *Co-ops, Communes, and Collectives: Experiments in Social Change in the 1960s and 1970s* (New York: Pantheon).

Castoriadis, Cornelius, 1988. *Political and Social Writings* (Minneapolis: University of Minnesota Press).

Castoriadis, Cornelius, 1984. *Workers' Councils and the Economics of a Self-Managed Society* (Philadelphia: Wooden Shoe Books). P.O. Box 25224, Philadelphia, PA 19119.

Clayre, Alasdair, 1980. *The Political Economy of Co-operation and Participation* (Oxford: Oxford University Press).

Cohen-Rosenthal, Edward, and Cynthia Burton, 1987. *Mutual Gains: A Guide to Union-Management Cooperation* (New York: Praeger).

Cole, Don, 1990. *Economy and Community: Lessons from Delinked Societies* (New York: Bootstrap Press).

Cole, George D. H., 1980. *Guild Socialism Restated* (New Brunswick, NJ: Transaction Books). Reprint of 1920 edition.

Cole, Robert E., 1979. *Work, Mobility, and Participation: A Comparative Study of American and Japanese Industry* (Berkeley: University of California Press).

Conte, Michael, and Arnold Tannenbaum, 1980. *Employee Ownership* (Ann Arbor: Survey Research Center, University of Michigan).

Cooley, Mike, 1982. *Architect or Bee? The Human/Technology Relationship* (Boston: South End Press).

Cornforth, Chris A., Thomas J. Lewis, and Roger Spear, 1988. *Developing Successful Worker Cooperatives* (London: Sage).

Craig, John C., 1980. *Managing Cooperative Organizations* (Saskatoon, Sask.: Co-operative College of Canada).

Crouch, Colin, and Frank A. Heller (eds.), 1983. *International Yearbook of Organizational Democracy*. Vol. 1, "Organizational Democracy and Political Processes" (New York: Wiley).

Curl, John, 1980. *History of Work Cooperation in America* (Berkeley: Homeward Press). P.O. Box 2307, Berkeley, CA 94702.

Dahl, Robert, 1985. *A Preface to Economic Democracy* (Berkeley: University of California Press).

Derber, Charles, 1989. *Power to the Highest Degree* (New York: Oxford University Press).

Duncan, Mel, 1990. "Making Minnesota Connections: From Economic Conversion to Progressive Coalitions." In Brecher and Costello, *Building Bridges*.

Earle, John, 1987. *The Italian Co-operative Movement: A Portrait of the Lega Nazionale delle Co-operative e Mutue* (Winchester, MA: Unwin Hyman).

Earle, John, 1990. "Italy's SACMI: 13 Subsidiaries in 6 Countries and Worker Owned," *Worker Co-op* 10, 1 (Summer).

Eccles, Tony, 1981. *Under New Management* (London: Pan Books).

Edwards, Richard C., Michael Reich, and David Gordon (eds.), 1979. *Contested Terrain: The Transformation of the Workplace in the Twentieth Century* (New York: Basic Books).

Einhorn, Eric, and John Logue (eds.), 1982. *Democracy on the Shop Floor? An American Look at Employee Influence in Scandinavia Today* (Kent, OH: Kent Popular Press).

Ellerman, David, 1987. "What is a Worker Cooperative?" Appendix in Bruyn, Severyn T., and James Meehan, *Beyond the Market and the State* (Philadelphia: Temple University Press).

Ellerman, David, 1990. *The Democratic Worker-Owned Firm: A New Model for the East and West* (Winchester, MA: Unwin Hyman).

Espinosa, Juan G., and Andrew Zimbalist, 1981. *Economic Democracy: Workers' Participation in Chilean Industry, 1970- 1973* (New York: Basic Books).

Etzioni, Amitai, 1988. *The Moral Dimension: Towards a New Economics* (New York: Free Press).

Evans, Larry, 1989. *Overtime: Punchin' Out with the Mill Hunk Herald* (Albuquerque, NM: West End Press). Available from Publishers Services, P.O. Box 2510, Novato, CA 94949.

Feldman, Richard, and Michael Betzold, 1988. *End of the Line: Autoworkers and the American Dream* (New York: Weidenfeld and Nicolson).

Fink, Leon, 1983. *Workingmen's Democracy: The Knights of Labor and American Politics* (Champaign: University of Illinois Press).

Fitz, Don, and David Roediger, 1990. *Within the Shell of the Old: Essays on Workers' Self-Organization* (Chicago: Charles H. Kerr).

Fowler, Susan J., and Rachel Willis, 1984. "Democratic Management and Learning: A Case Study of a Small Enterprise." In *Proceedings of the National Employee-Ownership and Participation Conference* (Greensboro, NC, October 12-14).

Fulton, Murray (ed.), 1990. *Cooperative Organizations and Canadian Society* (Toronto: University of Toronto Press).

Gorz, Andre, 1982. *Farewell to the Working Class* (Boston: South End Press).

Gorz, Andre, 1985. *Paths to Paradise* (Boston: South End Press).

Grazier, Peter B., 1989. *Before It's Too Late: Employee Involvement. . . An Idea Whose Time Has Come* (Chadds Ford, PA: Teambuilding, Inc.). 12 Pine Lane, Chadds Ford, PA 19317.

Greenberg, Edward S., 1986. *Workplace Democracy and the Political Effects of Participation* (Ithaca, NY: Cornell University Press).

Gunn, Christopher, 1984. *Workers' Self-Management in the United States* (Ithaca, NY: Cornell University Press).

Gunn, Christopher, and Hazel Dayton Gunn, 1991. *Reclaiming Capital—Democratic Initiatives and Community Development* (Ithaca, NY: Cornell University Press).

Gutchess, Jocelyn F., 1985. *Employment Security in Action: Strategies That Work* (New York: Pergamon Press).

Gutierrez-Johnson, Ana, 1982. *Industrial Democracy in Action: The Cooperative Complex of Mondragon*. Ph.D. dissertation, Cornell University.

Hackman, Richard J., and Greg Oldham, 1980. *Work Redesign* (Reading, MA: Addison-Wesley).

Hanagan, Michael P., 1980. *The Logic of Solidarity: Artisans and Industrial Workers in Three French Towns* (Champaign: University of Illinois Press).

Harrison, Bennett, and Barry Bluestone, 1988. *The Great U-Turn* (New York: Basic Books).

Hartzell, Hal, Jr., 1987. *Birth of a Co-operative: Hoedad's, Inc.* (Eugene, OR: Hulogosi Communications).

Henderson, Hazel, 1987. *The Politics of the Solar Age: Alternatives to Economics* (Garden City, NY: Anchor Press/Doubleday).

Hochner, Arthur, Cherlyn S. Granrose, Judith Goode, Elaine Simon, and Eileen Appelbaum, 1989. *Job Savings Strategies: Worker Buyouts and QWL* (Kalamazoo, MI: W.E. Upjohn Institute).

Hoerr, John, 1988. *And the Wolf Finally Came: The Decline of the American Steel Industry* (Pittsburgh: University of Pittsburgh Press).

Honingsberg, Peter J., Bernard Kamoroff, and Jim Beatty, 1982. *We Own It* (Laytonville, CA: Bell Springs). Available from Community Service, Inc., P.O. Box 243, Yellow Springs, OH 45387.

Ivancic, Catherine, and John Logue, 1986. *Employee Ownership and the States: Legislation, Implementation, and Models* (Kent, OH: Kent Popular Press).

Ivancic, Catherine, 1988. *Bringing Politics into Everyday Life: Effects of Democratic Participation in Employee-Owned Firms*. Thesis. Kent State University, Kent, OH.

Jackall, Robert, and Henry Levin (eds.), 1984. *Worker Cooperatives in America* (Berkeley: University of California Press).

Jacobs, Jane, 1985. *Cities and the Wealth of Nations: Principles of Economic Life* (New York: Vintage Books).

Jamson, June, and Ann B. Hellmark (eds.), 1985. *Labor Owned Firms and Workers' Cooperatives* (Aldershot, U.K.: Gower).

Jochim, Timothy C., 1982. *Employee Stock Ownership and Related Plans* (Westport, CT: Quorum Books).

Jones, Derek, and Jan Svejnar (eds.), 1982. *Participatory and Self-Managed Firms* (Lexington, MA: Lexington Books).

Jones, Derek, and Jan Svejnar (eds.), 1987. *Advances in the Economic Analysis of Participatory and Labor-Managed Firms, vol. 2* (Greenwich, CT: JAI Press).

Kanawaty, George, 1984. *Managing and Developing New Forms of Work Organization, 2d ed.* (Geneva: International Labour Office).

Kanter, Donald L., and Philip H. Mirvis, 1990. *The Cynical Americans: Living and Working in an Age of Discontent and Disillusion* (San Francisco: Jossey-Bass).

Kennedy, Donald (ed.), 1984. *Labor and Reindustrialization: Workers and Social Change* (University Park: Department of Labor Studies, Pennsylvania State University).

Kochan, Thomas A., 1984. *Worker Participation and American Unions* (Kalamazoo, MI: W.E. Upjohn Institute).

Kornbluh, Joyce, 1989. *Rebel Voices: An IWW Anthology* (Chicago: Charles H. Kerr).

Krimerman, Len, Frank Lindenfeld, Carol Korty, and Julian Benello (eds.), 1991. *From the Ground Up: Essays of C. George Benello* (Boston: South End Press).

Kruse, Douglas, 1984. *Employee Ownership and Employee Attitudes: Two Case Studies* (Norwood, PA: Norwood Editions).

Laurie, Bruce, 1989. *Artisans into Workers: Labor in Nineteenth Century America* (New York: Noonday Press).

Lindenfeld, Frank, 1990. "O&O: The Rise and Fall of a Great Idea," *Worker Co-op* 9, 4, (Spring).

Lindenfeld, Frank, and Joyce Rothschild-Whitt (eds.), 1982. *Workplace Democracy and Social Change* (Boston: Porter Sargent).

Linehan, Mary, and Vincent Tucker, 1983. *Workers' Co-operatives: Potential and Problems* (Cork: U.C.C. Bank of Ireland Centre for Co-operative Studies).

Logue, John, forthcoming. "Democratic Theory and Atheoretical Democracy: Creating Microdemocracies in the American Economy." in M. Donald Hancock, John Logue, and Bernt Schiller (eds.), *Managing Modern Capitalism: Comparative Strategies of Industrial Renewal and Workplace Reform* (Westport, CT: Greenwood Press).

Logue, John, James B. Quilligan, and Barbara J. Weissman, 1986. *Buyout! Employee Ownership as an Alternative to Plant Shutdowns: The Ohio Experience* (Kent, OH: Kent Popular Press).

Lutz, Mark A., and Kenneth Lux, 1988. *Humanistic Economics: The New Challenge* (New York: Bootstrap Press).

Lynd, Staughton, 1982. *The Fight against Shutdowns: Youngstown's Steel Mill Closings* (San Pedro, CA: Singlejack Books).

Lynd, Staughton, 1990. "From Protest to Economic Democracy," in Brecher and Costello, *Building Bridges.*

Mann, Eric, 1988. *Taking on General Motors* (Los Angeles: UCLA Industrial Relations Department). Available from Labor Distributors, 6454 Van Nuys Blvd., Suite 150, Van Nuys, CA 91401.

Mansbridge, Jane, 1980. *Beyond Adversary Democracy* (Chicago: University of Chicago Press).

Martin, Shan, 1983. *Managing without Managers: Alternative Work Arrangements in Public Organizations* (Beverly Hills, CA: Sage).

Mason, Ronald, 1982. *Participatory and Workplace Democracy: A Theoretical Critique of Liberalism* (Carbondale, IL: Southern Illinois University Press).

Meek, Christopher, Warner Woodworth, and W. Gibb Dyer, Jr., 1988. *Managing by the Numbers: Absentee Owners and the Decline of American Industry* (Reading, MA: Addison-Wesley).

Meeker-Lowry, Susan, 1987. *Economics as if the Earth Really Mattered: A Catalyst Guide to Socially Conscious Investing* (Philadelphia: New Society).

Meister, Albert, 1984. *Participation, Association, Development, and Change* (New Brunswick, NJ: Transaction Books).

Melman, Seymour, 1983. *Profits without Production* (New York: Knopf).

Melnyk, George, 1985. *The Search for Community: From Utopia to a Cooperative Society* (Montreal: Black Rose Books).

Montgomery, David, 1981. *Workers' Control in America* (Cambridge: Cambridge University Press).

Morrison, Roy, 1991. *We Build the Road as We Travel. Mondragon: A Cooperative Solution* (Philadelphia: New Society).

Mutual Aid Center et al., 1984. *The Prospects for Workers' Cooperatives in Europe*, 3 vols. (Luxembourg: Commission of the European Communities).

Naughton, Tony, 1981. *Work-Aid: Business Management for Co-operatives and Community Enterprises* (Edenbridge, Kent: Commonwork).

Nightingale, Donald V., 1982. *Workplace Democracy: An Inquiry into Employee Participation in Canadian Work Organizations* (Toronto: University of Toronto Press).

Office of the Historian, U.S. Department of Labor, 1977. *Labor Firsts in America* (Washington, DC: U.S. Government Printing Office).

Olson, Deborah Groban, 1982. "Union Experiences with Worker Ownership." *Wisconsin Law Review,* 5, 729-823.

O'Toole, James, 1981. *Making America Work: Productivity and Responsibility* (New York: Continuum).

Ouchi, William G., 1982. *Theory Z* (New York: Avon Books).

Parker, Mike, 1985. *Inside the Circle: A Union Guide to QWL* (Boston: South End Press).

Paton, Rob, 1989. *Reluctant Entrepreneurs* (Milton Keynes: The Open University Press).

Perry, Stewart E., 1987. *Communities on the Way: Rebuilding Local Economies in the United States and Canada* (Albany: SUNY Press).

Piore, Michael, and Charles Sabel, 1986. *The Second Industrial Divide: Possibilities for Prosperity* (New York: Basic Books).

Quarrey, Michael, Joseph Blasi, and Corey Rosen, 1986. *Taking Stock: Employee Ownership at Work* (Cambridge, MA: Ballinger).

Quarter, Jack, and George Melnyk (eds.), 1989. *Partners in Enterprise: The Worker Ownership Phenomenon* (Montreal: Black Rose Books).

Quarter, Jack, 1990. "A Worker Co-op Federation for Canada," *Worker Co-op* 9, 3 (Winter).

Quarter, Jack, and Paul Wilkenson, forthcoming. "Recent Trends in the Worker Ownership Movement in Canada," *Economic and Industrial Democracy*.

Rasmussen, A. Eric, 1981. *Financial Management in Cooperative Enterprises, 4th ed.* (Saskatoon, Sask.: Co-operative College of Canada).

Rausch, John S., 1985. "At Dungannon: The Struggle Continues." *Workplace Democracy* 12 (Fall).

Rifkin, Jeremy, and Randy Barber, 1978. *The North Will Rise Again: Pensions, Politics and Power in the 1980s* (Boston: Beacon).

Rosen, Corey, Katherine J. Klein, and Karen M. Young, 1986. *Employee Ownership in America: The Equity Solution* (Lexington, MA: Lexington Books).

Rosen, Corey, and Karen Young (eds.), 1991. *Understanding Employee Ownership* (Ithaca, NY: ILR Press).

Rosen, Michael L., 1987. "Producer Cooperatives, Education and the Dialectical Logic of Organization," *Praxis International* 7, 1 April.

Rothschild, Joyce, and J. Allen Whitt, 1986. *The Cooperative Workplace: Potentials and Dilemmas of Organizational Democracy and Participation* (Cambridge: Cambridge University Press).

Roy, Ewell Paul, 1981. *Cooperative Development, Principles, and Management*, 4th ed. (Danville, IL: Interstate Printers).

Russell, Raymond, 1985. *Sharing Ownership in the Workplace* (Albany: SUNY Press).

Schuster, Michael H., 1984. *Union-Management Cooperation: Structure, Process and Impact* (Kalamazoo, MI: W.E. Upjohn Institute).

Shostak, Arthur, 1990. *Robust Unionism* (Ithaca, NY: ILR Press).

Siegel, Irving H., and Edgar Weinberg, 1982. *Labor-Management Cooperation: The American Experience* (Kalamazoo, MI: W.E. Upjohn Institute).

Simmons, John, and William Mares, 1983. *Working Together: Participation from the Shop Floor to the Boardroom* (New York: Knopf).

Smiley, Robert W., Jr., and Ronald J. Gilbert (eds.), 1989. *Employee Stock Ownership Plans: Business Planning, Implementation, Law, and Taxation* (Larchmont, NY: Prentice Hall).

Stephen, Frank H., 1982. *The Performance of Labor-Managed Firms* (New York: St. Martin's Press).

Stephen, Frank H., 1984. *The Economic Analysis of Producers' Cooperatives* (New York: St. Martin's Press).

Stern, Robert N., K. Haydn Wood, and Tove H. Hammer, 1979. *Employee Ownership in Plant Shutdowns* (Kalamazoo, MI: W.E. Upjohn Institute).

Swidler, Ann, 1979. *Organization Without Authority: Dilemmas of Social Control in Free Schools* (Cambridge, MA: Harvard University Press).

Szell, Gyorgy, Paul Blyton, and Chris Cornforth (eds.), 1989. *The State, Trade Unions, and Self Management* (Hawthorne, NY: Aldine De Gruyter).

Thayer, Frederick, 1981. *An End to Hierarchy, an End to Competition* (New York: Franklin Watts).

Thimm, Alfred L., 1980. *The False Promise of Codetermination: The Changing Nature of European Workers' Participation* (Lexington, MA: Lexington Books).

Thomas, Alan, and Jenny Thornley (eds.), 1988. *Co-ops to the Rescue* (London: ICOM Publications).

Thomas, Henk, and Chris Logan, 1982. *Mondragon: An Economic Analysis* (London: George Allen and Unwin).

Thornley, Jenny, 1981. *Workers' Co-operatives: Jobs and Dreams* (London: Heinemann).

Toscano, David, 1983. *Property and Participation: Employee Ownership and Workplace Democracy in Three New England Firms* (New York: Irvington).

Vanek, Jaroslav, and L. Emmerii, 1979. *From the Old to a New Global Order* (The Hague: Institute of Social Studies).

Weiner, Hans, and Robert Oakeshott, 1987. *Worker Owners: Mondragon Revisited* (London: Anglo German Foundation).

Weitzman, Martin, 1986. *The Share Economy: Conquering Stagflation* (Cambridge, MA: Harvard University Press).

Whyte, William F., 1986. "Philadelphia Story." *Society* (March/April).

Whyte, William F., and Kathleen K. Whyte, 1988. *Making Mondragon: The Growth and Dynamics of the Worker Cooperative Complex* (Ithaca, NY: ILR Press).

Whyte, William F., et al., 1983. *Worker Participation and Ownership* (Ithaca, NY: ILR Press).

Wilpert, Bernhard, and Arndt Sorge (eds.), 1984. *Perspectives on Organizational Democracy* (New York: Wiley).

Winegrad, Dilys Pegler (ed.), 1990. *Benjamin Franklin: An American Encyclopaedist at the University of Pennsylvania* (Philadelphia: Trustees of the University of Pennsylvania).

Wineman, Steven, 1990. *The Politics of Human Services: A Radical Alternative to the Welfare State* (Boston: South End Press).

Wintner, Linda, 1983. *Employee Buyouts: An Alternative to Plant Closings* (New York: Conference Board).

Wisman, Jon (ed.), 1991. *Worker Empowerment: The Struggle for Workplace Democracy* (New York: Bootstrap Press).

Woodworth, Warner, Chris Meek, and William F. Whyte, 1985. *Industrial Democracy: Strategies for Community Revitalization* (Beverly Hills: Sage).

Young, Michael, and Marianne Riggs, 1983. *Resolution from Within: Cooperatives and Cooperation in British Industry* (London: Weidenfeld and Nicolson).

Zwerdling, Daniel, 1980. *Workplace Democracy* (New York: Harper and Row).

B. Central and Eastern Europe and the Third World

Abell, Peter, and Nicholas Mahoney, 1988. *Small Scale Industrial Producer Cooperatives in Developing Countries* (Oxford: Oxford University Press).

Bayat, Assef, 1991. *Work, Politics and Power: Workers Control and Self-Management in a Global Context* (New York: Monthly Review Press).

Bennoune, Mahfoud, 1988. *The Making of Contemporary Algeria* (Cambridge: Cambridge University Press).

Commisso, Ellen H., 1979. *Workers' Control under Plan and Market: Implications of Yugoslav Self-Management* (New Haven, CT: Yale University Press).

Denitch, Bodgan, 1990. *Limits and Possibilities: The Crisis of Yugoslav Socialism and State Socialist Systems* (Minneapolis: University of Minnesota Press).

Estrin, Saul, 1984. *Self-Management: Economic Theory and Yugoslav Practice* (Cambridge: Cambridge University Press).

Frölander-Ulf, Monica, and Frank Lindenfeld, 1985. *A New Earth: The Jamaican Sugar Workers' Cooperatives, 1975-1981* (Lanham, MD: University Press of America).

Horvat, Branco, 1982. *The Political Economy of Socialism: A Marxist Social Theory* (Oxford: Martin Robertson).

Keremetsky, Jacob, and John Logue, 1990. *Perestroika, Privatization, and Worker Ownership in the U.S.S.R.* (Kent, OH: Kent Popular Press).

Kester, Gerard, 1980. *Transition to Workers' Self-Management: Its Dynamics in the Decolonizing Economy of Malta* (The Hague: Institute for Social Studies). P.O. Box 90733, 2509 LS, The Hague, Netherlands).

LeGrand, Julian, and Saul Estrin (eds.), 1989. *Market Socialism* (New York: Oxford University Press).

McFarlane, Bruce, 1988. *Yugoslavia: Politics, Economics, and Society* (London: Pinter).

Nove, Alex, 1983. *The Economics of Feasible Socialism* (London: Allen and Unwin).

Pasic, Najdan (ed.), 1982. *Workers' Management in Yugoslavia: Recent Developments and Trends* (Oxford: Plunkett Foundation for Cooperative Studies). Available through State Mutual Books, 521 Fifth Ave., New York, NY 10175.

Sacks, Stephen R., 1983. *Self Management and Efficiency: Large Corporations in Yugoslavia* (London: Allen and Unwin).

Siebel, Hans Dieter and Ukandi G. Damachi, 1982. *Self-Management in Yugoslavia and the Developing World* (New York: St. Martin's Press).

Sirc, Ljubo, 1979. *The Yugoslav Economy under Self-Management* (London: Macmillan).

Sirianni, Carmen, 1982. *Workers' Control and Socialist Democracy: The Soviet Experience* (London: Verso Editions).

Stephens, Evelyne H., 1980. *The Politics of Workers' Participation: The Peruvian Approach in Cooperative Perspective* (New York: Academic Press).

Turok, Ben, 1979. *Development in Zambia* (London: Zed Books).

Vanek, Jaroslav, 1989. *Crisis and Reform: East and West; Essays in Social Economy.* Available from the author at Program on Participation and Labor Managed Systems, Dept. of Economics, Cornell University, Ithaca, NY 14850.

Von Freyhold, Michaela, 1979. *Ujamaa Villages in Tanzania* (New York: Monthly Review Press).

Yanowitch, Murray (ed.), 1979. *Soviet Work Attitudes: The Issue of Participation in Management* (New York: M.E. Sharpe).

C. Kibbutzim

Ben-Ner, A., 1981. *On the Economics of Communalism and Self-Management: The Israeli Kibbutz.* Ph.D dissertation, SUNY, Stony Brook.

Blasi, Joseph R., 1986. *The Communal Experience of the Kibbutz* (New Brunswick, NJ: Transaction Books).

Bowes, Alison M., 1989. *Kibbutz Goshen: An Israeli Commune* (Prospect Heights, IL: Waveland Press).

Cherns, Albert (ed.), 1980. *Quality of Working Life and the Kibbutz Experience* (Norwood, PA: Norwood Editions).

Krausz, Ernest (ed.), 1983. *The Sociology of the Kibbutz* (New Brunswick, NJ: Transaction Books).

Leviatan, Uri, and Menachem Rosner, 1983. *Democracy, Equality, and Change: The Kibbutz and Social Theory* (Darby, PA: Norwood Editions).

Rosner, Menachem, n.d. *Ownership, Participation, and Work Restructuring in the Kibbutz: A Comparative Perspective* (Haifa: Institute for Research on the Kibbutz and the Cooperative Idea). University of Haifa, Mt. Carmel, Haifa, Israel 31999.

Spiro, Melford E., 1989. *Gender and Culture: Kibbutz Women Revisited* (New York: Schocken Books).

D. Publications Available from Technical Assistance Groups

Centre for the Study of Co-Operatives Publications

(Available from the Centre for the Study of Co-operatives, Diefenbaker Centre, University of Saskatchewan, Saskatoon, Saskatchewan, S7N 0W0, Canada)

Apland, Lars. *Election of Directors in Saskatchewan Co-operatives: Process and Results.*

Axworthy, Christopher S. *Co-operatives and Their Employees: Towards a Harmonious Relationship.*

Axworthy, Christopher S. *Worker Co-operatives in Mondragon, the U.K., and France: Some Reflections.*

Axworthy, Christopher S., and David Perry. *Worker Co-operatives and Worker Ownership: Issues Affecting the Development of Worker Co-operatives in Canada.*

Bailey, Stuart. *Encouraging Democracy in Consumer and Producer Co-operatives.*

Corman, Jeff, and Murray Fulton. *Patronage Allocation, Growth, and Member Well-Being in Co-operatives.*

Daniel, Abraham. *A New Model for Producer Co-operatives in Israel.*

Ekelund, Finn Aage. *Co-operatives and Social Democracy: Elements of the Norwegian Case.*

Ekelund, Finn Aage. *The Property of the Common: Justifying Co-operative Activity.*

Fairbairn, Brett, June Bold, Murray Fulton, Lou Hammond Ketilson, and Daniel Ish. *Cooperatives and Community Development: Economics in Social Perspective.*

Fulton, Murray. *Co-operative Organizations in Western Canada.*

Halladay, Allan, and Colin Peile. *The Future of Worker Co-operatives in Hostile Enviroments: Some Reflections from Down Under.*

Ketilson, Lou Hammond, and Michael Quenell. *Community Based Models of Health Care: A Bibliography .*

Ketilson, Lou Hammond, Bonnie Kortuis, and Colin Boyd. *The Management of Co-operatives: A Bibliography.*

LeBrasseur, Rolland, Alain Bridault, David Gallingham, Gerald Lafreniere, and Terence Zinger. *Worker Co-operatives: An International Bibliography.*

Laycock, David. *Co-operative/Government Relations in Canada: Lobbying, Public-Policy Development and the Changing Co-operative System.*

Laycock, David. *Prairie Populists and the Idea of Co-operation, 1910-1945.*

McCarty, Skip (ed.). *Employment Co-operatives: An Investment in Innovation: Proceedings of the Saskatoon Worker Co-operative Conference.*

Mullord, Donald, Christopher S. Axworthy, and David Liston. *A History of Saskatchewan Co-operative Law—1900 to 1960.*

Wetzel, Kurt, and Daniel G. Gallagher. *Labour Relations in Co-operatives.*
Wilson, Barry, David Laycock, and Murray Fulton. *Farm Interest Groups and Canadian Agricultural Policy.*

ICA Publications
(Available from ICA Group, 20 Park Plaza, Suite 1127, Boston, MA 02116.)
Adams, Frank, and David Ellerman. *Your Own Boss: Democratic Worker Ownership.*
Adams, Frank T., and Gary B. Hansen. *ESOPs, Unions, and the Rank and File: An ICA Shirtpocket Book for Union Members in Businesses with ESOPs.*
Ellerman, David. *Entrepreneurship in the Mondragon Cooperatives.*
Ellerman, David. *The Legitimate Opposition at Work: The Union's Role in Large Democratic Firms.*
Ellerman, David. *Management Planning with Labor as a Fixed Cost: The Mondragon Annual Business Plan Manual.*
Ellerman, David. *The Mondragon Cooperative Movement.*
Ellerman, David, 1986. *Worker Ownership: Economic Democracy or Worker Capitalism?*
Ellerman, David. *Workers' Cooperatives: The Question of Legal Structure.*
Ellerman, David, and Peter Pitegoff. *The Democratic Corporation: The New Worker-Cooperative Statute in Massachusetts.*
Pitegoff, Peter, 1987. *The Democratic ESOP.*
Pitegoff, Peter. *The Massachusetts Law for Worker Cooperatives.*
Pitegoff, Peter. *Organizing Worker Cooperatives.*
Pitegoff, Peter, and David Ellerman. *ICA Model By-Laws for a Workers' Cooperative.*
Saglio, Janet, and Richard Hackman. *The Design of Governance Systems for Small Worker Cooperatives.*
Illustrated Guide to the Internal Capital Account System.

NCEO Publications
(Available from the National Center for Employee Ownership, 2201 Broadway, Suite 807, Oakland CA 94612-3024.)
Beyond Taxes: Managing an Employee Ownership Company.
Employee Ownership Bibliography.
Employee Ownership Casebook.
Employee Ownership Reader.
Employee Ownership Resource Guide.
Employee Participation Programs in Employee Ownership Companies.
International Developments in Employee Ownership.
Kieschnick, Michael, Julia Parzen, Corey Rosen, and Catherine Rosen, 1985. *Employee Buyout Handbook.*
Kuman, Matthew, and Corey Rosen. *Community Economic Development and Employee Ownership: A Resource Guide.*
Model ESOPs
Quarrey, Michael, and Corey Rosen, 1986. *Employee Ownership and Corporate Performance.*
Steiner, Sue, 1990. *Employee Ownership: Alternatives to ESOPs.*
Weissinger, Samuel, and Corey Rosen, 1986. *Employee Ownership: A Union Handbook.*
Yoffee, Michael, 1988. *Gainsharing and Employee Ownership.*

Other Resource Materials
Barry, Patrick, 1989. *No Time for Waste* (Center for Neighborhood Technology).

Community Based Development: Investing in Renewal, 1987 (National Congress for Community Economic Development).

Community Economic Development Strategies: Creating Successful Businesses, 1983 (National Economic Development and Law Center).

Community Land Trust Handbook, 1982 (Institute for Community Economics).

Community Land Trust Legal Manual (Institute for Community Economics).

Community Loan Fund Manual, 1987 (Institute for Community Economics).

Dodd, Gerard, et al. Management Workbooks for Self-Employed People (Dodd-Blair and Associates).

Erdman, Robin J., Harlan Gradin, and Robert O. Zdenek, 1985. Community Development Corporation Profile Book (National Congress for Community Economic Development).

Fixler, Philip, Employee Ownership and the Privatization of Local Government Services (Reason Foundation: Santa Monica, CA).

Goldberg, Lenny, 1983. Building Cooperatives in California: A Model for State Action (Center for Policy Alternatives).

Gould, Sara K., and Jing Lyman, 1987. A Working Guide to Women's Self-Employment (Corporation for Enterprise Development).

Greenwood, William Alvarado, 1979. Organizing Production Cooperatives (National Economic Development and Law Center).

Hansen, Gary B., 1984. Cooperative Approaches for Dealing with Plant Closings: A Resource Guide for Employers and Communities (Utah Center for Productivity and Quality of Working Life).

Hansen, Gary B., 1984. Organizing the Delivery of Services to Workers Facing Plant Shutdowns: Lessons from California and Canada (Utah Center for Productivity and Quality of Working Life).

Hansen, Gary B., and Frank T. Adams, 1987. "Saving Jobs and Putting Democracy to Work: Labor Management Cooperation at Seymour Specialty Wire," Labor Management Cooperation Brief, no. 11, September (U.S. Department of Labor).

Hansen, Gary B., and Marion T. Bentley, 1981. Problems and Solutions in a Plant Shutdown: A Handbook for Community Involvement (Utah Center for Productivity and Quality of Working Life).

Hansen, Gary B., Marion T. Bentley, and Mark H. Skidmore, 1982. Plant Shutdowns, People, and Communities: A Selected Bibliography (Utah Center for Productivity and Quality of Working Life).

Hatch, C. R., 1988. Flexible Manufacturing Networks: Cooperation for Competitiveness in a Global Economy (Corporation for Enterprise Development).

Herbert, Gabriele, 1987. Favorable and Unfavorable Conditions for a Regional Development of Common Ownership Enterprises (International Institute for Self-management).

Kaswan, Jaques, 1988. Cooperative Democracy (Berkeley, CA: Alternatives Center). 2375 Shattuck Ave., Berkeley, CA 94704.

Kerson, Roger, and Greg LeRoy, 1989. State and Local Initiatives on Development Subsidies and Plant Closings (Federation for Industrial Retention and Renewal).

Kobak, Sue Ellen, and Nina McCormack. Developing Feasibility Studies for Community-Based Business Venture (Highland Center).

Lamas, Andrew (ed.), 1983. Employee Ownership: A Strategy for Jobs. Edited conference transcripts and commentary. (Philadelphia: PACE, 2100 Chestnut Street, Phila., PA 19103).

LeRoy, Greg, Dan Swinney, and Elaine Charpentier, 1988. Early Warning Manual against Plant Closings, 2d ed. (Midwest Center for Labor Research).

Lewis, Helen, and John Gaventa. *Jellico Handbook: A Teacher's Guide to Community-Based Learning* (Highlander Center).

Logan, Patricia (ed.), 1982. *Community Energy Cooperatives: How to Organize, Manage, and Finance Them* (Center for Policy Alternatives).

Luttrell, Wendy. *Claiming What Is Ours: An Economics Experience Workbook* (Highlander Center).

Lynch, John E. (ed.), 1990. *Plant Closures and Community Recovery* (National Council for Urban Economic Development).

MacLeod, Greg, 1986. *New Age Business: Community Corporations That Work* (Canadian Council on Social Development).

McLenighan, Valjean, 1990. *Sustainable Manufacturing: Saving Jobs, Saving the Environment* (Center for Neighborhood Technology).

No Time to Waste: *How Communiteis Can Reep Benefits from the Shift to Recycling*, 1990 (Center for Neighboorhood Technology).

O'Connell, Mary, et al., 1986. *Working Neighborhoods: Taking Charge of Your Local Economy* (Center for Neighborhood Technology).

Parzen, Julia, Catherine Squire, and Michael Kieschnick, 1983. *Buyout: A Guide for Workers Facing Plant Closings* (Sacramento: California Department of Economic and Business Development).

Schweke, William, and Rodney Stares, 1986. *Sowing the Seeds of Economic Renewal: A Manual for Dislocated Communities* (Center for Enterprise Development).

Schweke, William, and Lee Webb, 1982. *Putting America Back to Work: What States and Cities Can Do* (Center for Policy Alternatives).

Shavelson, Jeff, 1990. *A Third Way. A Sourcebook: Innovations in Community-Owned Enterprises* (Washington, DC: National Center for Economic Alternatives).

Strickland, Susan, 1982. *HRD Enterprises Limited: A Case Study in Productive Alternatives for Public Transfer Payments* (Institute for Enterprise Development).

Surpin, Rick. *Cooperative Home Care Associates: A Status Report* (Community Service Society, New York).

Surpin, Rick, 1984. *Enterprise Development and Worker Ownership: A Strategy for Community Economic Development* (Community Service Society).

Surpin, Rick, 1988. *The Neighborhood Toolbox* (Center for Neighborhood Technology).

U.S. Catholic Bishops, *Economic Justice for All: Pastoral Letter on the Economy* (U.S. Catholic Conference).

Wade, Jerry L., and Carolyn E. Cook, 1986. *Alternative Economic Activities: Catalog of Ideas* (Department of Community Development, University of Missouri-Columbia).

Wilkins, R., and June Holley, 1990. *Development of Flexible Manufacturing Networks: A Conceptual Framework* (Worker Owned Network).

Worker Ownership: An Employee Buyout Handbook (Pennsylvania MILRITE Council).

MAGAZINES, NEWSLETTERS, ETC.

This is a partial list of periodicals that specialize in the themes of workers' participation, workplace democracy, and worker ownership.

Alternative Economic Development Ideas, 62B Clark Hall, University of Missouri-Columbia, Columbia, MO 65211.

Autogestions, Editions Privat, 14 rue des Arts, F. 31000 Toulouse, France.

Catalyst, 64 Main St., Montpelier, VT 05602. (800) 535-3551.

CDCU Report, 29 John St., Suite 1603, New York, NY 10038.

Community Economics, 57 School Street, Springfield, MA 01105-1331. (413) 746-8660.

Community Jobs, 1520 16th St. NW, Washington, DC 20036. (202) 387-7702.

Community Matters, 100 S. Morgan St., Chicago, IL 60607.

Co-Op America Quarterly: A Magazine for Building Economic Alternatives, Co-op America, 2100 M St. NW Suite 403, Washington, DC 20063. (800) 424-COOP.

Cooperative Grocer, P.O. Box 597, Athens, OH 45701. (614) 592-3854.

Cooperative Notes, Commonwealth, Inc., 1221 Elm St., Youngstown, OH 44505.

The Corporate Examiner, 475 Riverside Drive, Room 566, New York, NY 10115.

Dollars and Sense, 38 Union Square, Somerville, MA 02143. (617) 628-8411.

Economic and Industrial Democracy, Sage Publications Ltd., 28 Banner St., London EC1Y 8QE, England.

Employee Ownership, 2201 Broadway, Suite 807, Oakland, CA 94612. (415) 272-9461.

Everyone's Backyard, Citizens Clearinghouse for Hazardous Wastes, P.O. Box 926, Arlington, VA 22216.

Grassroots Economic Organizing (GEO) Newsletter, P.O. Box 5065, New Haven, CT 06525.

ICA Bulletin, 20 Park Place, Suite 1127, Boston, MA 02116.

In Business, Box 323, 18 S. Seventh St., Emmaus, PA. (215) 967-4135.

In Context, P.O. Box 2107, Sequim, WA 98382.

Jobs for People Newsletter, 1216 E. McMillan, Suite 304, Cincinnati, OH 45206.

The Journal of Economic Democracy, c/o COPE International, Dept. of Economics, Bloomsburg University, Bloomsburg, PA 17815

The Journal of Employee Ownership and Finance, The National Center for Employee Ownership, 2201 Broadway, Suite 807, Oakland, CA 94612. (415) 272-9461.

Labor Notes, P.O. Box 2000, Detroit, MI 48220. (313) 883-5580.

Labor Research Review. Midwest Center for Labor Research, 3411 West Diversey Ave., Suite 14, Chicago, IL 60647. (312) 278-5418.

Making Waves—A Newsletter for CED Practitioners in Canada, West Coast Development Group, 3024 Second Ave., Port Alberni, B.C. V9Y 1Y9, Canada.

Multinational Monitor, P.O. Box 19405, Washington, DC 20036. (202) 833-3932.

Neighborhood Funding Bulletin Board , Development Training Institute, 4806 Seton Drive, Baltimore, MD 21215.

The Neighborhood Works, 2125 W. North Ave., Chicago, IL 60647. (312) 278-4800.

Networker News, 94 N. Columbus Rd., Athens, OH 45701.

New Options, P.O. Box 19324, Washington, DC 20036.

News, FIRR, 3411 W. Diversey Ave., #10, Chicago, IL 60647.

Owners at Work, Northeast Ohio Employee Ownership Center, Department of Political Science, Kent State University, Kent, OH 44242.

Planners Network Newsletter, 1901 Que St., NW, Washington, DC 20009. (202) 234-9382.

Plowshare Press, 222C View St., Mountain View, CA 94041.

Project for Kibbutz Studies, Harvard University Center for Jewish Studies, 129 Vanserg Hall, 10 Divinity Ave., Cambridge, MA 02138.

The Real Story, REAL Enterprise, Chicopee Complex, 1180 E. Broad St., Athens, GA 30602.

Resources for Community-Based Economic Development, 2025 Eye St. N.W., Suite 901, Washington, DC 20006.

Socialism and Democracy, Graduate Center, CUNY, 33 West 42d St., New York, NY 10036.

Tri-State Conference Call, 300 Saline St., Pittsburgh, PA 15207.

Worker Co-op, P.O. Box 101, Station G, Toronto, Ontario M4M 3E8, Canada.

VIDEOS ON WORKER CO-OPS AND WORKER OWNERSHIP

Note: Many of these videos are also available for rent.

Title:	Length in Minutes	Price	Available From
A Working Alternative		$27.95	LYDIA
Principles of Participation		$27.95 (Both for $50)	1257 E. Sienna Heights Dr. Adrian, MI 49221 (517) 265-5135, x292
The Mondragon Experiment	57		Canadian Cooperative Assn.,
My Own Boss			275 Bank St., Suite 400
Worker Coops in Canada: An Idea Whose Time Has Come			Ottawa, Ontario K2P 2L6 Canada
The Mondragon Cooperatives	33	$50/90*	The Alternatives Center
Planning and Facilitating Effective Democratic Meetings	56	$95/200*	2375 Shattuck Ave. Berkeley, CA 94707 (415) 644-8336
Cooperative Voices: Past, Present, and Future	30	$75	Michigan Alliance of Cooperatives P.O. Box 8032 Ann Arbor, MI 48107 (313) 663-3624
NCEO 1989 Annual Conference			Chicago Video Transfer 230 N. Michigan, Suite 1518 Chicago, IL 60601 (312) 236-2600
Introduction to ESOPs	40	$50/75§	National Center for
Introduction to ESOPs for Employees	30	$50/75§	Employee Ownership
Managing an ESOP Company	30	$50/75§	2201 Broadway, Suite 807 Oakland, CA 94612
On Their Own Terms: The Worker Cooperative Experience in Nova Scotia, Canada		$30	Extension Department St. Francis Xavier Univ. Antigonish, Nova Scotia Canada

*   Small groups/large organizations.
§   Member/nonmember prices; speeches by Corey Rosen, Executive Director, NCEO.

Recharge South Side Steel	16		Steel Valley Authority 230 Third St. Rankin, PA 15104 (412) 351-7779
Alternative Economic Development from the Inside Out	20		Clearinghouse for Community Economic Development 628 Clark Hall Univ. of Missouri-Columbia Columbia, MO 65211 (314) 882-2937
Workers Own, a Video about Worker Cooperatives	50		Worker Ownership Development Foundation 348 Danforth Ave., #212 Toronto, Ontario M4K 1N8 Canada (416) 461-6992
Building a Sustainable Economy	26		Center for Economic Conversion 222C View St. Mountain View, CA 94041 (415) 968-8798
We're the Boss	29	$30/45*	National Film Board of Canada D-5, P.O. Box 6100 Montreal, Quebec H3C 3H5 Canada
The Cheticamp Experience	30	$35	Acadian Co-op Council P.O. Box 667, Cheticamp Nova Scotia B0E 1H0 Canada
The Frisbee Success Story			Center for Defense Information 1500 Massachusetts Ave. N.W. Washington, DC 20005 (202) 862-0700

*   Individual/Institutional

Audio Cassettes on Employee Ownership

Twenty-four individual tapes from the 10th annual conference of the National Center for Employee Ownership and a set of tapes from an International Symposium at Harvard Univerisity are available from Conference Audio Services, 806 Lombard St., San Francisco, CA 94133. (415) 775-TAPE.

Appendix 1

Largest Majority-Owned ESOPs, May 1991*

Company	Location	Business	No. of Employees
Publix Supermarkets	Lakeland, FL	Supermarkets	65,000
HealthTrust	Nashville, TN	Hospital Management	30,000
Avis, Inc.	Westbury, NY	Rental Cars	13,500
Science Applications	La Jolla, CA	Research and Development	13,000
EPIC Healthcare	Irving, TX	Hospital Management	13,000
Parsons Corporation	Pasadena, CA	Engineering	8,500
Amsted Industries	Chicago, IL	Industr. Mfr.	8,300
Austin Industries	Dallas, TX	Construction	7,800
Avondale Shipyards	New Orleans, LA	Shipbuilding	7,500
Weirton Steel Corp.	Weirton, WV	Steel Mfr.	7,200
The Journal Company	Milwaukee, WI	Newspapers/Media	6,200
Wyatt Cafeterias, Inc.	Dallas, TX	Cafeterias	6,000
W.L. Gore Associates	Newark, DE	High-tech Mfr.	5,000
Republic Eng'rd Steel	Massillon, OH	Steel Mfr.	4,900
Graybar Electric	St. Louis, MO	Elect. Eqpmnt.	4,800
Treasure Chest Adv.	Glendora, CA	Printing	4,000
Nat'l Steel & Shipbldng.	San Diego, CA	Shipbuilding	4,000
CH2M Hill, Inc.	Corvallis, OR	Engnrng., Arch.	4,000
Davey Tree Expert Co.	Kent, OH	Tree Service	3,800
Norcal Solid Waste Systs.	San Francisco, CA	Waste Disposal	3,000
Lifetouch	Minneapolis, MN	Photography	3,000
Northwestern Steel & Wire	Sterling, IL	Steel Mfr.	2,800
Arthur D. Little	Cambridge, MA	Consulting	2,600
American Cast Iron Pipe	Birmingham, AL	Iron Pipe	2,600

*   Source: National Center for Employee Ownership. This list includes the
    largest employee-ownership firms (by employment size) that, as of May
    1991, were at least 50% employee owned.

Swank, Inc.	Attleboro, MA	Leather Goods	2,300
Phelps, Inc.	Greenley, CO	Construction	2,200
Herbereger's	St. Cloud, MN	Retail	2,200
Reliable Stores	Columbia, MD	Dept. Stores	2,100
ABC Liquors	Orlando, FL	Liquor Stores	2,100
McLouth Steel	Trenton, MI	Steel Mfr.	2,000
Houchens Food Stores	Bowling Green, KY	Supermarkets	2,000
Cranston Print Works	Cranston, RI	Textiles	1,700
Okonite Company	Ramsey, NJ	Wire & Cable Mfr.	1,700
Rural/Metro Corp.	Scottsdale, AZ	Emergency Svcs.	1,600
Bur. of Natl. Affrs. Inc.	Washington, DC	Publishing	1,590
North American Rayon	Elizabethton, TN	Rayon Mfr.	1,500
AECOM	Los Angeles, CA	Energy Tech.	1,250
National Health Corp ESOP	Murfreesboro, TN	Healthcare	1,200
Texas Foundries	Lufkin, TX	Foundry	1,200
Erickson's	Hudson, WI	Supermarkets	1,100
BCM Engineers	Plymouth Mtg., PA	Engineering	1,100
Mutual Savings Life	Decatur, AL	Insurance	1,050
Burns & McDonnell Engr.	Kansas City, MO	Engineering	1,050
Halmode Apparel	Roanoke, VA	Textiles	1,050
Ecker Enterprises	Chicago, IL	Printing	1,000
Guckenheimer	Redwood City, CA	Food Dist.	1,000
Jerell, Inc.	Dallas, TX	Dress Mfr.	1,000
Kolbe and Kolbe	Wausau, WI	Window Mfr.	1,000
Rosauer's	Spokane, WA	Supermarkets	1,000

Appendix 2
ESOP Tax Benefits

[The information about tax advantages of ESOPs presented here was condensed from memos prepared by tax lawyers Peter R. Pitegoff and Deborah Groban Olson—Eds.]

A company can use an employee stock ownership plan (ESOP) to become employee owned and receive significant tax benefits in the process. The most important tax benefit to the company is that it can borrow money from a bank and get a tax deduction for repayment of the principal of the loan. ESOPs give rise to other tax benefits as well—some to the employee-owned company, others to outside parties to encourage employee ownership. Following are some of the most important tax advantages.

Tax-Favored Financing. A company with an ESOP can get a tax deduction for repayment of a loan. The company adopts an ESOP and establishes a trust as a separate legal entity to hold company stock. The ESOP trust borrows money from a bank and uses that money to purchase some or all of the company stock. The loan money passes through the trust to the company and the stock is held in the trust for the employees. The company repays the principal and interest of the bank loan through the ESOP trust, and gets a tax deduction for those payments. This deduction of both interest and principal payments of the loan is a significant tax advantage, since the company ordinarily could deduct only the interest payments if it had no ESOP and borrowed money directly from the bank.

Tax-Deferred Benefits to the Employees. An employee generally is not taxed on his ESOP benefits until she or he leaves the company. When the company makes payments to the ESOP, company shares are allocated to ESOP accounts in the name of the employees. If the company does well, the value of these stock shares may increase in value (capital gain). When an employee leaves the company, she or he is entitled to the stock or the cash value of stock in her or his account. The employees are *not* liable for income tax on the ESOP contribution, nor for capital gain tax on ESOP holdings, until they are paid out upon termination or retirement.

Benefit to the Lender. A bank gets a tax benefit for lending money to an ESOP. The bank is taxed on only one-half of the income it receives on interest from such a loan. In some cases, this can result in ESOP loans at a reduced rate, if the bank is willing to pass part of its tax benefit on to the ESOPs.

Capital Gain Rollover. An owner of a company gets a tax benefit for selling stock to an ESOP. A shareholder of a company can sell company stock to an ESOP and defer any capital gain tax on the proceeds of that sale. The selling shareholder must reinvest the proceeds in stock of another corporation, and will not pay any capital gain tax until she or he sells these "replacement securities." For a seller to qualify for this tax benefit, the ESOP must hold at least 30 percent of the company stock after the sale.

Deductible Dividends. A company can deduct the amount of cash dividends paid to employees on stock held by the ESOP. The dividends must be paid in cash directly to the employees within ninety days after the end of the plan year. Ordinarily, a company gets no tax deduction for dividends paid to shareholders.

Special Benefits for Majority ESOPs (November 1989)

ESOP law was significantly changed in 1989 in order to increase revenue, to curb perceived abuses of ESOP tax benefits by large businesses, and to expand employee rights. Some of the major changes include the following:

- Dividends used by ESOPs to repay stock acquisition loans are deductible only if the dividends are from stock acquired with the ESOP loan.
- The maximum annual individual contribution dollar limit for ESOP participants was lowered from $60,000 to $30,000 to conform with that of other defined contribution plans.
- Partial ESOP lender interest exclusion requires that the ESOP own more than 50 percent of the company's stock and that stock voting rights are passed through to plan participants.
- Capital gains deferral for an owner who sells stock to an ESOP is permitted only if she or he owned the stock for at least 3 years before the sale to the ESOP.

About the Contributors

Frank T. Adams has been Director of Educational Services of the ICA Group and has written numerous books and articles on worker ownership education, including *The Shirt Pocket Guide: ESOPs, Unions and the Rank and File.*

Andrew R. Banks is Associate Director of the Center for Labor Research and Studies at Florida International University in Miami and an associate editor of *Labor Research Review.*

Daniel Bell is a staff member of the Northeast Ohio Ownership Center and author of *Bringing Your Employees into the Business.*

Jim Benn is the Director of the Federation for Industrial Retention and Renewal, which has over 20 labor-community affiliates.

Joseph R. Blasi is a professor at the Rutgers University Institute of Management and Labor Relations, New Brunswick, New Jersey. He is co-author, with Douglas L. Kruse, of *The New Owners.*

Matt Borenstein has taught at the New Haven, Connecticut, High School in the Community since 1971. He holds a Ph.D. in Theoretical Physics from Yale University.

Christine Clamp is a faculty member of the Graduate Program in Community Economic Development at New Hampshire College in Manchester, New Hampshire.

Lance Compa is a staff member of the United Electrical, Radio and Machine Workers in Washington, DC. He has written widely on labor strategy and worker ownership.

Steven L. Dawson served as the Executive Director of the Industrial Cooperative Association (now the ICA Group) during its first decade. He now lives in New Hampshire where he publishes a state-wide newspaper.

Ron Ehrenreich, a community activist in Syracuse, New York, is Treasurer of the Syracuse Cooperative Credit Union.

Richard Feldman is the Director of the Seattle Worker Center. He also works with the Puget Sound Cooperative Federation.

Gary B. Hansen is Professor of Economics and Director of Business and Economic Development at Utah State University in Logan, Utah, where he has pioneered the development of educational programs and extension services for worker cooperatives.

Eric Hart has worked in cooperative printshops and is now studying workplace democracy in a graduate program at Cornell University.

Hal Hartzell lives and works in Eugene, Oregon. He has been participating in cooperatives for two decades and is the author of *Birth of a Cooperative*, a first-hand account of the formative years of Hoedads, Inc.

John Isbister is Provost and professor of economics at Merrill College, University of California at Santa Cruz. He has been the Treasurer of the Santa Cruz Community Credit Union since 1979.

Catherine Ivancic is a staffmember of the Northeast Ohio Employee Ownership Center. She has co-authored many publications on employee ownership.

Len Krimerman is Professor of Philosophy at the University of Connecticut. He is co-editor of the *Grassroots Economic Organizing (GEO) Newsletter* and co-editor of *From the Ground Up: Essays on Grassroots and Workplace Democracy by C. George Benello*.

Andrew T. Lamas is Director of the technical assistance organization PACE of Philadelphia, with which he has been associated since the early 1980s.

Pete Leki is a member of the Editorial Committee of *Labor Today*.

Frank Lindenfeld is Professor of Sociology at Bloomsburg University, Bloomsburg, PA. He is co-author, with Monica Frölander-Ulf, of *A New Earth: The Jamaican Sugar Workers' Cooperatives, 1975-1981*.

Michael Locker is co-founder and President of Working Equity, Inc. and of Locker Associates. Both are economic consulting firms that specialize in corporate feasibility studies for labor unions.

John Logue is a professor of Political Science at Kent State University, Kent, Ohio, and the Director of the Northeast Ohio Employee Ownership Center.

Carolyn McKecuen is founder and Director of Watermark Artisans, a cooperative in North Carolina.

Kevin McQueen is Assistant Vice President and a loan officer of the NCB Development Corporation, affiliated with the National Cooperative Bank.

Christopher Meek is a professor of organizational behavior at Brigham Young University in Provo, Utah. He has researched and written extensively on worker ownership and participation.

Deborah Groban Olson is an attorney specializing in ESOP conversions. She was formerly director of the Michigan Employee Ownership Council.

Dorris Pickens is President of the Neighborhood Institute, a local development affiliate of the South Shore Bank in Chicago.

Gregg Ramm, a member of the technical assistance staff of the Institute for Community Economics, served as an organizer and initial coordinator of the National Association of Community Development Loan Funds.

Christine Rico is the former coordinator of the Interfaith Center on Corporate Responsibility's Alternative Investment Fund and provided educational and technical assistance to Cooperative Home Care Associates.

Corey Rosen is the founder and Executive Director of the National Center for Employee Ownership in Oakland, California, and co-author of numerous publications on employee ownership and ESOPs.

Janet Saglio is Vice President and senior business consultant of the ICA Group and co-author of a handbook on governance of employee-owned companies.

Mark Satin is the editor of *New Options* newsletter.

Dan Swinney was Vice President of United Steel Workers of America Local 8787 and is a founder, Board member and Director of the Midwest Center for Labor Research.

Chuck Turner was for many years the Educational Director of the ICA Group. He is the founder of the Greater Roxbury Workers' Association and Director of the Center for Community Action, both in Roxbury, Massachusetts.

Jackie Van Anda has been a labor organizer for the Amalgamated Textile and Clothing Workers Union, Financial Manager of the War Resisters League, and the Deputy Director of a local development corporation in New York City.

Chris Weiss is a member of the MS Foundation for Women and Women's World Banking.

Lynn Williams has been President of the 650,000 member United Steel Workers of America since 1983. He has helped provide support for employee buyouts of numerous steel companies.

Charlene Renberg Winters is a staff writer for the Brigham Young University publication, *BYU Today*.

Karen M. Young is Associate Director of the National Center for Employee Ownership in Oakland, California, and a co-author of *Employee Ownership in America*.

INDEX